ST. DRAGON GIRL

VOLUME SEVEN

 Story & Art by **Natsumi Matsumoto**

ST.♥ DRAGON GIRL

CHARACTERS

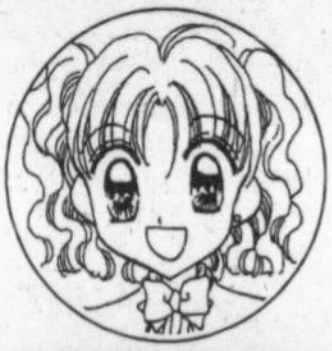

Shunran Kou

Ryuga's cousin and Momoka's best friend. Has psychic abilities.

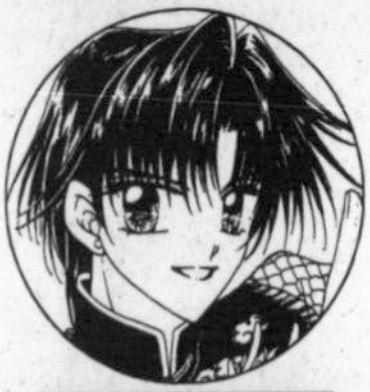

Ryuga Kou

Momoka's childhood friend and magic master.

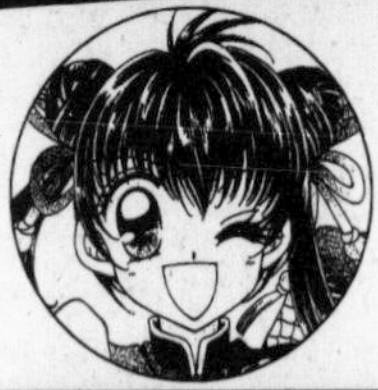

Momoka Sendou

She's possessed by a dragon spirit Ryuga summoned. She loves Ryuga. ♥

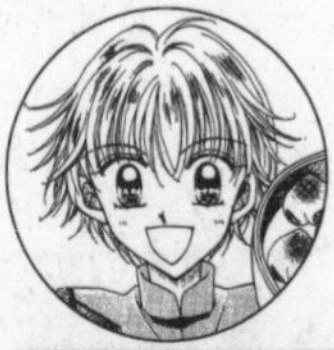

Touya Shirai

He's actually Yutengenyo, but he's reformed now. He loves Momoka. ♥

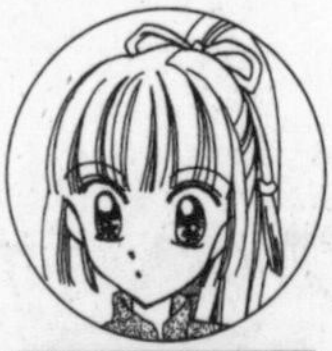

Ageha Inui

Momoka's friend. Member of the kenpo club.

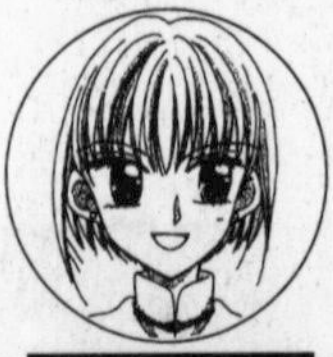

Raika Kou

Ryuga's distant relative. Can emit electricity.

STORY THUS FAR

Momoka is a member of the kenpo club at Yokohama's Tourin Academy. Her friends Ryuga and Shunran belong to a family of magic masters who can control dragons. Ever since the dragon Ryuga summoned possessed Momoka, she's been in danger many times. But every time, they manage to control the dragon and fight together.

Momoka is asked to do kung fu stunts for a martial arts movie, but Ryuga seems to be growing closer to the lead actress, Sara. Suspicious, Momoka follows him to Sara's house, where Sara's true identity is revealed: she's a nine-tailed fox! Sara steals Momoka's feelings of love for Ryuga and her memory of him. But when Ryuga risks his life to save Momoka, she regains her memory once again.

They've overcome so much danger together, but their stubborn personalities stand in the way of them revealing their true feelings... What will happen with these two?

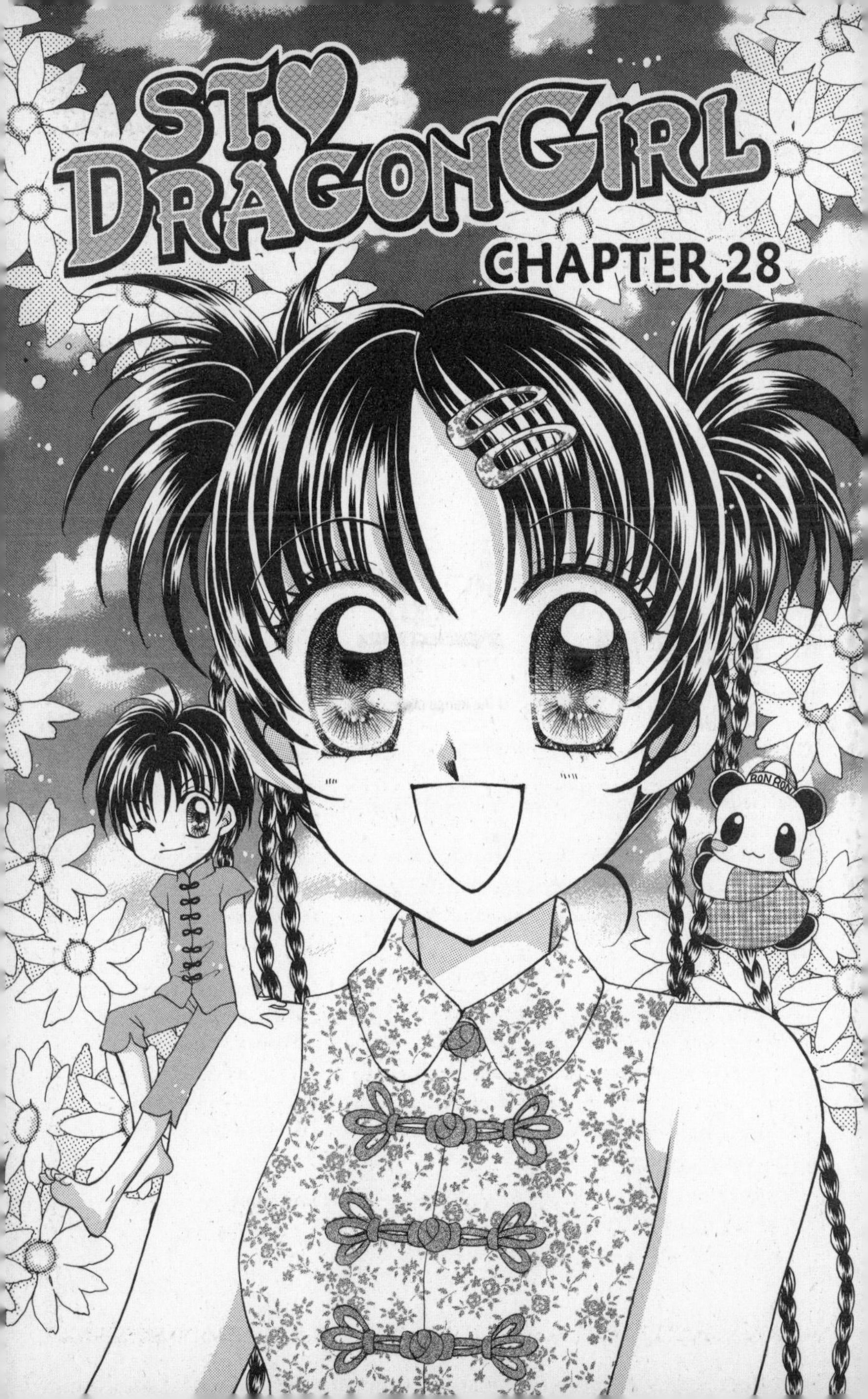
ST. DRAGON GIRL
CHAPTER 28
RON RON

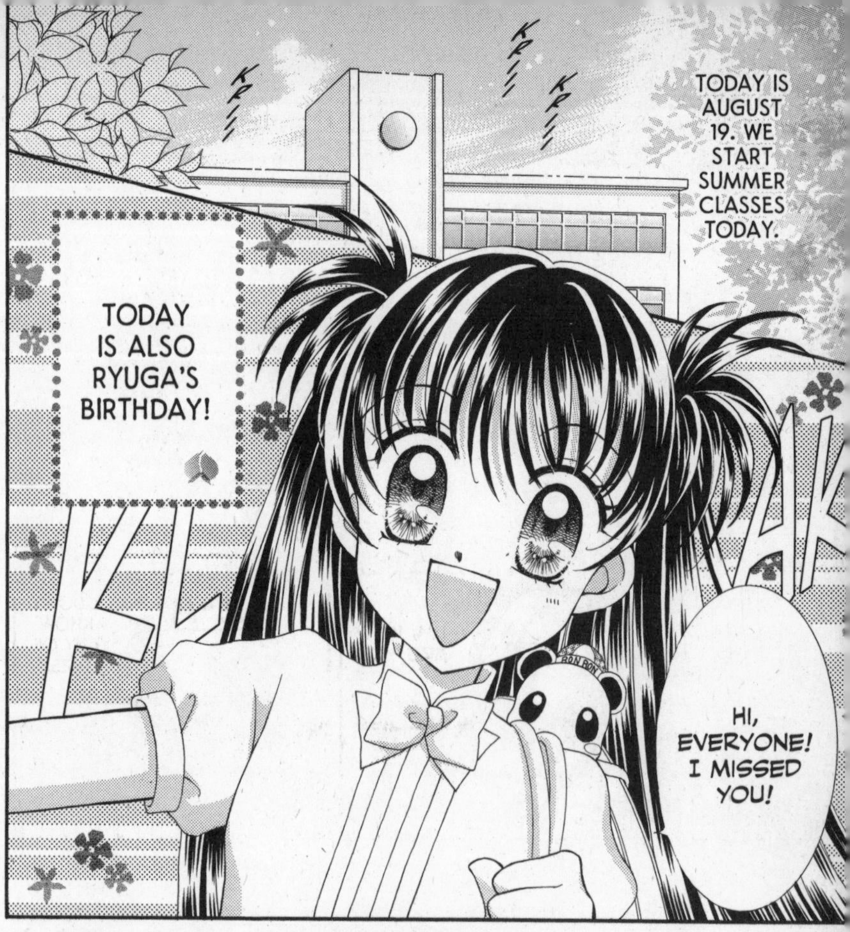
TODAY IS AUGUST 19. WE START SUMMER CLASSES TODAY.
TODAY IS ALSO RYUGA'S BIRTHDAY!
HI, EVERYONE! I MISSED YOU!

Xi Chen

Birthday: Unknown
Birthplace: China, most likely

She's a fairy who lives inside a pocket watch. She can stop time and can send the owner of the watch to the past or future.

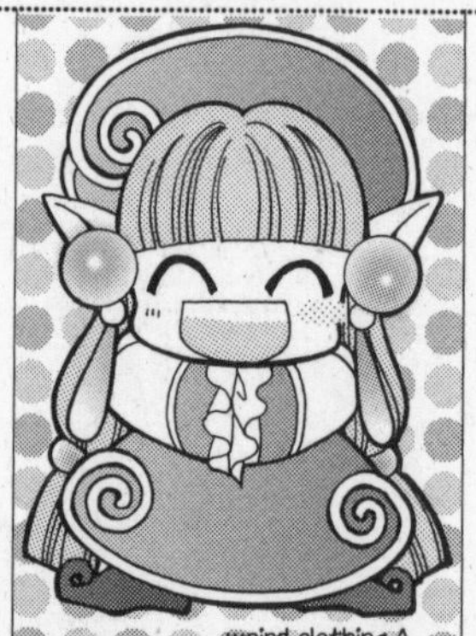
weird clothing

She's tiny and loves playing tricks. But she is very powerful.
Xi Chen is really interesting. She was waiting in the antique shop when Momoka bought the watch.

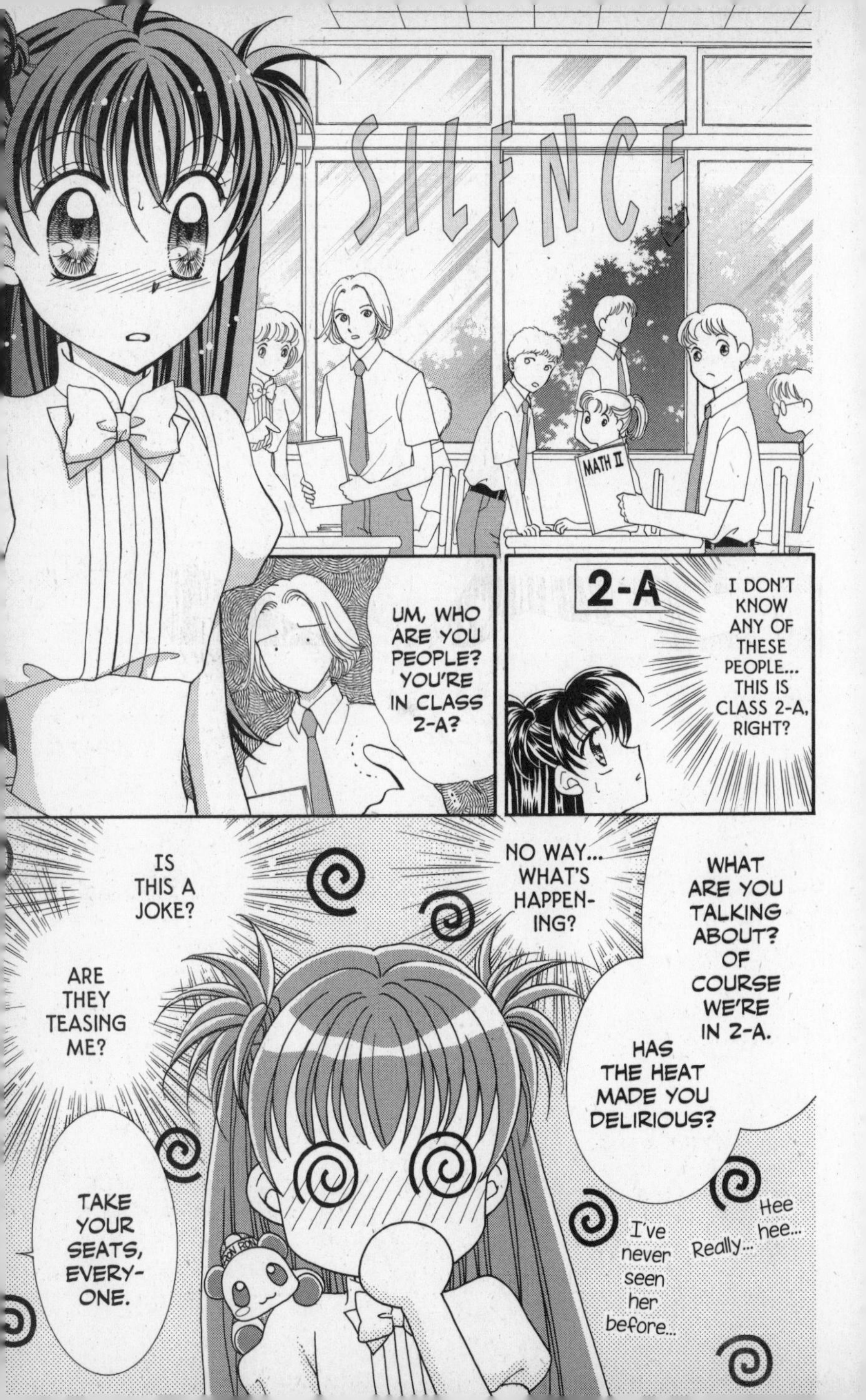
SILENCE
MATH II
2-A
I DON'T KNOW ANY OF THESE PEOPLE... THIS IS CLASS 2-A, RIGHT?
UM, WHO ARE YOU PEOPLE? YOU'RE IN CLASS 2-A?
WHAT ARE YOU TALKING ABOUT? OF COURSE WE'RE IN 2-A.
HAS THE HEAT MADE YOU DELIRIOUS?
Hee hee...
Really...
I've never seen her before...
NO WAY... WHAT'S HAPPEN-ING?
IS THIS A JOKE?
ARE THEY TEASING ME?
TAKE YOUR SEATS, EVERY-ONE.

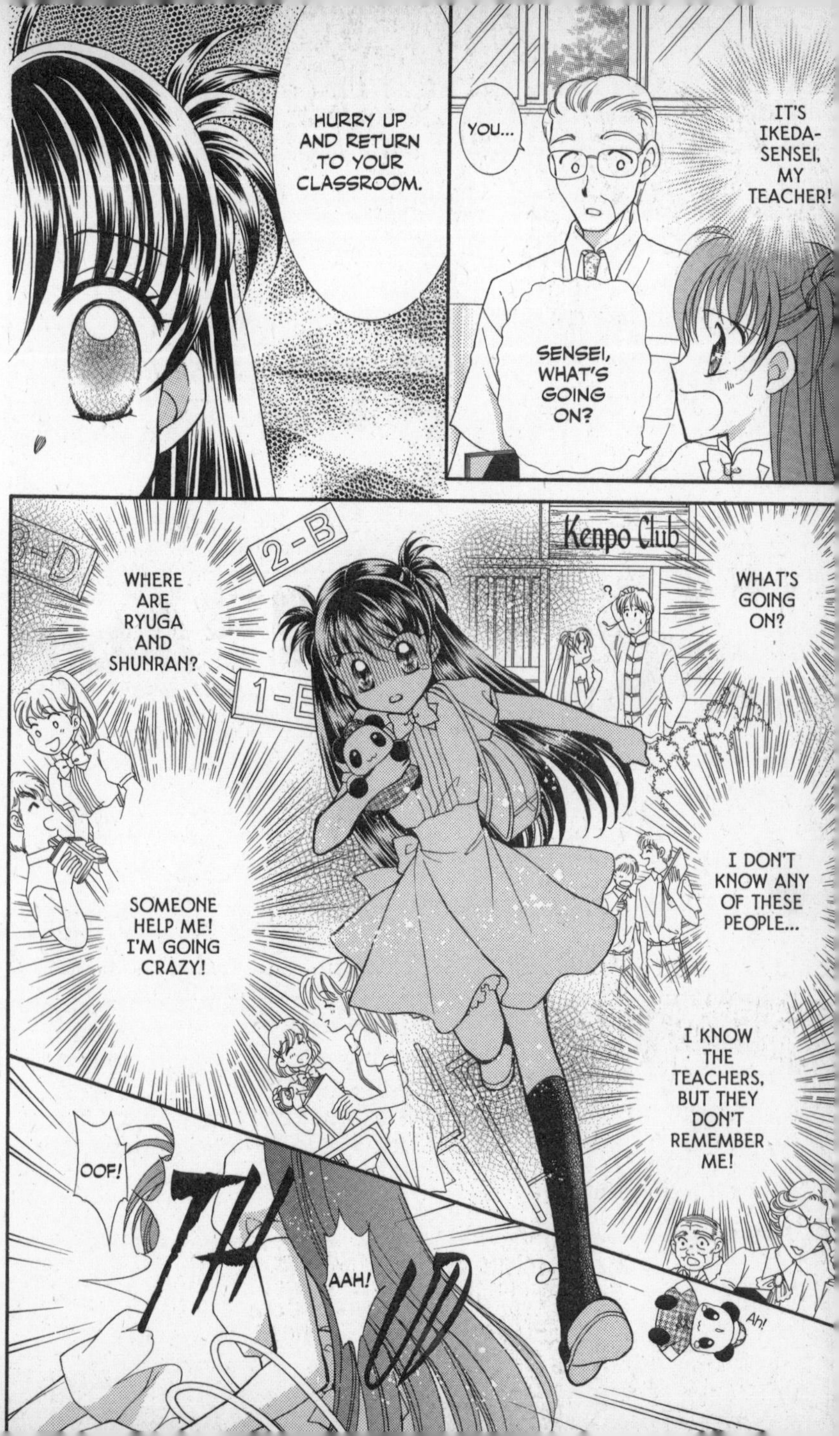
IT'S IKEDA-SENSEI, MY TEACHER!
YOU...
SENSEI, WHAT'S GOING ON?
HURRY UP AND RETURN TO YOUR CLASSROOM.
Kenpo Club
WHAT'S GOING ON?
I DON'T KNOW ANY OF THESE PEOPLE...
I KNOW THE TEACHERS, BUT THEY DON'T REMEMBER ME!
2-B
WHERE ARE RYUGA AND SHUNRAN?
SOMEONE HELP ME! I'M GOING CRAZY!
Ah!
AAH!
OOF!

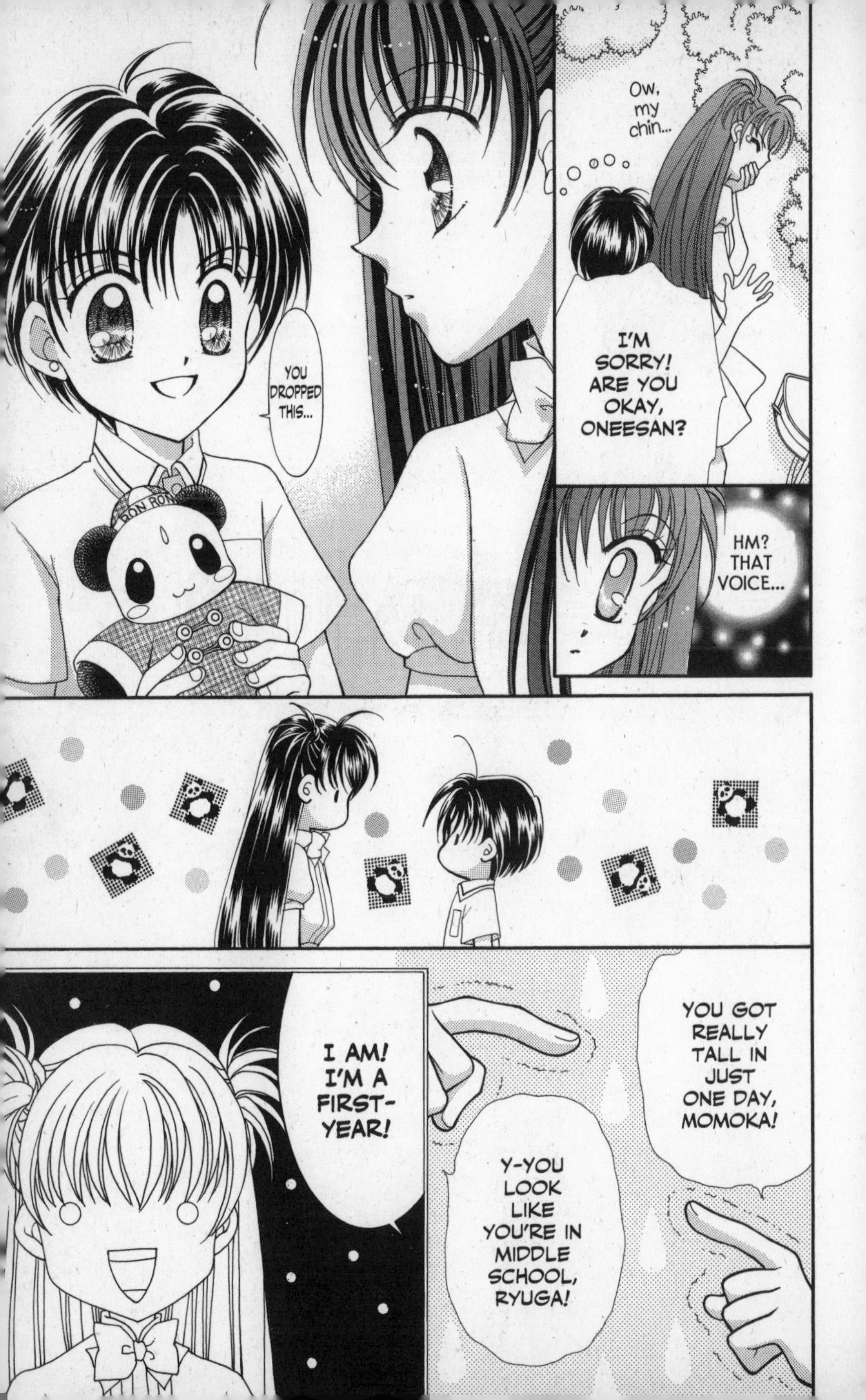
Ow, my chin...
I'M SORRY! ARE YOU OKAY, ONEESAN?
HM? THAT VOICE...
YOU DROPPED THIS...
RON RON
YOU GOT REALLY TALL IN JUST ONE DAY, MOMOKA!
Y-YOU LOOK LIKE YOU'RE IN MIDDLE SCHOOL, RYUGA!
I AM! I'M A FIRST-YEAR!

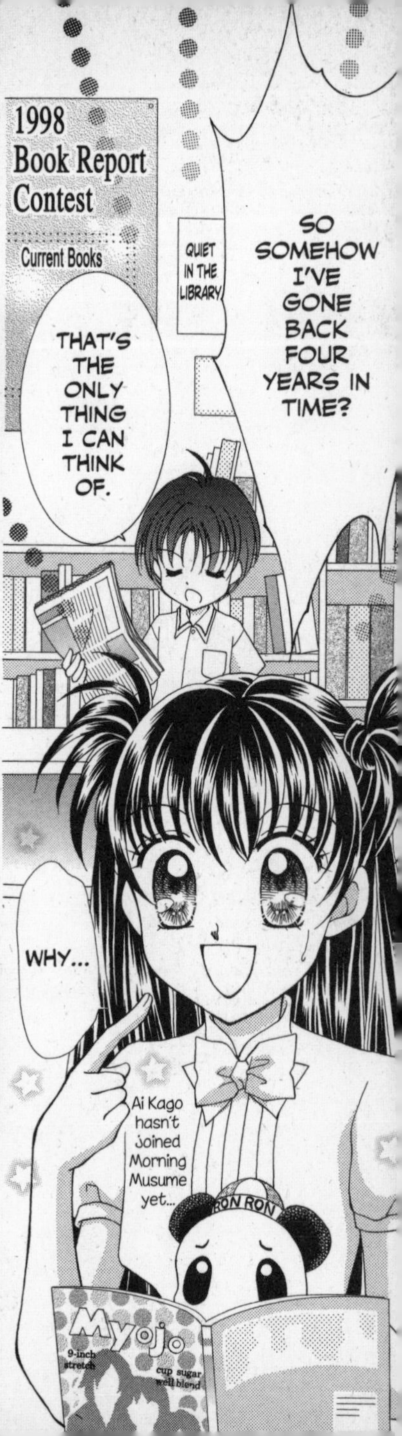
1998
Book Report
Contest
Current Books
QUIET IN THE LIBRARY
SO SOMEHOW I'VE GONE BACK FOUR YEARS IN TIME?
THAT'S THE ONLY THING I CAN THINK OF.
WHY...
Ai Kago hasn't joined Morning Musume yet...
RON RON
Myojo
9-inch stretch
cup sugar well blend

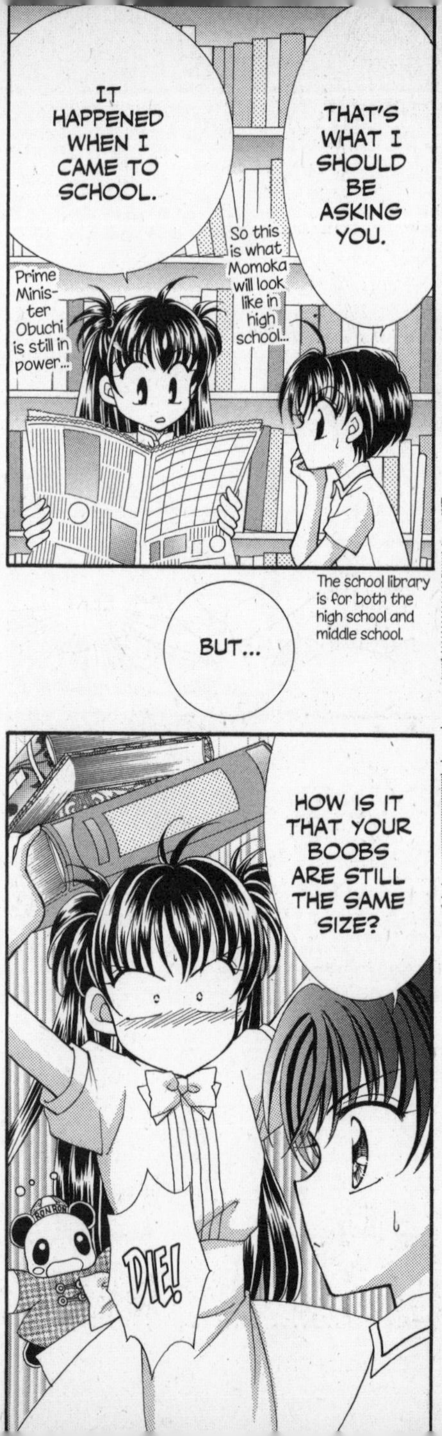
THAT'S WHAT I SHOULD BE ASKING YOU.
So this is what Momoka will look like in high school...
IT HAPPENED WHEN I CAME TO SCHOOL.
Prime Minister Obuchi is still in power...
The school library is for both the high school and middle school.
BUT...
HOW IS IT THAT YOUR BOOBS ARE STILL THE SAME SIZE?
DIE!
RON RON

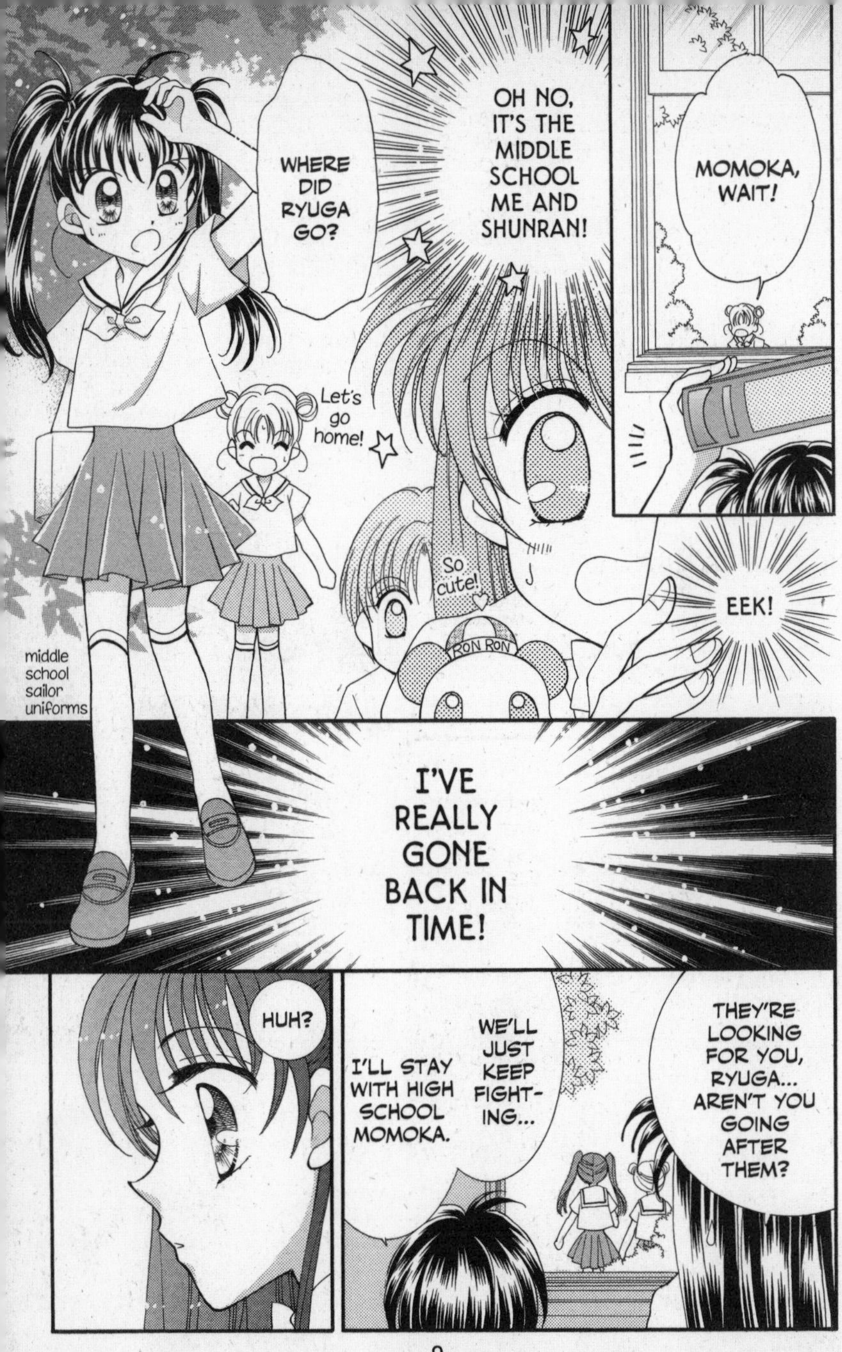

MOMOKA, WAIT!
EEK!
OH NO, IT'S THE MIDDLE SCHOOL ME AND SHUNRAN!
So cute!
WHERE DID RYUGA GO?
Let's go home!
middle school sailor uniforms
I'VE REALLY GONE BACK IN TIME!
THEY'RE LOOKING FOR YOU, RYUGA... AREN'T YOU GOING AFTER THEM?
WE'LL JUST KEEP FIGHTING...
I'LL STAY WITH HIGH SCHOOL MOMOKA.
HUH?

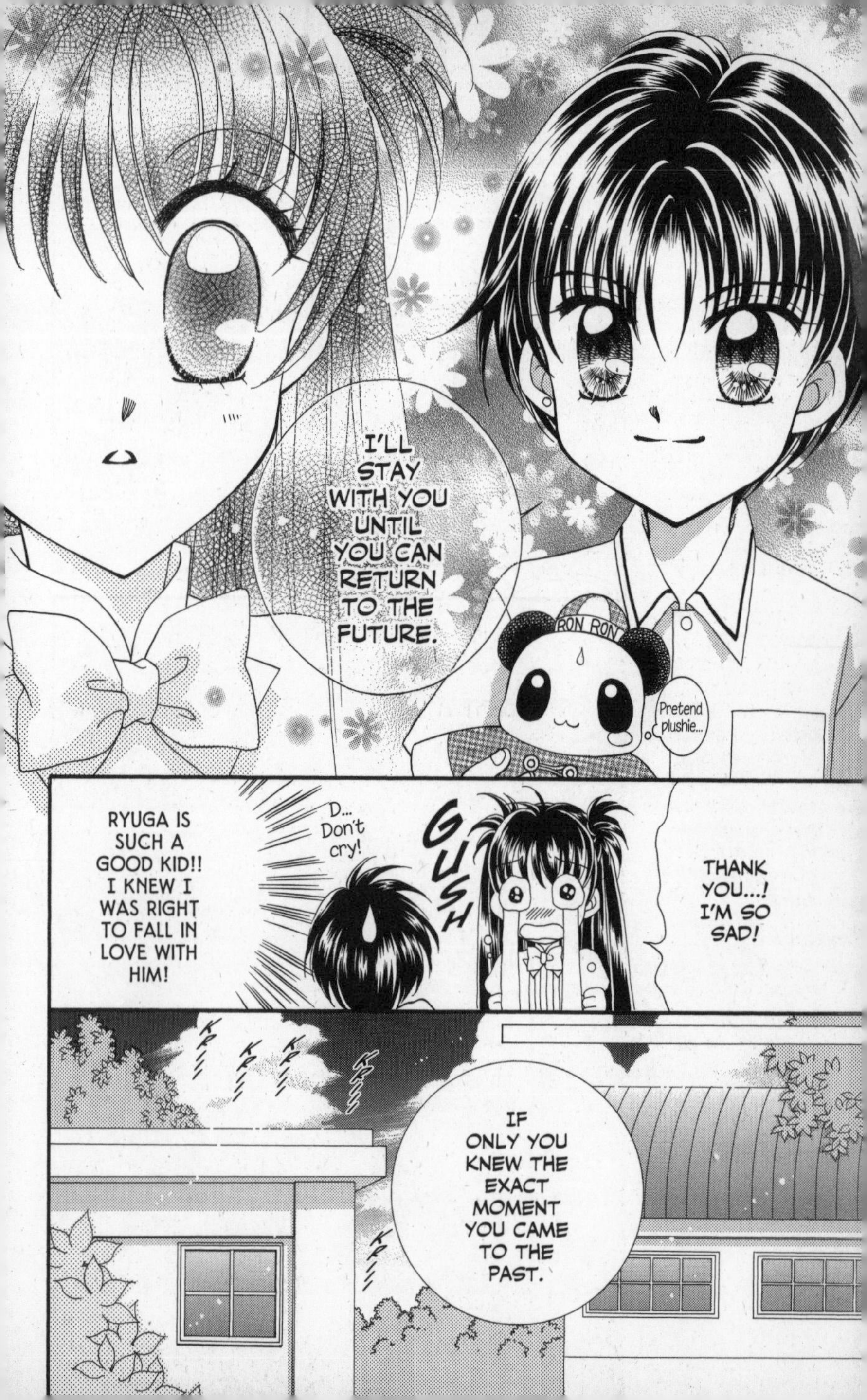
I'LL STAY WITH YOU UNTIL YOU CAN RETURN TO THE FUTURE.
Pretend plushie...
RON RON
THANK YOU...! I'M SO SAD!
GUSH
D... Don't cry!
RYUGA IS SUCH A GOOD KID!! I KNEW I WAS RIGHT TO FALL IN LOVE WITH HIM!
IF ONLY YOU KNEW THE EXACT MOMENT YOU CAME TO THE PAST.
KRI
KRI
KRI
KRI
KRI

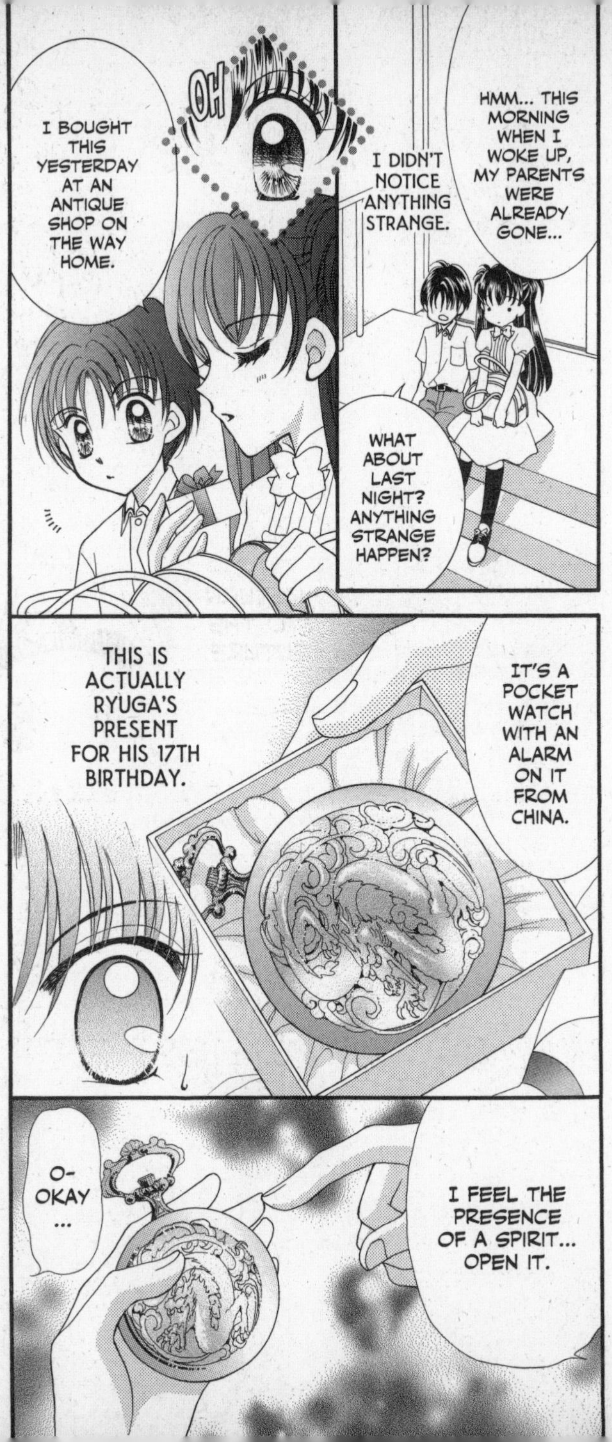
HMM... THIS MORNING WHEN I WOKE UP, MY PARENTS WERE ALREADY GONE...
I DIDN'T NOTICE ANYTHING STRANGE.
WHAT ABOUT LAST NIGHT? ANYTHING STRANGE HAPPEN?
OH
I BOUGHT THIS YESTERDAY AT AN ANTIQUE SHOP ON THE WAY HOME.
IT'S A POCKET WATCH WITH AN ALARM ON IT FROM CHINA.
THIS IS ACTUALLY RYUGA'S PRESENT FOR HIS 17TH BIRTHDAY.
I FEEL THE PRESENCE OF A SPIRIT... OPEN IT.
O-OKAY ...

1

Hello! ♡
This is Matsumoto. How are you? Thanks for reading the latest volume of *St.♥Dragon Girl!*

It had always been my dream to make a manga series longer than two volumes, so I can't believe this is already the seventh! I've been drawing this series for almost four years now. I'm able to continue drawing Momoka and her friends because of the continued support of the publisher, my assistants, my family and my fans.

I'm a really lucky person. I'm thankful to you from the bottom of my heart! I'll continue doing my best, so please keep supporting me!

1/20/2003

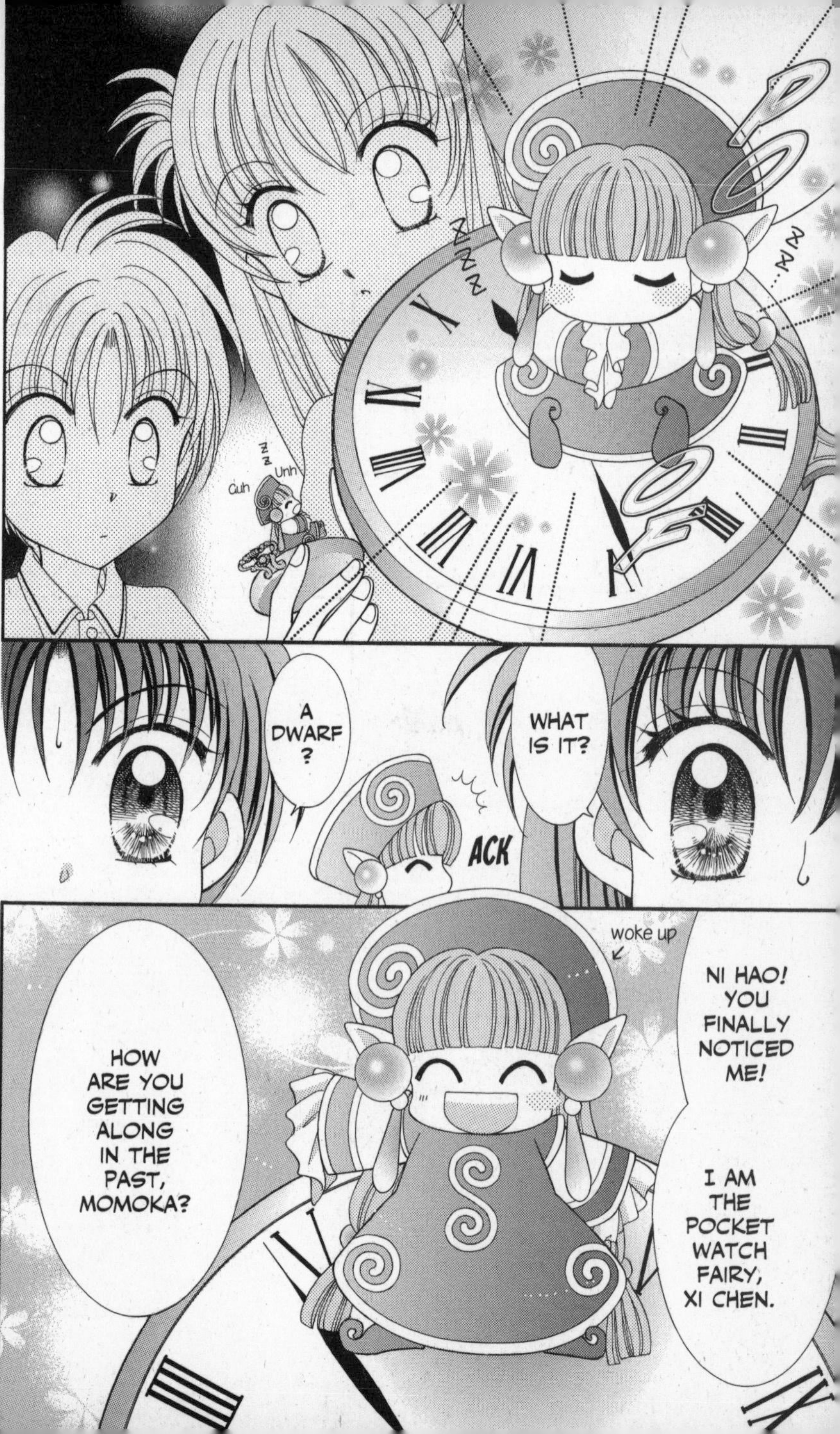
Unh
Guh
WHAT IS IT?
ACK
A DWARF?
woke up
NI HAO! YOU FINALLY NOTICED ME!
I AM THE POCKET WATCH FAIRY, XI CHEN.
HOW ARE YOU GETTING ALONG IN THE PAST, MOMOKA?

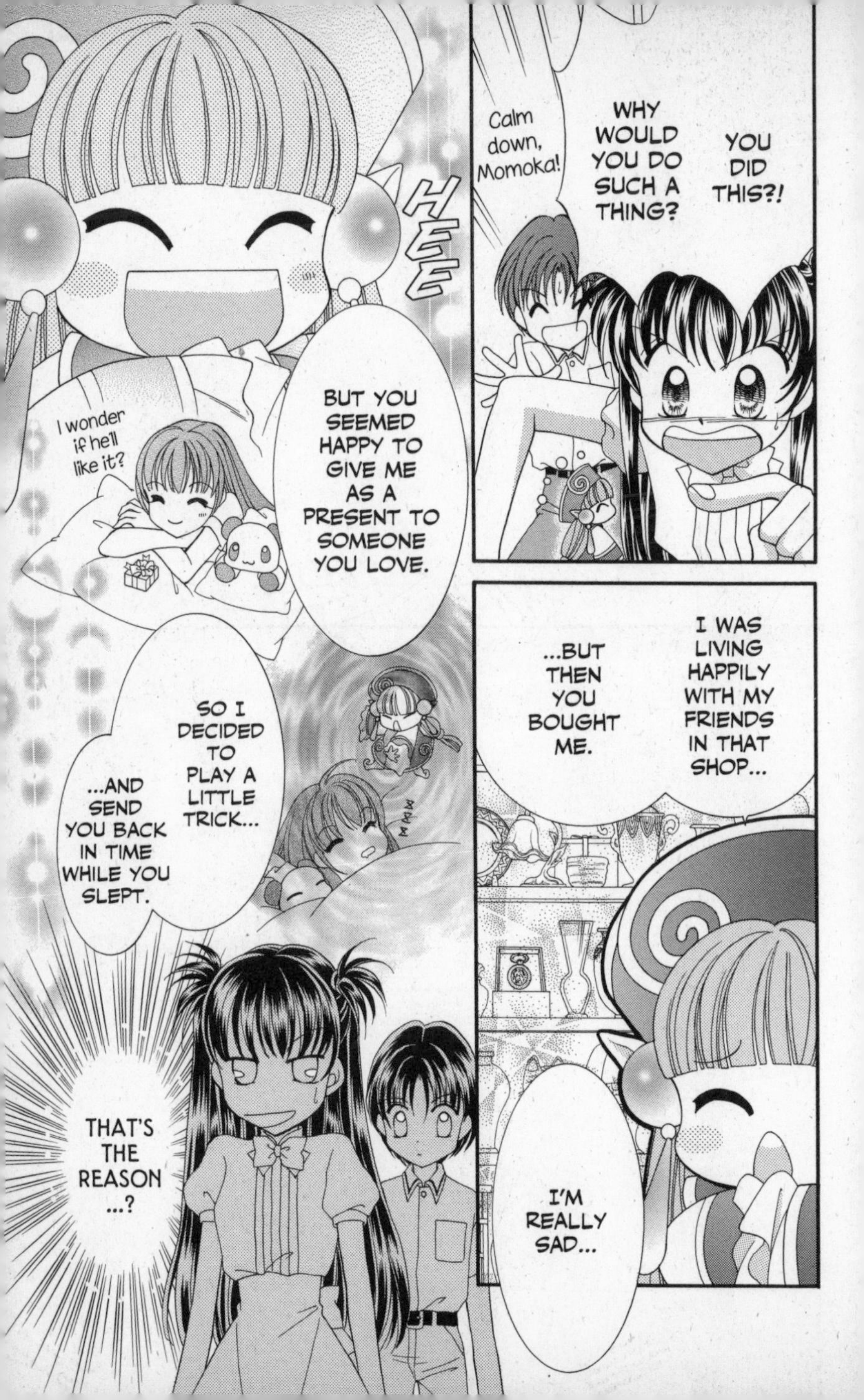
YOU DID THIS?!
WHY WOULD YOU DO SUCH A THING?
Calm down, Momoka!
I WAS LIVING HAPPILY WITH MY FRIENDS IN THAT SHOP...
...BUT THEN YOU BOUGHT ME.
I'M REALLY SAD...
HEE
BUT YOU SEEMED HAPPY TO GIVE ME AS A PRESENT TO SOMEONE YOU LOVE.
I wonder if he'll like it?
SO I DECIDED TO PLAY A LITTLE TRICK...
...AND SEND YOU BACK IN TIME WHILE YOU SLEPT.
THAT'S THE REASON ...?

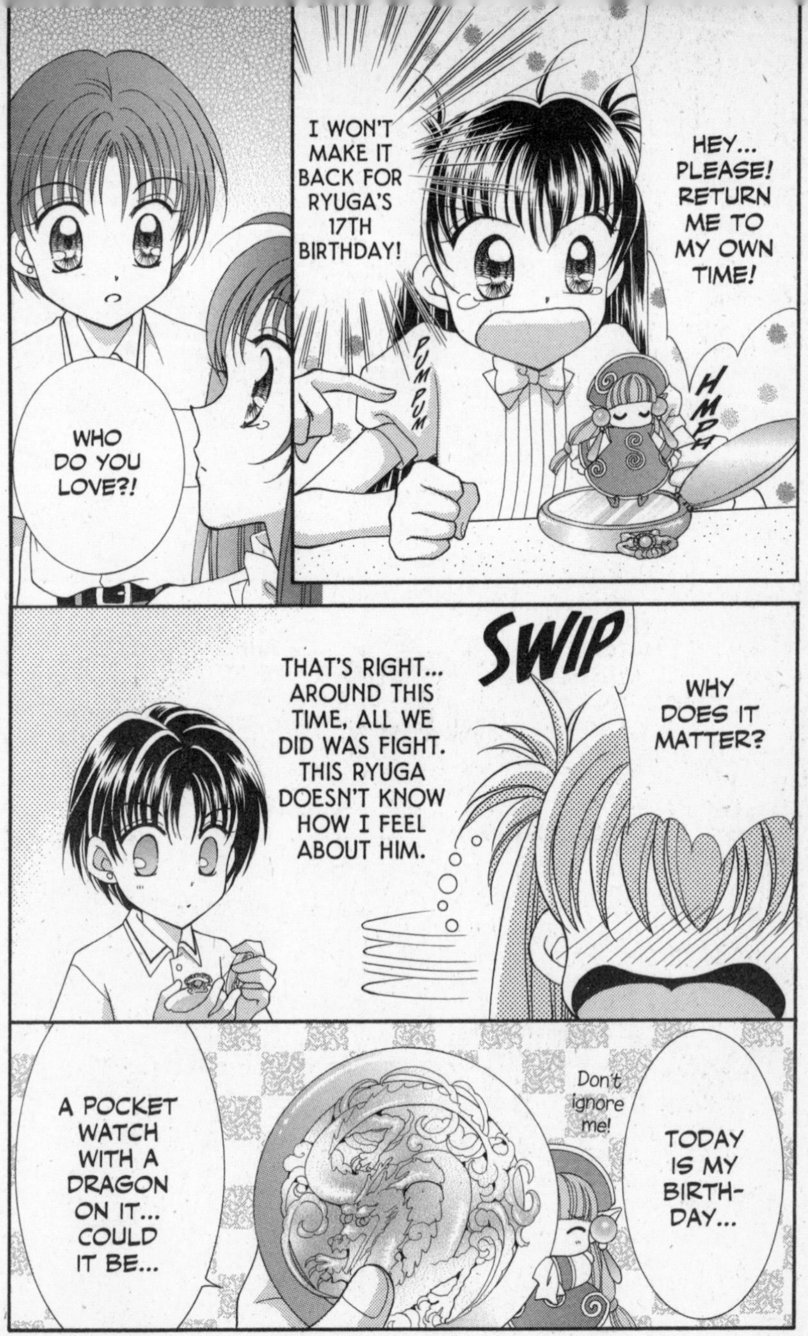
HEY... PLEASE! RETURN ME TO MY OWN TIME!
I WON'T MAKE IT BACK FOR RYUGA'S 17TH BIRTHDAY!
HMPH
PUM PUM
WHO DO YOU LOVE?!
WHY DOES IT MATTER?
SWIP
THAT'S RIGHT... AROUND THIS TIME, ALL WE DID WAS FIGHT. THIS RYUGA DOESN'T KNOW HOW I FEEL ABOUT HIM.
TODAY IS MY BIRTH-DAY...
Don't ignore me!
A POCKET WATCH WITH A DRAGON ON IT... COULD IT BE...

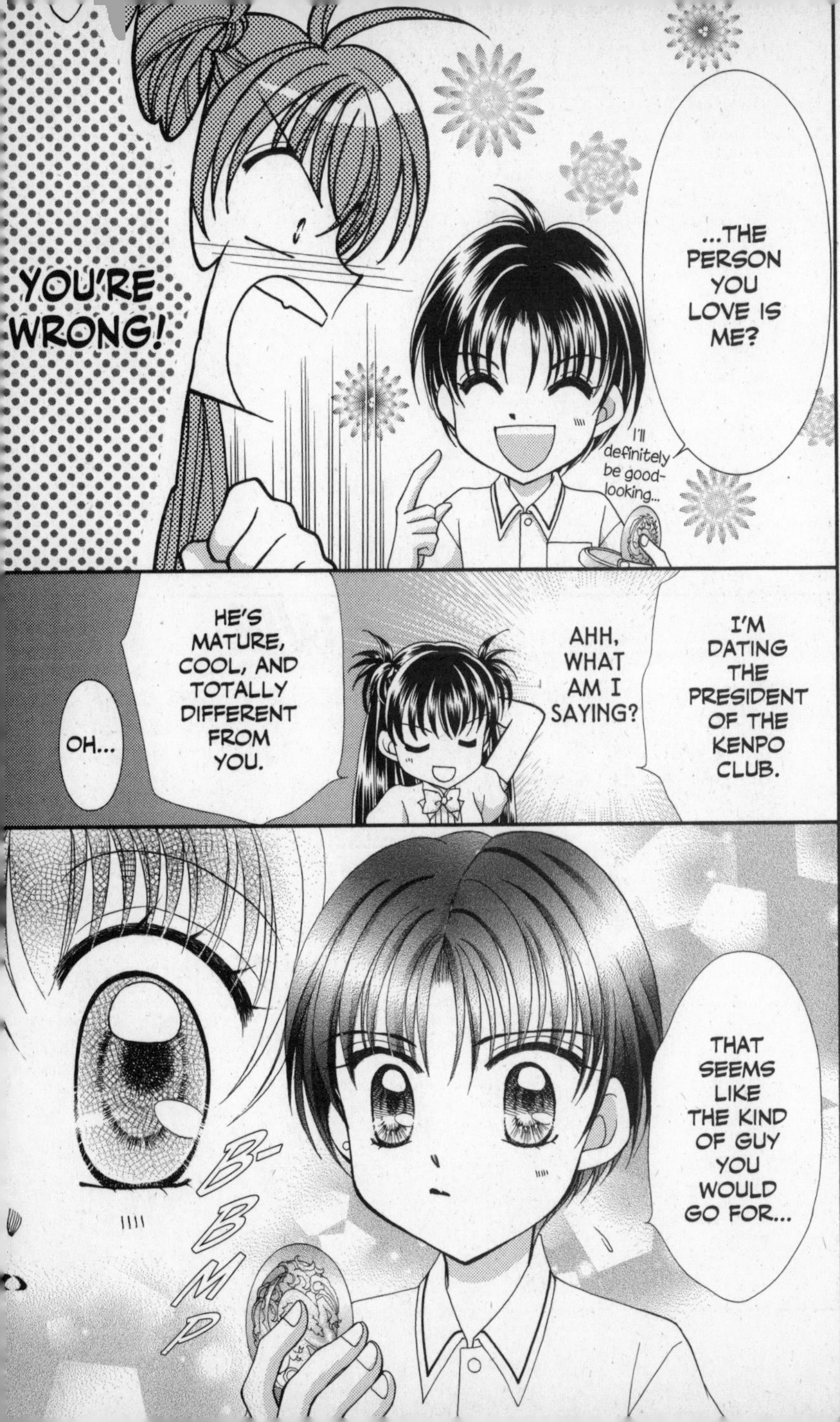
...THE PERSON YOU LOVE IS ME?
I'll definitely be good-looking...
YOU'RE WRONG!
I'M DATING THE PRESIDENT OF THE KENPO CLUB.
AHH, WHAT AM I SAYING?
HE'S MATURE, COOL, AND TOTALLY DIFFERENT FROM YOU.
OH...
THAT SEEMS LIKE THE KIND OF GUY YOU WOULD GO FOR...
B-BMP

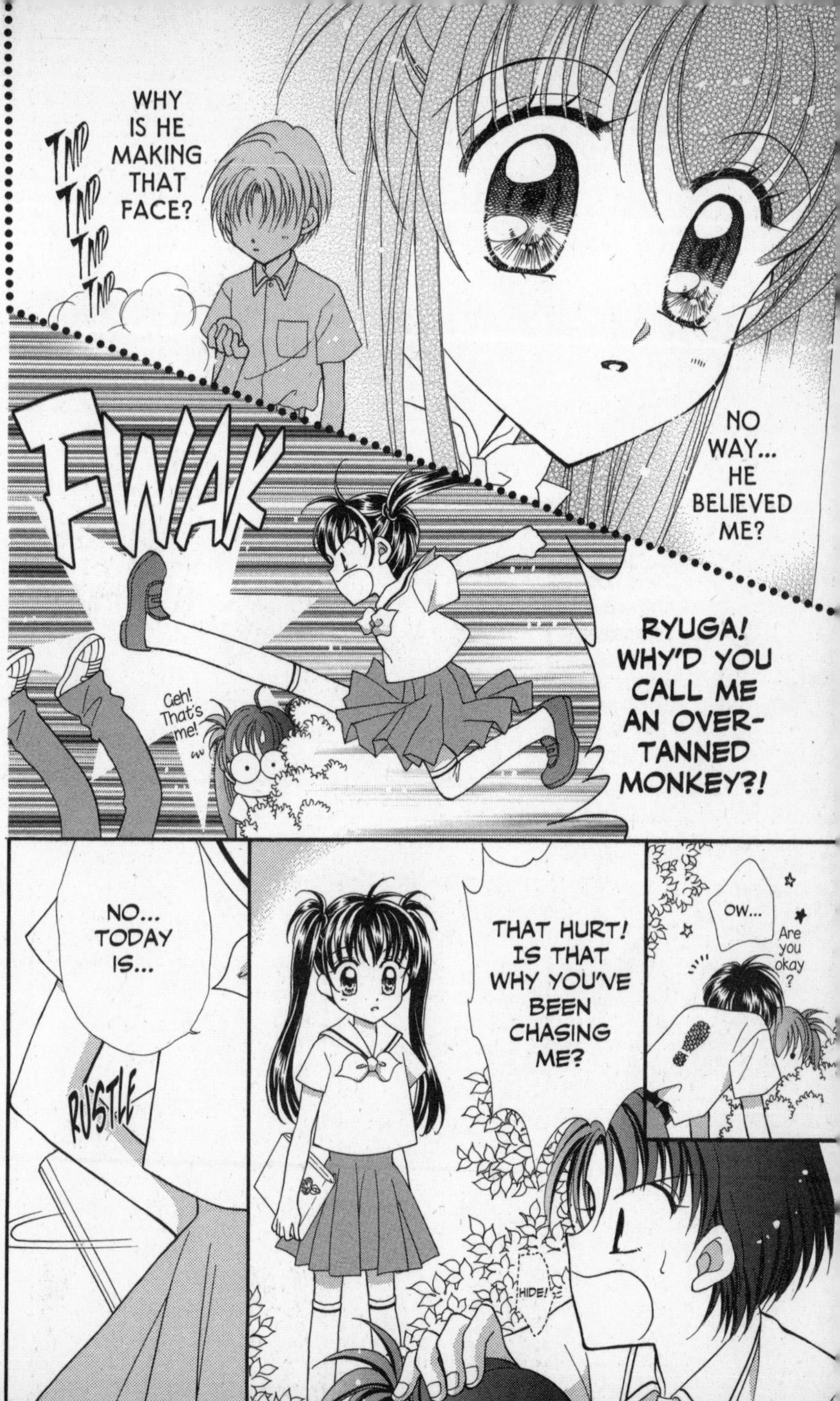
WHY IS HE MAKING THAT FACE?
TMP TMP TMP TMP
NO WAY... HE BELIEVED ME?
RYUGA! WHY'D YOU CALL ME AN OVER-TANNED MONKEY?!
FWAK
Geh! That's me!
OW...
Are you okay?
THAT HURT! IS THAT WHY YOU'VE BEEN CHASING ME?
HIDE!
NO... TODAY IS...
RUSTLE

2

I had always wanted to do a time-travel story like Xi Chen's.

Four years in the past didn't change the scenery too much, but it was hard to distinguish between the young versions of Ryuga and Momoka and their high school counterparts. If it had been a different era, it would've been easier! (laugh) But I like these kinds of stories, so I enjoyed it.

Xi Chen, the pocket-watch fairy, is the smallest creature I've drawn yet! Her name is the Chinese reading for "time." Too easy? ◊

If I had a pocket watch like this, I'd travel in time and go to any time period I wanted. But my assistant said that there'd also be the fear that Xi Chen would just take me wherever she wanted! (laugh) But I'd love to have Ryuga go all kinds of places and eras too... ◊

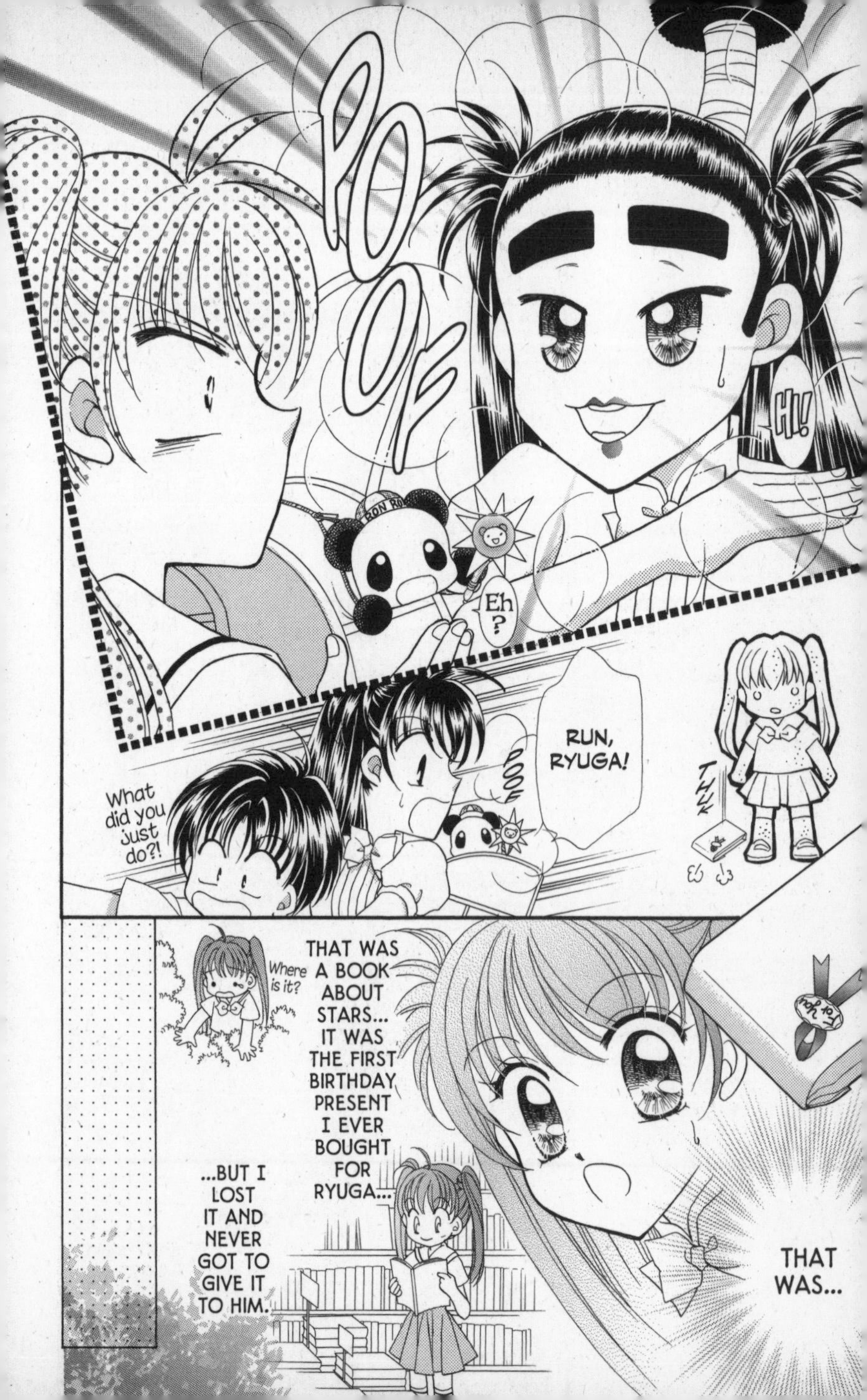
HI!
POOF
Eh?
RUN, RYUGA!
POOF
What did you just do?!
THUNK
THAT WAS...
THAT WAS A BOOK ABOUT STARS... IT WAS THE FIRST BIRTHDAY PRESENT I EVER BOUGHT FOR RYUGA...
...BUT I LOST IT AND NEVER GOT TO GIVE IT TO HIM.
Where is it?

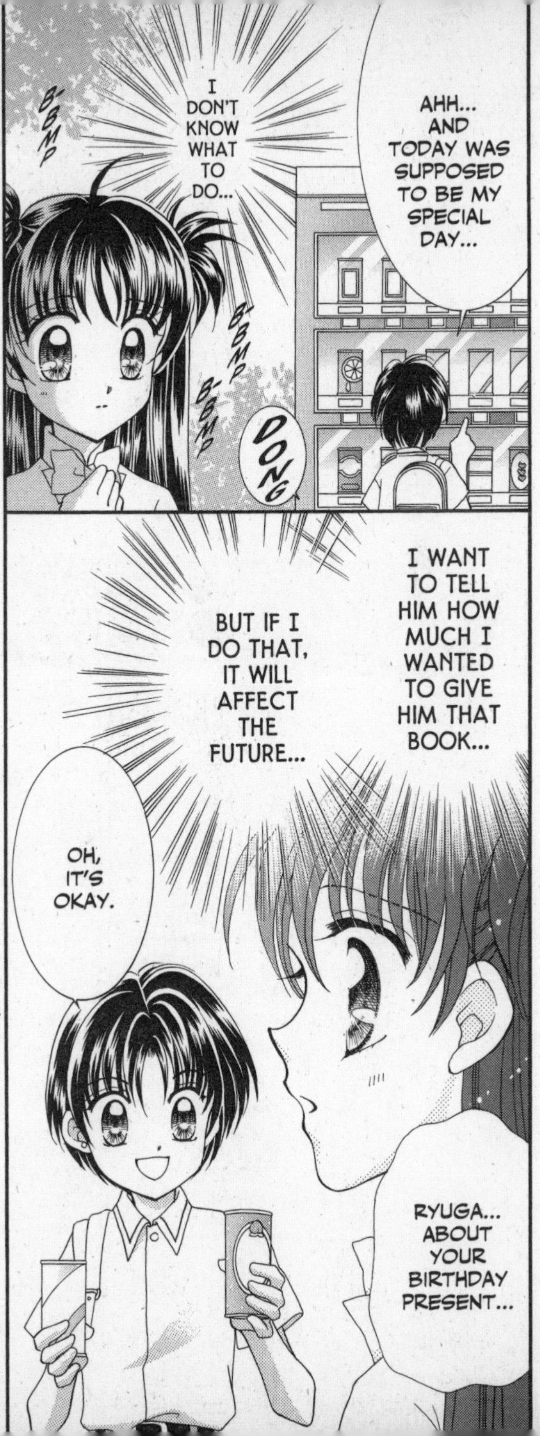
AHH... AND TODAY WAS SUPPOSED TO BE MY SPECIAL DAY...
I DON'T KNOW WHAT TO DO...
B-BUMP
B-BUMP
B-BUMP
DONG
I WANT TO TELL HIM HOW MUCH I WANTED TO GIVE HIM THAT BOOK...
BUT IF I DO THAT, IT WILL AFFECT THE FUTURE...
RYUGA... ABOUT YOUR BIRTHDAY PRESENT...
OH, IT'S OKAY.

3

By the way, I had mentioned in *St.♥Dragon Girl* volume 6 that I had bought a lot of souvenirs from Chinatown. Thanks for all your letters! Congratulations to those who won.

Actually, um, the way I wrote it was confusing, and I think that it sounded like whoever wrote letters would get a souvenir. I'm sorry—that was a mistake. But I chose the winners. I'm really sorry!!! I'm sorry I caused so much confusion.

I wanted to give out more presents, so I bought 500 small souvenirs from Chinatown, but even that wasn't enough for how many people wrote to me! And I figured it would take too long to send them all, so I gave up.

I'm sorry to all those who were waiting for something. But I'll definitely do another souvenir giveaway at some point.

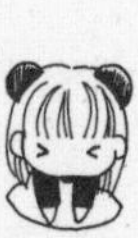

I'm sorry!

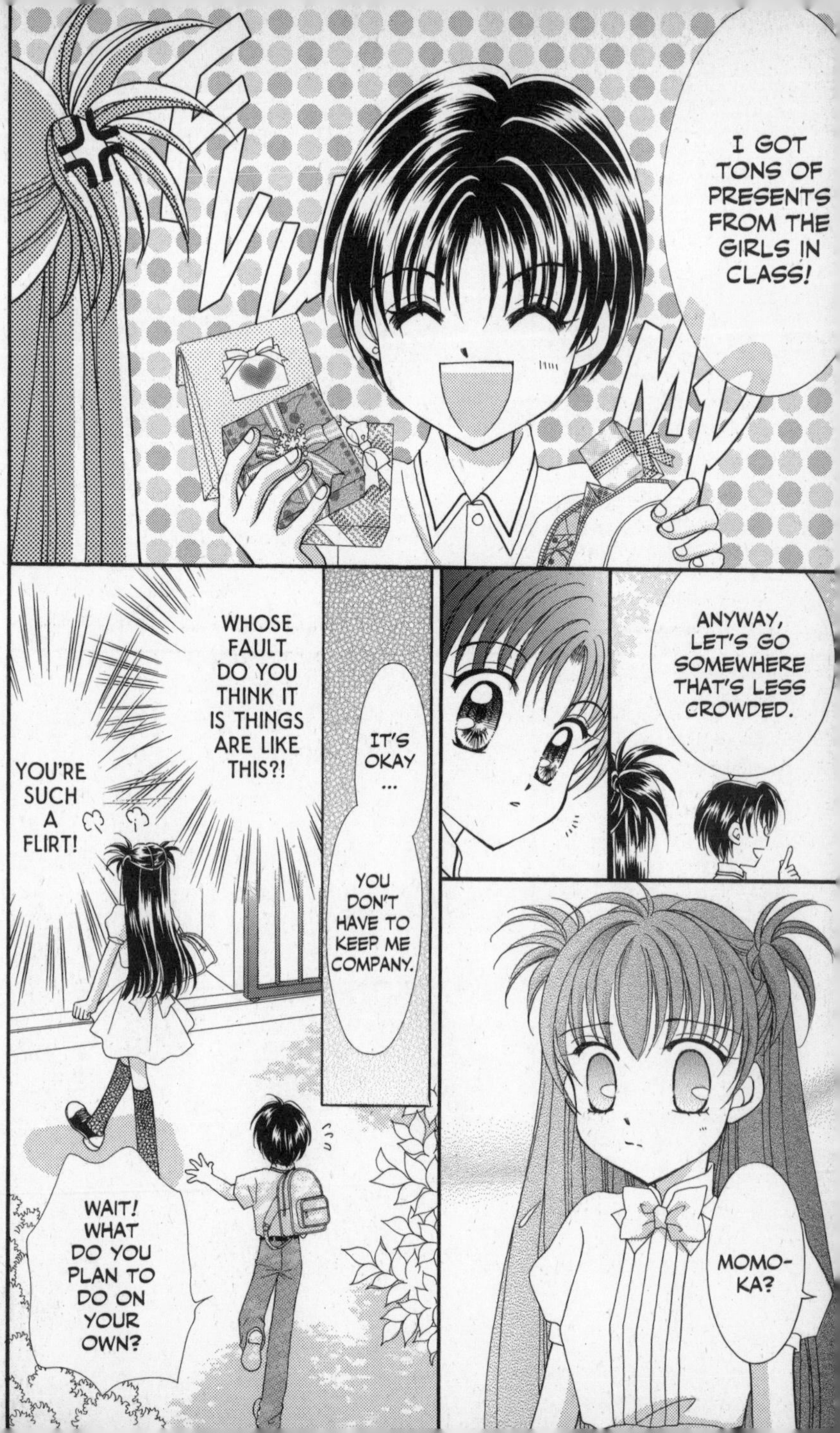
I GOT TONS OF PRESENTS FROM THE GIRLS IN CLASS!
ANYWAY, LET'S GO SOMEWHERE THAT'S LESS CROWDED.
MOMO-KA?
IT'S OKAY ...
YOU DON'T HAVE TO KEEP ME COMPANY.
WHOSE FAULT DO YOU THINK IT IS THINGS ARE LIKE THIS?!
YOU'RE SUCH A FLIRT!
WAIT! WHAT DO YOU PLAN TO DO ON YOUR OWN?

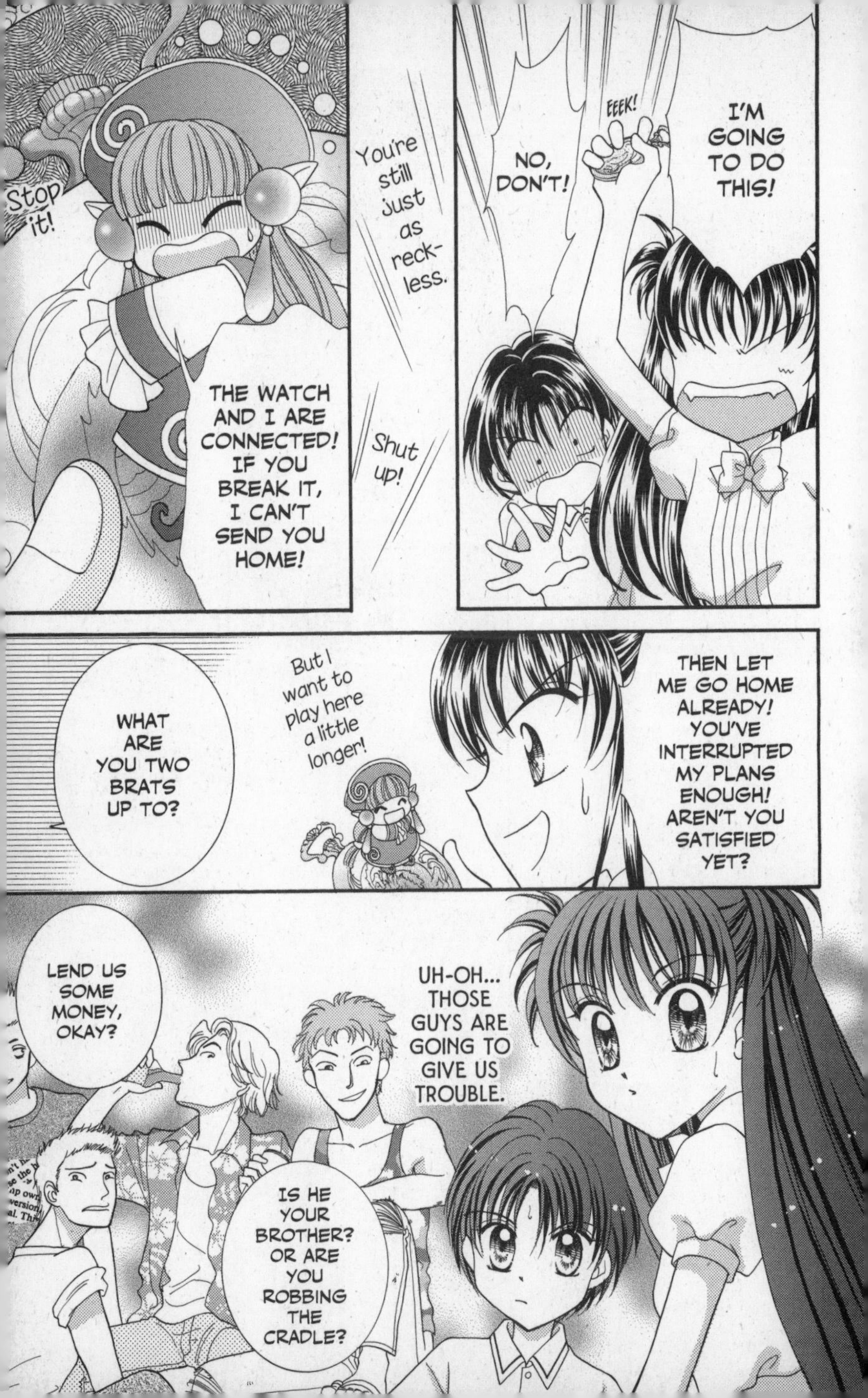
I'M GOING TO DO THIS!
EEEK!
NO, DON'T!
You're still just as reck-less.
Shut up!
THE WATCH AND I ARE CONNECTED! IF YOU BREAK IT, I CAN'T SEND YOU HOME!
Stop it!
THEN LET ME GO HOME ALREADY! YOU'VE INTERRUPTED MY PLANS ENOUGH! AREN'T YOU SATISFIED YET?
But I want to play here a little longer!
WHAT ARE YOU TWO BRATS UP TO?
UH-OH... THOSE GUYS ARE GOING TO GIVE US TROUBLE.
LEND US SOME MONEY, OKAY?
IS HE YOUR BROTHER? OR ARE YOU ROBBING THE CRADLE?

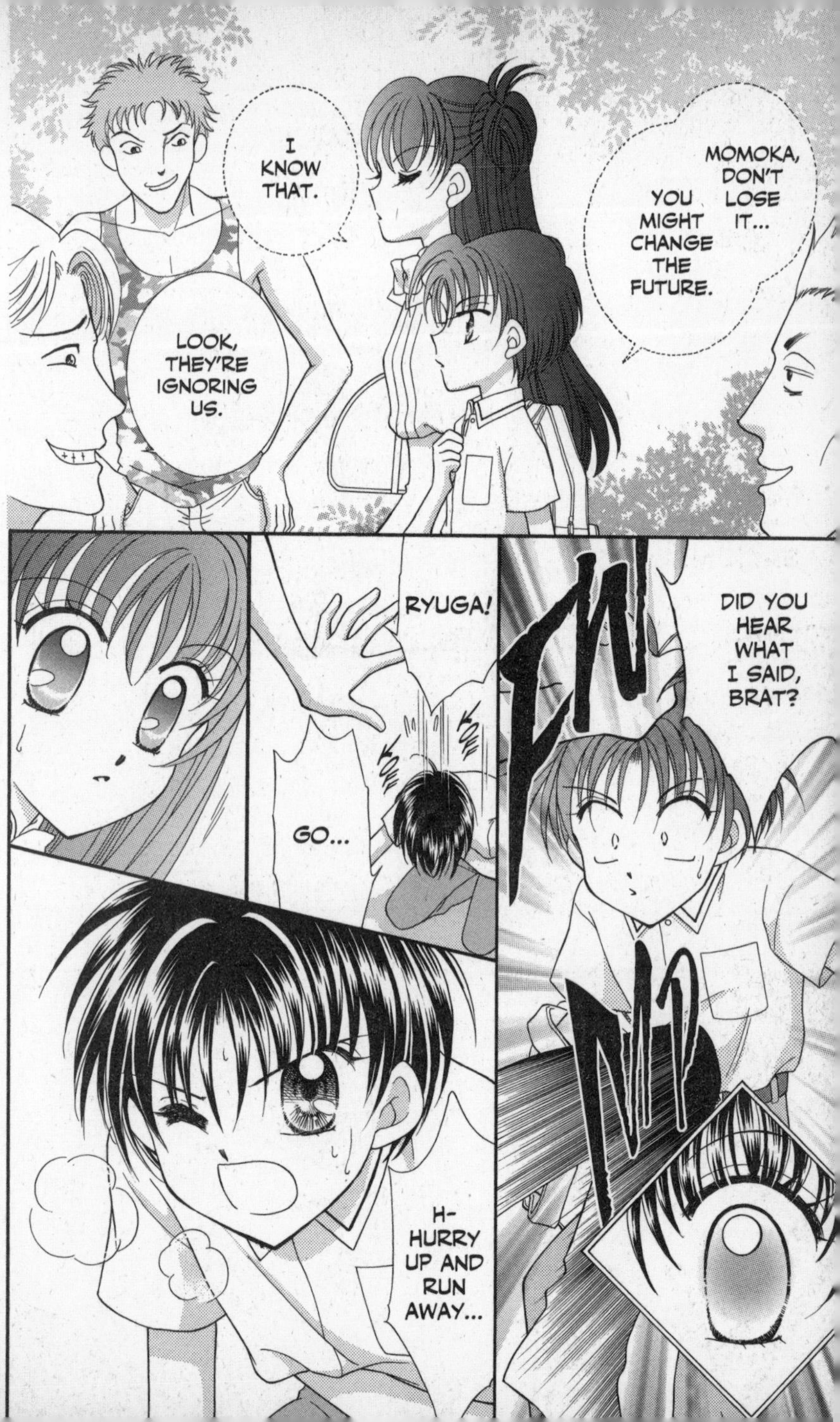
MOMOKA, DON'T LOSE IT...
YOU MIGHT CHANGE THE FUTURE.
I KNOW THAT.
LOOK, THEY'RE IGNORING US.
DID YOU HEAR WHAT I SAID, BRAT?
RYUGA!
GO...
H-HURRY UP AND RUN AWAY...

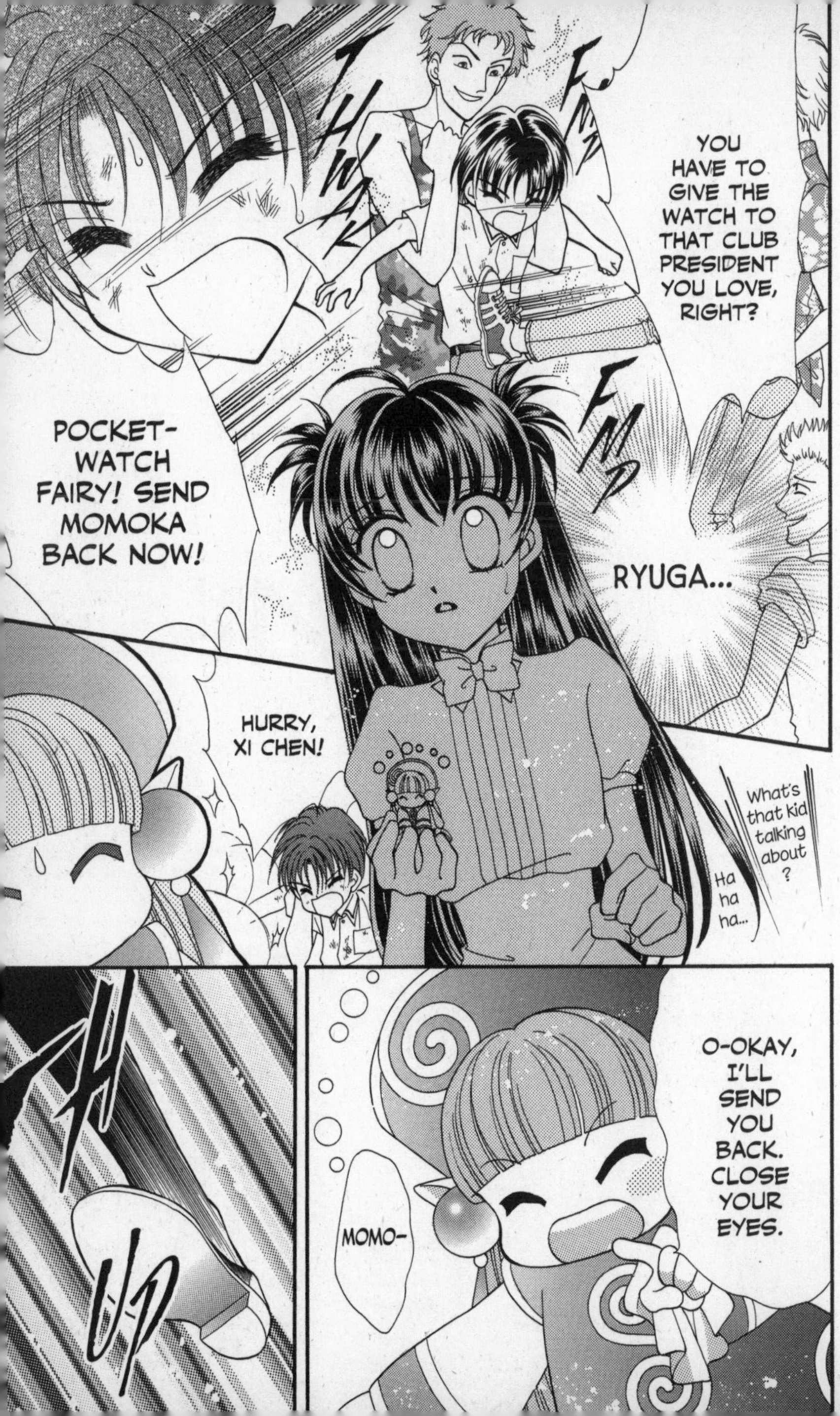
YOU HAVE TO GIVE THE WATCH TO THAT CLUB PRESIDENT YOU LOVE, RIGHT?
POCKET-WATCH FAIRY! SEND MOMOKA BACK NOW!
RYUGA...
What's that kid talking about?
Ha ha ha...
HURRY, XI CHEN!
O-OKAY, I'LL SEND YOU BACK. CLOSE YOUR EYES.
MOMO-

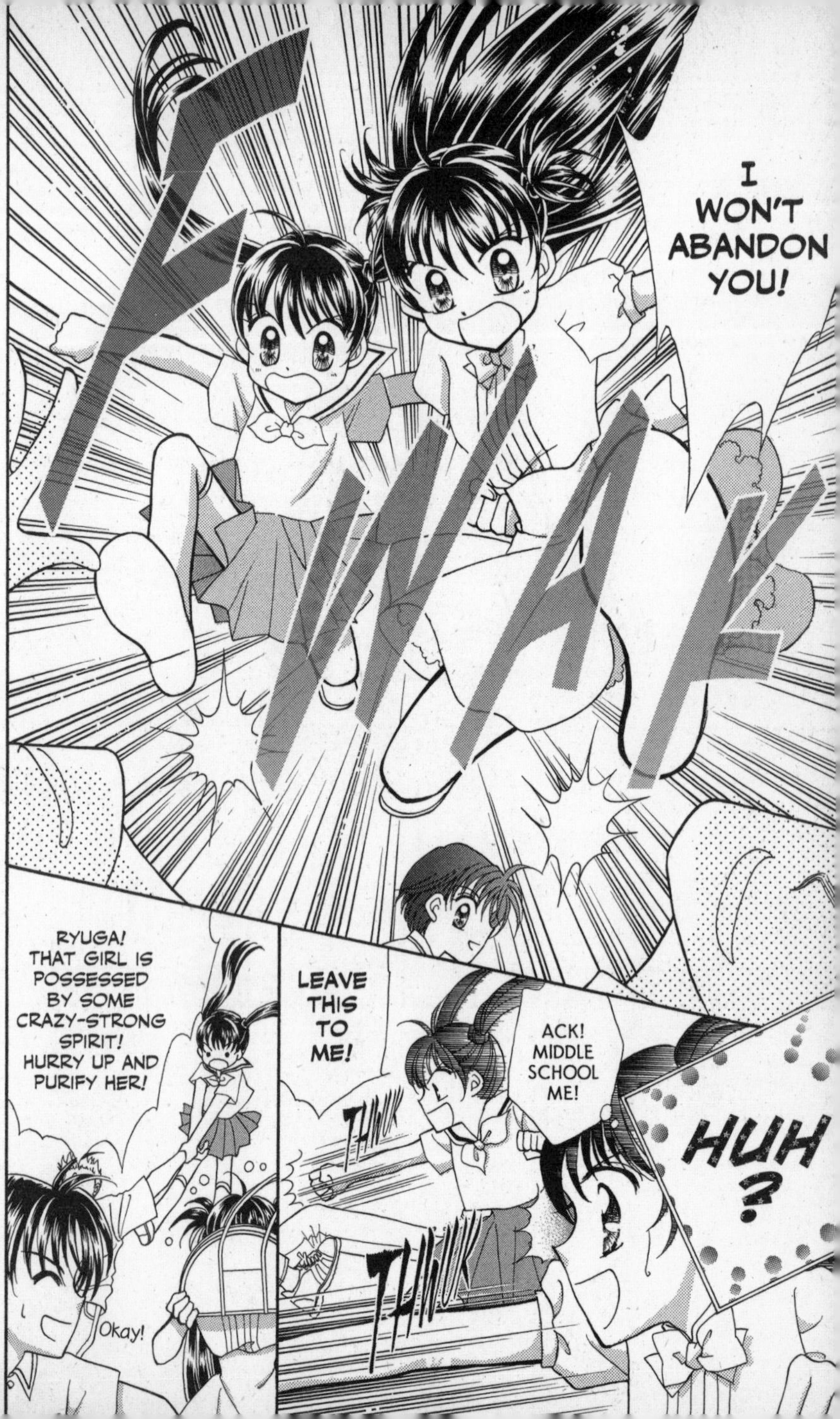
I WON'T ABANDON YOU!
HUH?
ACK! MIDDLE SCHOOL ME!
LEAVE THIS TO ME!
RYUGA! THAT GIRL IS POSSESSED BY SOME CRAZY-STRONG SPIRIT! HURRY UP AND PURIFY HER!
Okay!

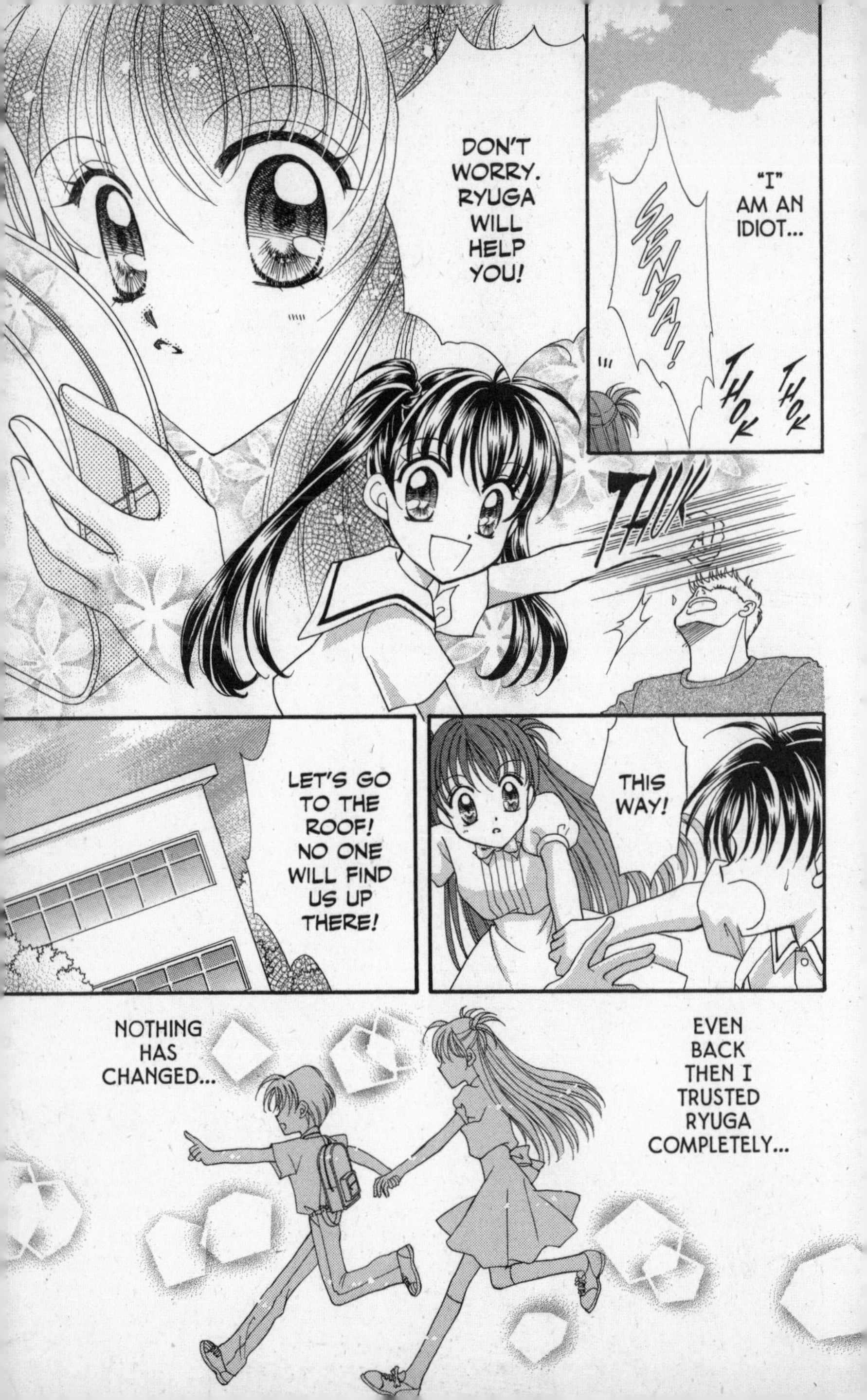
"I" AM AN IDIOT...
SENPAI!
THOK THOK
DON'T WORRY. RYUGA WILL HELP YOU!
THUK
THIS WAY!
LET'S GO TO THE ROOF! NO ONE WILL FIND US UP THERE!
EVEN BACK THEN I TRUSTED RYUGA COMPLETELY...
NOTHING HAS CHANGED...

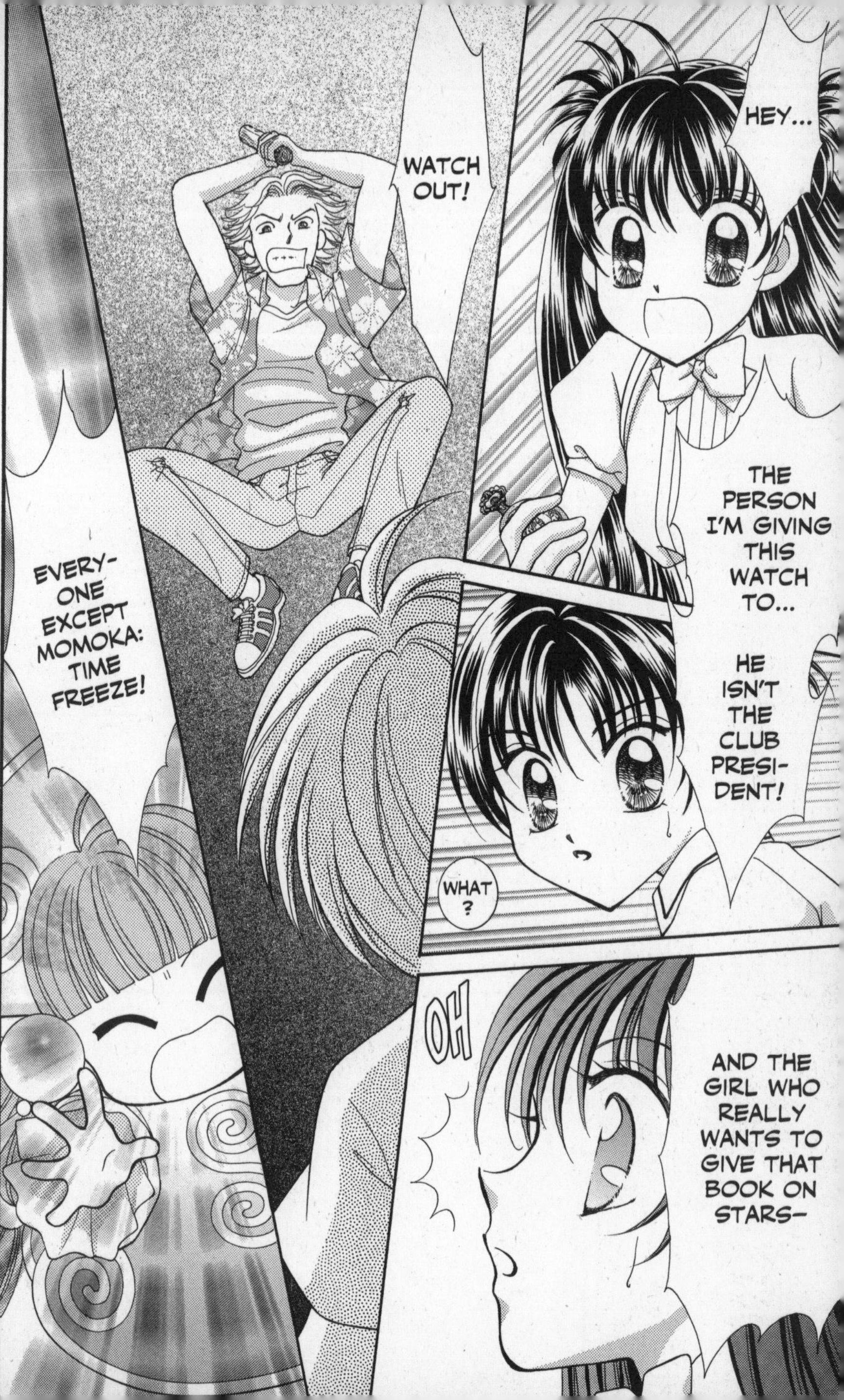
HEY...
THE PERSON I'M GIVING THIS WATCH TO...
HE ISN'T THE CLUB PRESIDENT!
WHAT?
OH
AND THE GIRL WHO REALLY WANTS TO GIVE THAT BOOK ON STARS—
WATCH OUT!
EVERY-ONE EXCEPT MOMOKA: TIME FREEZE!

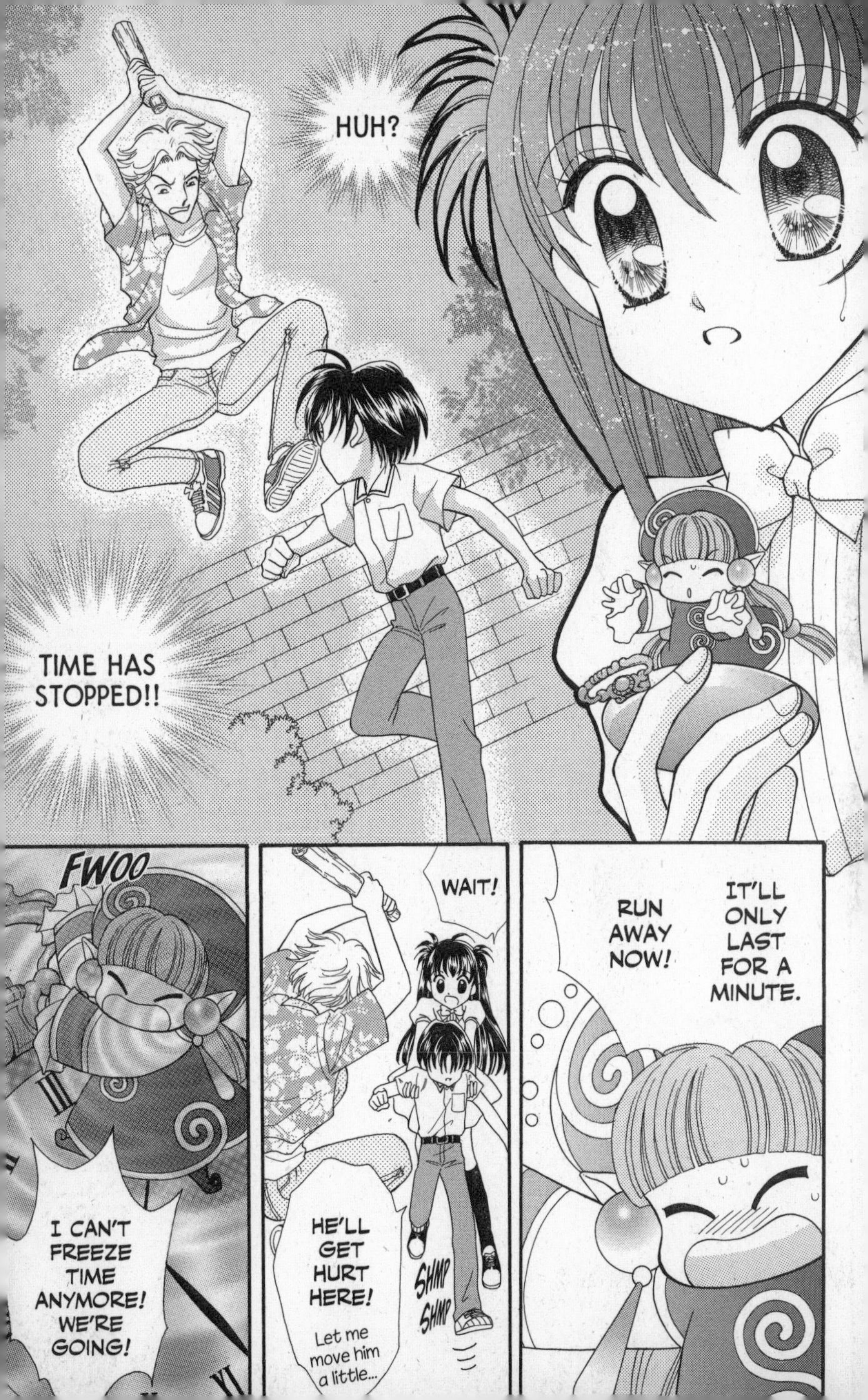
HUH?
TIME HAS STOPPED!!
IT'LL ONLY LAST FOR A MINUTE.
RUN AWAY NOW!
WAIT!
HE'LL GET HURT HERE!
Let me move him a little...
SHMP SHMP
FWOO
I CAN'T FREEZE TIME ANYMORE! WE'RE GOING!

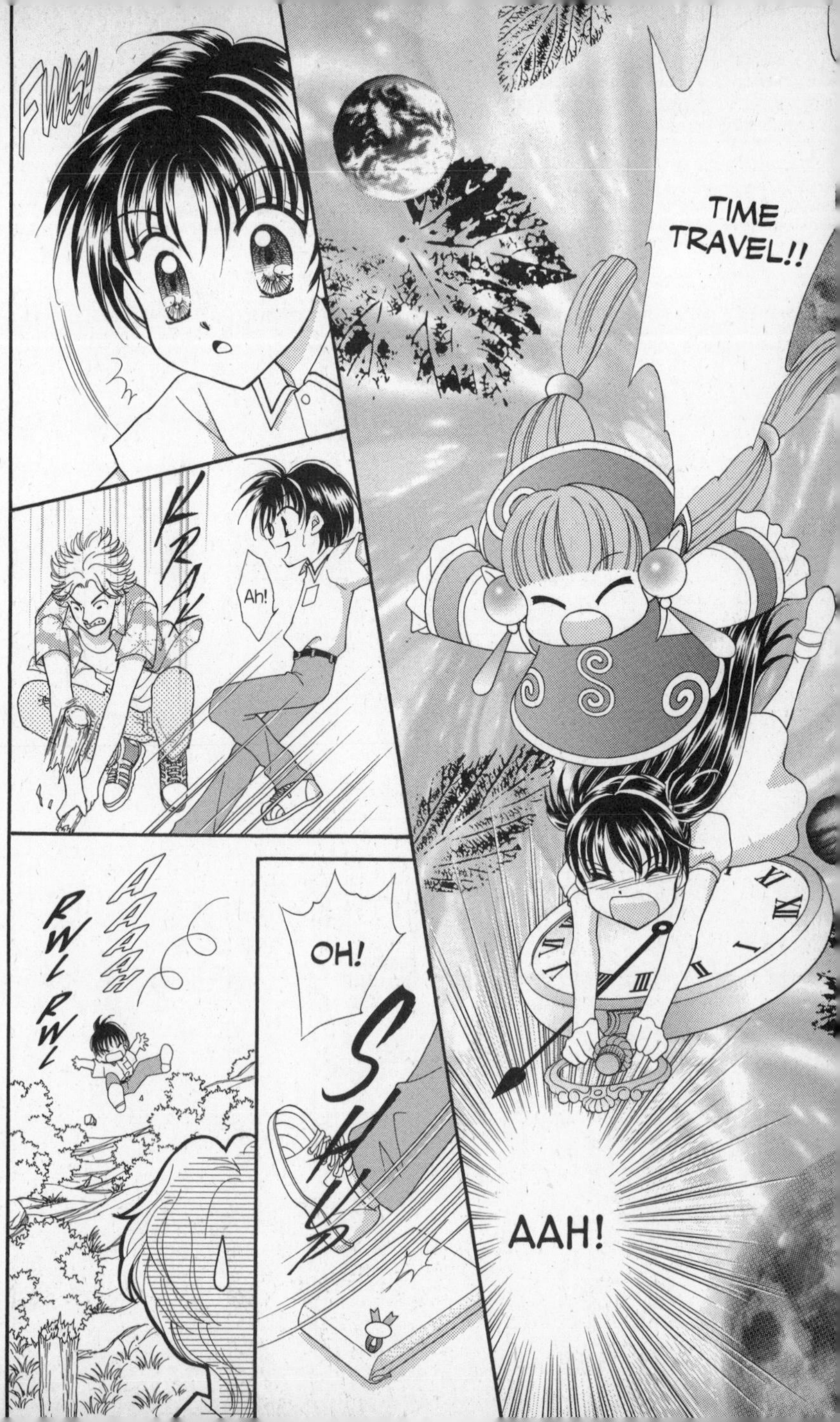
TIME TRAVEL!!
AAH!
FWISH
KRAK
Ah!
OH!
SHUP
AAAAH
RWL RWL

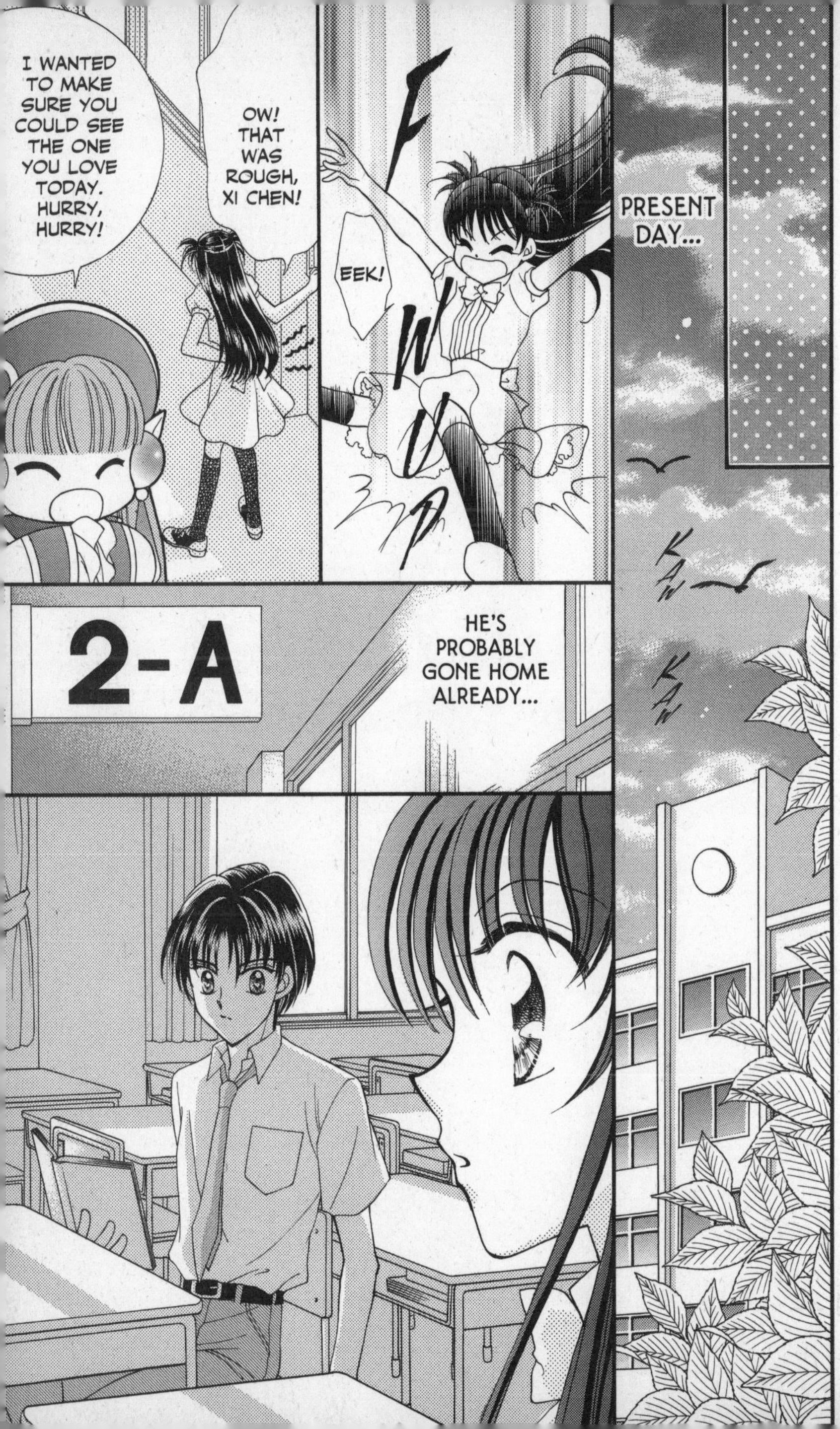
PRESENT DAY...
KAW
KAW
EEK!
FWUMP
OW! THAT WAS ROUGH, XI CHEN!
I WANTED TO MAKE SURE YOU COULD SEE THE ONE YOU LOVE TODAY. HURRY, HURRY!
HE'S PROBABLY GONE HOME ALREADY...
2-A

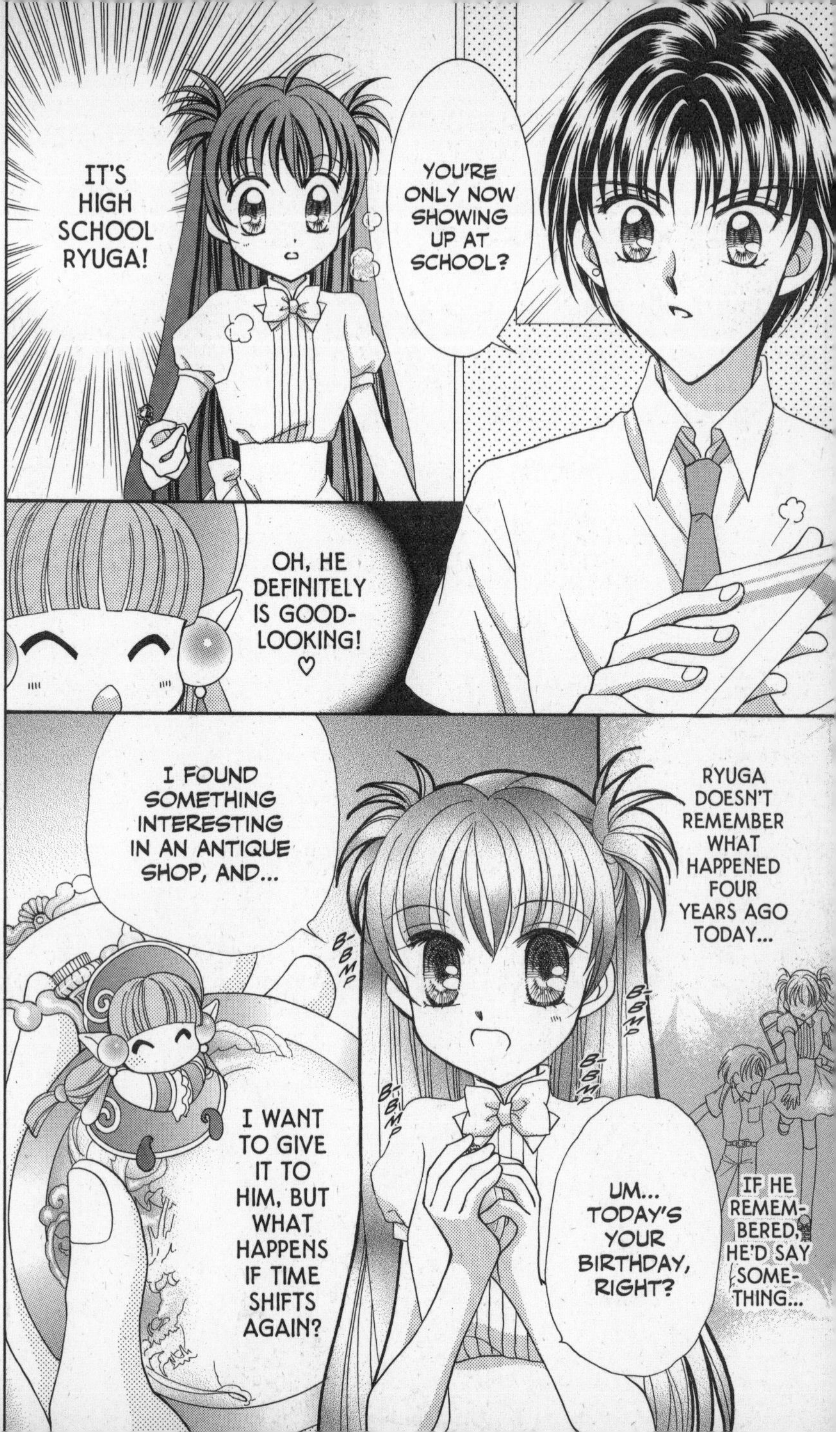
YOU'RE ONLY NOW SHOWING UP AT SCHOOL?
IT'S HIGH SCHOOL RYUGA!
OH, HE DEFINITELY IS GOOD-LOOKING! ♡
RYUGA DOESN'T REMEMBER WHAT HAPPENED FOUR YEARS AGO TODAY...
IF HE REMEMBERED, HE'D SAY SOMETHING...
B-BMP
B-BMP
B-BMP
UM... TODAY'S YOUR BIRTHDAY, RIGHT?
I FOUND SOMETHING INTERESTING IN AN ANTIQUE SHOP, AND...
B-BMP
I WANT TO GIVE IT TO HIM, BUT WHAT HAPPENS IF TIME SHIFTS AGAIN?

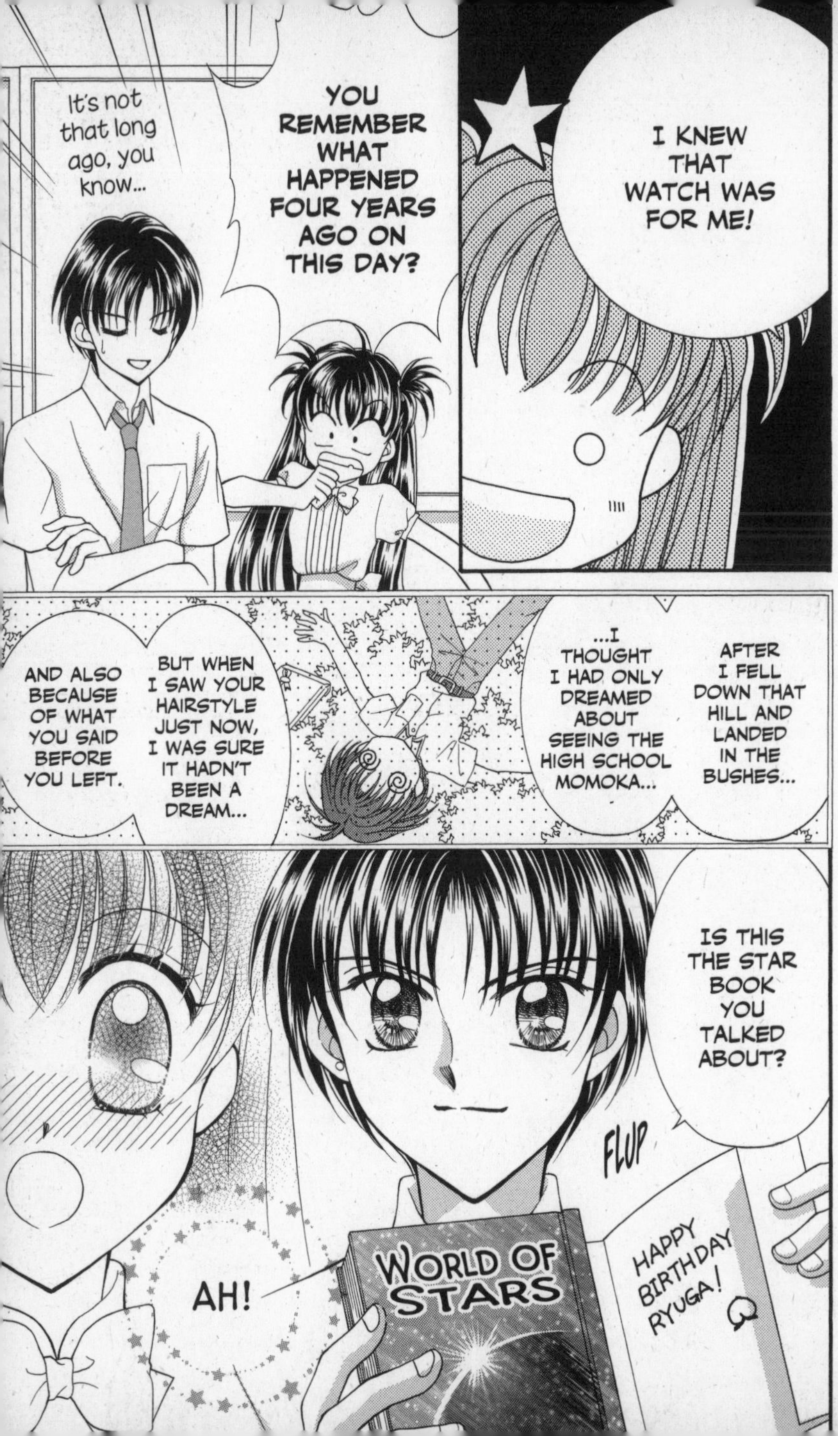
I KNEW THAT WATCH WAS FOR ME!
YOU REMEMBER WHAT HAPPENED FOUR YEARS AGO ON THIS DAY?
It's not that long ago, you know...
AFTER I FELL DOWN THAT HILL AND LANDED IN THE BUSHES...
...I THOUGHT I HAD ONLY DREAMED ABOUT SEEING THE HIGH SCHOOL MOMOKA...
BUT WHEN I SAW YOUR HAIRSTYLE JUST NOW, I WAS SURE IT HADN'T BEEN A DREAM...
AND ALSO BECAUSE OF WHAT YOU SAID BEFORE YOU LEFT.
IS THIS THE STAR BOOK YOU TALKED ABOUT?
FLUP
HAPPY BIRTHDAY RYUGA!
WORLD OF STARS
AH!

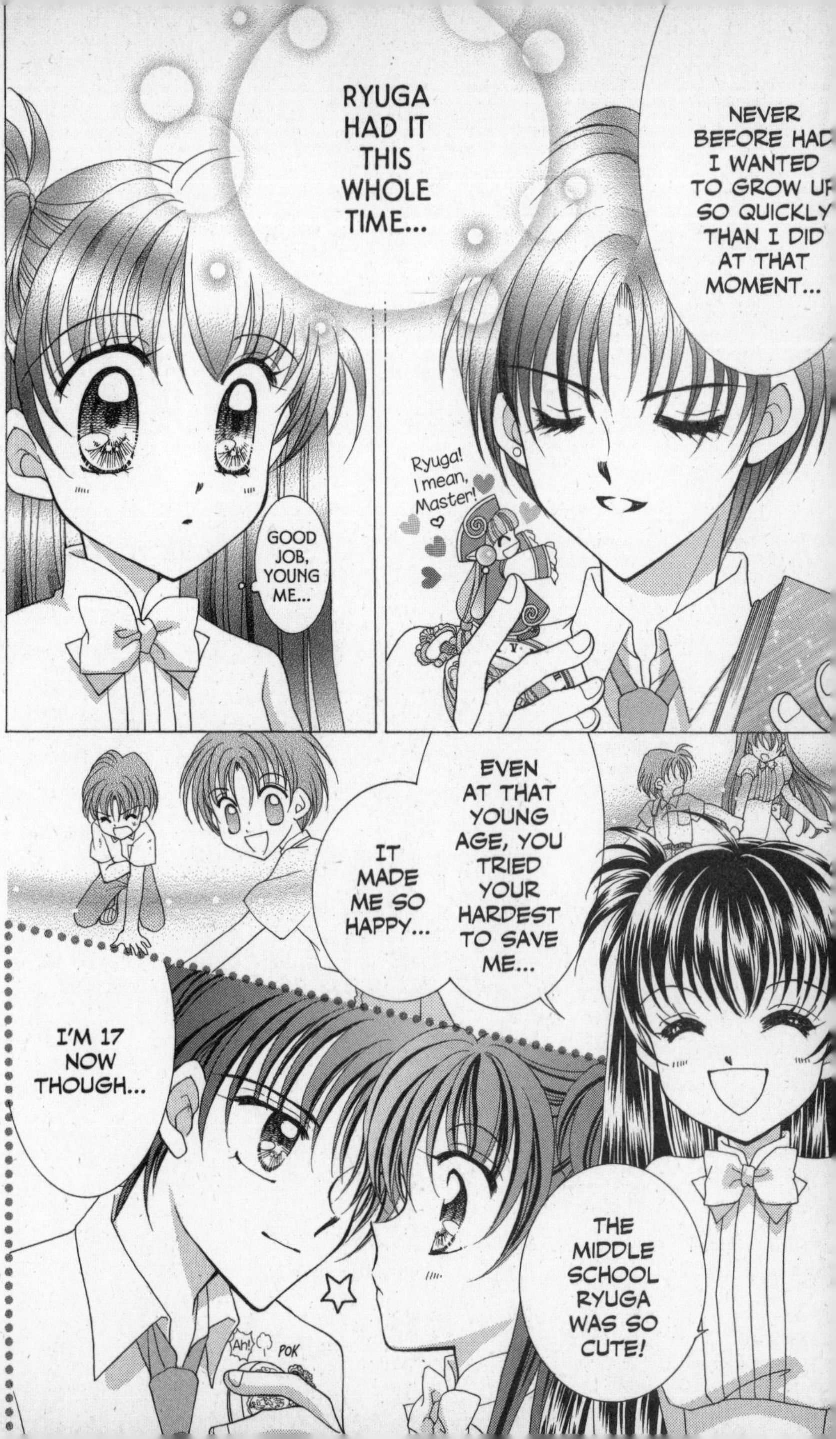

NEVER BEFORE HAD I WANTED TO GROW UP SO QUICKLY THAN I DID AT THAT MOMENT...
Ryuga! I mean, Master!
RYUGA HAD IT THIS WHOLE TIME...
GOOD JOB, YOUNG ME...
EVEN AT THAT YOUNG AGE, YOU TRIED YOUR HARDEST TO SAVE ME...
IT MADE ME SO HAPPY...
THE MIDDLE SCHOOL RYUGA WAS SO CUTE!
I'M 17 NOW THOUGH...
Ah!
POK

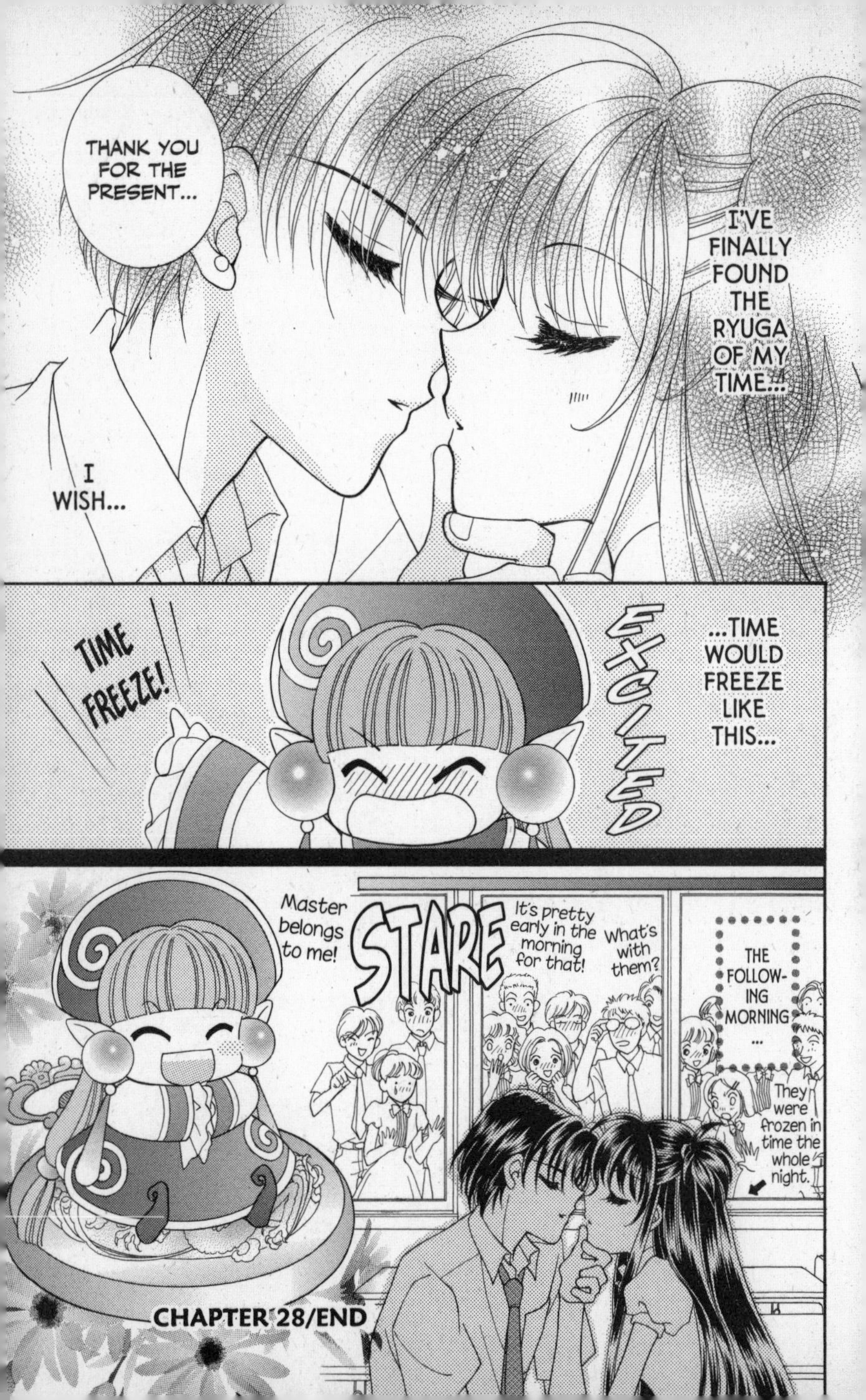
I'VE FINALLY FOUND THE RYUGA OF MY TIME...!
THANK YOU FOR THE PRESENT...
I WISH...
...TIME WOULD FREEZE LIKE THIS...
EXCITED
TIME FREEZE!
THE FOLLOWING MORNING...
They were frozen in time the whole night.
What's with them?
It's pretty early in the morning for that!
STARE
Master belongs to me!
CHAPTER 28/END

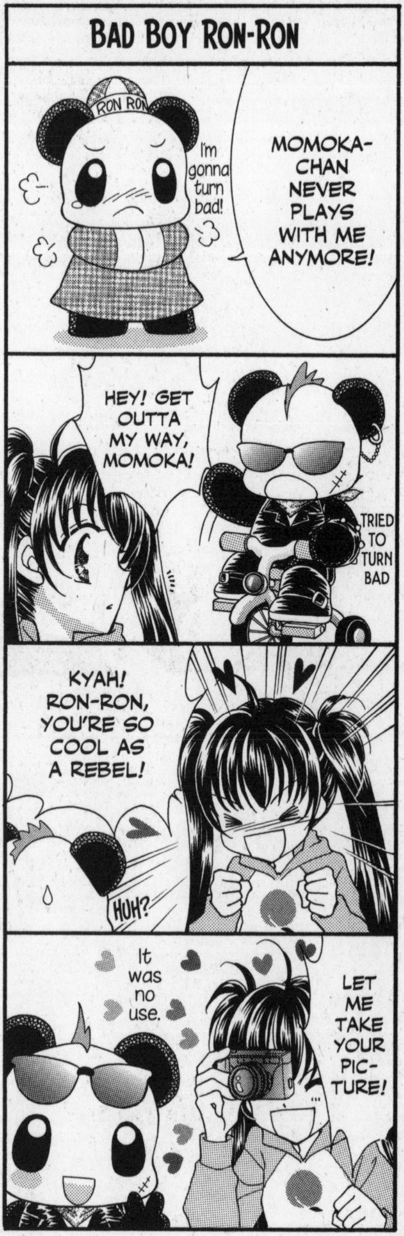
BAD BOY RON-RON
RON RON
MOMOKA-CHAN NEVER PLAYS WITH ME ANYMORE!
I'm gonna turn bad!
HEY! GET OUTTA MY WAY, MOMOKA!
TRIED TO TURN BAD
KYAH! RON-RON, YOU'RE SO COOL AS A REBEL!
HUH?
LET ME TAKE YOUR PIC-TURE!
It was no use.

♥ I sent signed manga to those who sent in these comic strips. ♥

This idea was from Kaori Kudou from Okayama Prefecture. ▶

She drew it in her letter, and I arranged it into a comic strip. Kaori-chan's Ron-Ron is really cute. I was so happy! I don't know your address, so please tell me what it is!

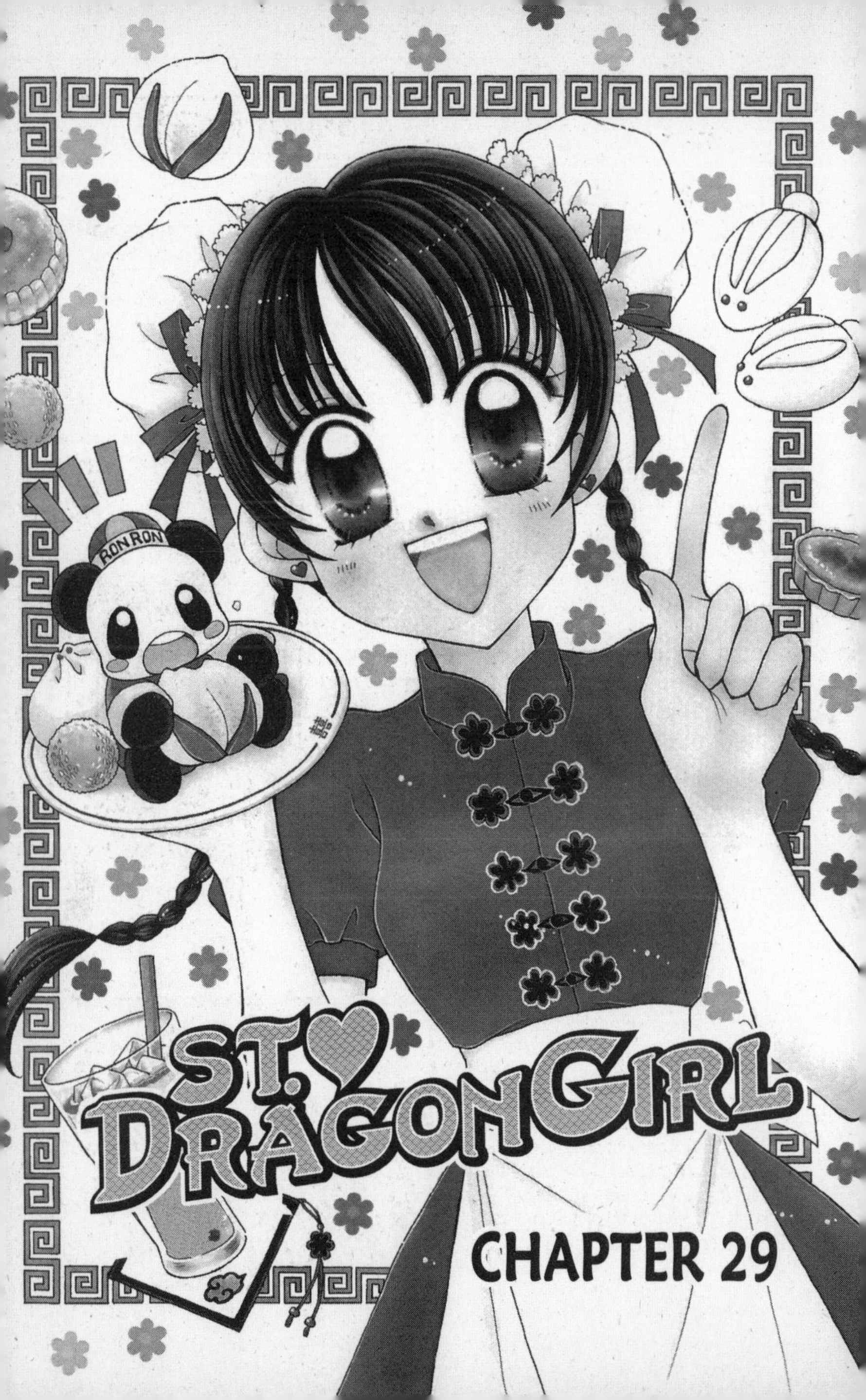
RON RON
ST.♥DRAGON GIRL
CHAPTER 29

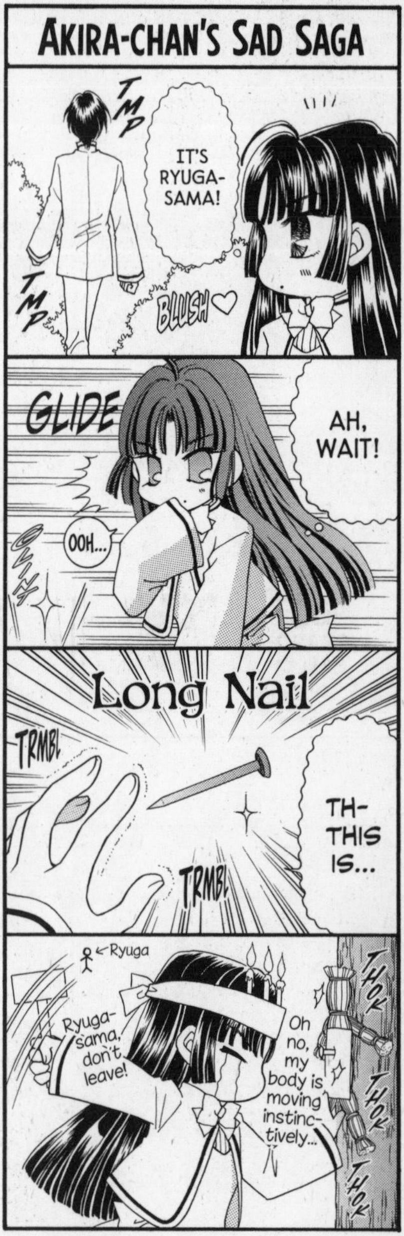
AKIRA-CHAN'S SAD SAGA
IT'S RYUGA-SAMA!
BLUSH
TMP
TMP
AH, WAIT!
GLIDE
OOH...
Long Nail
TH-THIS IS...
TRMBL
TRMBL
←Ryuga
Oh no, my body is moving instinctively...
Ryuga-sama, don't leave!
THOK
THOK
THOK

Idea from Kumiko Saito from Tokyo ▶

Did she automatically make a voodoo doll after she saw a nail? (laugh) Thanks for the hilarious Akira-chan comic! But who is Akira cursing all of a sudden... Could it be me?

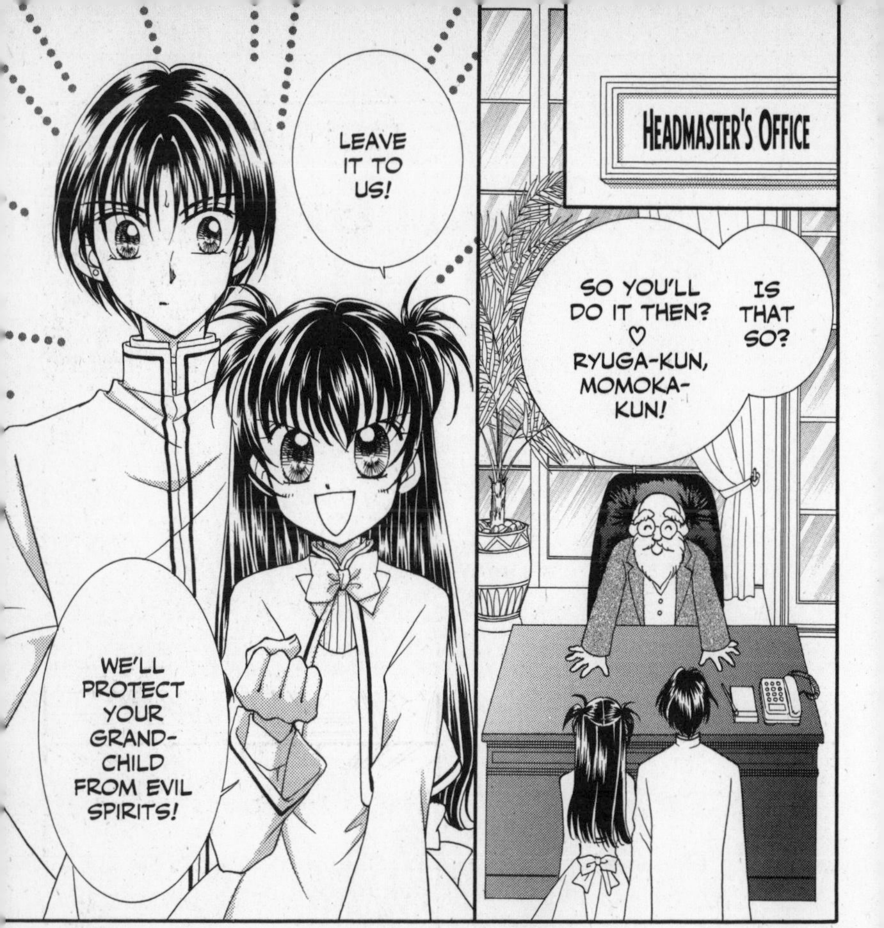
HEADMASTER'S OFFICE
SO YOU'LL DO IT THEN? ♡ RYUGA-KUN, MOMOKA-KUN!
IS THAT SO?
LEAVE IT TO US!
WE'LL PROTECT YOUR GRAND-CHILD FROM EVIL SPIRITS!

Misuzu Fujimiya

Birthday: October 4.
Libra. Blood Type: A.
10 years old.

She's the headmaster's granddaughter. Her mother died when she was young, and her father was transferred overseas for his job. She's an only child.

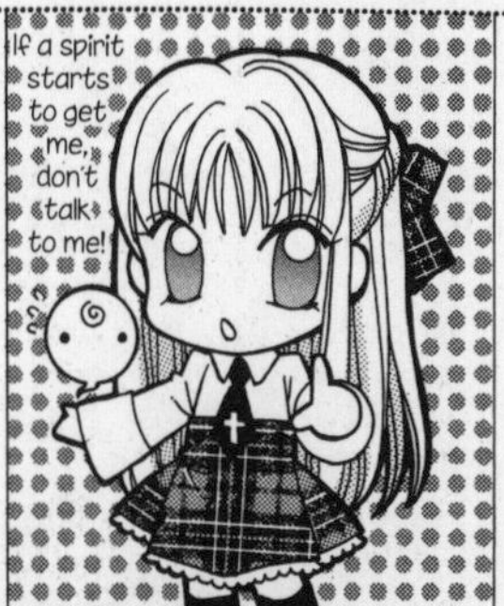
If a spirit starts to get me, don't talk to me!

She doesn't get scared even when she sees spirits. Instead, she befriends them. She's a brave elementary school kid. With such a strange personality, it's hard for her true feelings to come through, so she's easily misunderstood. She's actually quite lonely. Her hobbies are reading books and watching TV.

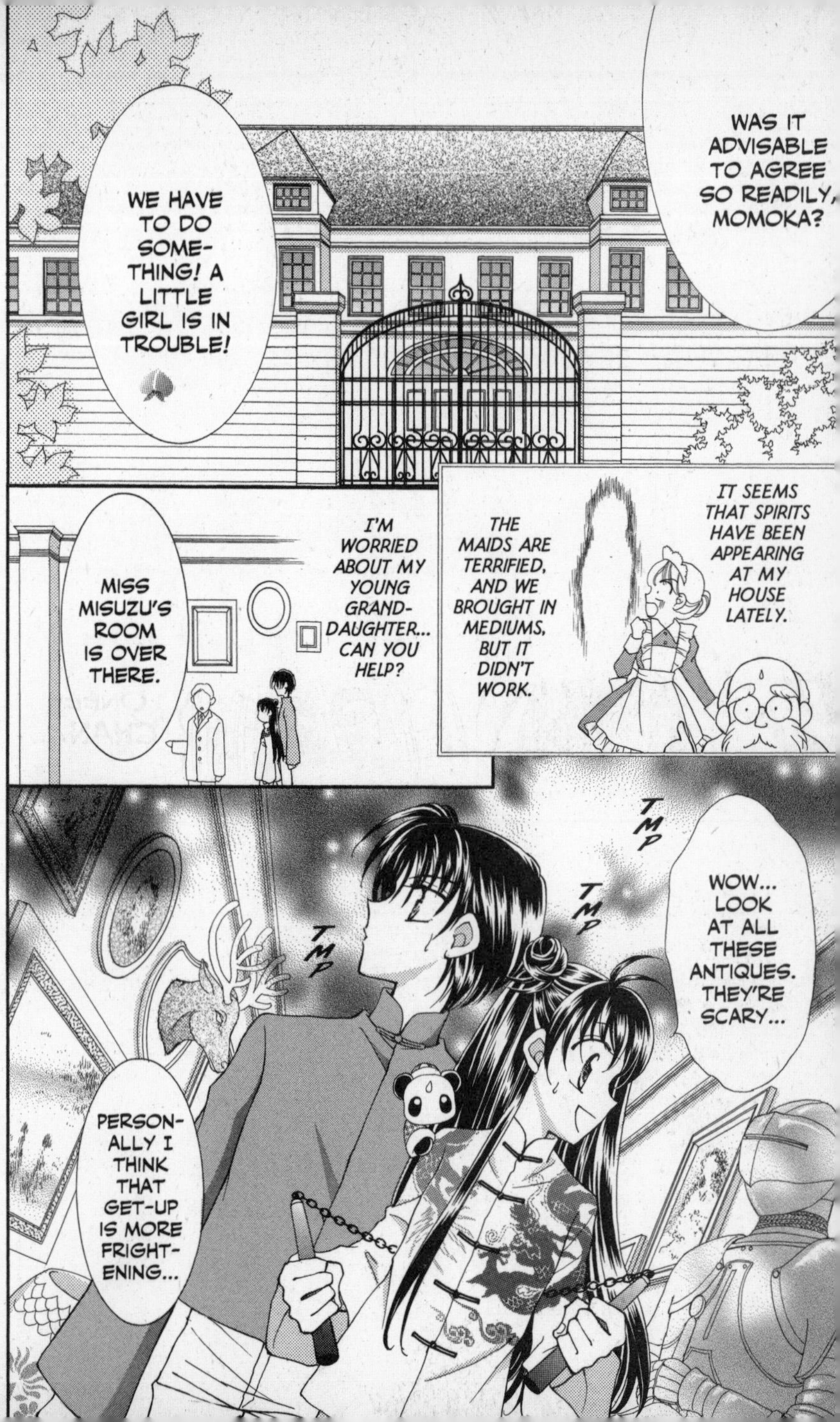
WAS IT ADVISABLE TO AGREE SO READILY, MOMOKA?
WE HAVE TO DO SOMETHING! A LITTLE GIRL IS IN TROUBLE!
IT SEEMS THAT SPIRITS HAVE BEEN APPEARING AT MY HOUSE LATELY.
THE MAIDS ARE TERRIFIED, AND WE BROUGHT IN MEDIUMS, BUT IT DIDN'T WORK.
I'M WORRIED ABOUT MY YOUNG GRAND-DAUGHTER... CAN YOU HELP?
MISS MISUZU'S ROOM IS OVER THERE.
TMP
TMP
TMP
WOW... LOOK AT ALL THESE ANTIQUES. THEY'RE SCARY...
PERSON-ALLY I THINK THAT GET-UP IS MORE FRIGHT-ENING...

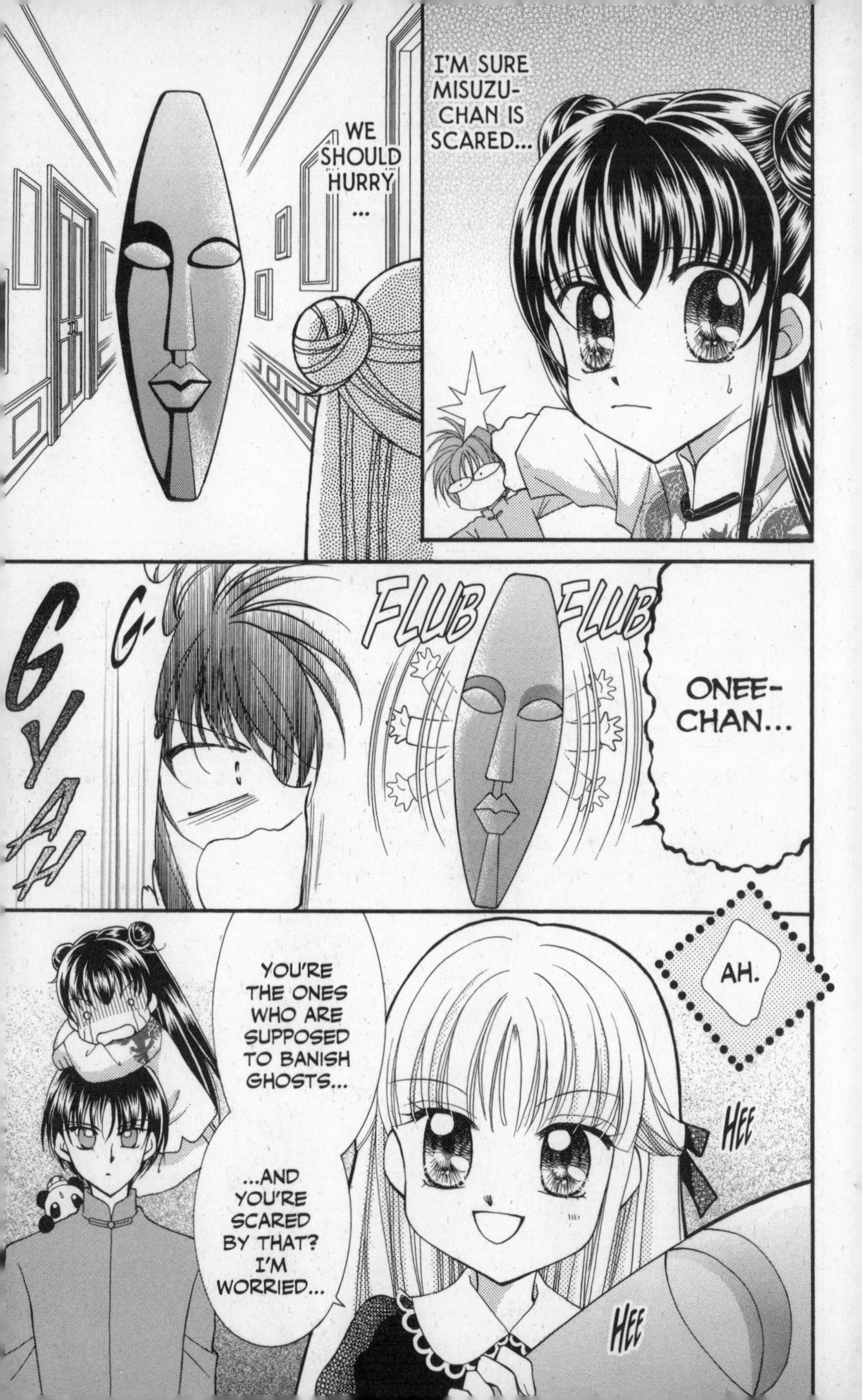
I'M SURE MISUZU-CHAN IS SCARED...
WE SHOULD HURRY ...
ONEE-CHAN...
FLUB FLUB
G-
GYAH
AH.
HEE
HEE
YOU'RE THE ONES WHO ARE SUPPOSED TO BANISH GHOSTS...
...AND YOU'RE SCARED BY THAT? I'M WORRIED...

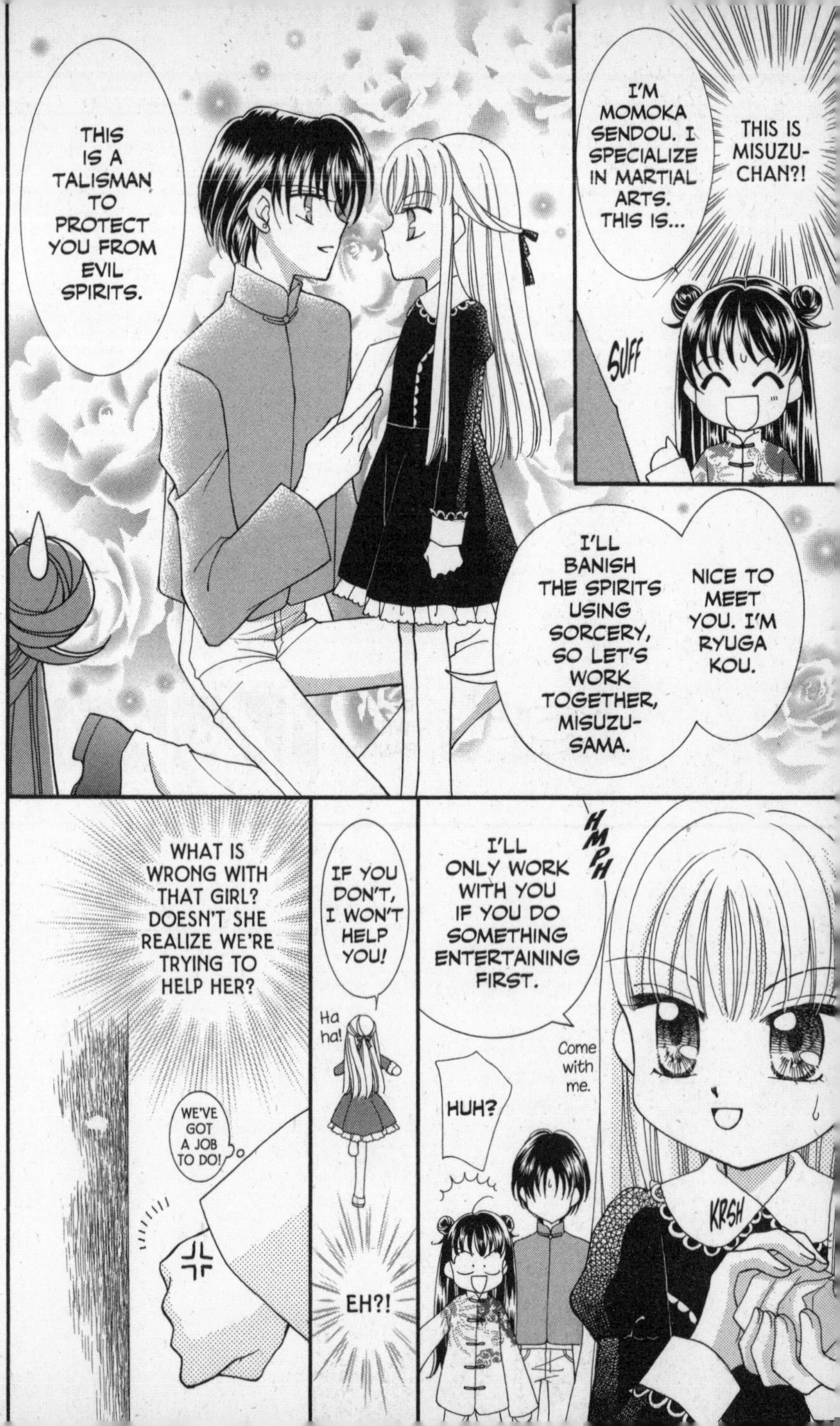
I'M MOMOKA SENDOU. I SPECIALIZE IN MARTIAL ARTS. THIS IS...
THIS IS MISUZU-CHAN?!
SUFF
NICE TO MEET YOU. I'M RYUGA KOU.
I'LL BANISH THE SPIRITS USING SORCERY, SO LET'S WORK TOGETHER, MISUZU-SAMA.
THIS IS A TALISMAN TO PROTECT YOU FROM EVIL SPIRITS.
HMPH
I'LL ONLY WORK WITH YOU IF YOU DO SOMETHING ENTERTAINING FIRST.
Come with me.
HUH?
KRSH
IF YOU DON'T, I WON'T HELP YOU!
Ha ha!
EH?!
WHAT IS WRONG WITH THAT GIRL? DOESN'T SHE REALIZE WE'RE TRYING TO HELP HER?
WE'VE GOT A JOB TO DO!

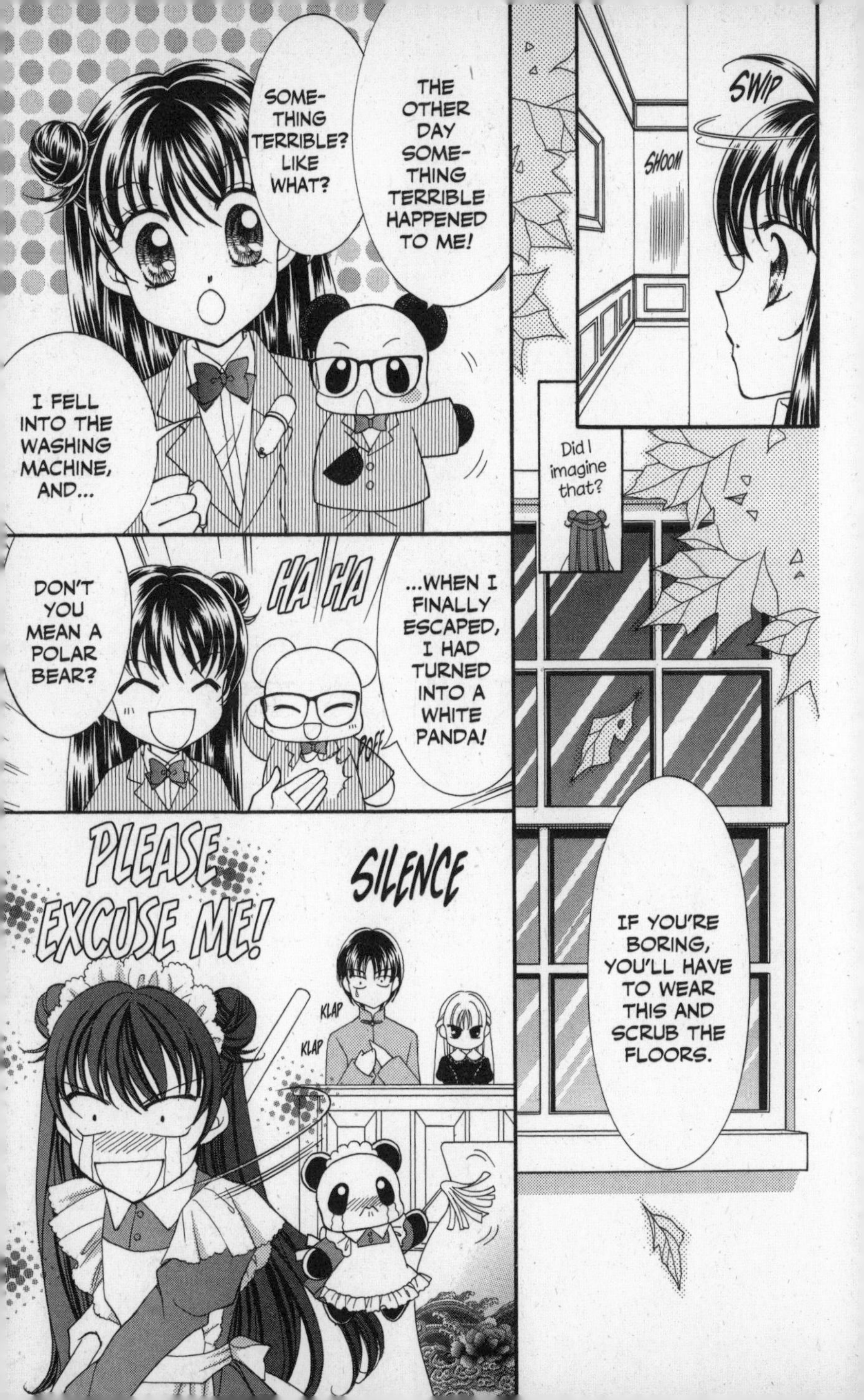
SWIP
SHOOM
Did I imagine that?
IF YOU'RE BORING, YOU'LL HAVE TO WEAR THIS AND SCRUB THE FLOORS.
THE OTHER DAY SOME-THING TERRIBLE HAPPENED TO ME!
SOME-THING TERRIBLE? LIKE WHAT?
I FELL INTO THE WASHING MACHINE, AND...
...WHEN I FINALLY ESCAPED, I HAD TURNED INTO A WHITE PANDA!
HA HA
POFF
DON'T YOU MEAN A POLAR BEAR?
SILENCE
PLEASE EXCUSE ME!
KLAP
KLAP

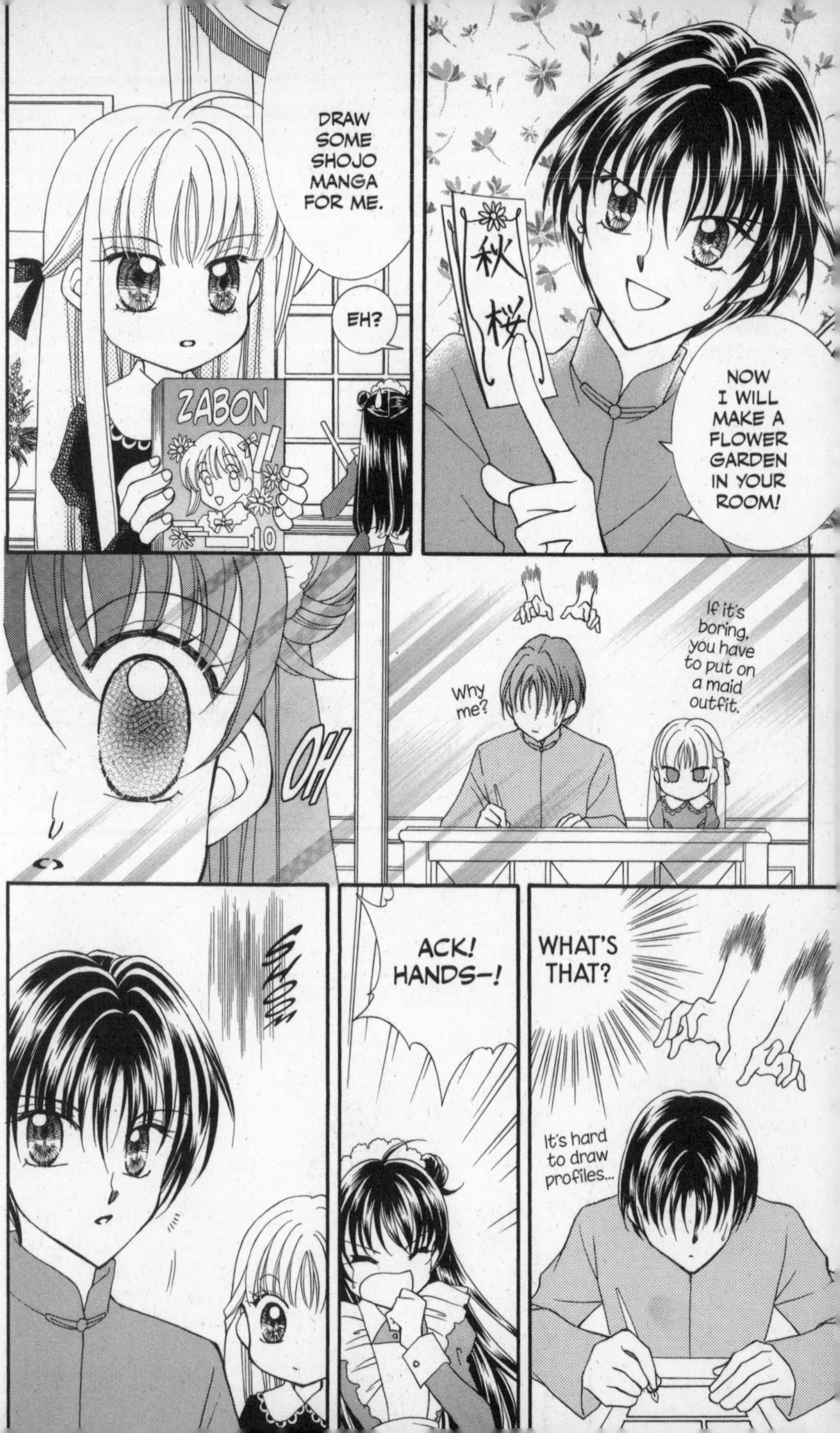
秋桜
NOW I WILL MAKE A FLOWER GARDEN IN YOUR ROOM!
DRAW SOME SHOJO MANGA FOR ME.
EH?
ZABON
10
If it's boring, you have to put on a maid outfit.
Why me?
OH
WHAT'S THAT?
It's hard to draw profiles...
ACK! HANDS—!

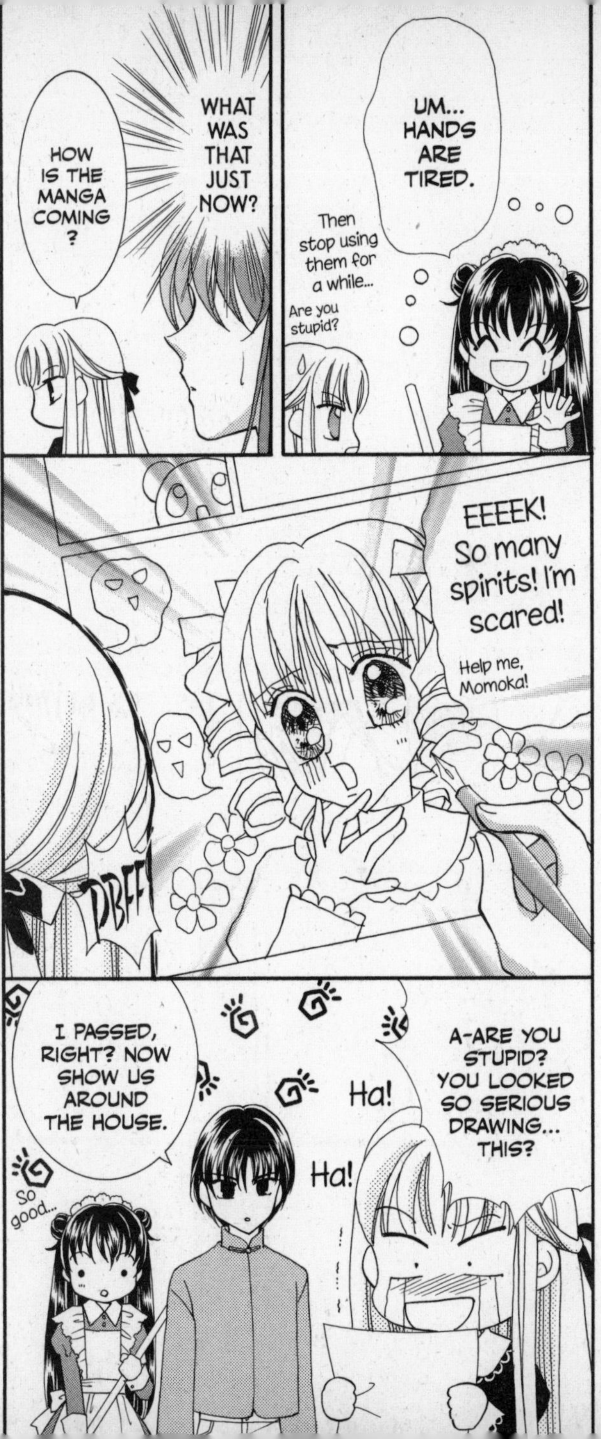
UM... HANDS ARE TIRED.
Then stop using them for a while...
Are you stupid?
WHAT WAS THAT JUST NOW?
HOW IS THE MANGA COMING?
EEEEK! So many spirits! I'm scared!
Help me, Momoka!
DBFF
A-ARE YOU STUPID? YOU LOOKED SO SERIOUS DRAWING... THIS?
Ha!
Ha!
I PASSED, RIGHT? NOW SHOW US AROUND THE HOUSE.
So good...

4

When I wrote this story, I was very busy with various summer events and with my editors changing.

I'm really fond of Misuzu. And Momoka and Ron-Ron's comedy act. (laugh)

I'm really interested in haunted houses.

A long time ago I wrote a manga called "Tarot♡ Labyrinth" about a scary haunted house and school. If you like haunted houses, you should read it!♡
And watch the commercial for it.
Where is that thing anyway?

My dream is to someday go on a haunted-house tour in England. Then I'll get to visit the grave of one of my favorite occult authors, Arthur Machen. Anyone want to come with me?

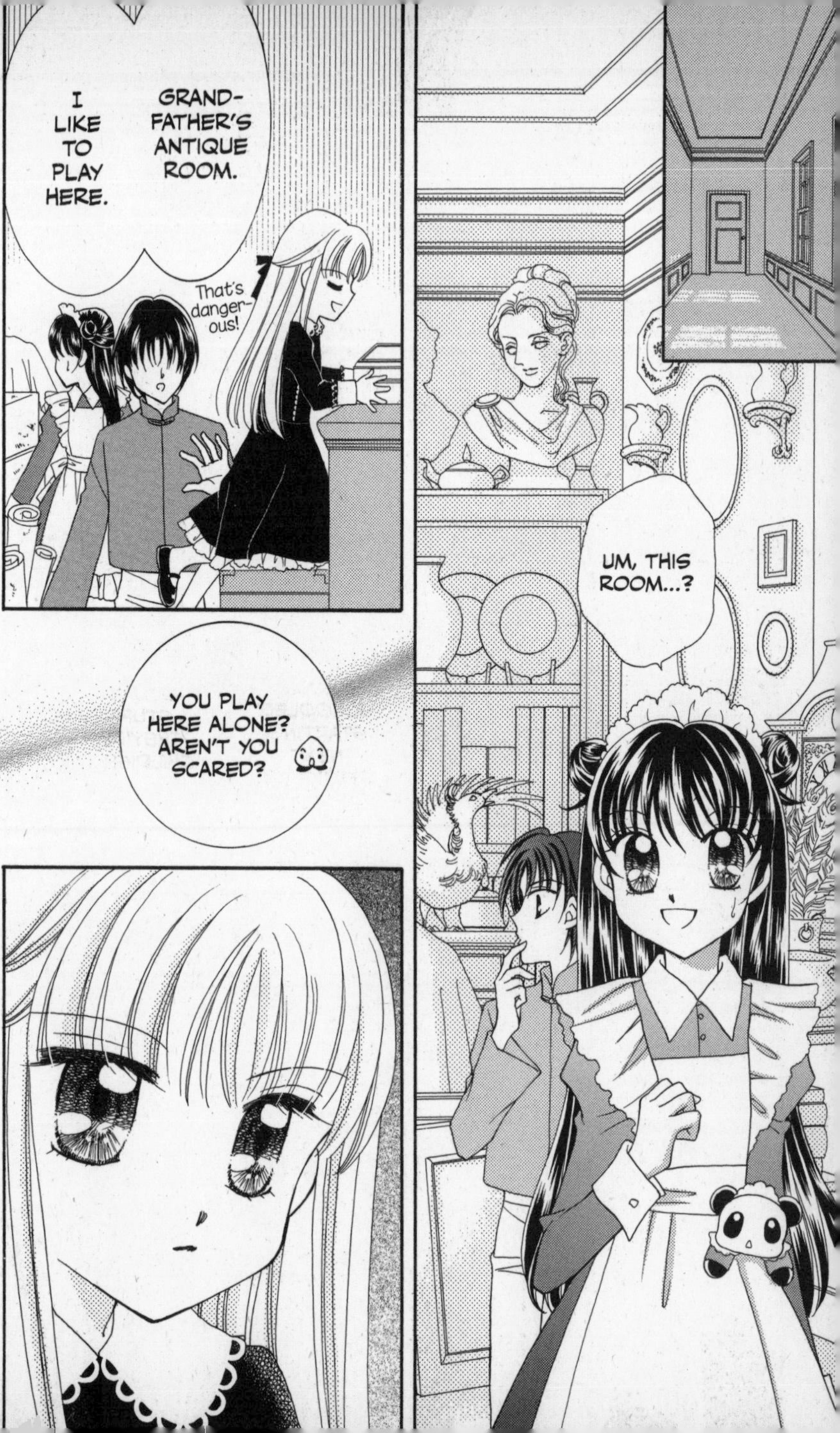
UM, THIS ROOM...?
GRAND-FATHER'S ANTIQUE ROOM.
I LIKE TO PLAY HERE.
That's danger-ous!
YOU PLAY HERE ALONE? AREN'T YOU SCARED?

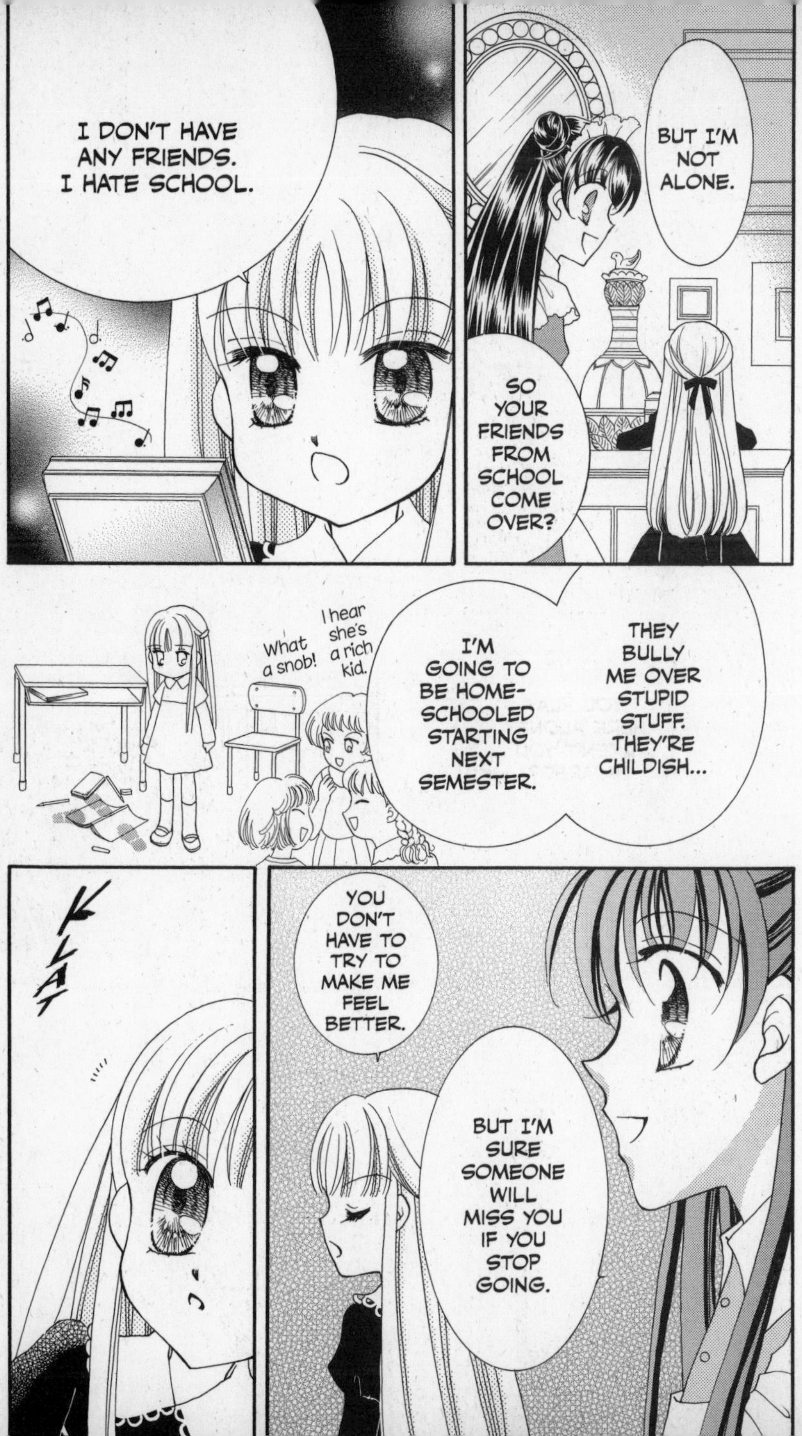
BUT I'M NOT ALONE.
SO YOUR FRIENDS FROM SCHOOL COME OVER?
I DON'T HAVE ANY FRIENDS. I HATE SCHOOL.
THEY BULLY ME OVER STUPID STUFF. THEY'RE CHILDISH...
I'M GOING TO BE HOME-SCHOOLED STARTING NEXT SEMESTER.
I hear she's a rich kid.
What a snob!
YOU DON'T HAVE TO TRY TO MAKE ME FEEL BETTER.
BUT I'M SURE SOMEONE WILL MISS YOU IF YOU STOP GOING.
KLAK

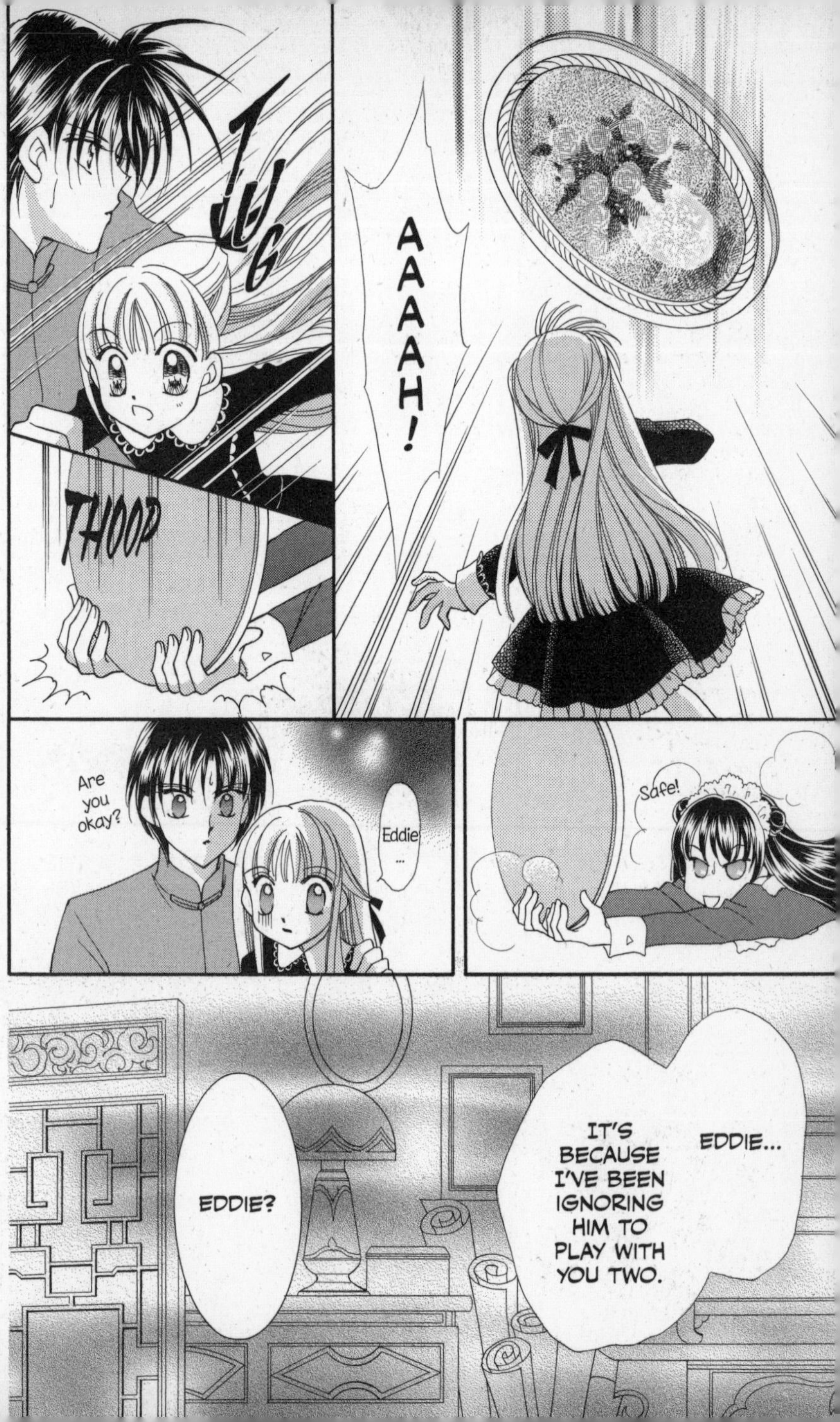
AAAAH!
JUG
THOOP
Safe!
Eddie ...
Are you okay?
EDDIE...
IT'S BECAUSE I'VE BEEN IGNORING HIM TO PLAY WITH YOU TWO.
EDDIE?

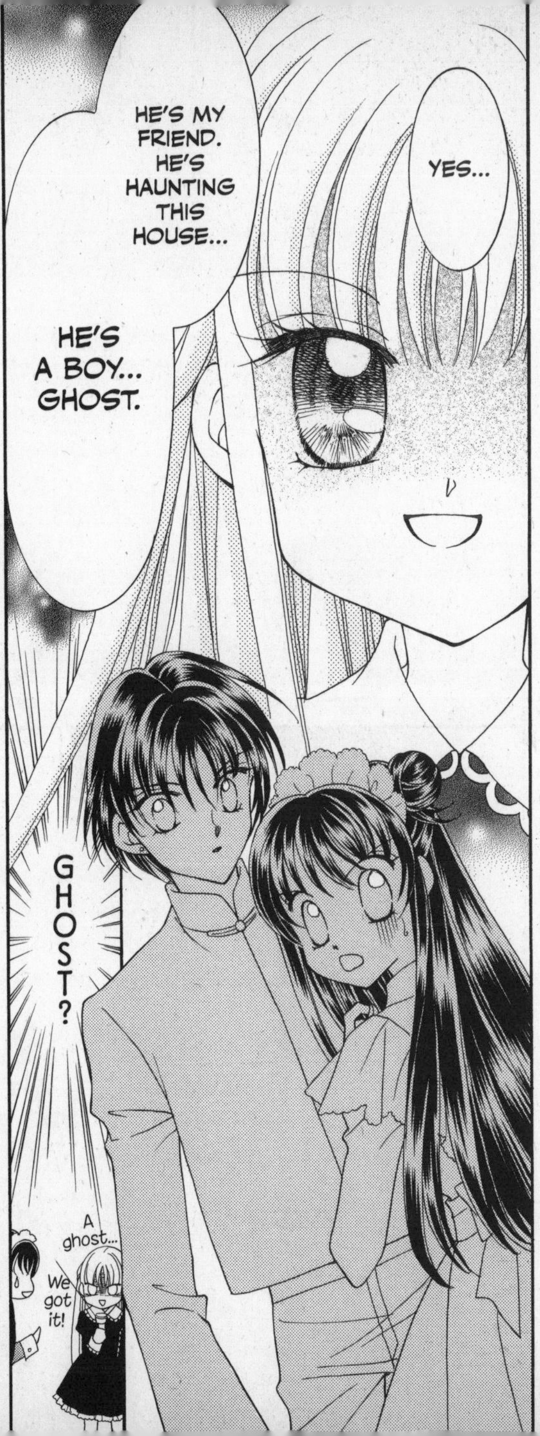
YES...
HE'S MY FRIEND. HE'S HAUNTING THIS HOUSE...
HE'S A BOY... GHOST.
GHOST?
A ghost...
We got it!

5

An interesting horror movie I saw recently was Nicole Kidman's *The Others.* Two children and their mother live in a large old house. The dad is away at war and hasn't come home. They start to feel the presence of something... The twist at the end was really sad. But it was really moving to see the mother trying to protect her children.

It's not a horror movie, but *Harry Potter and the Chamber of Secrets* was also pretty scary. Hogwarts is so large... The writing in blood on the wall... The creepy voices that only Harry can hear... That's the kind of world that I love! And I guess they have toilet ghosts in England too! (laugh)

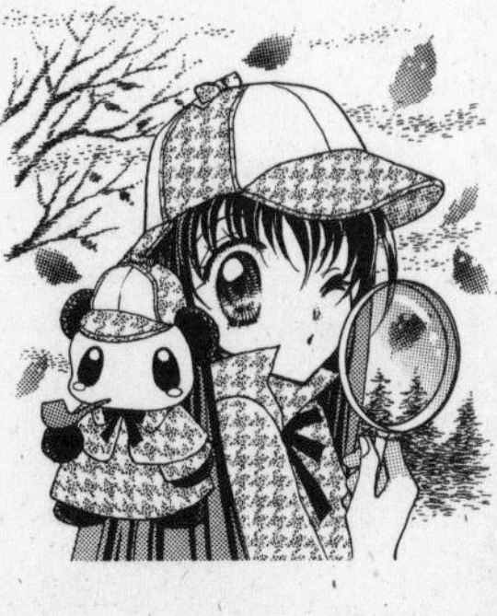

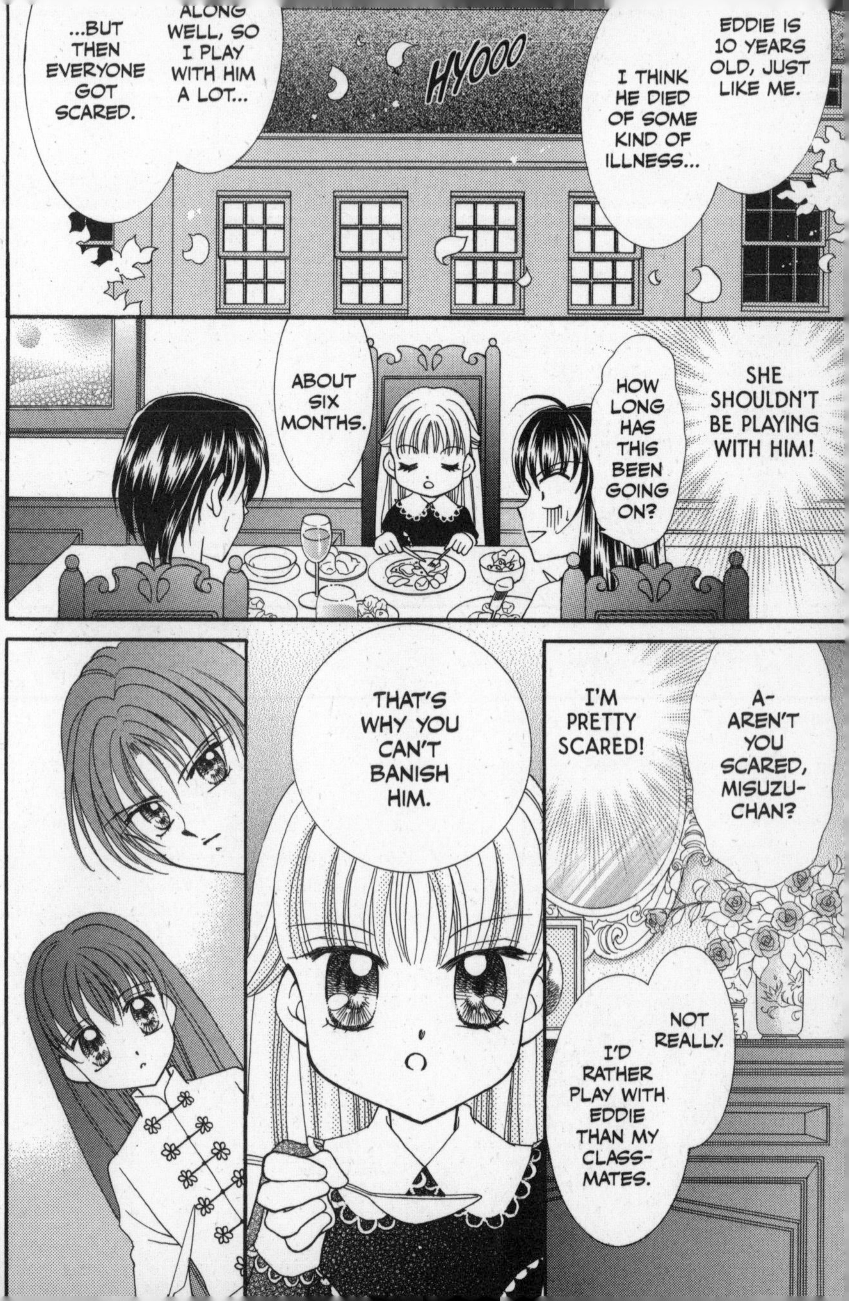
EDDIE IS 10 YEARS OLD, JUST LIKE ME.
I THINK HE DIED OF SOME KIND OF ILLNESS...
HYOOO
ALONG WELL, SO I PLAY WITH HIM A LOT...
...BUT THEN EVERYONE GOT SCARED.
SHE SHOULDN'T BE PLAYING WITH HIM!
HOW LONG HAS THIS BEEN GOING ON?
ABOUT SIX MONTHS.
A-AREN'T YOU SCARED, MISUZU-CHAN?
I'M PRETTY SCARED!
NOT REALLY. I'D RATHER PLAY WITH EDDIE THAN MY CLASS-MATES.
THAT'S WHY YOU CAN'T BANISH HIM.

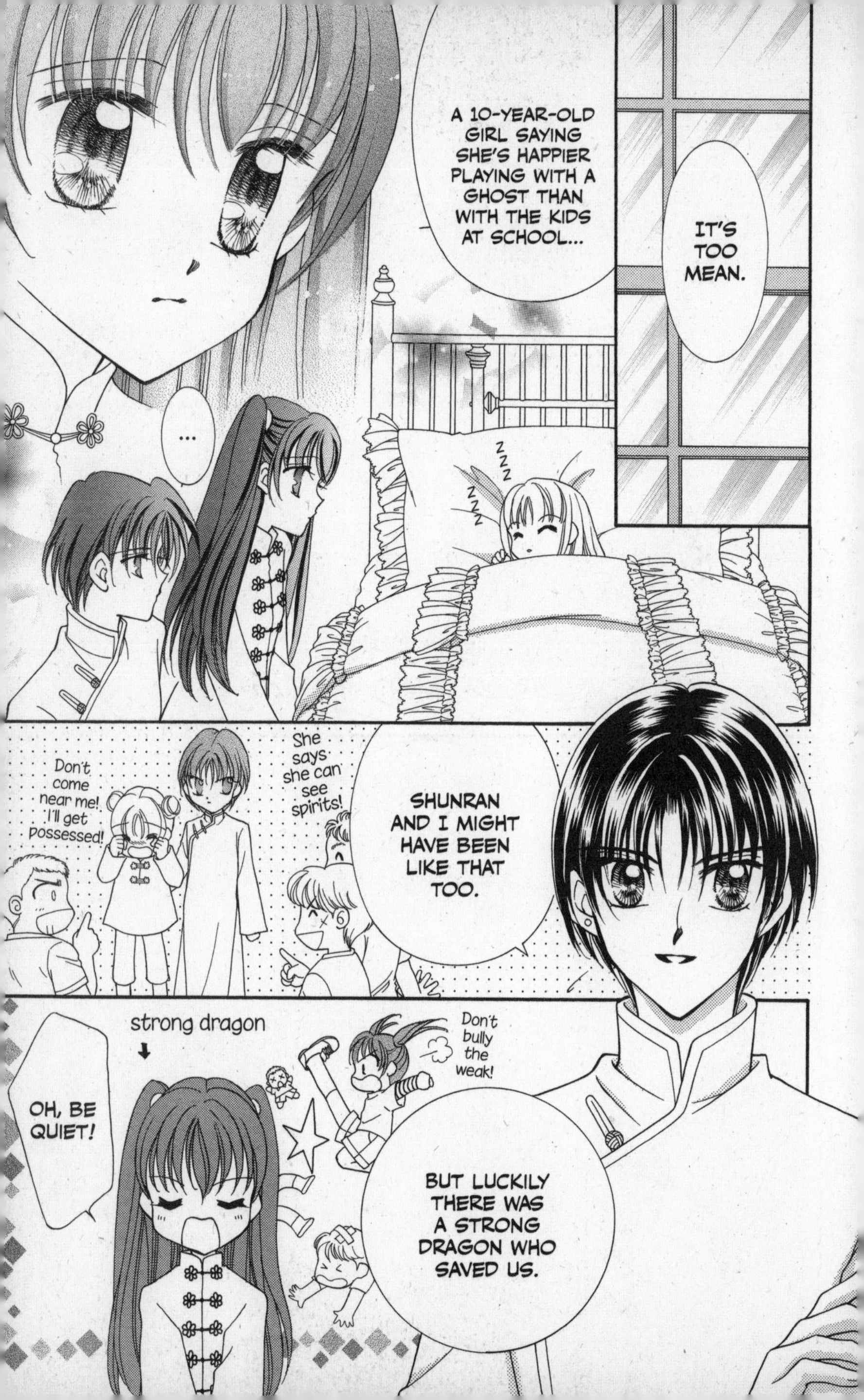
A 10-YEAR-OLD GIRL SAYING SHE'S HAPPIER PLAYING WITH A GHOST THAN WITH THE KIDS AT SCHOOL...
IT'S TOO MEAN.
...
SHUNRAN AND I MIGHT HAVE BEEN LIKE THAT TOO.
She says she can see spirits!
Don't come near me! I'll get possessed!
BUT LUCKILY THERE WAS A STRONG DRAGON WHO SAVED US.
Don't bully the weak!
strong dragon
OH, BE QUIET!

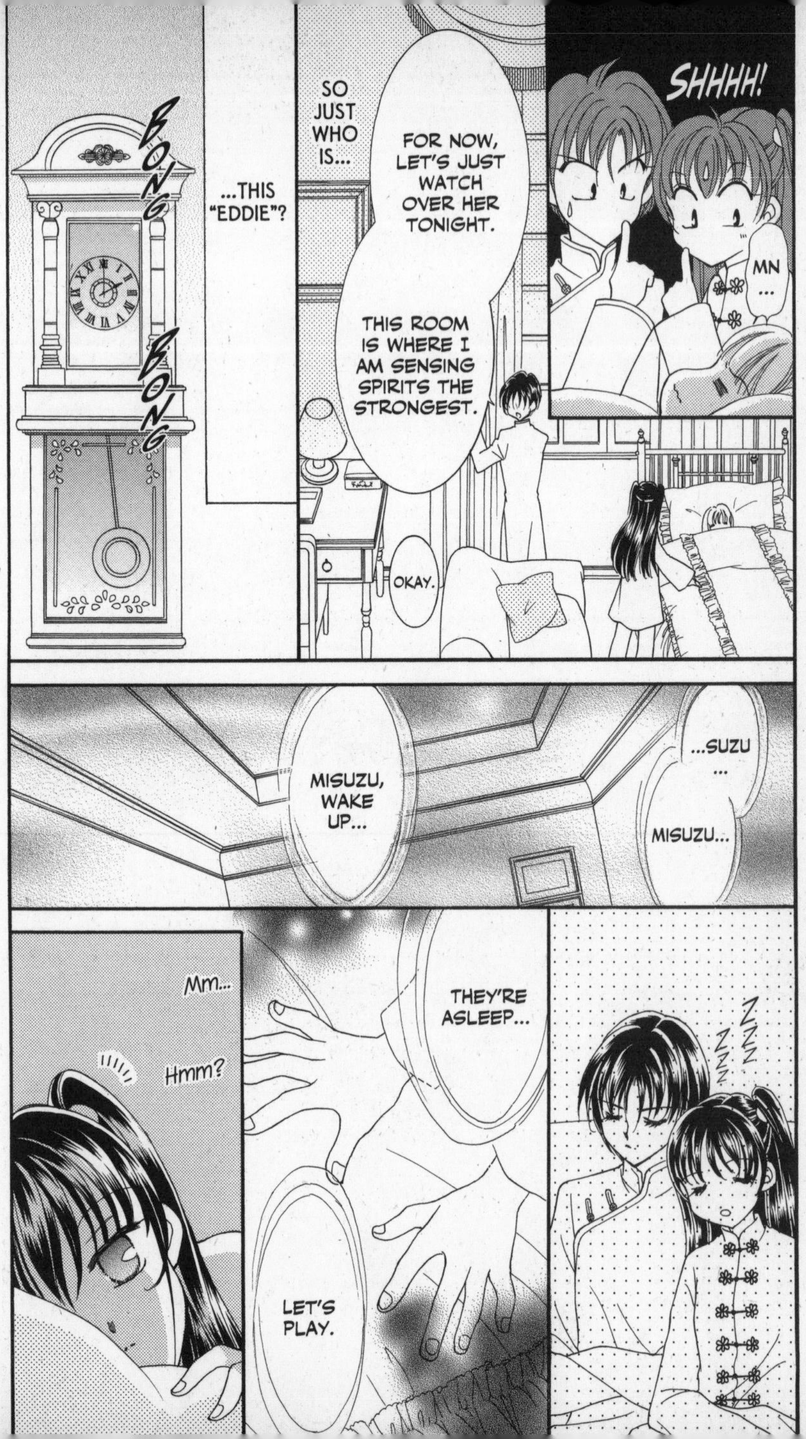
FOR NOW, LET'S JUST WATCH OVER HER TONIGHT.
THIS ROOM IS WHERE I AM SENSING SPIRITS THE STRONGEST.
OKAY.
SHHHH!
MN...
SO JUST WHO IS...
...THIS "EDDIE"?
BONG
BONG
...SUZU...
MISUZU...
MISUZU, WAKE UP...
ZZZ
THEY'RE ASLEEP...
LET'S PLAY.
Mm...
Hmm?

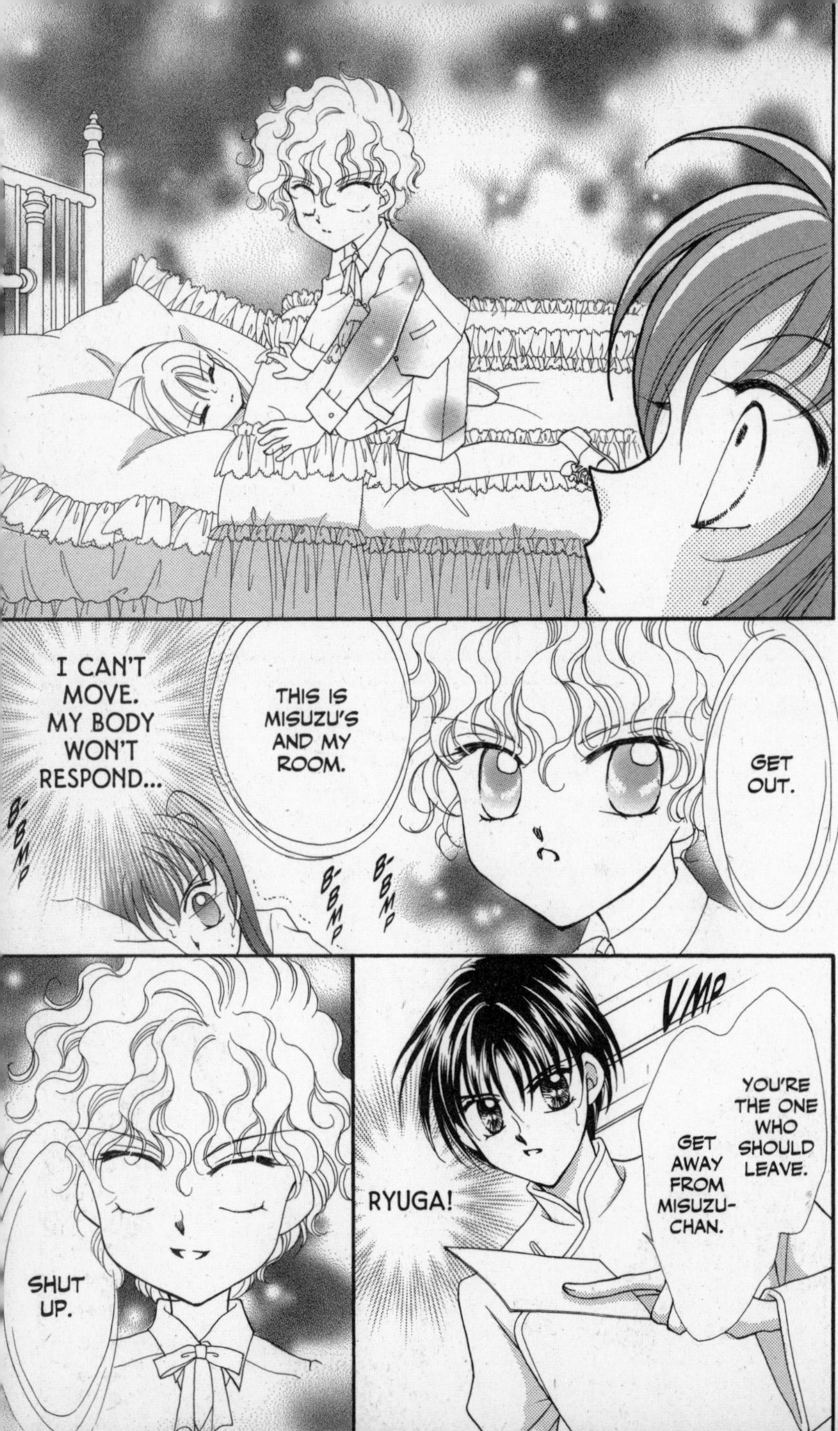

THIS IS MISUZU'S AND MY ROOM.
GET OUT.
I CAN'T MOVE. MY BODY WON'T RESPOND...
B-BMP
B-BMP
B-BMP
VMP
YOU'RE THE ONE WHO SHOULD LEAVE.
GET AWAY FROM MISUZU-CHAN.
RYUGA!
SHUT UP.

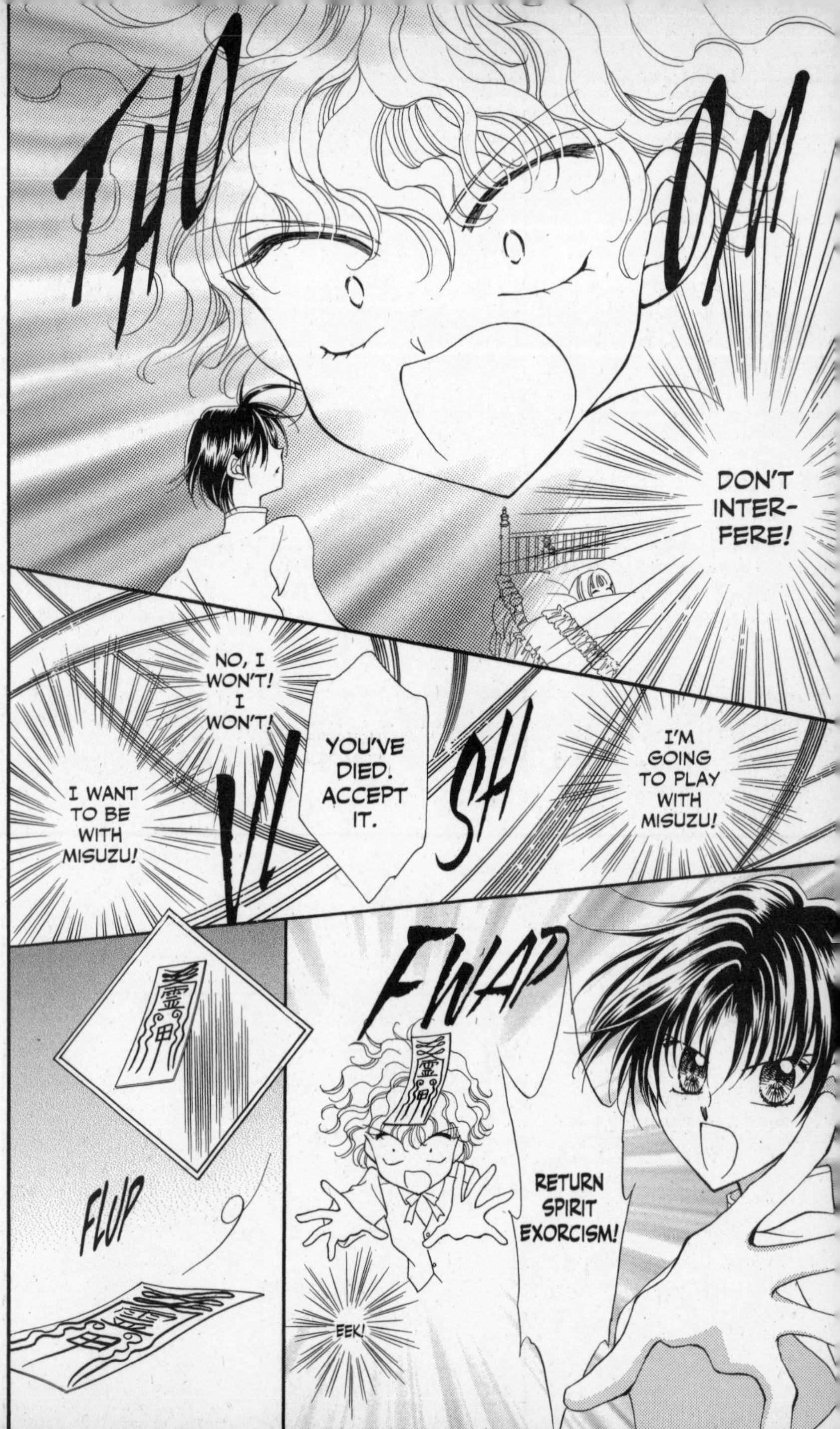
THOOM
DON'T INTERFERE!
I'M GOING TO PLAY WITH MISUZU!
VISH
YOU'VE DIED. ACCEPT IT.
NO, I WON'T! I WON'T!
I WANT TO BE WITH MISUZU!
FWAP
RETURN SPIRIT EXORCISM!
EEK!
FLUP

6

More about the Harry Potter movie... This time Hermione and Hagrid really moved me. I cried twice. I really like Emma Watson, the actress who plays Hermione. (She's so cute! ♡) And Daniel, who plays Harry, grew a lot since the last movie. I'm looking forward to the third movie! ♡

After the movie, I bought some Harry Potter goods: playing cards, a key chain, and a letter opener in the shape of the Gryffindor sword. I'll open all the fan letters with it!

I also want to go to the school where the movie was filmed. Great Britain is a small country, but there are tons of places I want to visit. I want to go to Stonehenge, Loch Ness, Kensington Park, Madame Tussauds Wax Museum, etc. And if I'm going all the way there, I hope I see some crop circles! (laugh)

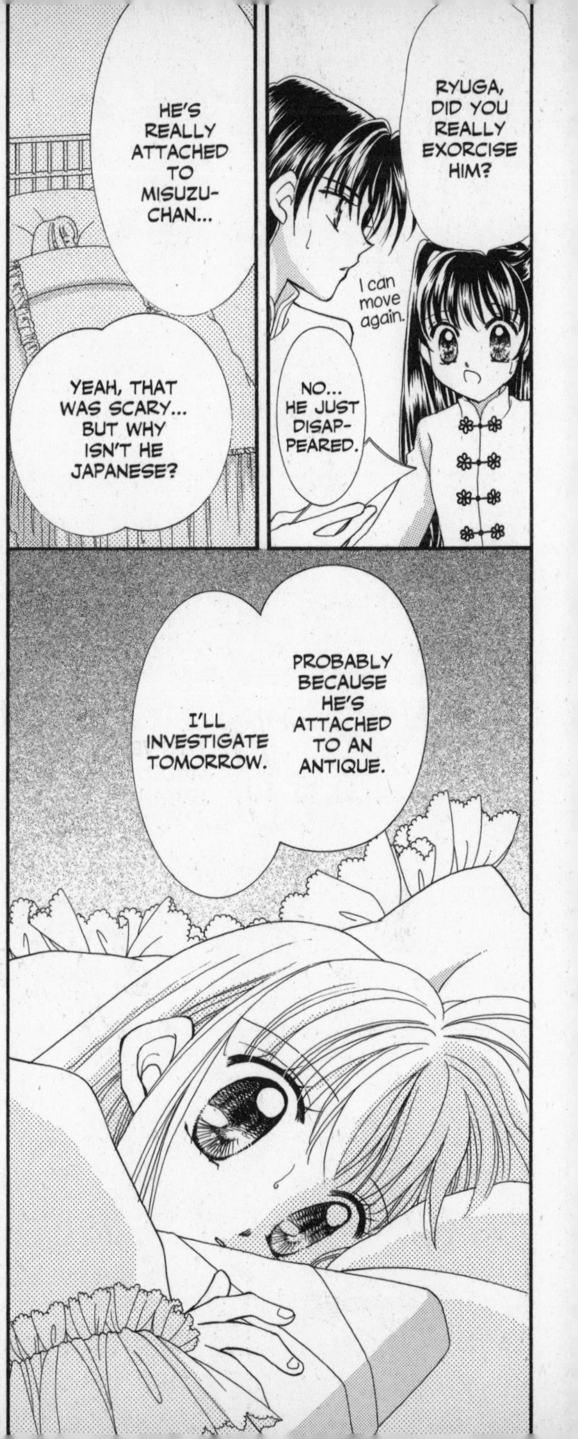
RYUGA, DID YOU REALLY EXORCISE HIM?
I can move again.
NO... HE JUST DISAPPEARED.
HE'S REALLY ATTACHED TO MISUZU-CHAN...
YEAH, THAT WAS SCARY... BUT WHY ISN'T HE JAPANESE?
PROBABLY BECAUSE HE'S ATTACHED TO AN ANTIQUE.
I'LL INVESTIGATE TOMORROW.

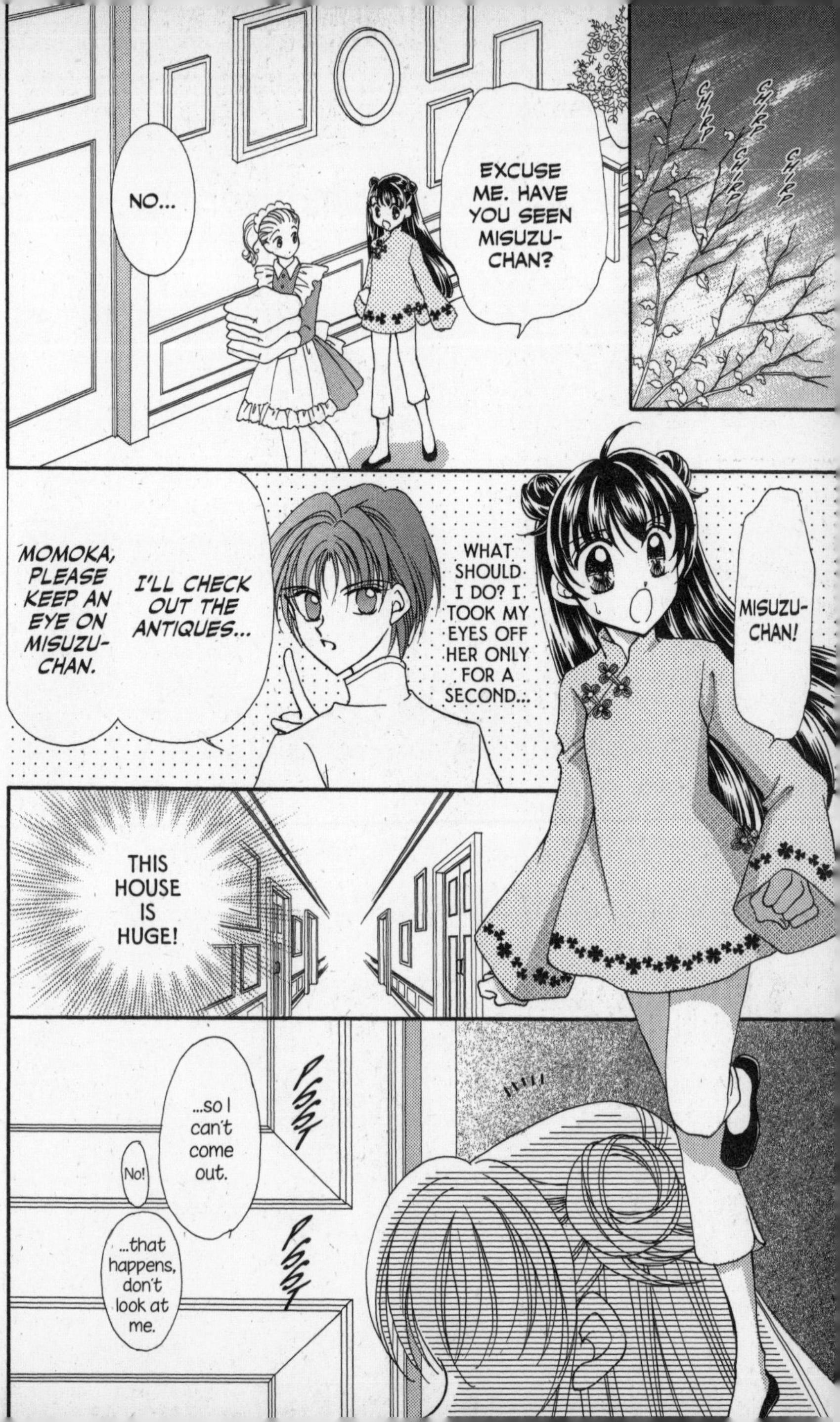
CHIRP CHIRP
CHIRP CHIRP
EXCUSE ME. HAVE YOU SEEN MISUZU-CHAN?
NO...
MISUZU-CHAN!
WHAT SHOULD I DO? I TOOK MY EYES OFF HER ONLY FOR A SECOND...
I'LL CHECK OUT THE ANTIQUES...
MOMOKA, PLEASE KEEP AN EYE ON MISUZU-CHAN.
THIS HOUSE IS HUGE!
...so I can't come out.
No!
...that happens, don't look at me.

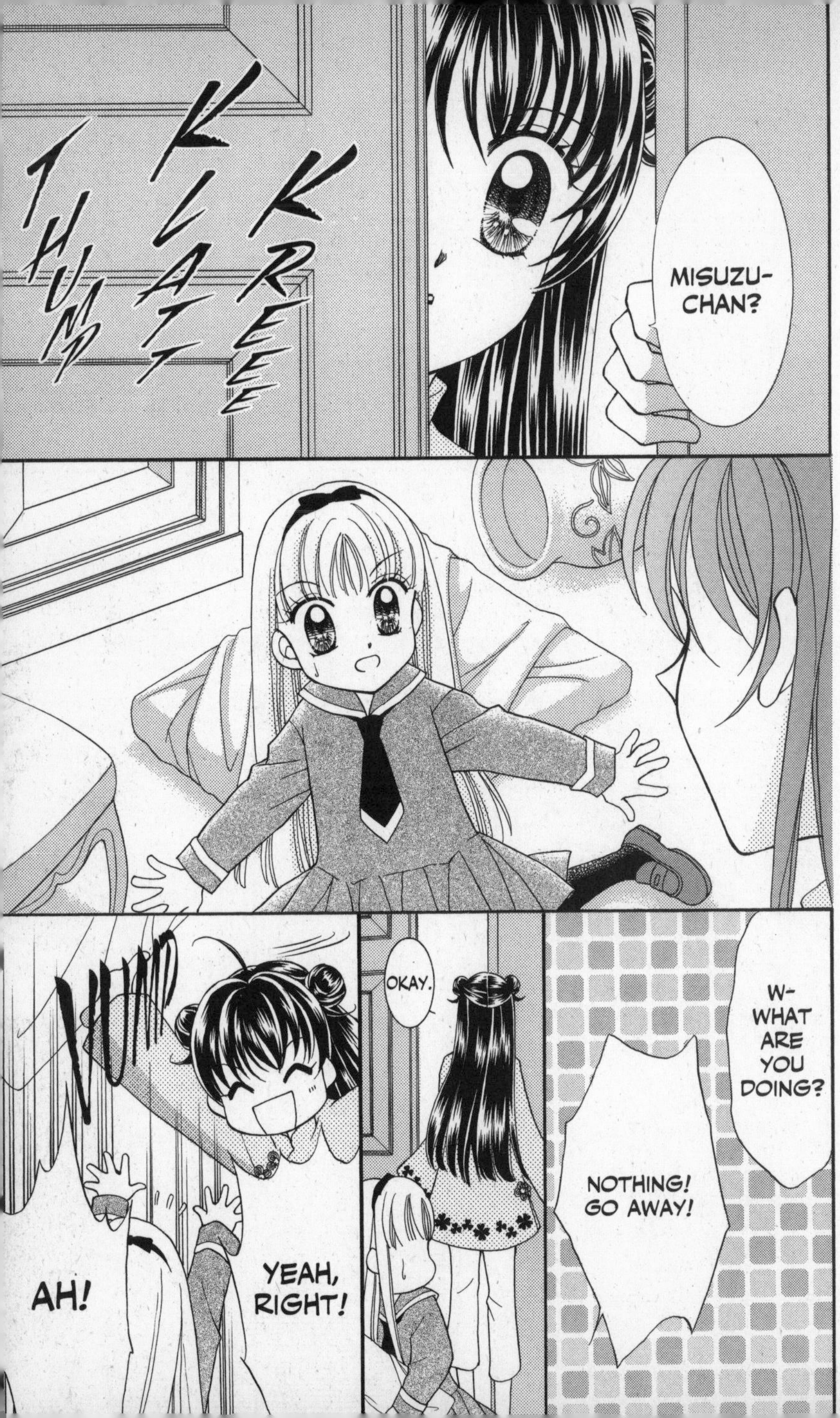
MISUZU-CHAN?
KREEE
KLATT
THUMP
W-WHAT ARE YOU DOING?
NOTHING! GO AWAY!
OKAY.
VUMP
YEAH, RIGHT!
AH!

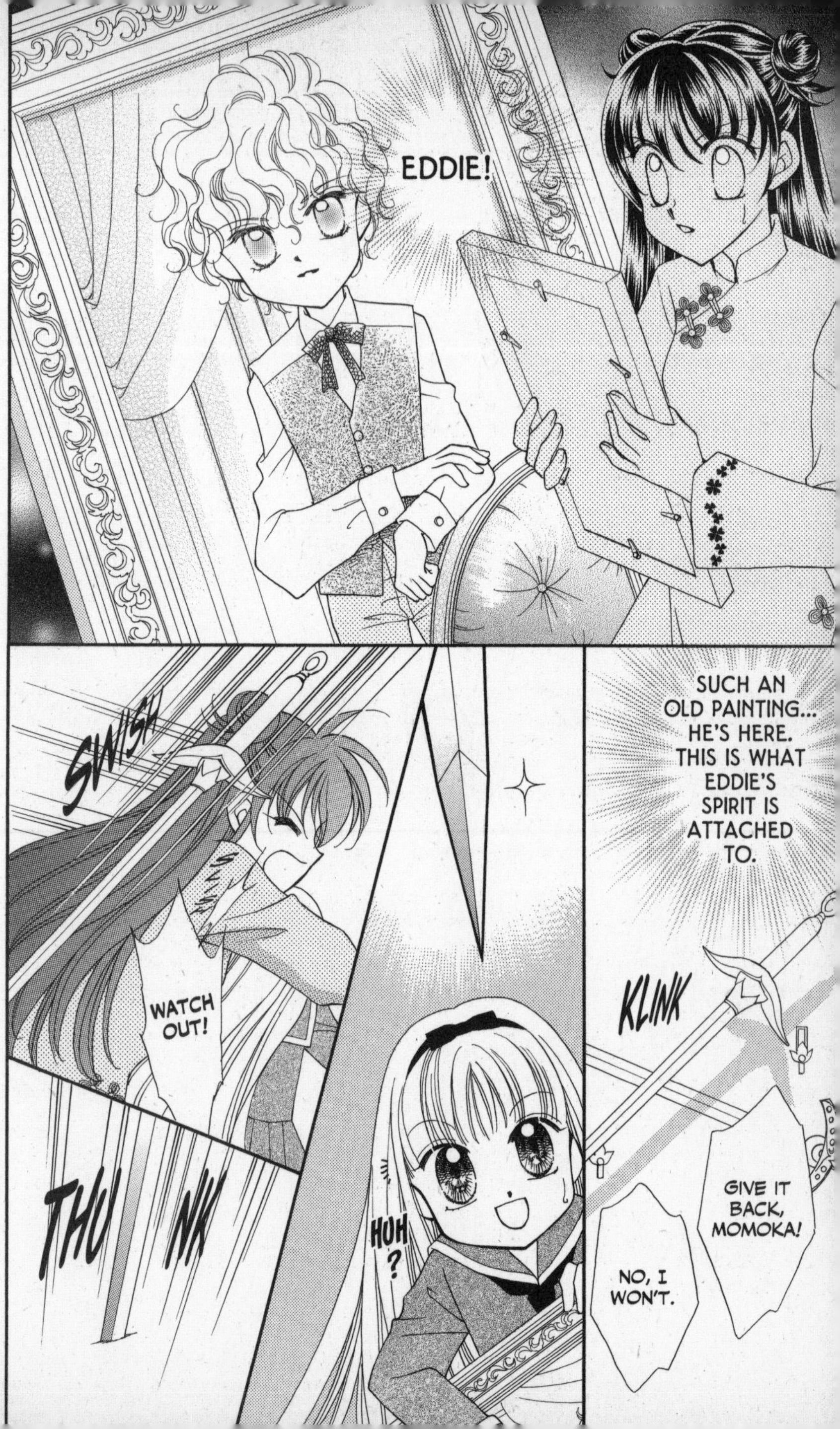
EDDIE!
SUCH AN OLD PAINTING... HE'S HERE. THIS IS WHAT EDDIE'S SPIRIT IS ATTACHED TO.
KLINK
GIVE IT BACK, MOMOKA!
NO, I WON'T.
SWISH
WATCH OUT!
HUH?
THU NK

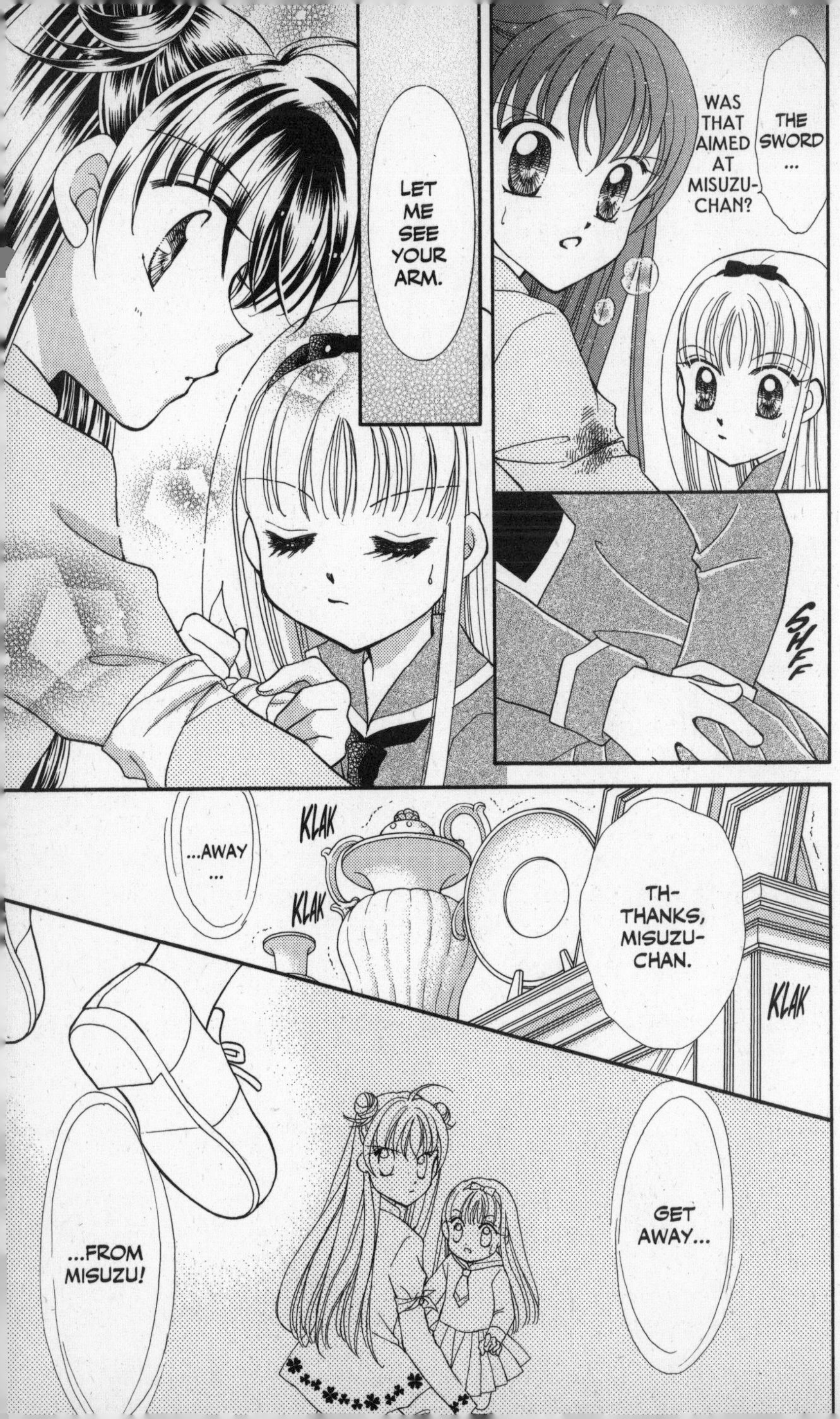
THE SWORD ...
WAS THAT AIMED AT MISUZU-CHAN?
SHFF
LET ME SEE YOUR ARM.
TH-THANKS, MISUZU-CHAN.
KLAK
KLAK
KLAK
...AWAY ...
GET AWAY...
...FROM MISUZU!

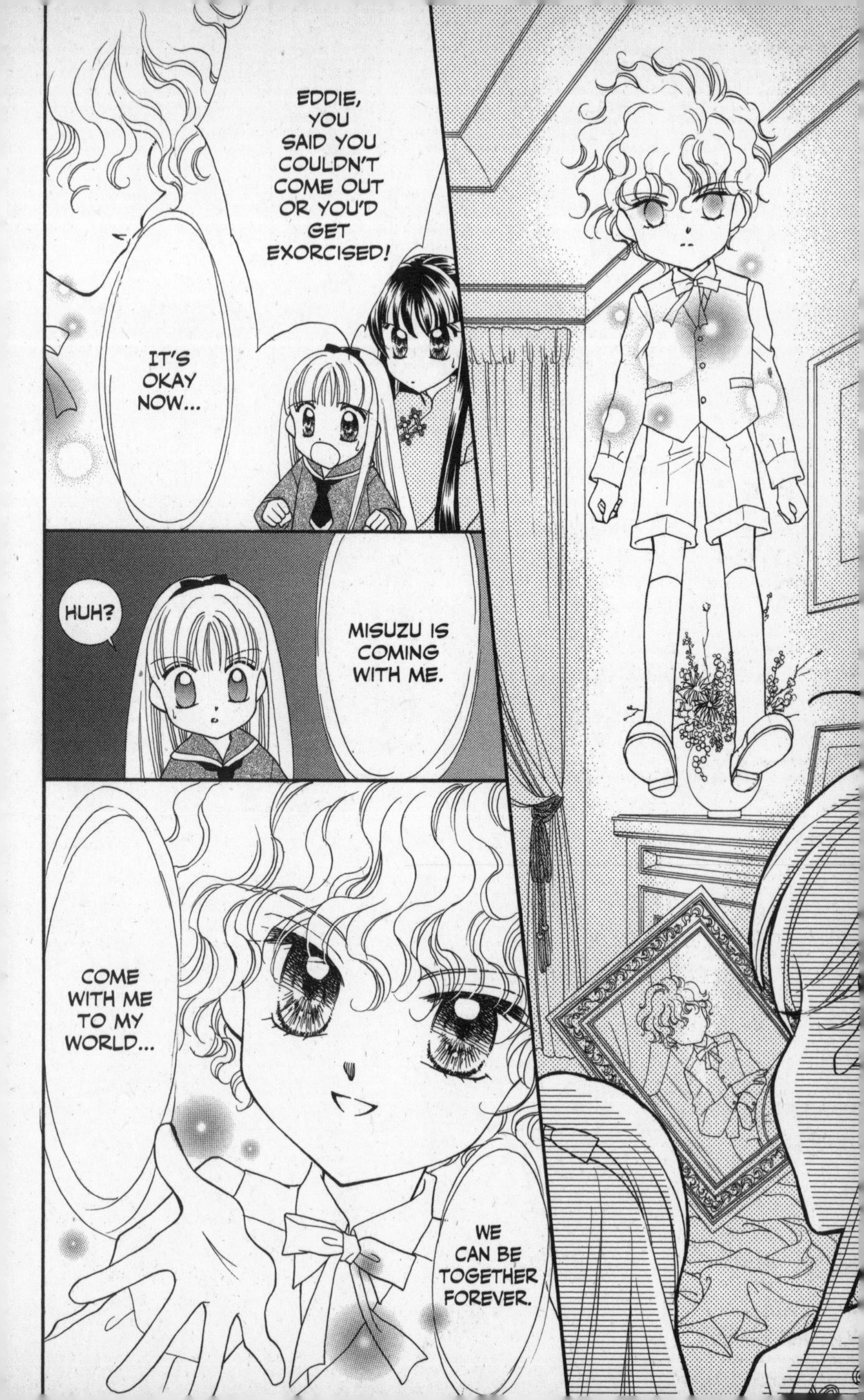
EDDIE, YOU SAID YOU COULDN'T COME OUT OR YOU'D GET EXORCISED!
IT'S OKAY NOW...
MISUZU IS COMING WITH ME.
HUH?
COME WITH ME TO MY WORLD...
WE CAN BE TOGETHER FOREVER.

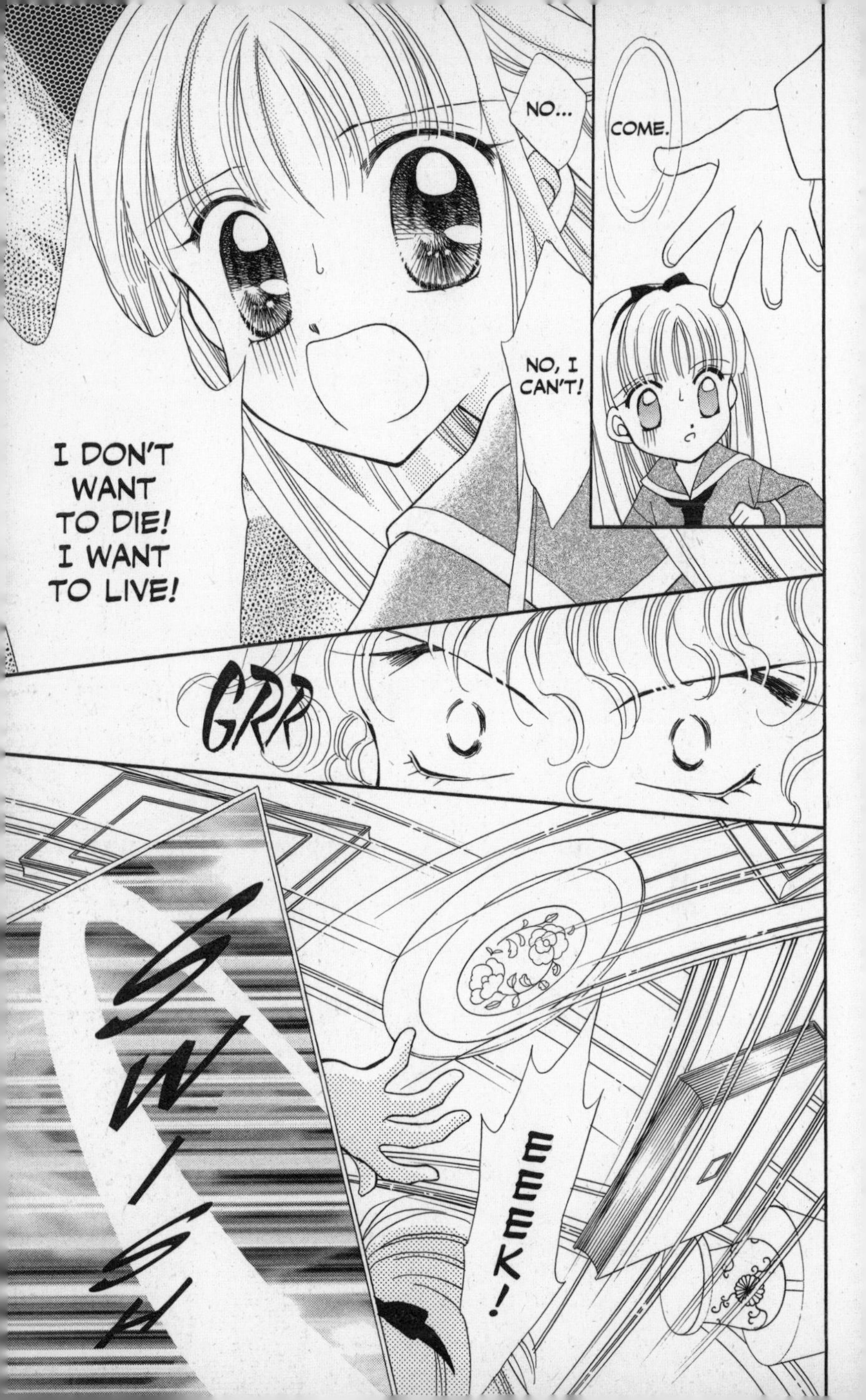
COME.
NO...
NO, I CAN'T!
I DON'T WANT TO DIE! I WANT TO LIVE!
GRR
EEEEK!
SWISH

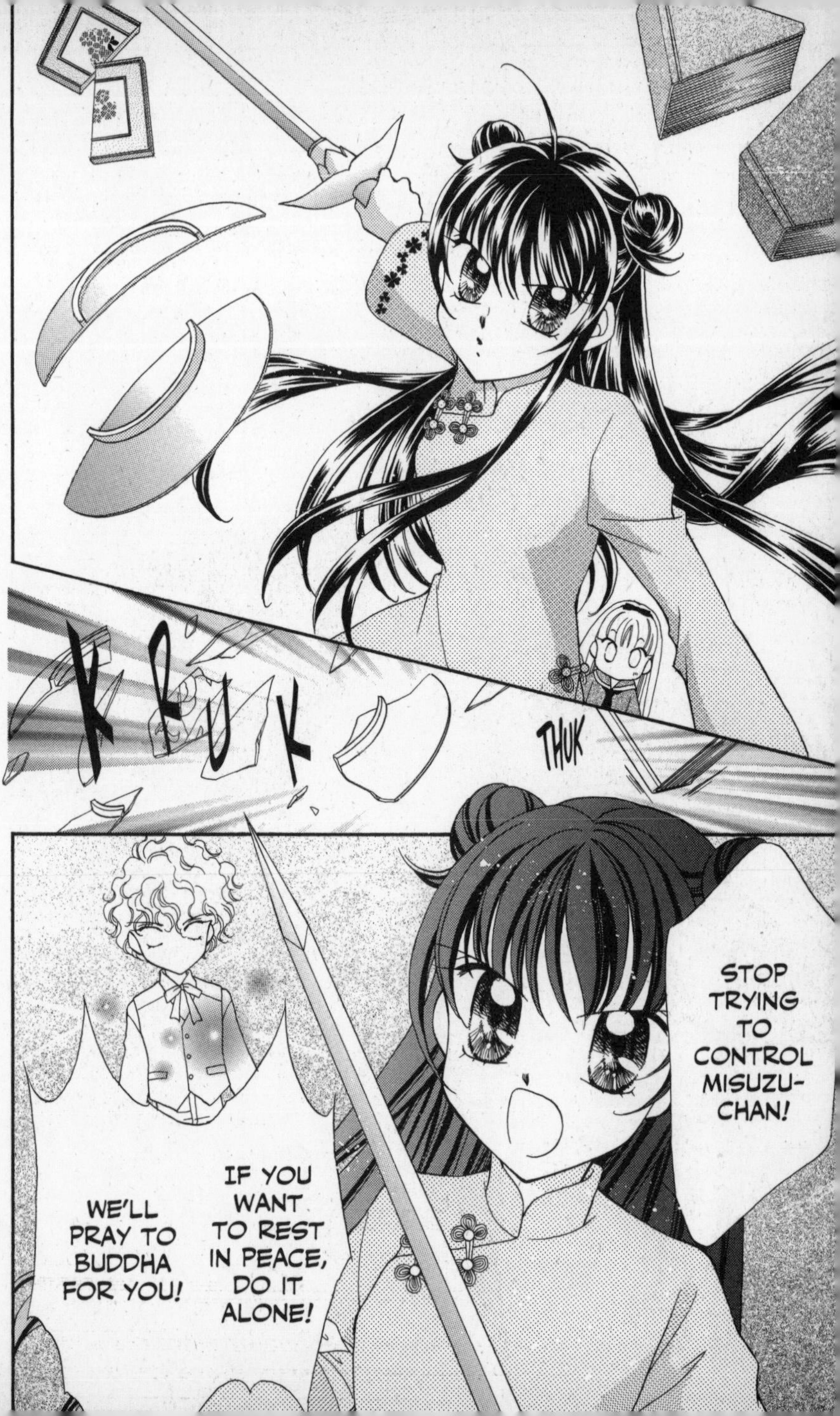
THUK
KRUK
STOP TRYING TO CONTROL MISUZU-CHAN!
IF YOU WANT TO REST IN PEACE, DO IT ALONE!
WE'LL PRAY TO BUDDHA FOR YOU!

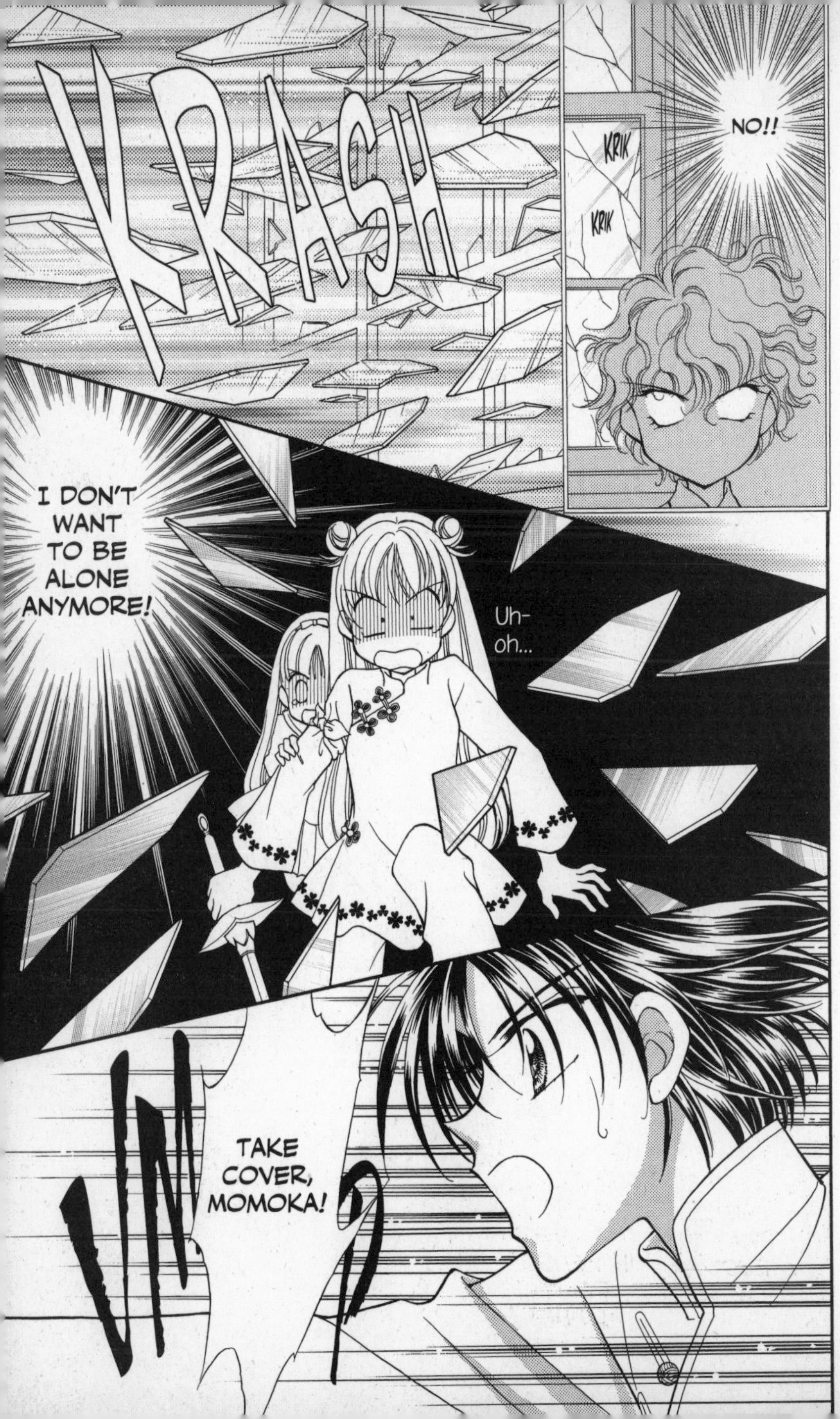
KRIK
KRIK
NO!!
KRASH
I DON'T WANT TO BE ALONE ANYMORE!
Uh-oh...
TAKE COVER, MOMOKA!

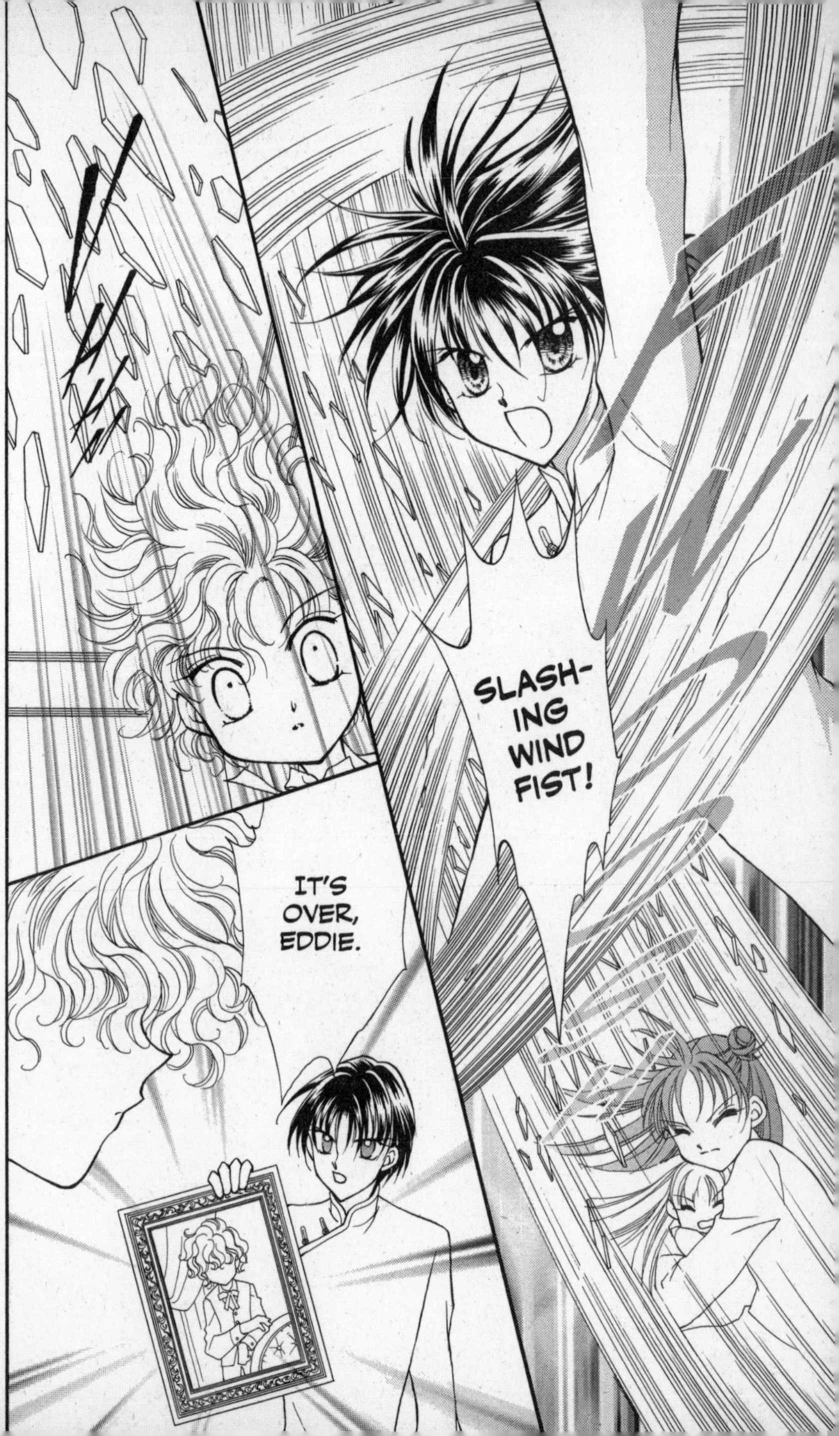
SLASH-
ING
WIND
FIST!
IT'S
OVER,
EDDIE.

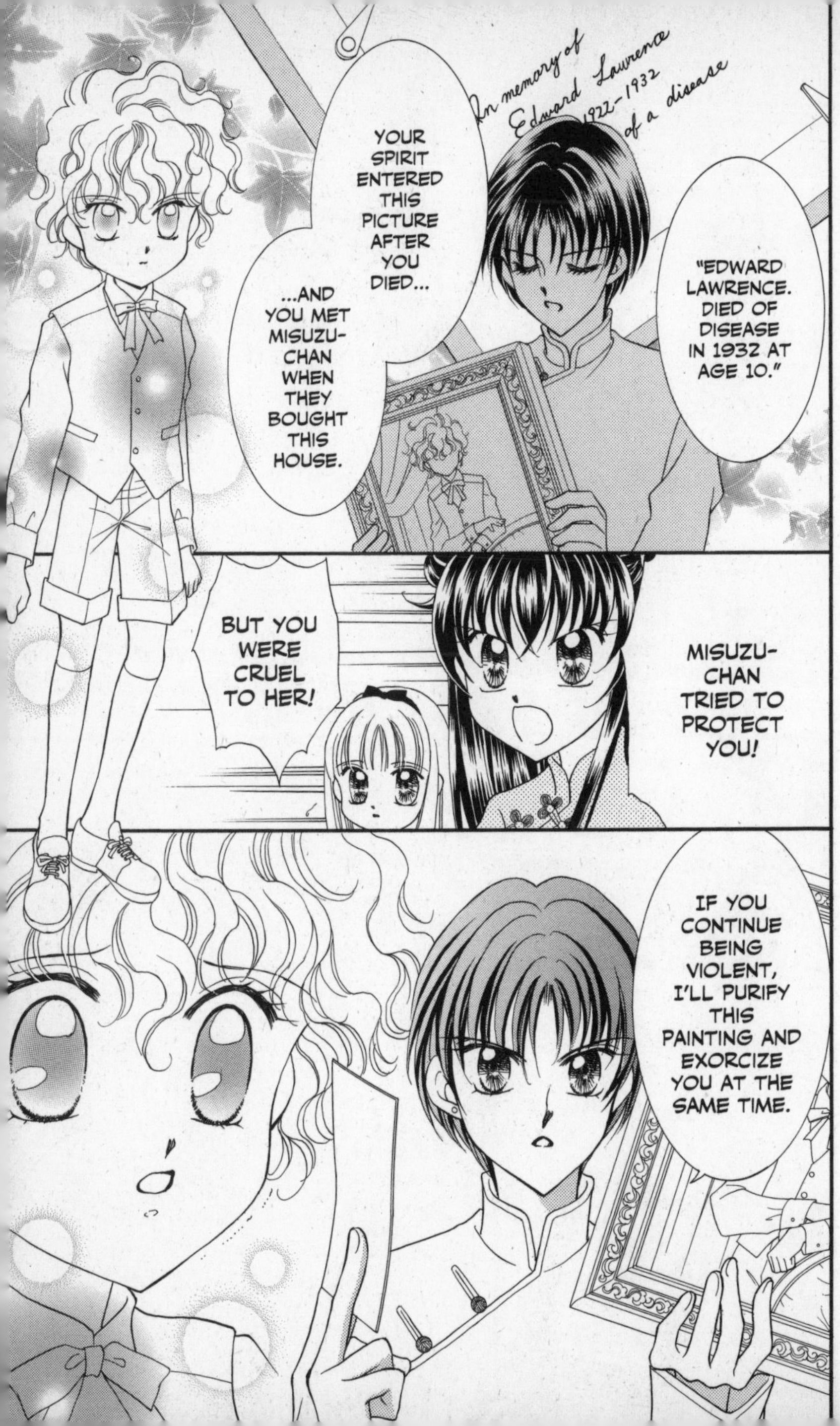
In memory of Edward Lawrence 1922-1932 of a disease
"EDWARD LAWRENCE. DIED OF DISEASE IN 1932 AT AGE 10."
YOUR SPIRIT ENTERED THIS PICTURE AFTER YOU DIED...
...AND YOU MET MISUZU-CHAN WHEN THEY BOUGHT THIS HOUSE.
MISUZU-CHAN TRIED TO PROTECT YOU!
BUT YOU WERE CRUEL TO HER!
IF YOU CONTINUE BEING VIOLENT, I'LL PURIFY THIS PAINTING AND EXORCIZE YOU AT THE SAME TIME.

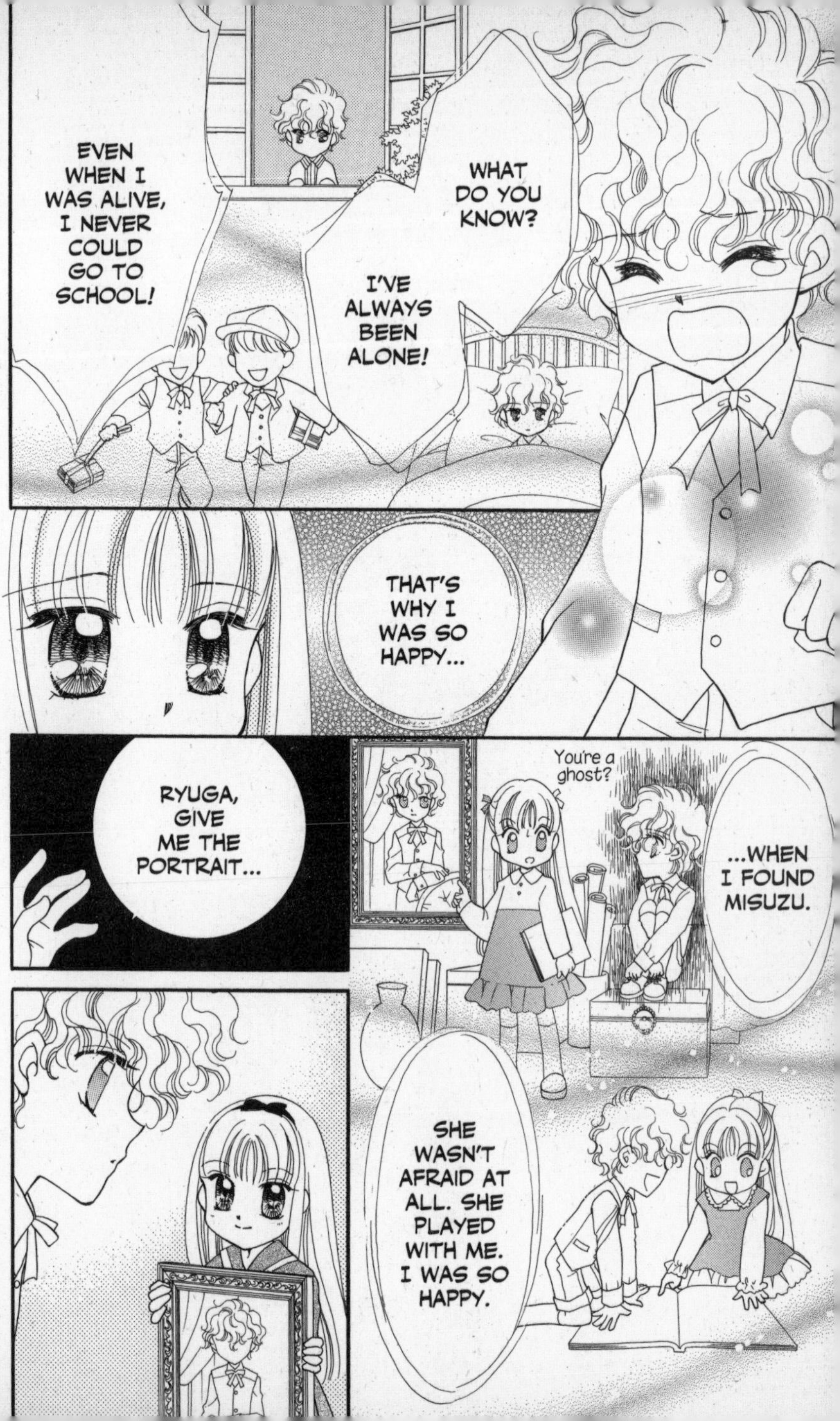
WHAT DO YOU KNOW?
I'VE ALWAYS BEEN ALONE!
EVEN WHEN I WAS ALIVE, I NEVER COULD GO TO SCHOOL!
THAT'S WHY I WAS SO HAPPY...
You're a ghost?
...WHEN I FOUND MISUZU.
SHE WASN'T AFRAID AT ALL. SHE PLAYED WITH ME. I WAS SO HAPPY.
RYUGA, GIVE ME THE PORTRAIT...

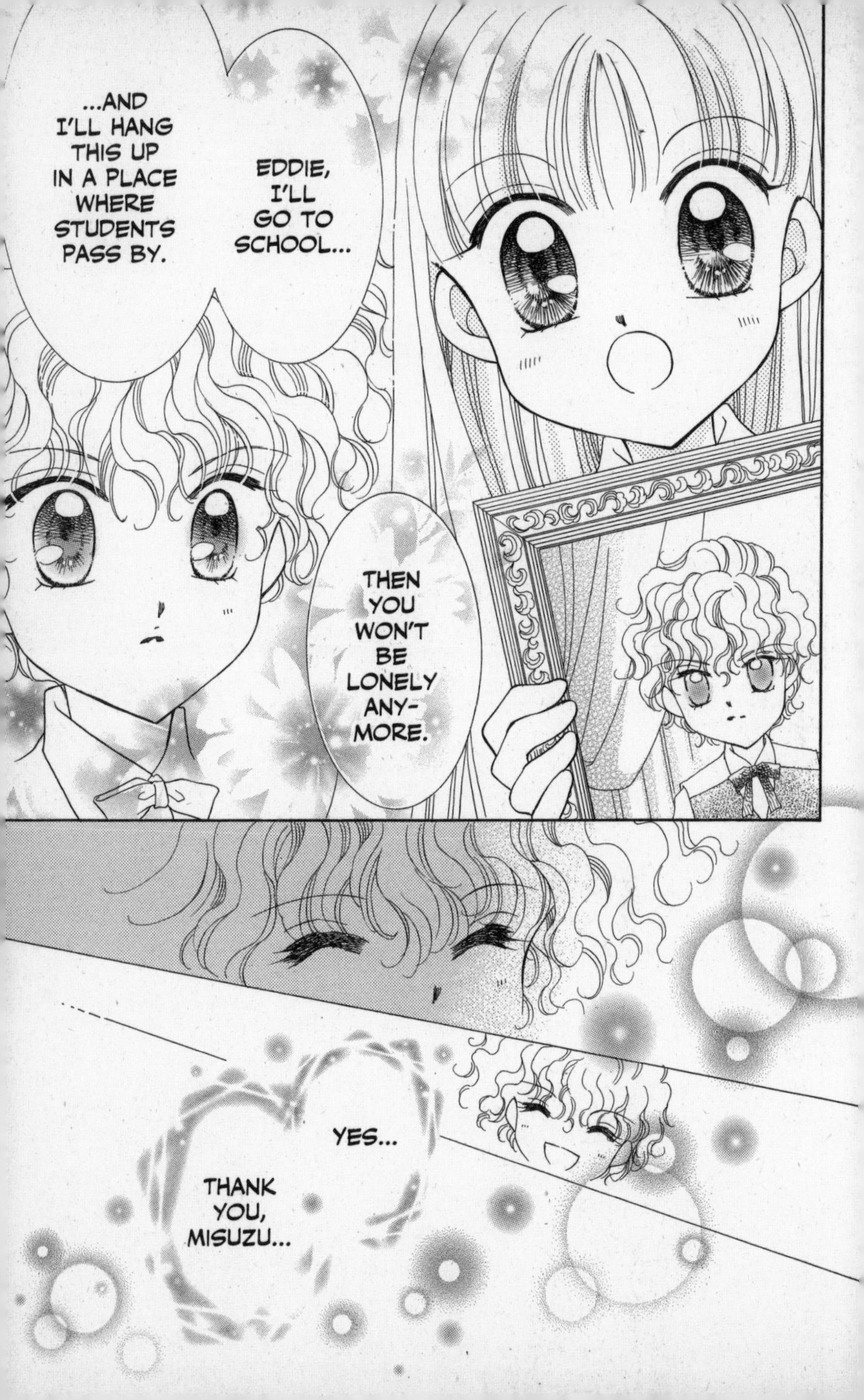
EDDIE, I'LL GO TO SCHOOL...
...AND I'LL HANG THIS UP IN A PLACE WHERE STUDENTS PASS BY.
THEN YOU WON'T BE LONELY ANY-MORE.
YES...
THANK YOU, MISUZU...

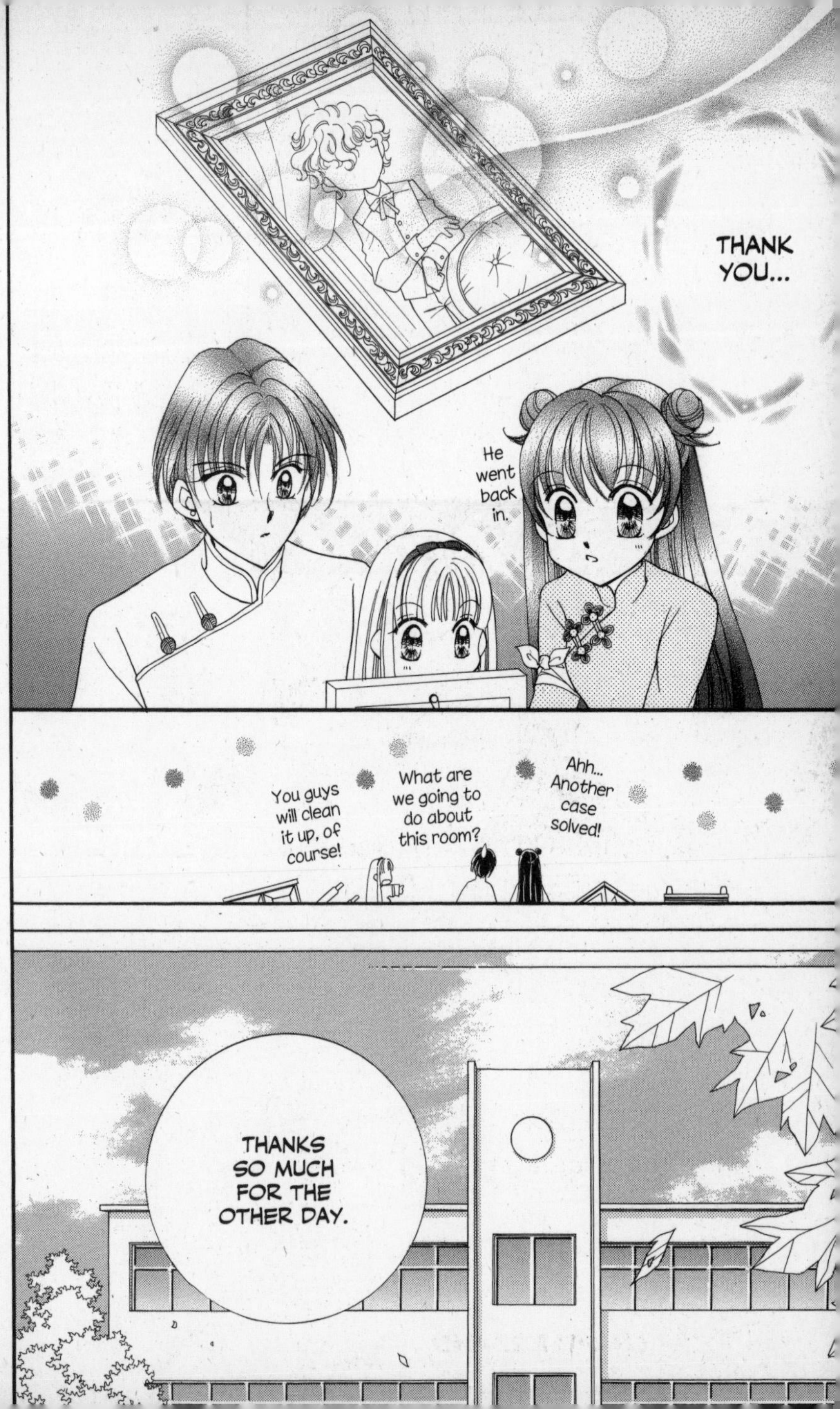
THANK YOU...
He went back in.
Ahh... Another case solved!
What are we going to do about this room?
You guys will clean it up, of course!
THANKS SO MUCH FOR THE OTHER DAY.

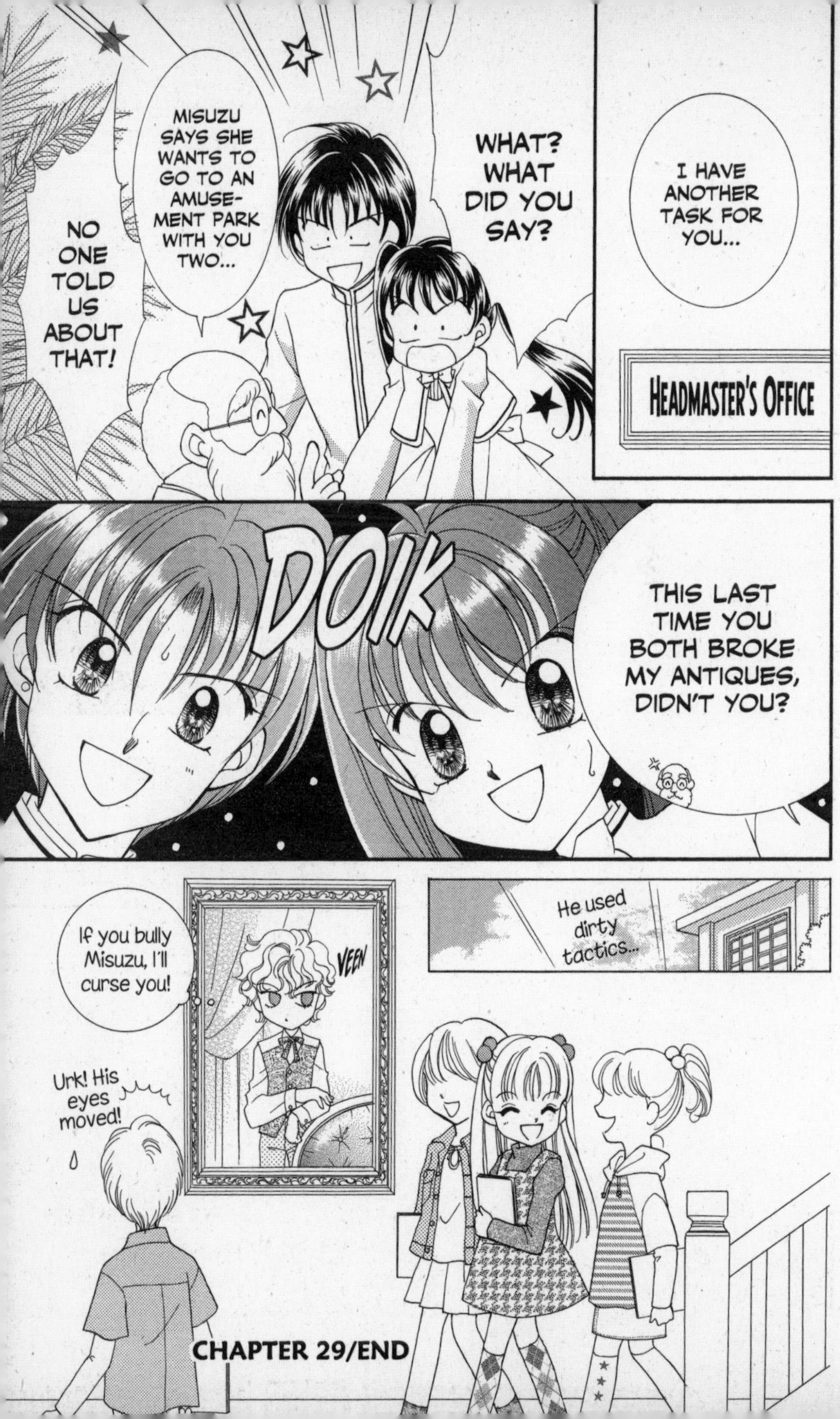
HEADMASTER'S OFFICE
I HAVE ANOTHER TASK FOR YOU...
WHAT? WHAT DID YOU SAY?
MISUZU SAYS SHE WANTS TO GO TO AN AMUSEMENT PARK WITH YOU TWO...
NO ONE TOLD US ABOUT THAT!
THIS LAST TIME YOU BOTH BROKE MY ANTIQUES, DIDN'T YOU?
DOIK
He used dirty tactics...
If you bully Misuzu, I'll curse you!
VEEN
Urk! His eyes moved!
CHAPTER 29/END

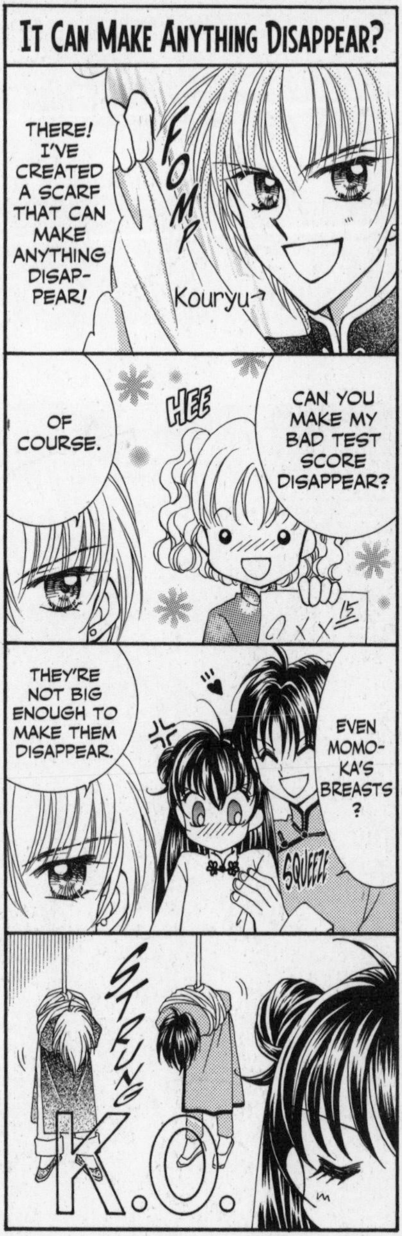
IT CAN MAKE ANYTHING DISAPPEAR?
FOMP
THERE! I'VE CREATED A SCARF THAT CAN MAKE ANYTHING DISAP-PEAR!
Kouryu→
CAN YOU MAKE MY BAD TEST SCORE DISAPPEAR?
HEE
OF COURSE.
EVEN MOMO-KA'S BREASTS?
SQUEEZE
THEY'RE NOT BIG ENOUGH TO MAKE THEM DISAPPEAR.
STRUNG
K.O.

This was an idea from Marie Yano-chan in Hokkaido. ▶

I think Marie-chan's comic shows she understands *St.♥Dragon Girl* more than I do! (laugh) But anyway, it's been a long time since we've seen Kouryu-sama! I was so happy about all these comic strips—thanks, everyone!

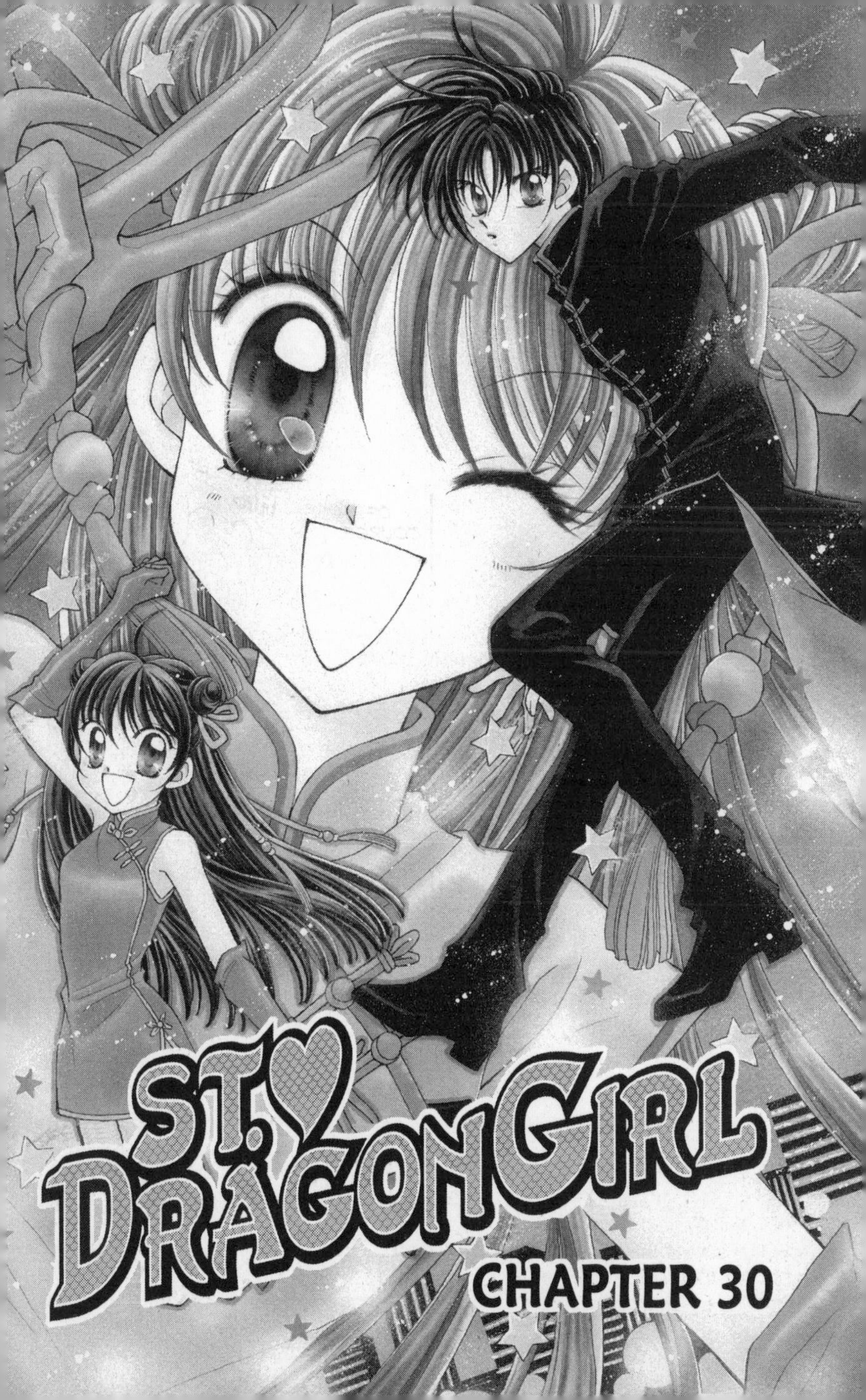
ST.♥DRAGON GIRL
CHAPTER 30

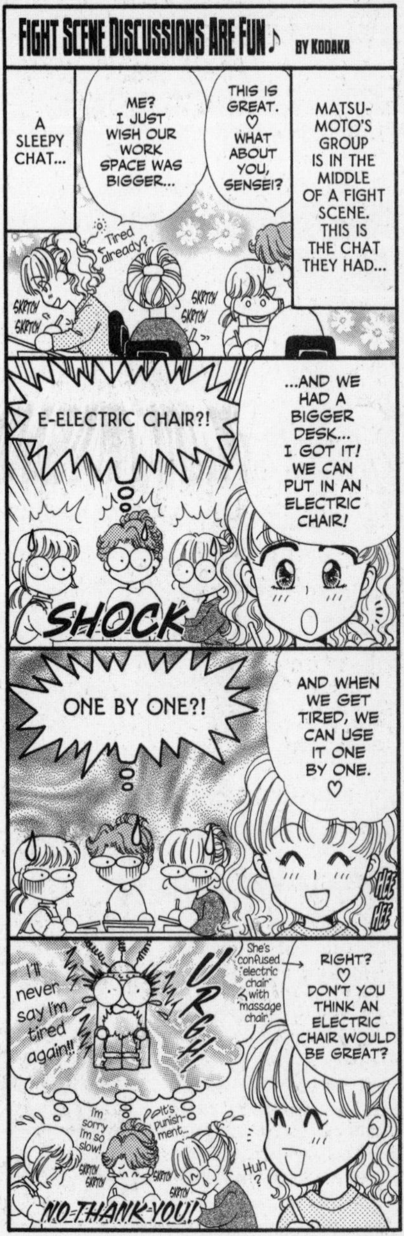
FIGHT SCENE DISCUSSIONS ARE FUN♪ BY KODAKA
MATSU-MOTO'S GROUP IS IN THE MIDDLE OF A FIGHT SCENE. THIS IS THE CHAT THEY HAD...
THIS IS GREAT. ♡ WHAT ABOUT YOU, SENSEI?
ME? I JUST WISH OUR WORK SPACE WAS BIGGER...
A SLEEPY CHAT...
← Tired already?
SKRTCH SKRTCH
SKRTCH SKRTCH
...AND WE HAD A BIGGER DESK... I GOT IT! WE CAN PUT IN AN ELECTRIC CHAIR!
E-ELECTRIC CHAIR?!
SHOCK
AND WHEN WE GET TIRED, WE CAN USE IT ONE BY ONE. ♡
HEE HEE
ONE BY ONE?!
RIGHT? ♡ DON'T YOU THINK AN ELECTRIC CHAIR WOULD BE GREAT?
She's confused "electric chair" with "massage chair."
URGH
I'll never say I'm tired again!!
Huh?
It's punish-ment...
I'm sorry I'm so slow!
SKRTCH SKRTCH
SKRTCH
NO THANK YOU!

By Kodaka ▶

This actually happened at work once. I meant "massage chair" but said "electric chair" instead. I'm brain-dead when I work on fight scenes. But I really want one! A full-body massage chair!

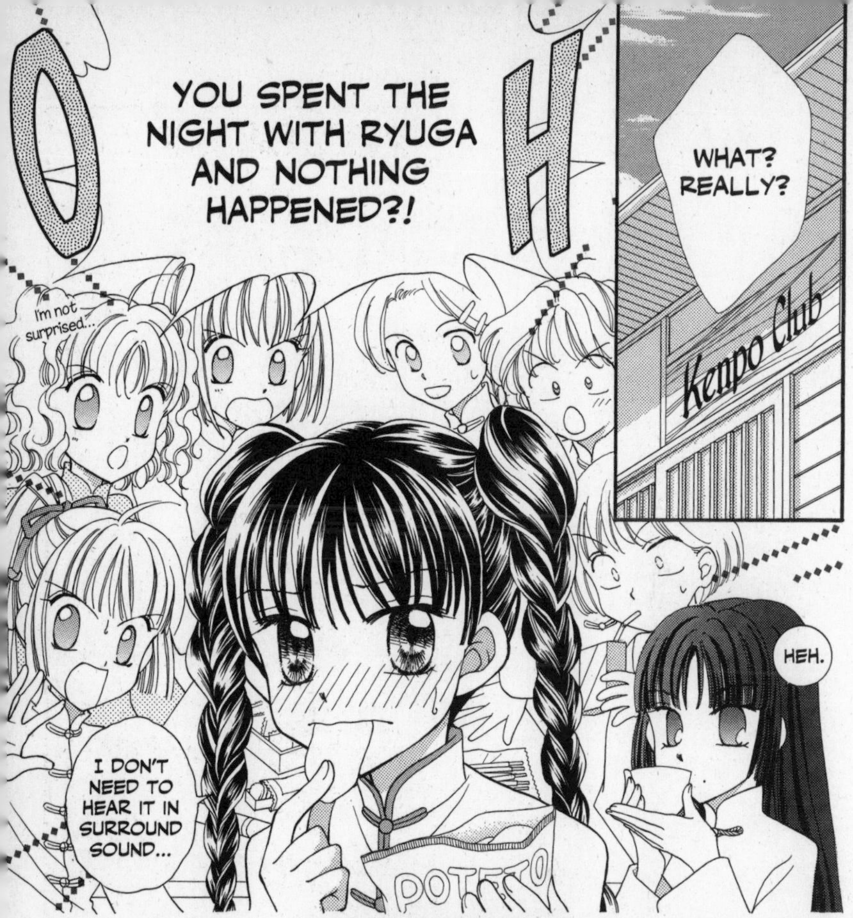
WHAT? REALLY?
OH
YOU SPENT THE NIGHT WITH RYUGA AND NOTHING HAPPENED?!
I'm not surprised...
HEH.
I DON'T NEED TO HEAR IT IN SURROUND SOUND...

Mao Hikami

Birthday: December 5.
17 years old.
Sagittarius. Blood Type: B.
Red hair.

He's from a family of magic masters. He's a half-demon. He appears to be a child, but when the sun sets, he turns into an adult. With the power of his familiars, Miya and Kuu, he can remain as an adult throughout the day.

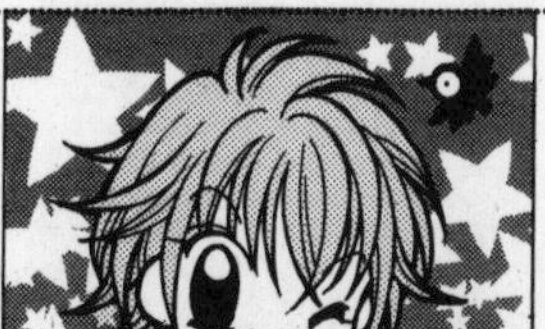

He's a naive boy. At 17, he wants a dinosaur. You want to say, "Is he okay?" but for some reason he's really popular with readers. Some people even want Mao and Momoka to get together! They do have a lot in common—they act impulsively and cause lots of trouble! (laugh) He has summoning powers. He has one younger sister.

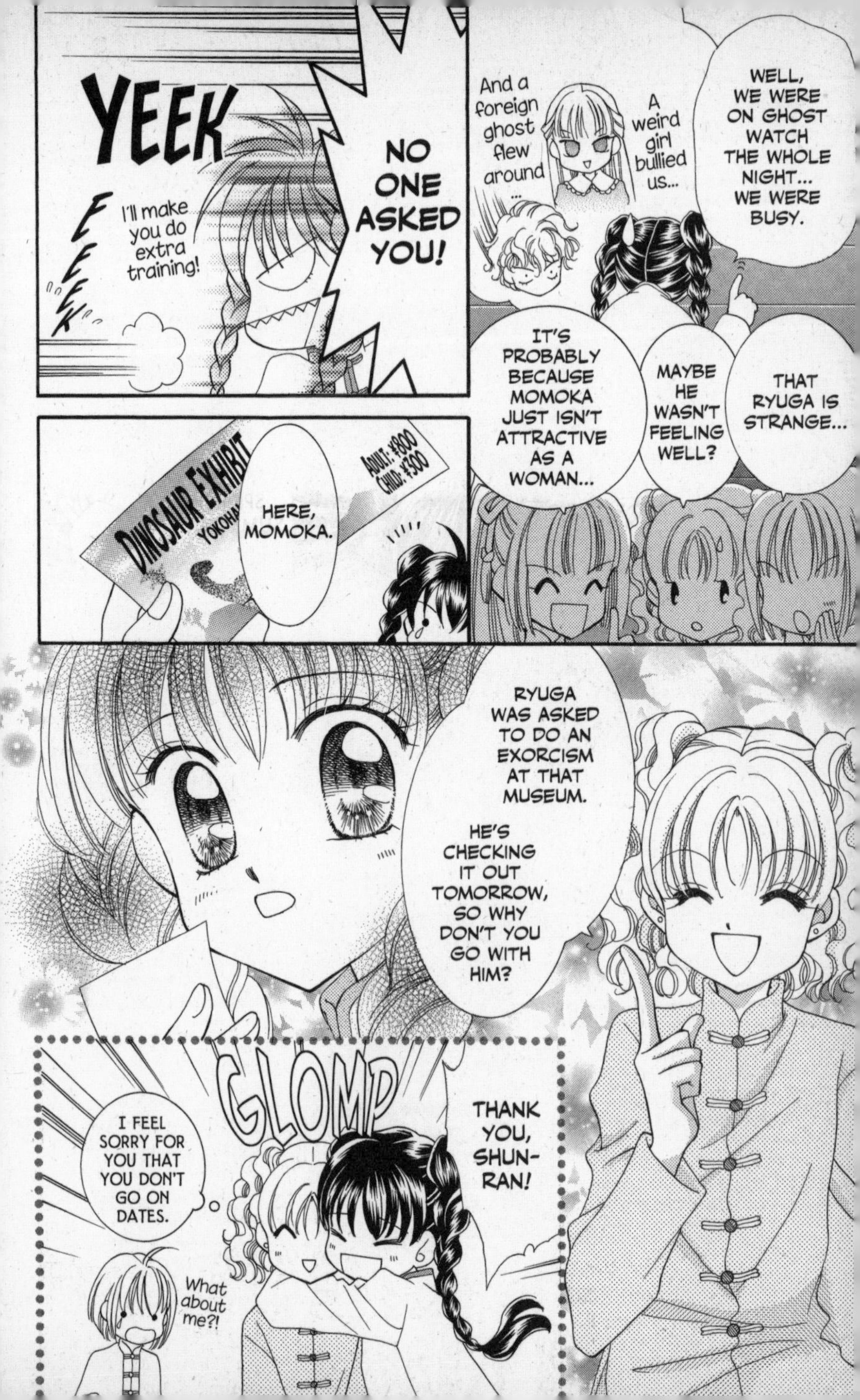
WELL, WE WERE ON GHOST WATCH THE WHOLE NIGHT... WE WERE BUSY.
A weird girl bullied us...
And a foreign ghost flew around...
THAT RYUGA IS STRANGE...
MAYBE HE WASN'T FEELING WELL?
IT'S PROBABLY BECAUSE MOMOKA JUST ISN'T ATTRACTIVE AS A WOMAN...
NO ONE ASKED YOU!
YEEK
EEEEK
I'll make you do extra training!
ADULT: ¥800 CHILD: ¥300
DINOSAUR EXHIBIT
YOKOHA
HERE, MOMOKA.
RYUGA WAS ASKED TO DO AN EXORCISM AT THAT MUSEUM.
HE'S CHECKING IT OUT TOMORROW, SO WHY DON'T YOU GO WITH HIM?
THANK YOU, SHUN-RAN!
GLOMP
I FEEL SORRY FOR YOU THAT YOU DON'T GO ON DATES.
What about me?!

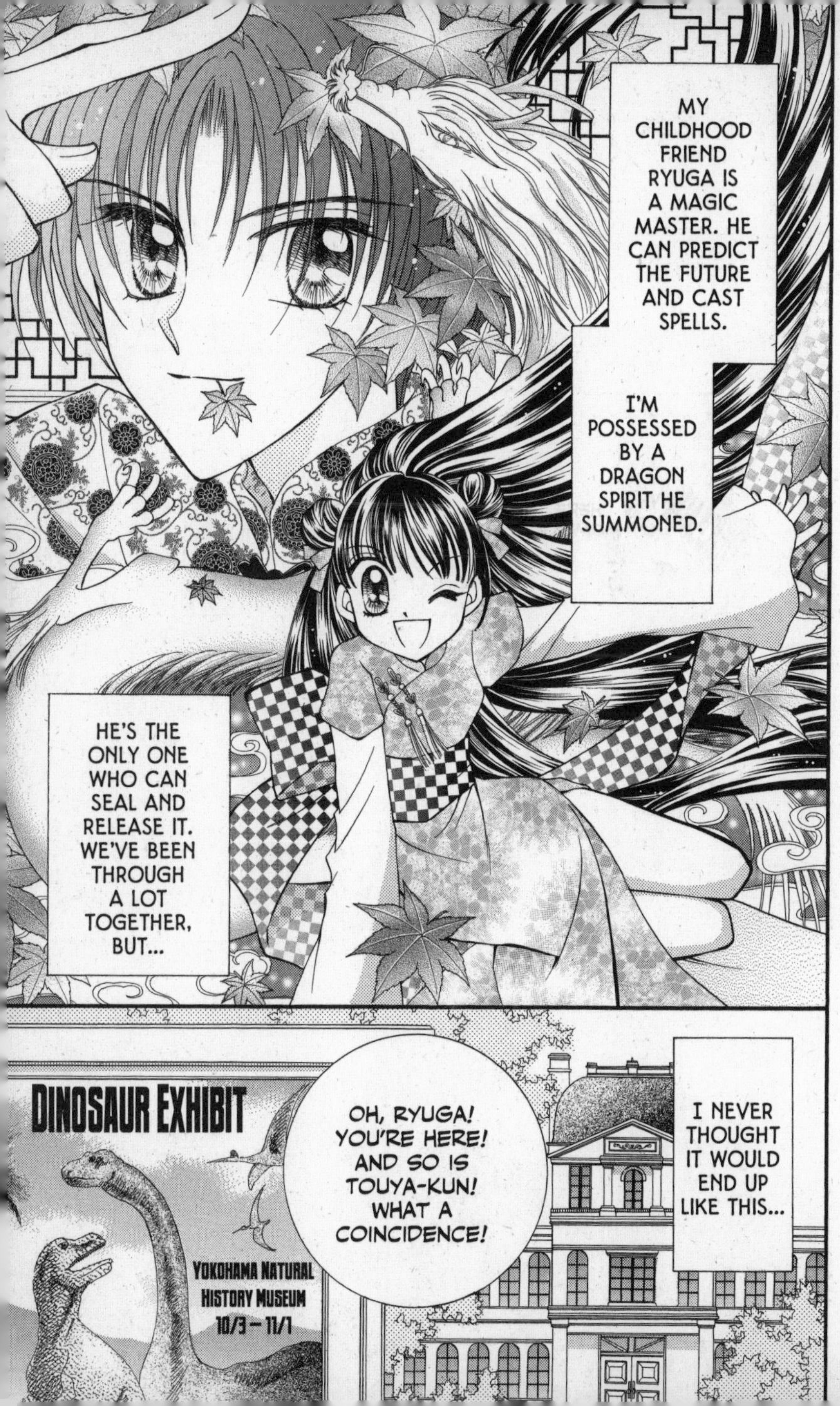
MY CHILDHOOD FRIEND RYUGA IS A MAGIC MASTER. HE CAN PREDICT THE FUTURE AND CAST SPELLS.
I'M POSSESSED BY A DRAGON SPIRIT HE SUMMONED.
HE'S THE ONLY ONE WHO CAN SEAL AND RELEASE IT. WE'VE BEEN THROUGH A LOT TOGETHER, BUT...
I NEVER THOUGHT IT WOULD END UP LIKE THIS...
OH, RYUGA! YOU'RE HERE! AND SO IS TOUYA-KUN! WHAT A COINCIDENCE!
DINOSAUR EXHIBIT
YOKOHAMA NATURAL HISTORY MUSEUM
10/3 – 11/1

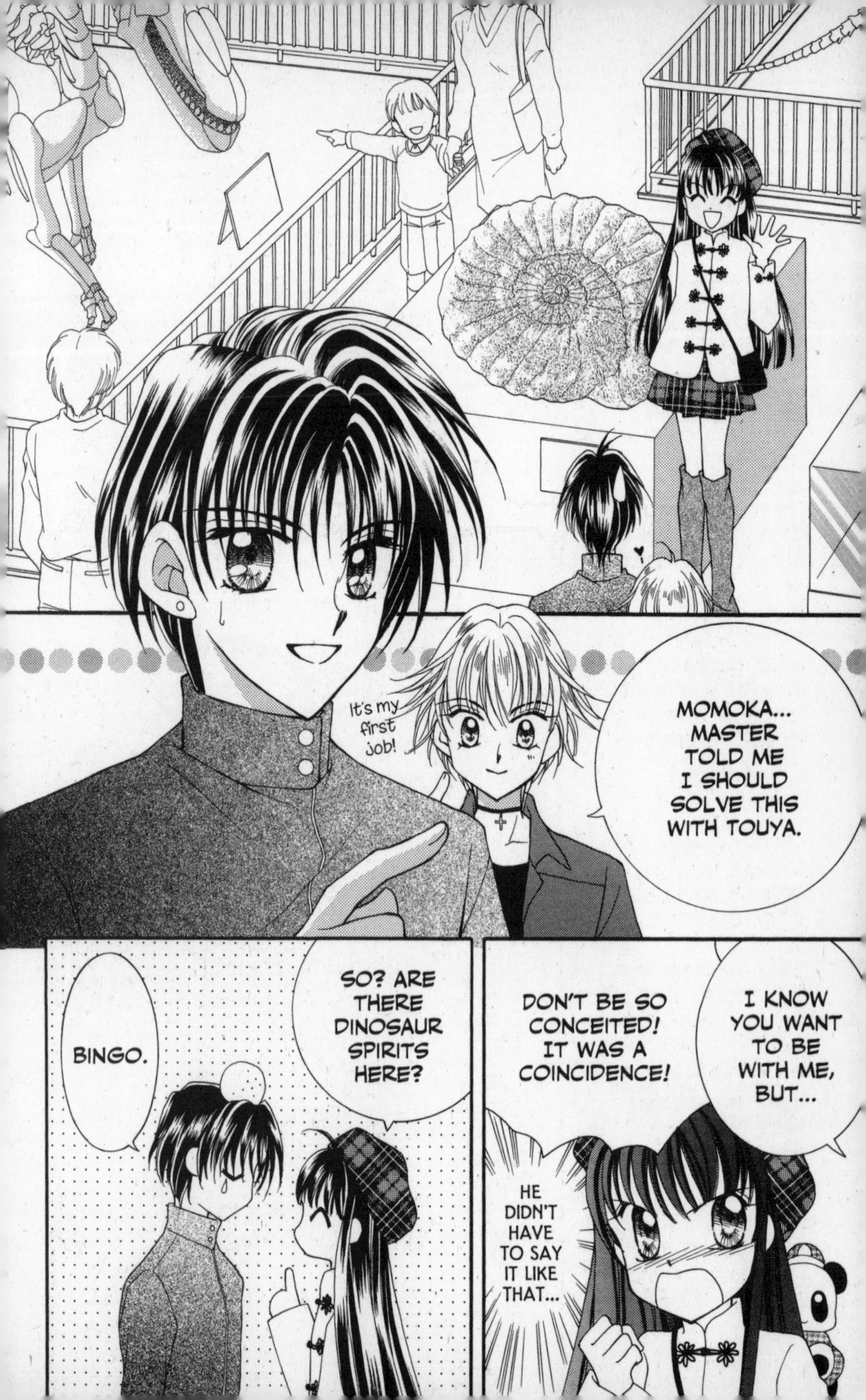
MOMOKA... MASTER TOLD ME I SHOULD SOLVE THIS WITH TOUYA.
It's my first job!
SO? ARE THERE DINOSAUR SPIRITS HERE?
BINGO.
I KNOW YOU WANT TO BE WITH ME, BUT...
DON'T BE SO CONCEITED! IT WAS A COINCIDENCE!
HE DIDN'T HAVE TO SAY IT LIKE THAT...

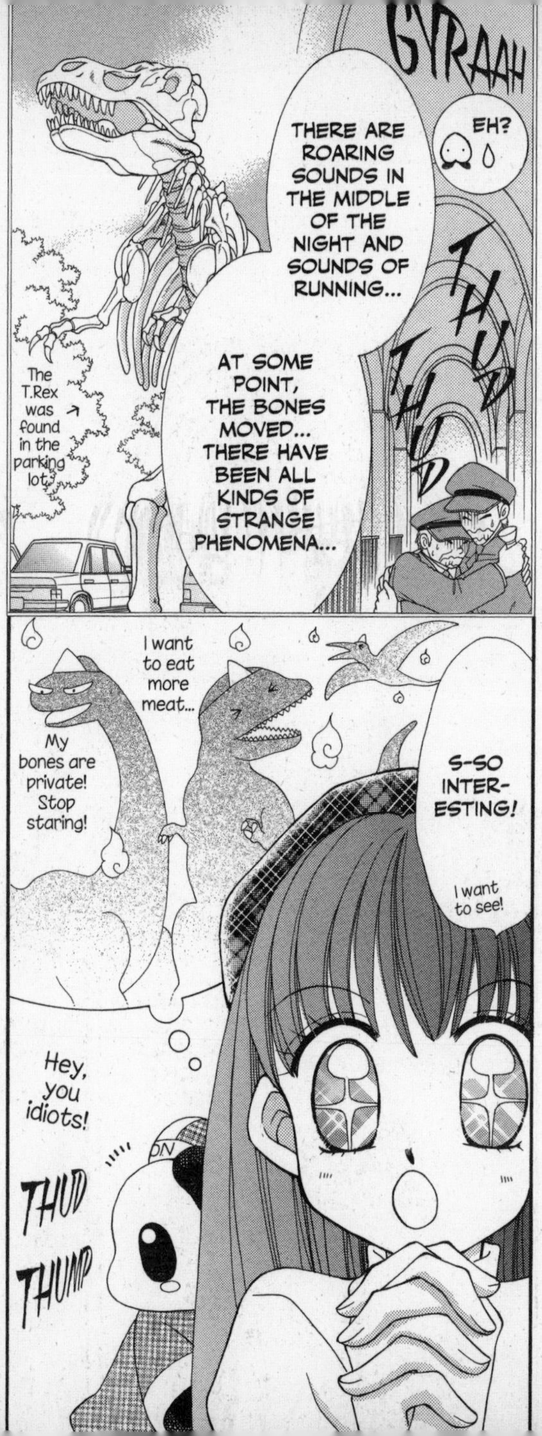
GYRAAH
EH?
THERE ARE ROARING SOUNDS IN THE MIDDLE OF THE NIGHT AND SOUNDS OF RUNNING...
THUD THUD
AT SOME POINT, THE BONES MOVED... THERE HAVE BEEN ALL KINDS OF STRANGE PHENOMENA...
The T.Rex was found in the parking lot.
S-SO INTER-ESTING!
I want to see!
I want to eat more meat...
My bones are private! Stop staring!
Hey, you idiots!
THUD
THUMP

7

In this chapter a new character, Mao, makes his first appearance. His interests will be revealed as we go along.

I love dinosaurs and museums. I've felt that way since I was little! The pencil board I use is a dinosaur one I bought from a museum. At my parents' house, they have a (small) ammonite fossil and a plastic model of a dinosaur skeleton.

The main character in my first manga was a girl who kept a dinosaur in her apartment. It was a long time ago.

But I didn't get too detailed. At that time, my assistant told me the brachiosaurus's neck didn't turn upward, but then I saw *Jurassic Park* on TV and that brachiosaurus's neck did turn upward! Oh well. So after that I didn't bother about it, and now I'm sticking to magic! (laugh)

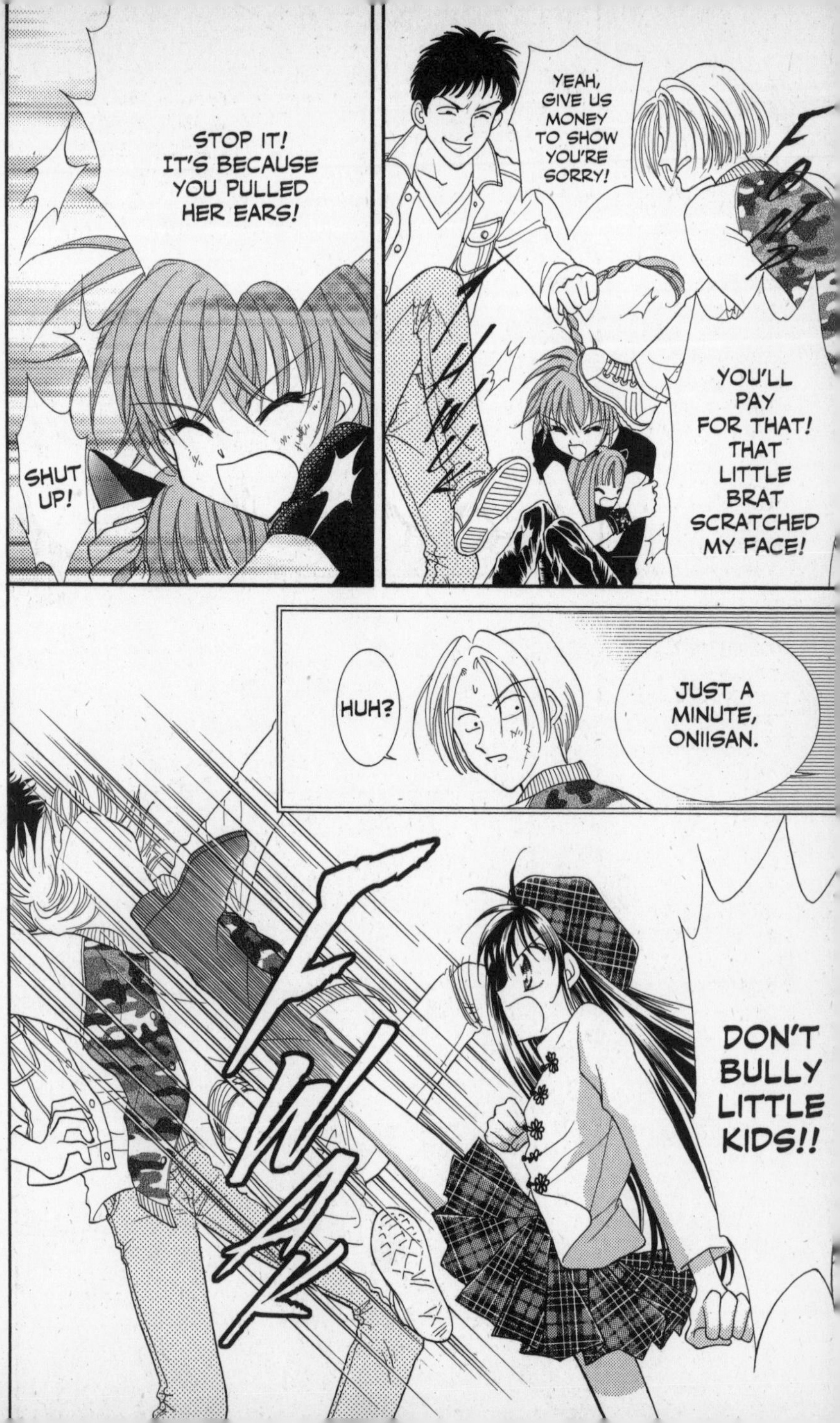
YOU'LL PAY FOR THAT! THAT LITTLE BRAT SCRATCHED MY FACE!
YEAH, GIVE US MONEY TO SHOW YOU'RE SORRY!
STOP IT! IT'S BECAUSE YOU PULLED HER EARS!
SHUT UP!
JUST A MINUTE, ONIISAN.
HUH?
DON'T BULLY LITTLE KIDS!!

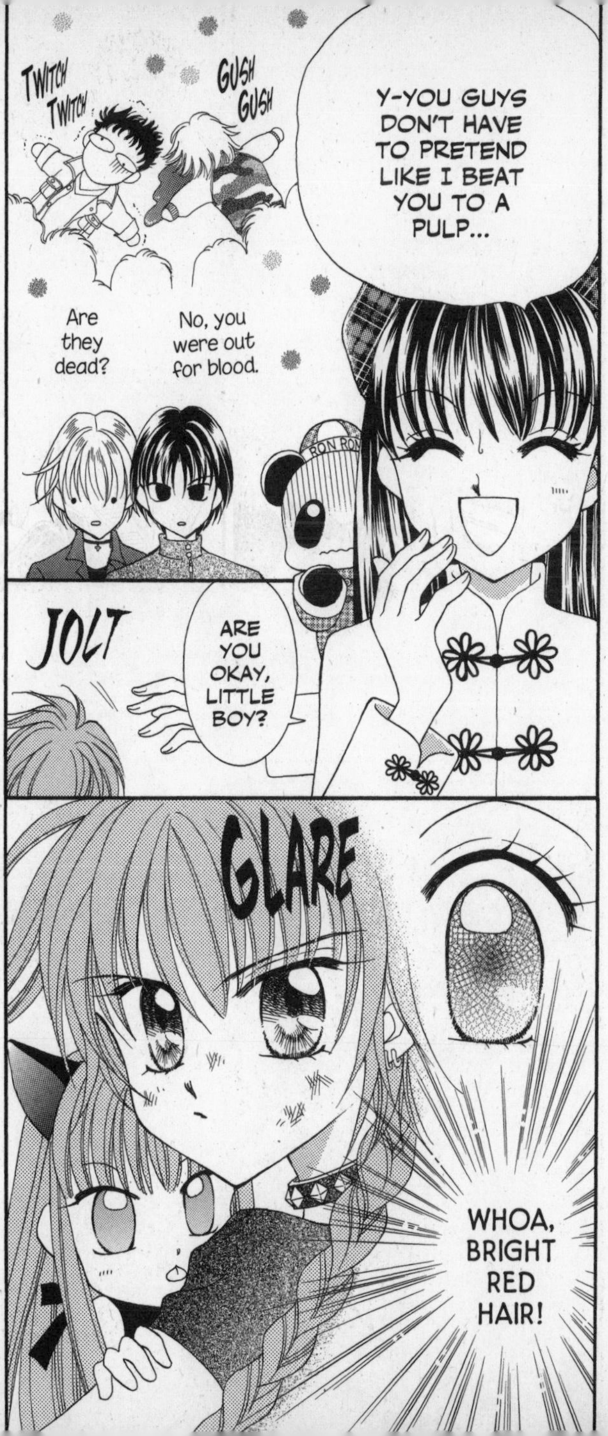
Y-YOU GUYS DON'T HAVE TO PRETEND LIKE I BEAT YOU TO A PULP...
GUSH GUSH
TWITCH TWITCH
No, you were out for blood.
Are they dead?
RON ROM
ARE YOU OKAY, LITTLE BOY?
JOLT
GLARE
WHOA, BRIGHT RED HAIR!

8

I really like Mao's personality. He's silly (sometimes ;), but he's individualistic. I like creating chibi characters, so it was fun to draw Miya and Kuu. When night falls, they grow up, but the next day they return to being small again. It's because their chibi forms are so cute! I have fun drawing them.

Miya and Kuu are familiars. They're like "shikigami," a sorcerer's divine agents. To Mao, they're like pets or siblings! He loves cats. (Miya is a cat...)

These two are very helpful to Mao, but they remain a mystery...

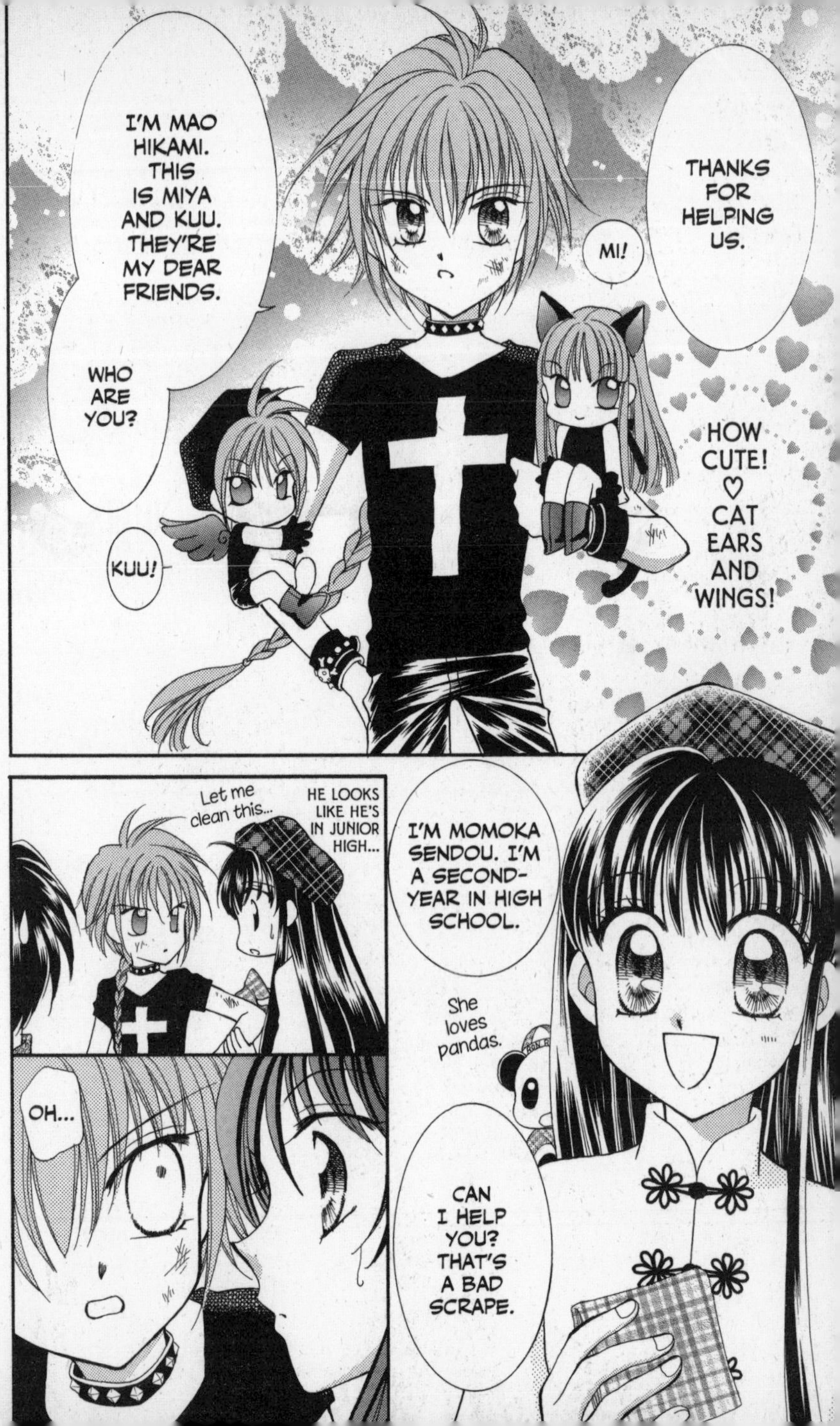
THANKS FOR HELPING US.
MI!
I'M MAO HIKAMI. THIS IS MIYA AND KUU. THEY'RE MY DEAR FRIENDS.
WHO ARE YOU?
HOW CUTE! ♡ CAT EARS AND WINGS!
KUU!
I'M MOMOKA SENDOU. I'M A SECOND-YEAR IN HIGH SCHOOL.
She loves pandas.
CAN I HELP YOU? THAT'S A BAD SCRAPE.
HE LOOKS LIKE HE'S IN JUNIOR HIGH...
Let me clean this...
OH...

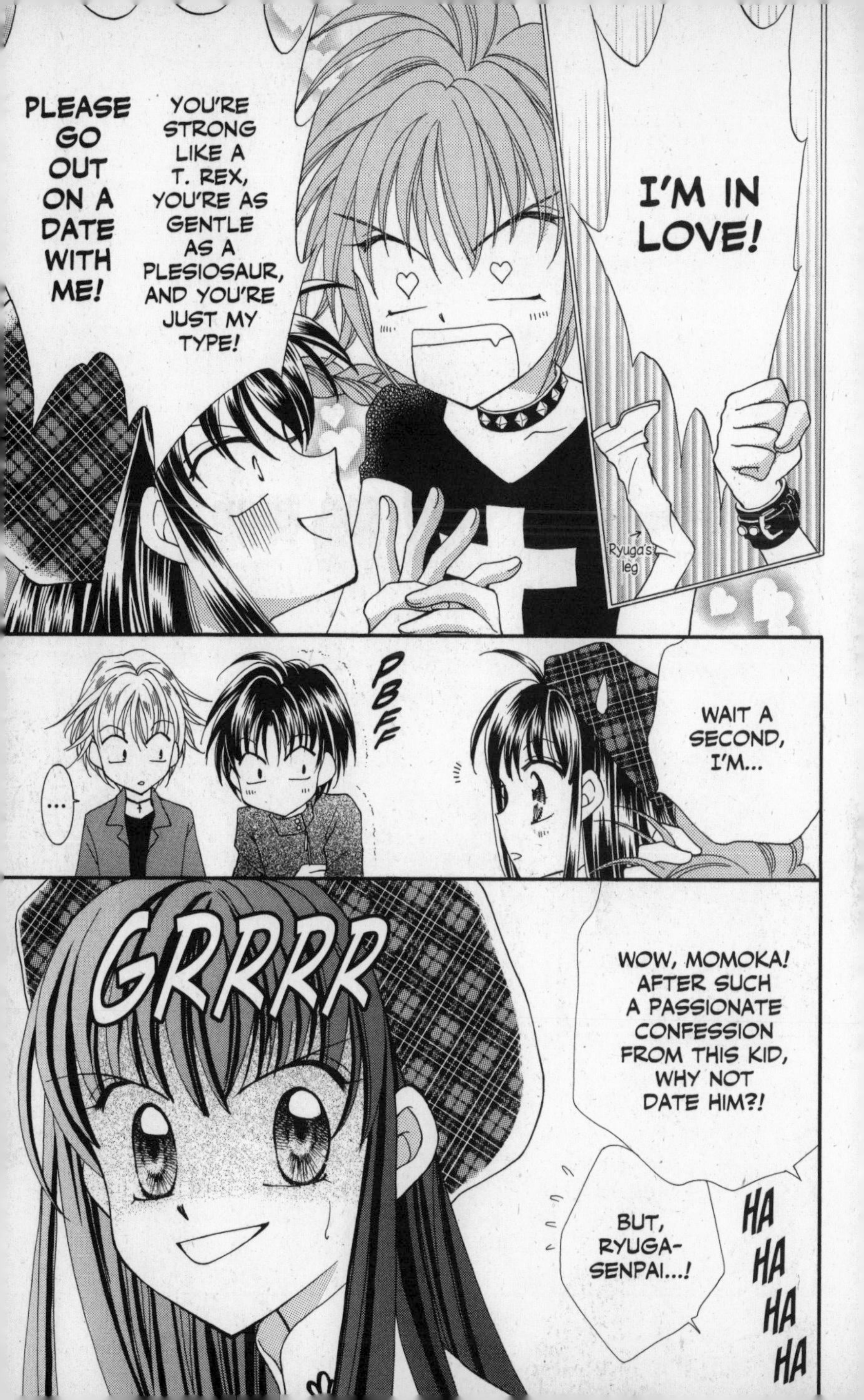
I'M IN LOVE!
YOU'RE STRONG LIKE A T. REX, YOU'RE AS GENTLE AS A PLESIOSAUR, AND YOU'RE JUST MY TYPE!
PLEASE GO OUT ON A DATE WITH ME!
Ryuga's leg
WAIT A SECOND, I'M...
PBFF
...
WOW, MOMOKA! AFTER SUCH A PASSIONATE CONFESSION FROM THIS KID, WHY NOT DATE HIM?!
HA HA HA HA HA
BUT, RYUGA-SENPAI...!
GRRRR

If you had just been honest, this wouldn't have happened...
LET'S GO, MAO-KUN.
STUPID RYUGA! HE'S SO INSENSITIVE!
I HOPE A DINOSAUR GHOST STOMPS ON HIM!
THOSE TWO ARE YOUR SERVANTS?
Right?
RIGHT ?
Servants?
fish → cookie
NO, THE DARK-HAIRED ONE IS MY CHILDHOOD FRIEND. THE BLOND GOES TO OUR SCHOOL, BUT HE'S A YEAR YOUNGER.
THOUGH I WANT TO BE MORE THAN A CHILDHOOD FRIEND TO RYUGA...
ARE YOU SIBLINGS—

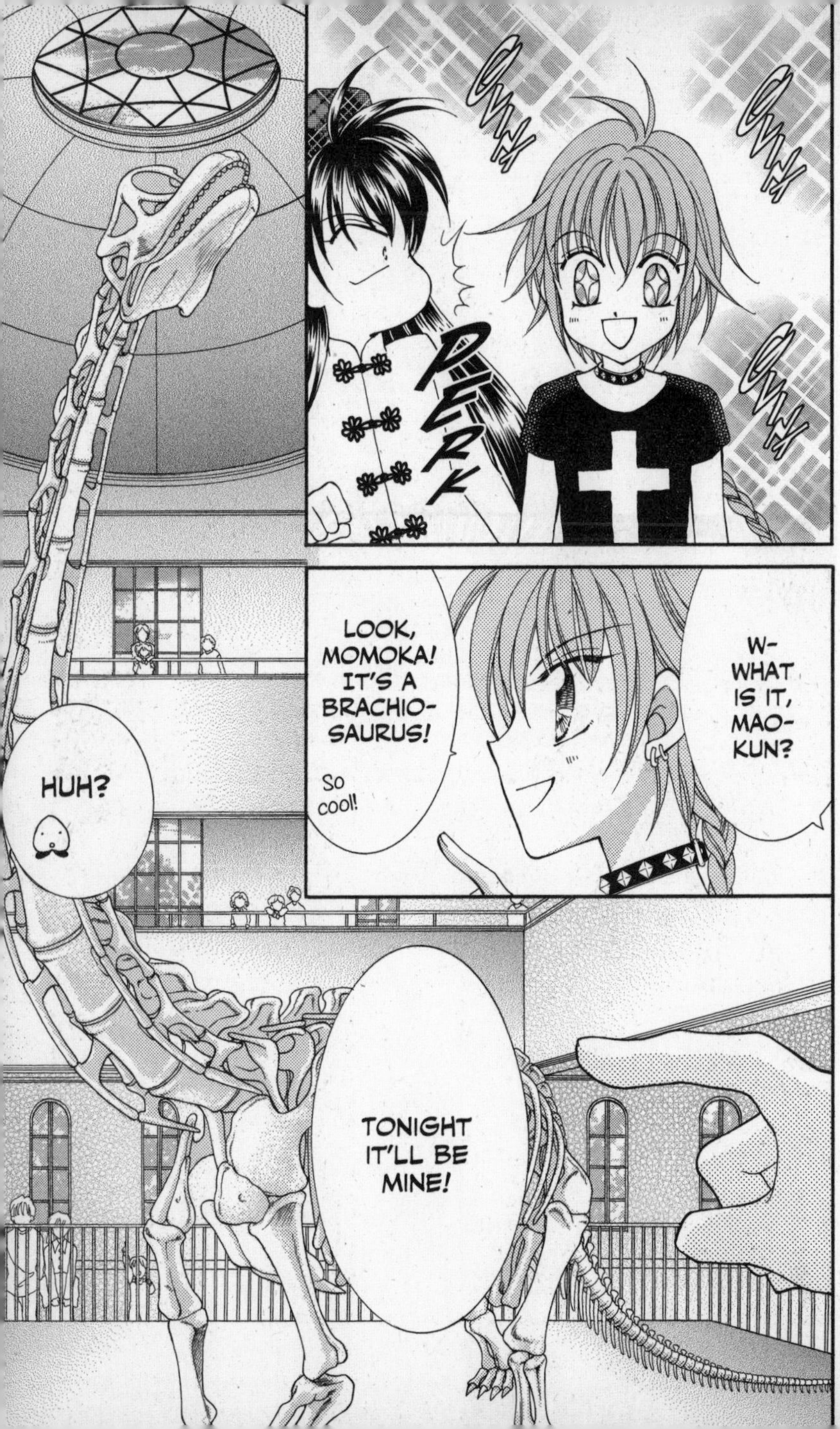
GAWK
GAWK
GAWK
PERK
W-WHAT IS IT, MAO-KUN?
LOOK, MOMOKA! IT'S A BRACHIO-SAURUS!
So cool!
HUH?
TONIGHT IT'LL BE MINE!

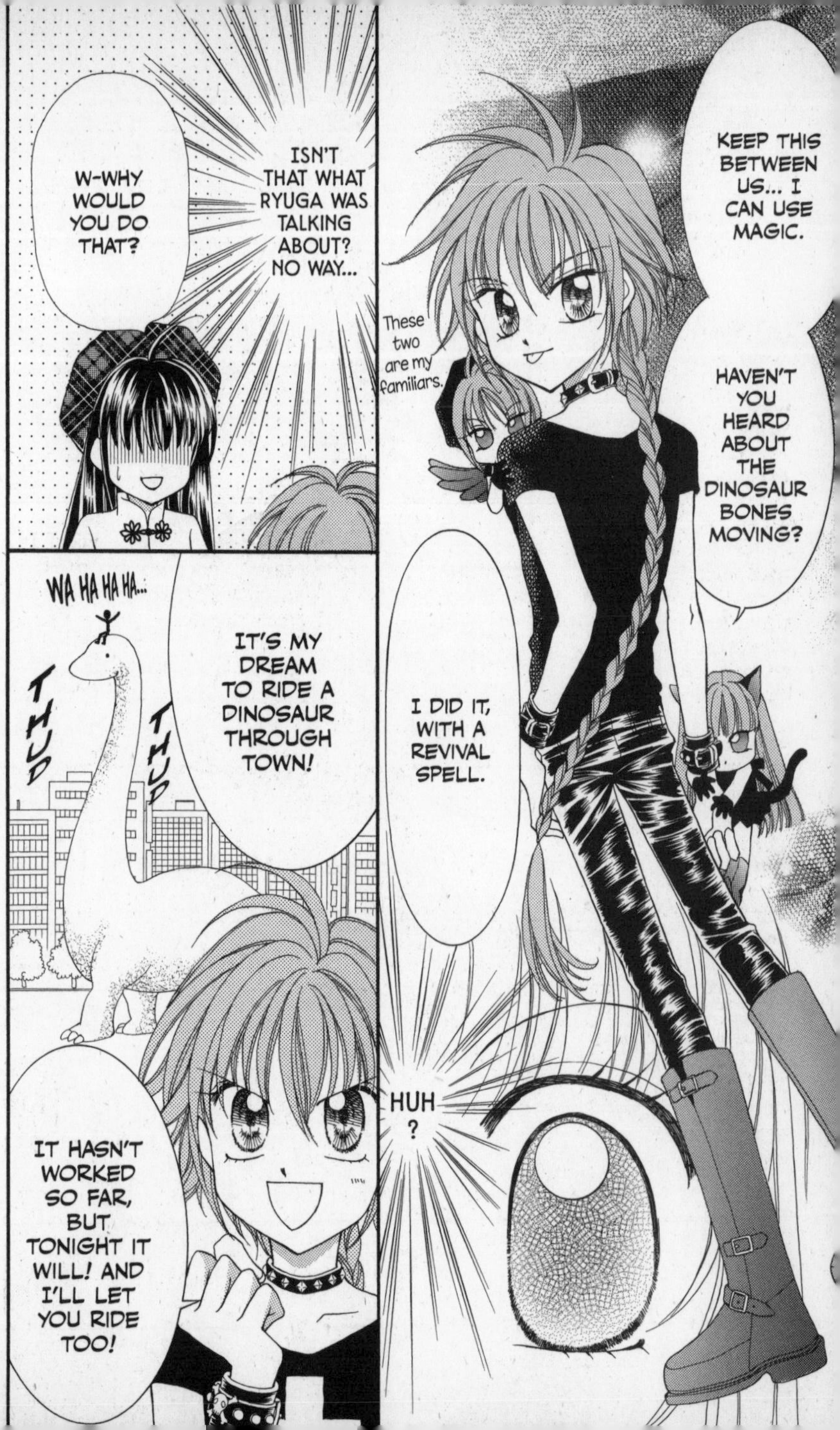
KEEP THIS BETWEEN US... I CAN USE MAGIC.
These two are my familiars.
HAVEN'T YOU HEARD ABOUT THE DINOSAUR BONES MOVING?
I DID IT, WITH A REVIVAL SPELL.
HUH?
ISN'T THAT WHAT RYUGA WAS TALKING ABOUT? NO WAY...
W-WHY WOULD YOU DO THAT?
IT'S MY DREAM TO RIDE A DINOSAUR THROUGH TOWN!
WA HA HA HA...
THUD
THUD
IT HASN'T WORKED SO FAR, BUT TONIGHT IT WILL! AND I'LL LET YOU RIDE TOO!

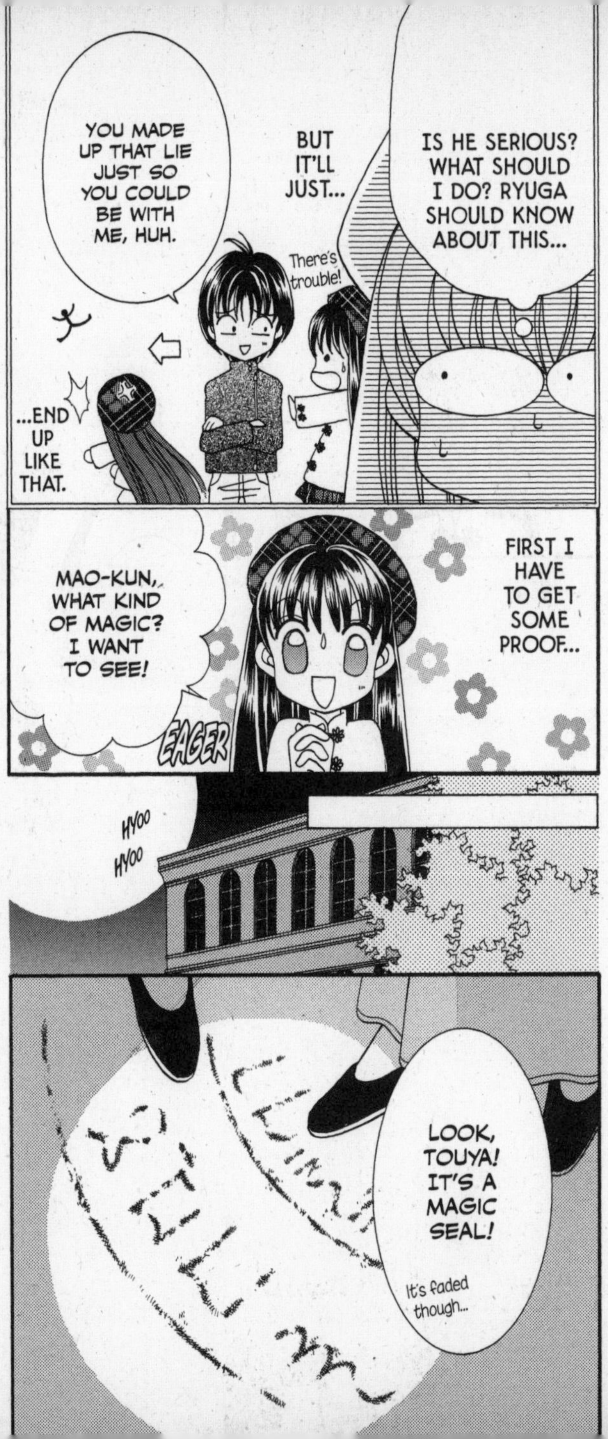
IS HE SERIOUS? WHAT SHOULD I DO? RYUGA SHOULD KNOW ABOUT THIS...
BUT IT'LL JUST...
There's trouble!
YOU MADE UP THAT LIE JUST SO YOU COULD BE WITH ME, HUH.
...END UP LIKE THAT.
FIRST I HAVE TO GET SOME PROOF...
MAO-KUN, WHAT KIND OF MAGIC? I WANT TO SEE!
EAGER
HYOO HYOO
LOOK, TOUYA! IT'S A MAGIC SEAL!
It's faded though...

9

By the way, I used "magic seals" for the first time in a long time in this story. In my other manga, *Kimi Dake no Devil,* they appeared in scenes too. Ah, how nostalgic! In that story, the seals were more like a magic square. But please know that in *St.♥Dragon Girl* the seal is more like a magic circle.

At my house, I have lots of books—not only on dinosaurs, but I have books on demons and magic as well. When I started this manga, my number of books about martial arts also increased, as did the ones on sorcery. Sometimes when I look at my bookshelf, I feel like I might have picked the wrong job! (laugh)

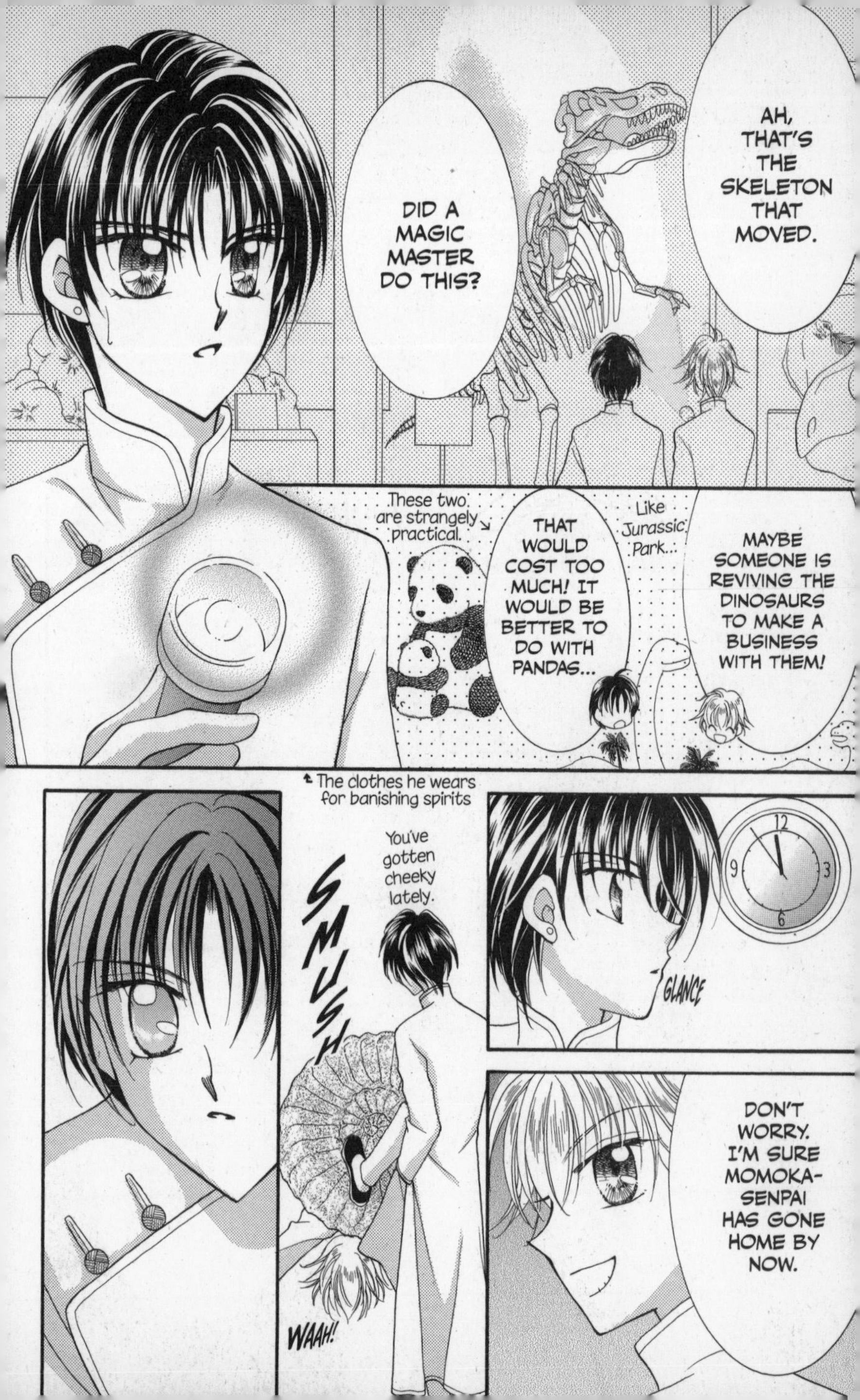
AH, THAT'S THE SKELETON THAT MOVED.
DID A MAGIC MASTER DO THIS?
MAYBE SOMEONE IS REVIVING THE DINOSAURS TO MAKE A BUSINESS WITH THEM!
Like Jurassic Park...
THAT WOULD COST TOO MUCH! IT WOULD BE BETTER TO DO WITH PANDAS...
These two are strangely practical.
The clothes he wears for banishing spirits
GLANCE
DON'T WORRY. I'M SURE MOMOKA-SENPAI HAS GONE HOME BY NOW.
SMUSH
You've gotten cheeky lately.
WAAH!

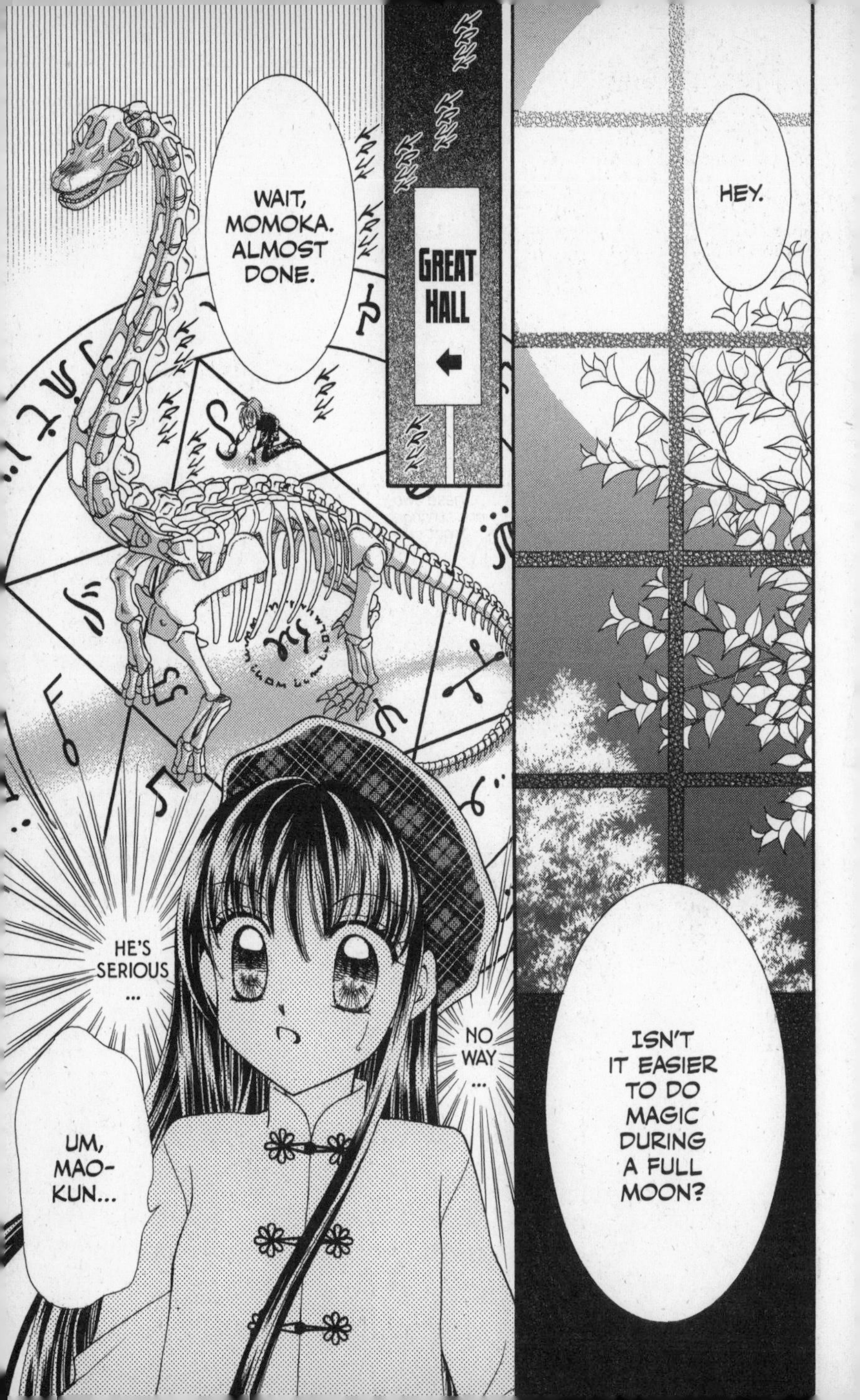
HEY.
ISN'T IT EASIER TO DO MAGIC DURING A FULL MOON?
KRUK
GREAT HALL
WAIT, MOMOKA. ALMOST DONE.
HE'S SERIOUS ...
NO WAY ...
UM, MAO-KUN...

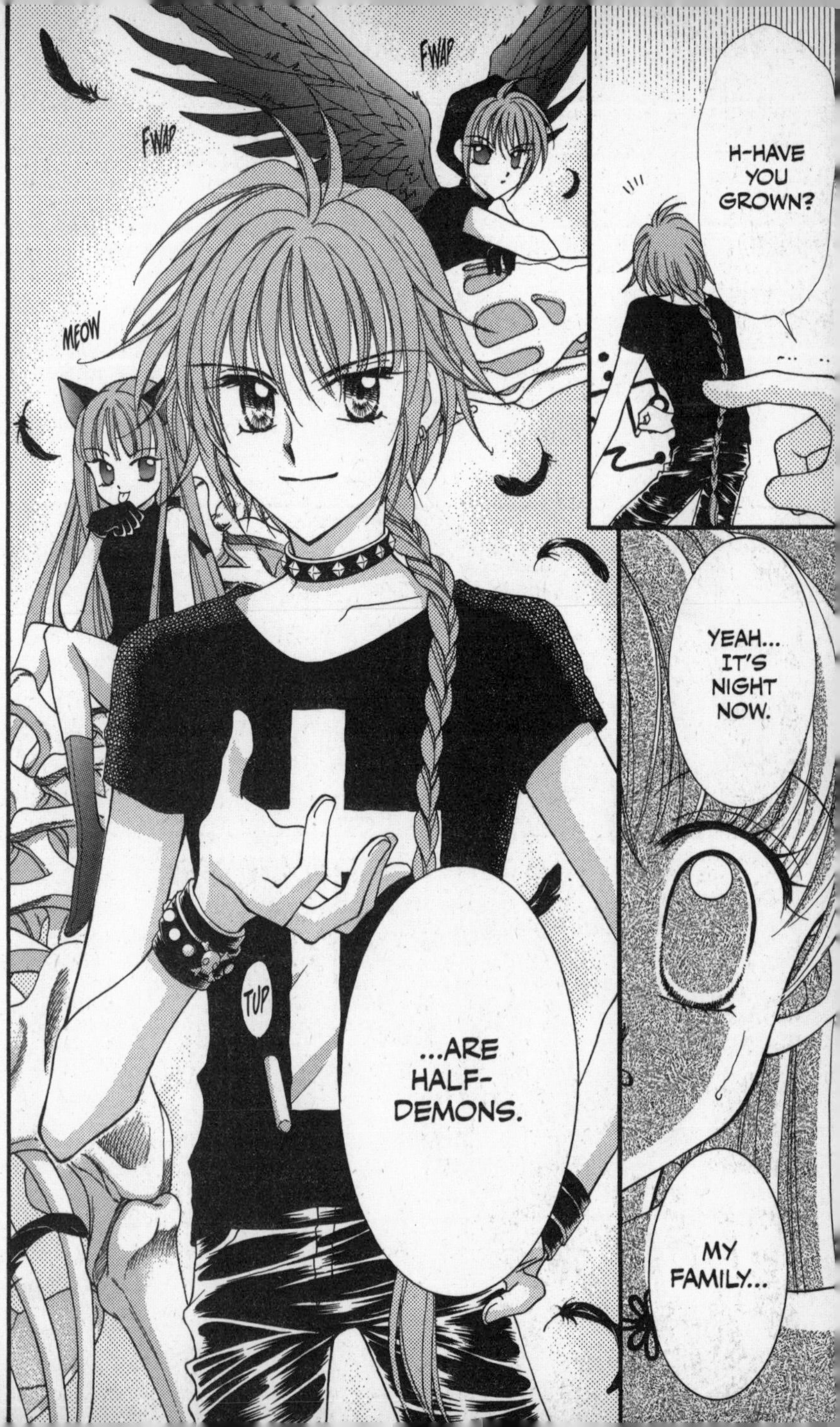
H-HAVE YOU GROWN?
...
YEAH... IT'S NIGHT NOW.
MY FAMILY...
F-WAP
F-WAP
MEOW
TUP
...ARE HALF-DEMONS.

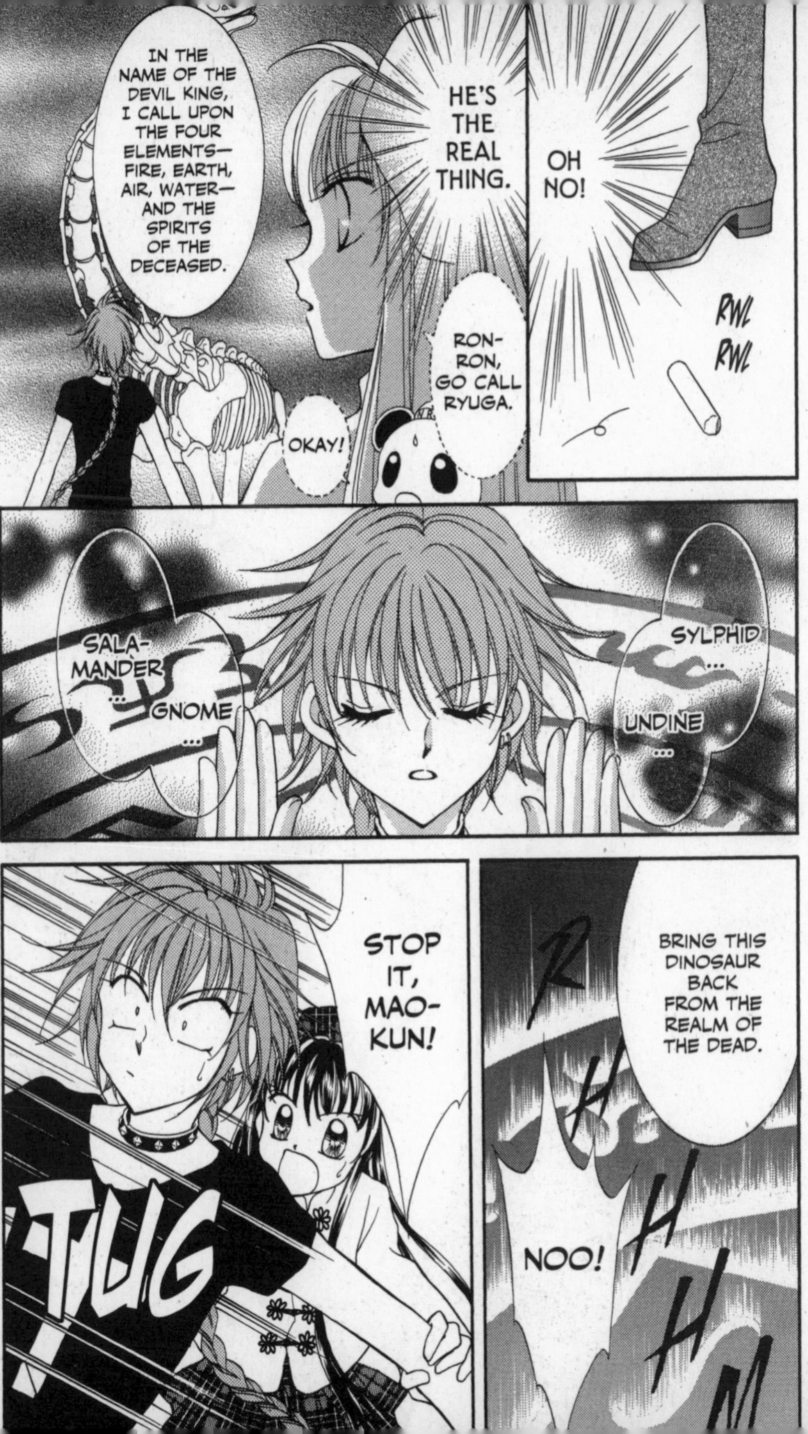
OH NO!
RWL RWL
HE'S THE REAL THING.
IN THE NAME OF THE DEVIL KING, I CALL UPON THE FOUR ELEMENTS—FIRE, EARTH, AIR, WATER—AND THE SPIRITS OF THE DECEASED.
RON-RON, GO CALL RYUGA.
OKAY!
SYLPHID ...
UNDINE ...
SALA-MANDER ...
GNOME ...
BRING THIS DINOSAUR BACK FROM THE REALM OF THE DEAD.
RHHHHM
NOO!
STOP IT, MAO-KUN!
TUG!

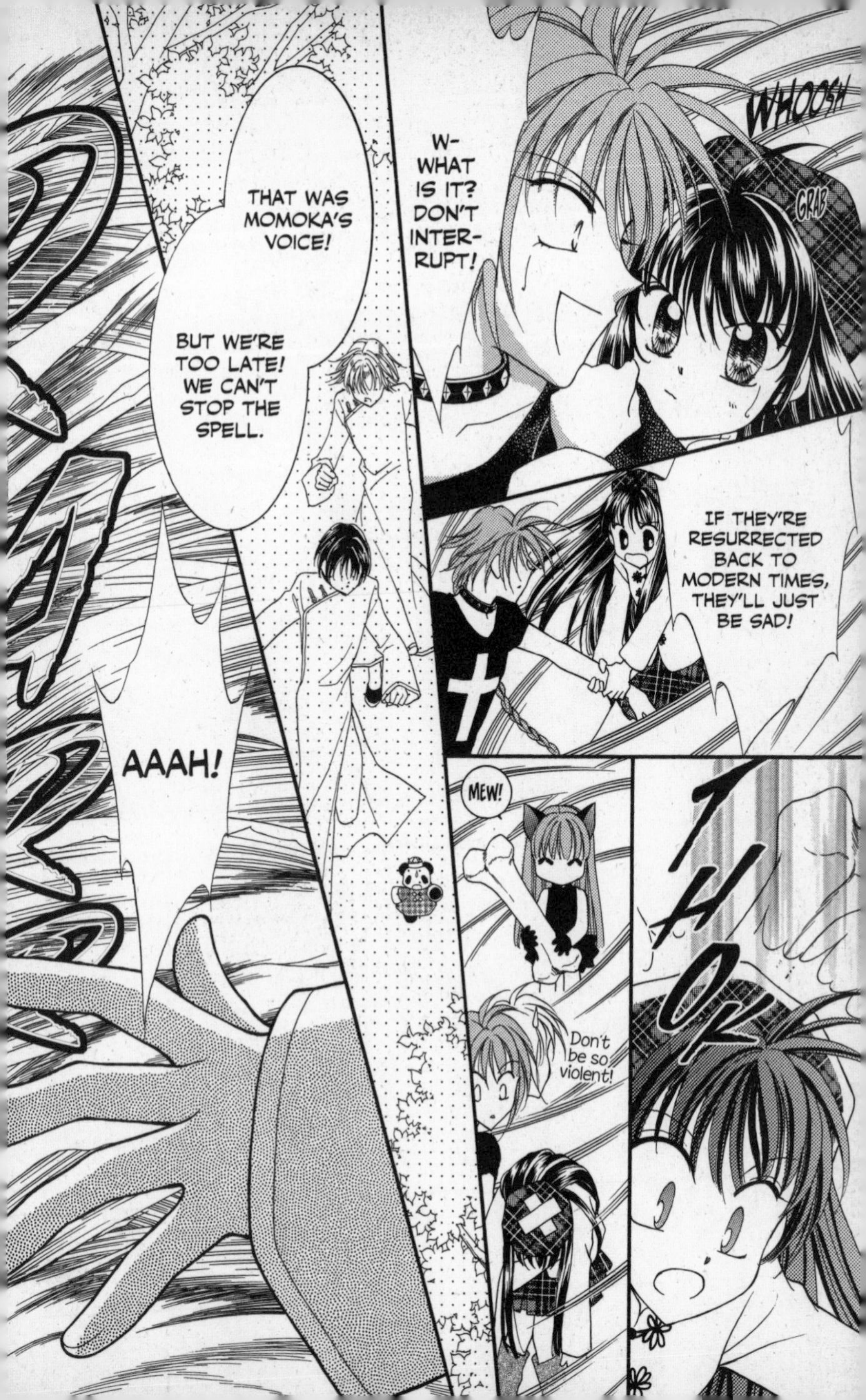
WHOOSH
GRAB
W-WHAT IS IT? DON'T INTER-RUPT!
IF THEY'RE RESURRECTED BACK TO MODERN TIMES, THEY'LL JUST BE SAD!
THWOK
MEW!
Don't be so violent!
THAT WAS MOMOKA'S VOICE!
BUT WE'RE TOO LATE! WE CAN'T STOP THE SPELL.
AAAH!

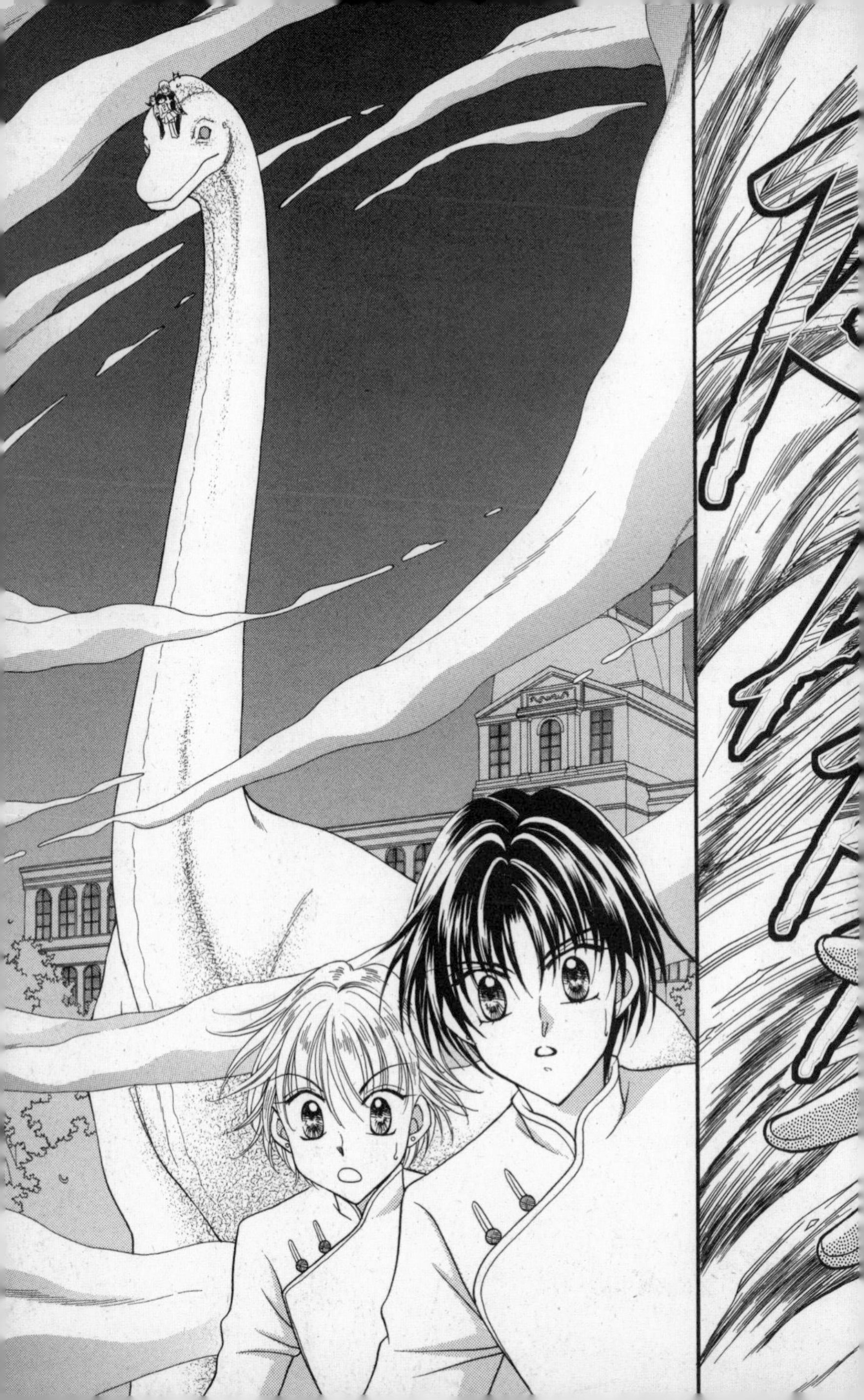

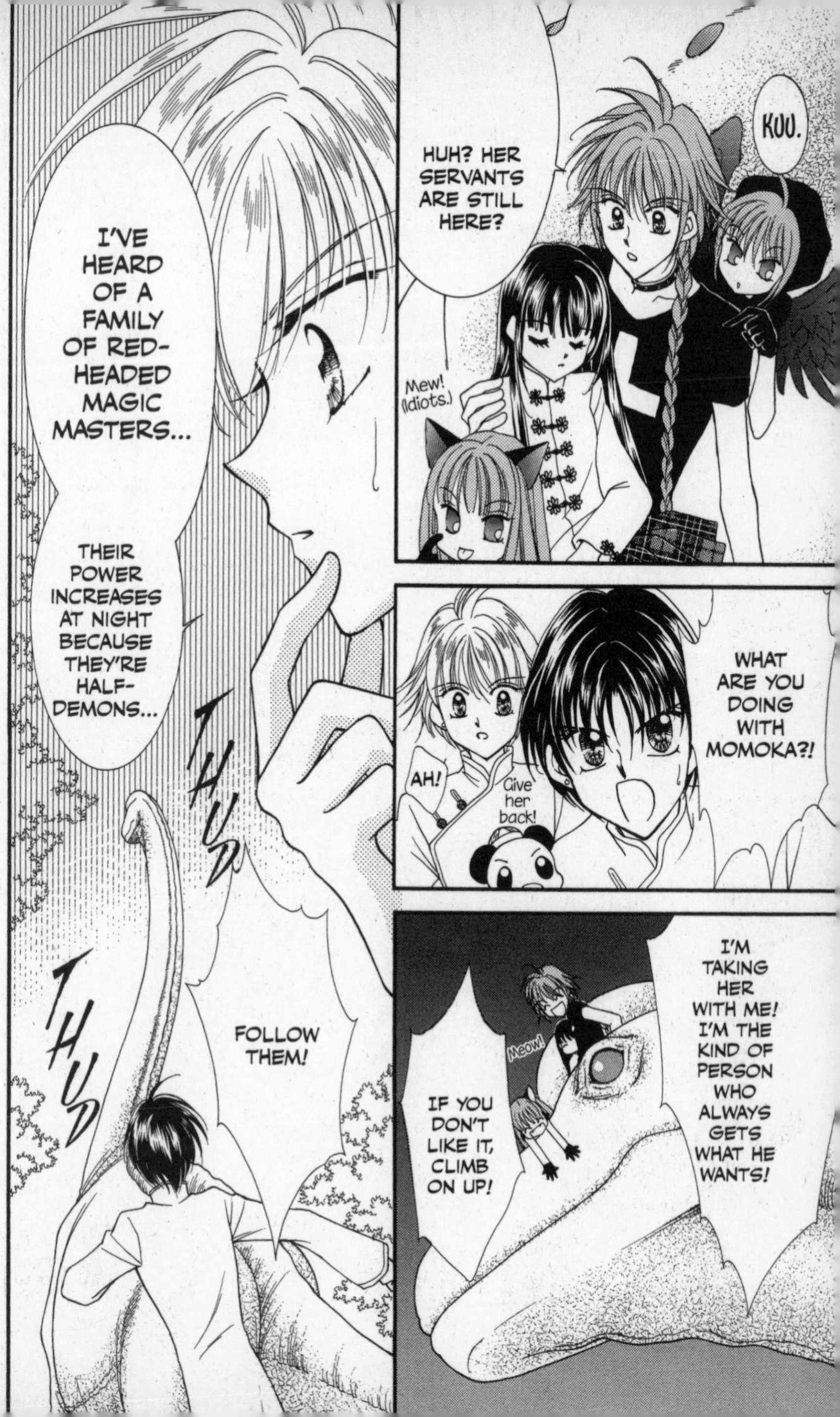
KUU.
HUH? HER SERVANTS ARE STILL HERE?
Mew! (Idiots.)
WHAT ARE YOU DOING WITH MOMOKA?!
Give her back!
AH!
I'M TAKING HER WITH ME! I'M THE KIND OF PERSON WHO ALWAYS GETS WHAT HE WANTS!
Meow!
IF YOU DON'T LIKE IT, CLIMB ON UP!
I'VE HEARD OF A FAMILY OF RED-HEADED MAGIC MASTERS...
THEIR POWER INCREASES AT NIGHT BECAUSE THEY'RE HALF-DEMONS...
THUD
FOLLOW THEM!
THUD

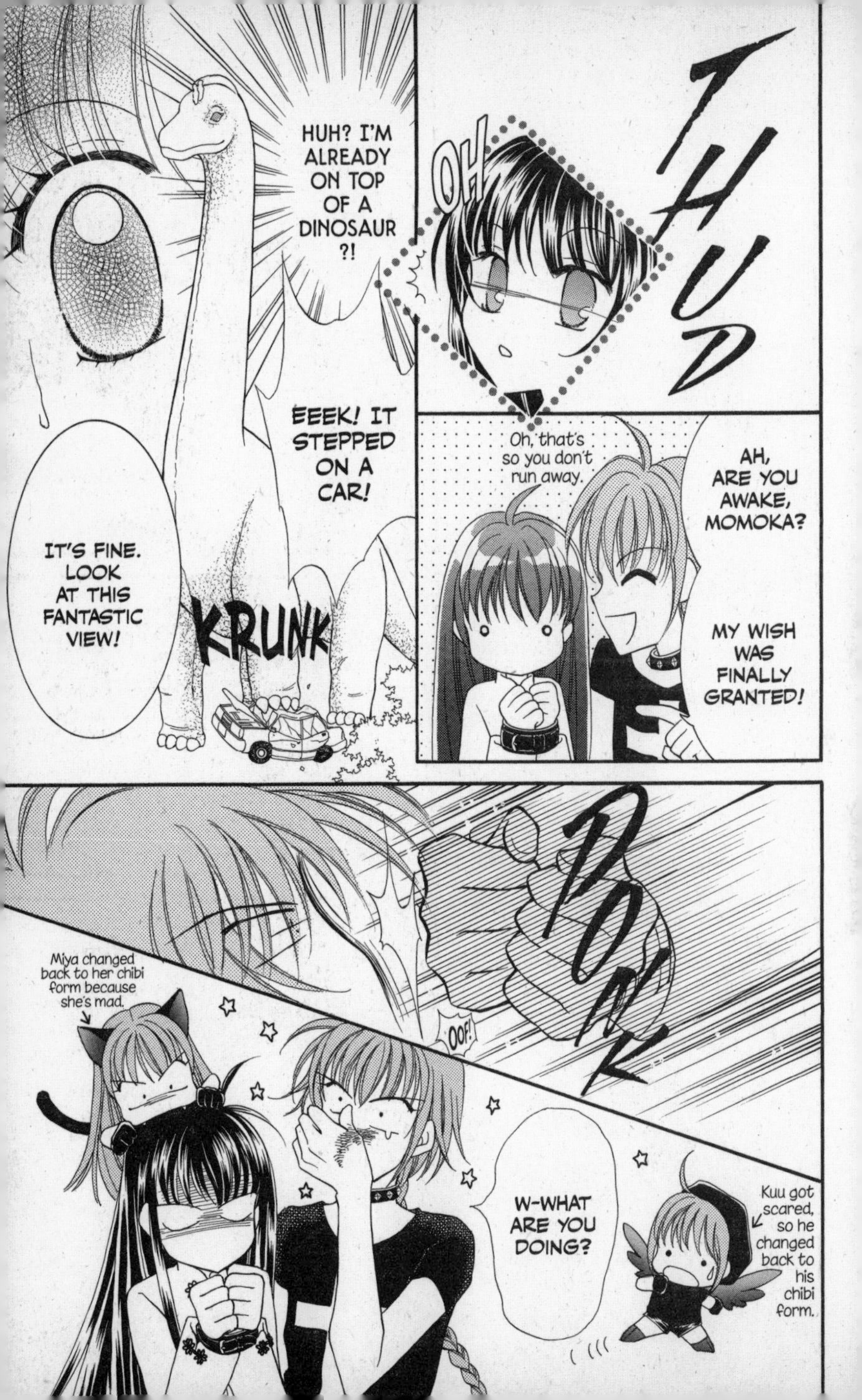
THUD
OH
AH, ARE YOU AWAKE, MOMOKA?
MY WISH WAS FINALLY GRANTED!
Oh, that's so you don't run away.
HUH? I'M ALREADY ON TOP OF A DINOSAUR ?!
EEEK! IT STEPPED ON A CAR!
KRUNK
IT'S FINE. LOOK AT THIS FANTASTIC VIEW!
POW
OOF!
Kuu got scared, so he changed back to his chibi form.
W-WHAT ARE YOU DOING?
Miya changed back to her chibi form because she's mad.

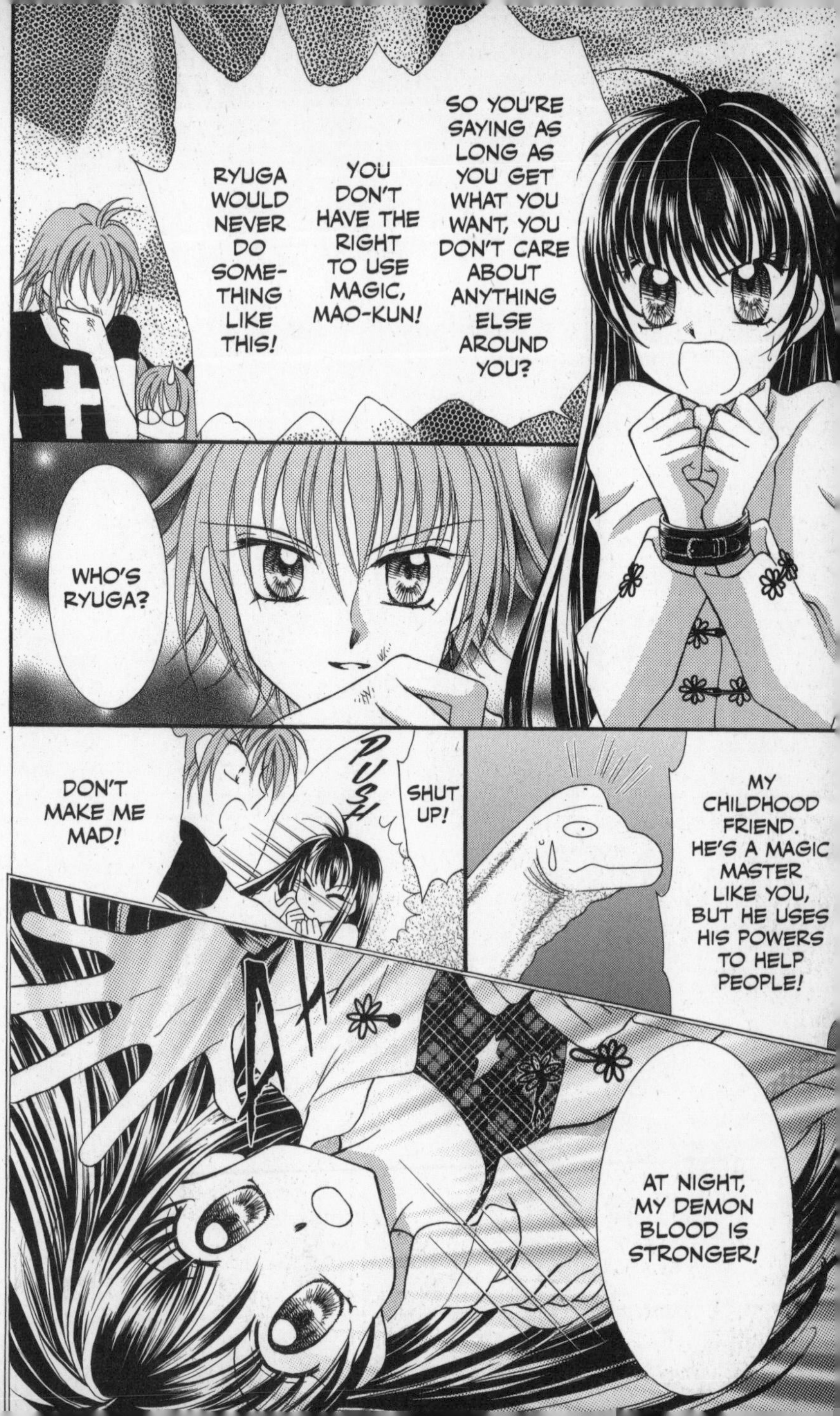
SO YOU'RE SAYING AS LONG AS YOU GET WHAT YOU WANT, YOU DON'T CARE ABOUT ANYTHING ELSE AROUND YOU?
YOU DON'T HAVE THE RIGHT TO USE MAGIC, MAO-KUN!
RYUGA WOULD NEVER DO SOME-THING LIKE THIS!
WHO'S RYUGA?
MY CHILDHOOD FRIEND. HE'S A MAGIC MASTER LIKE YOU, BUT HE USES HIS POWERS TO HELP PEOPLE!
SHUT UP!
PUSH
DON'T MAKE ME MAD!
AT NIGHT, MY DEMON BLOOD IS STRONGER!

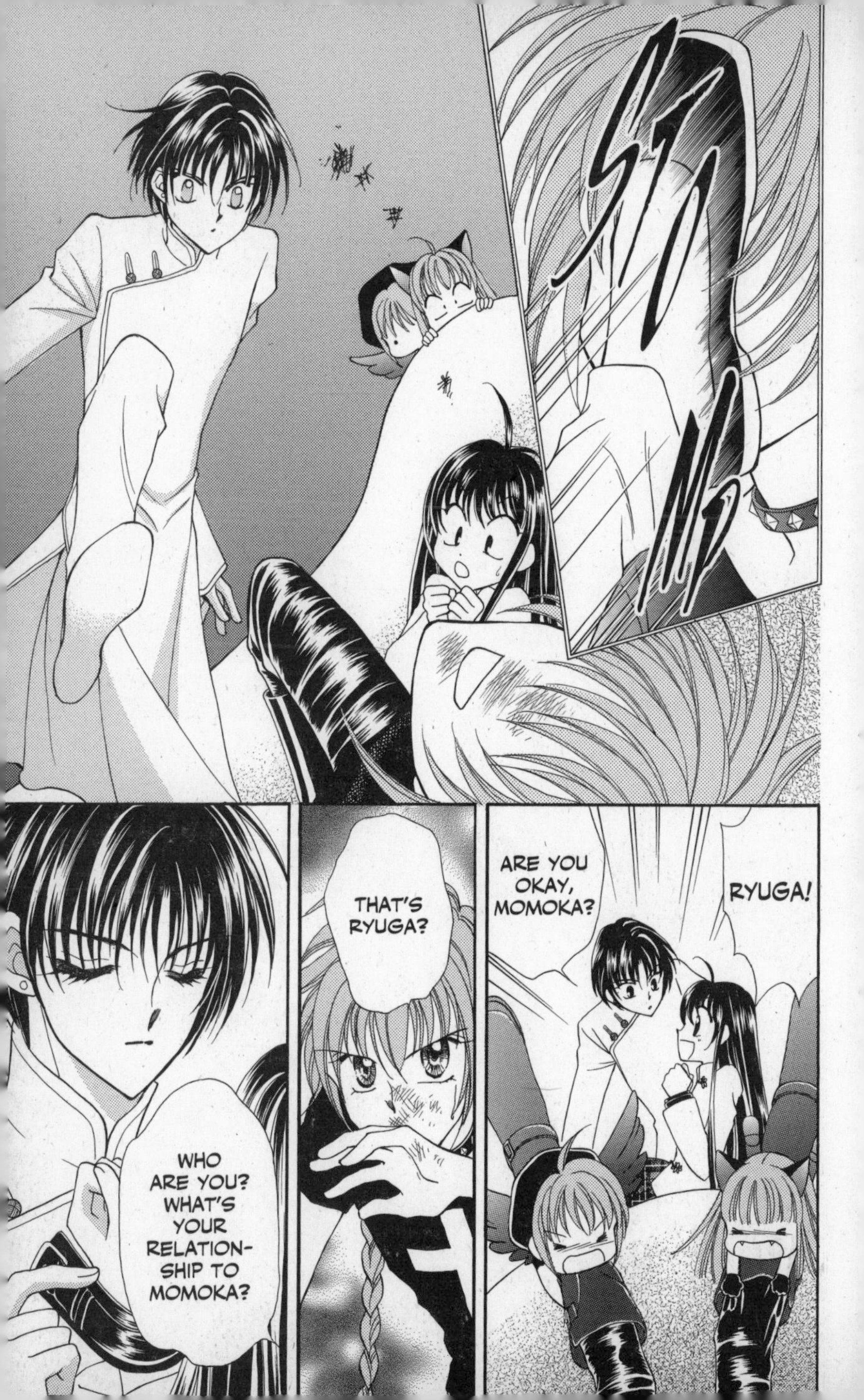
RYUGA!
ARE YOU OKAY, MOMOKA?
THAT'S RYUGA?
WHO ARE YOU? WHAT'S YOUR RELATIONSHIP TO MOMOKA?

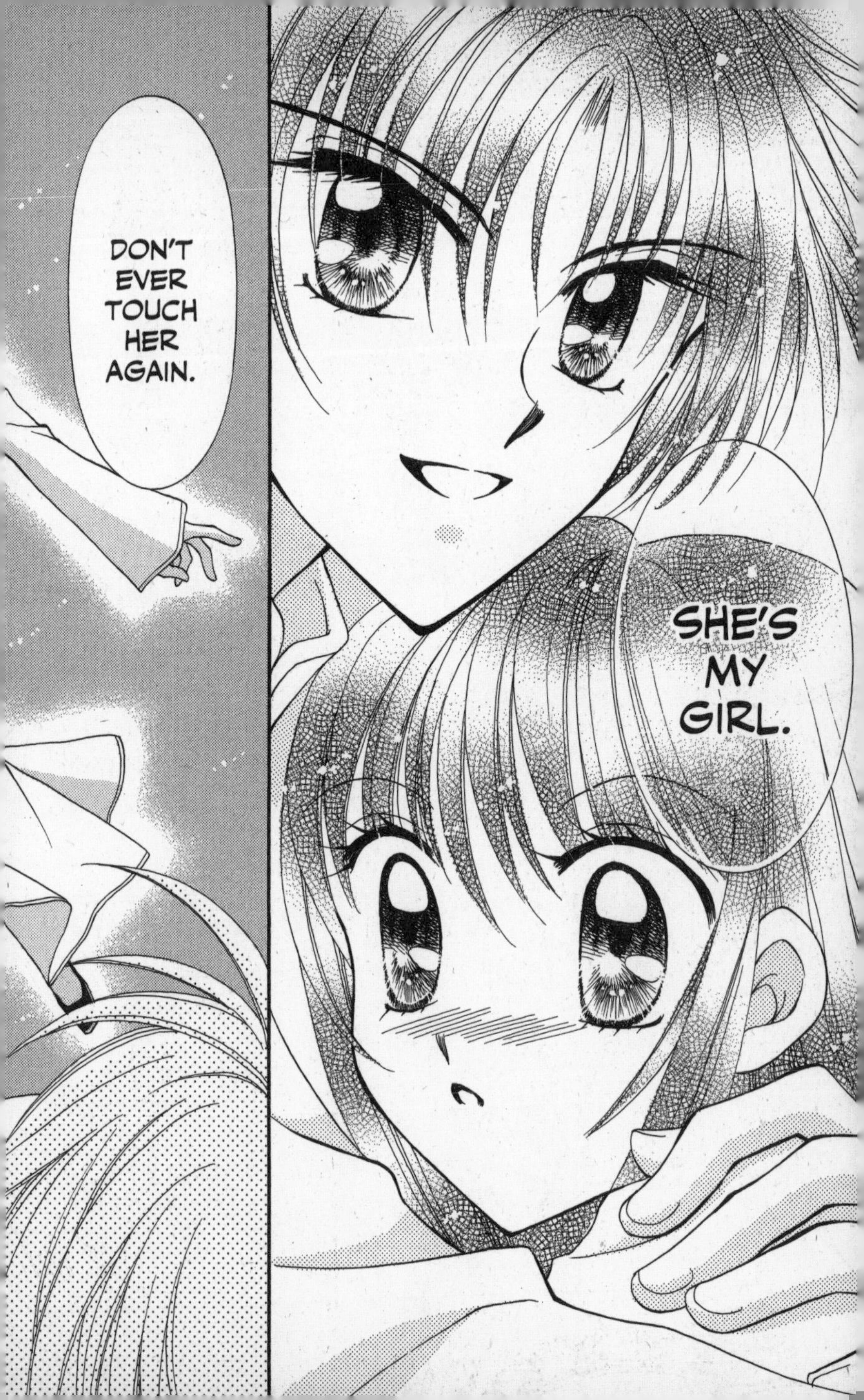
SHE'S MY GIRL.
DON'T EVER TOUCH HER AGAIN.

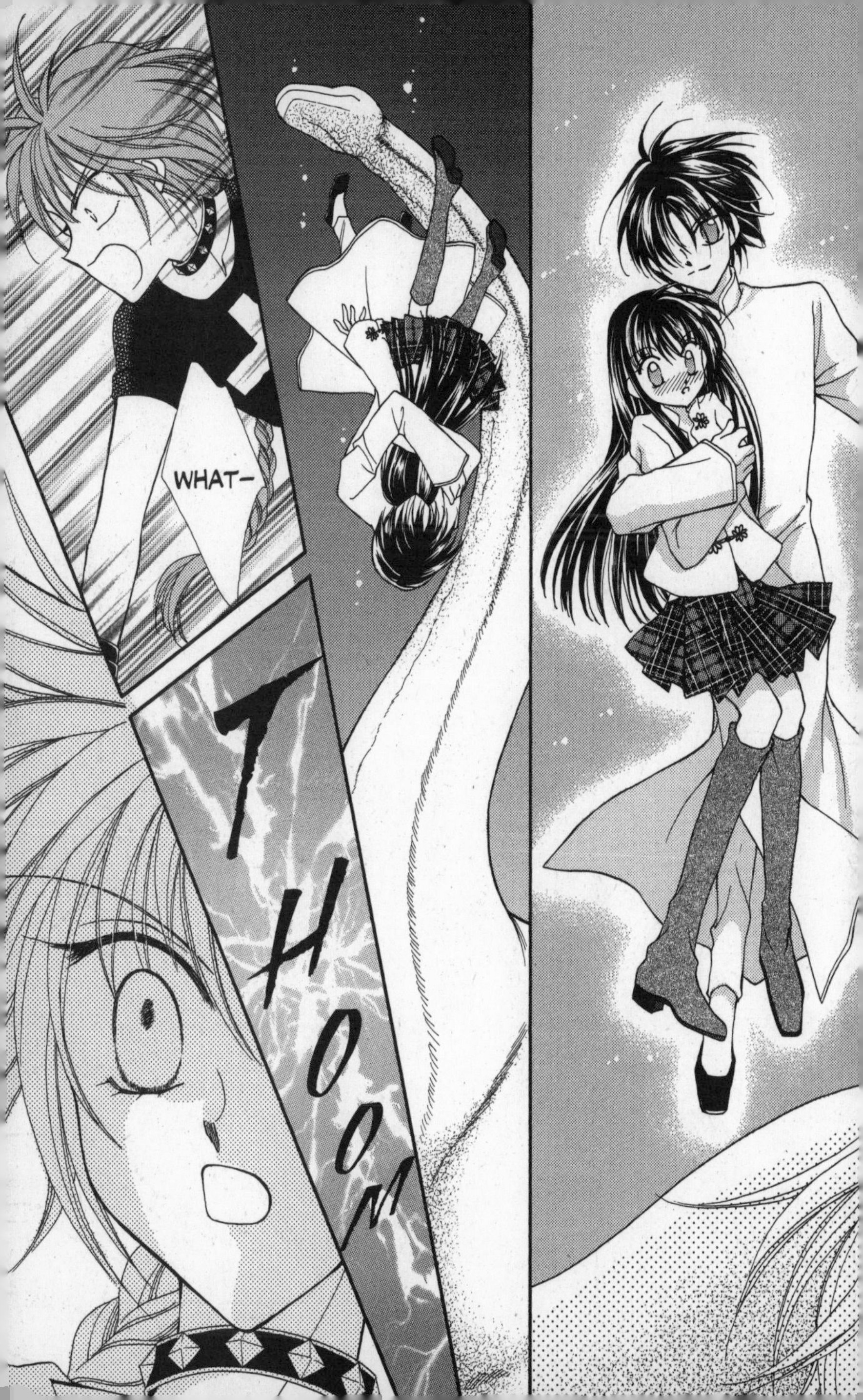
WHAT–
THOOM

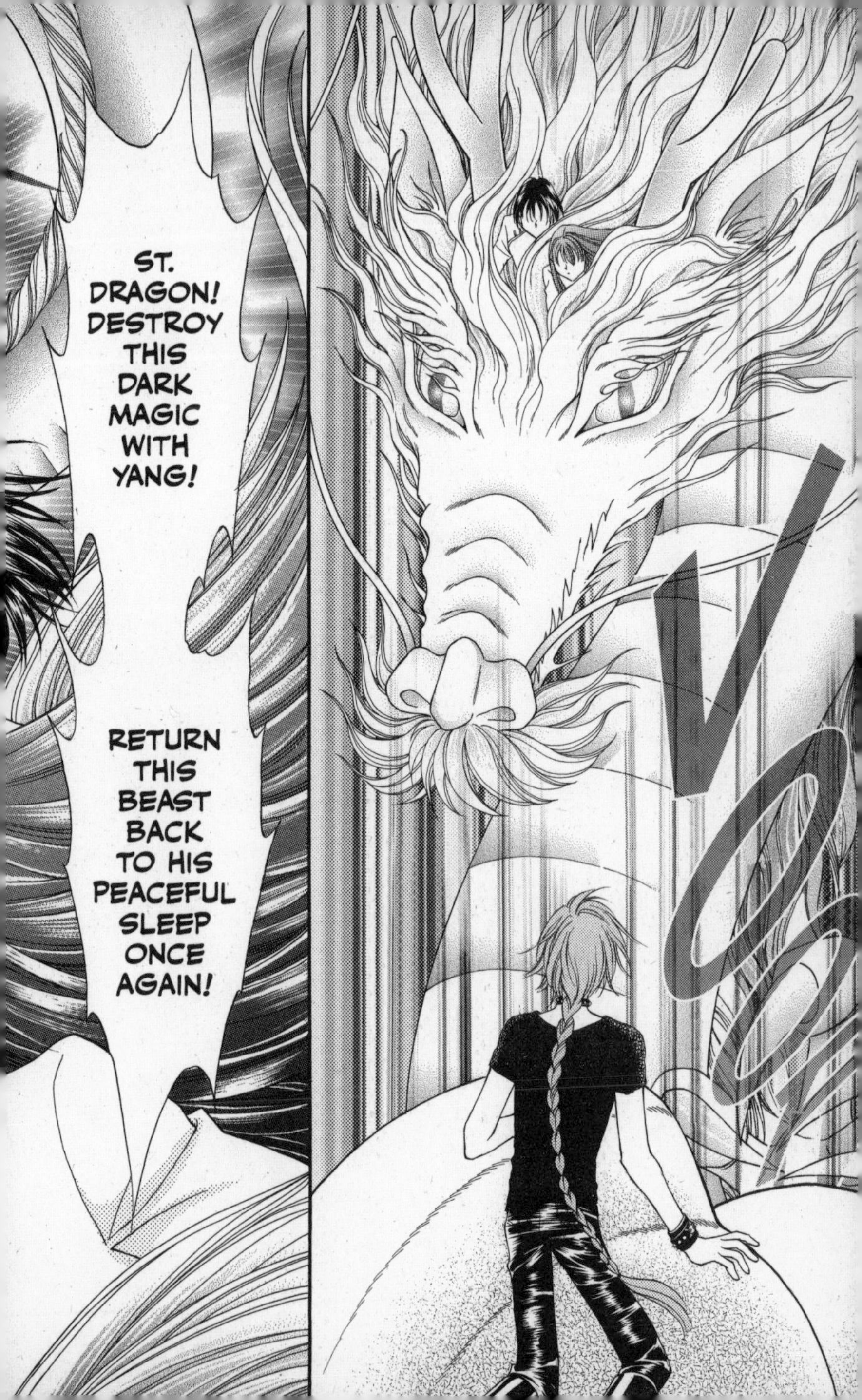
ST. DRAGON! DESTROY THIS DARK MAGIC WITH YANG!
RETURN THIS BEAST BACK TO HIS PEACEFUL SLEEP ONCE AGAIN!

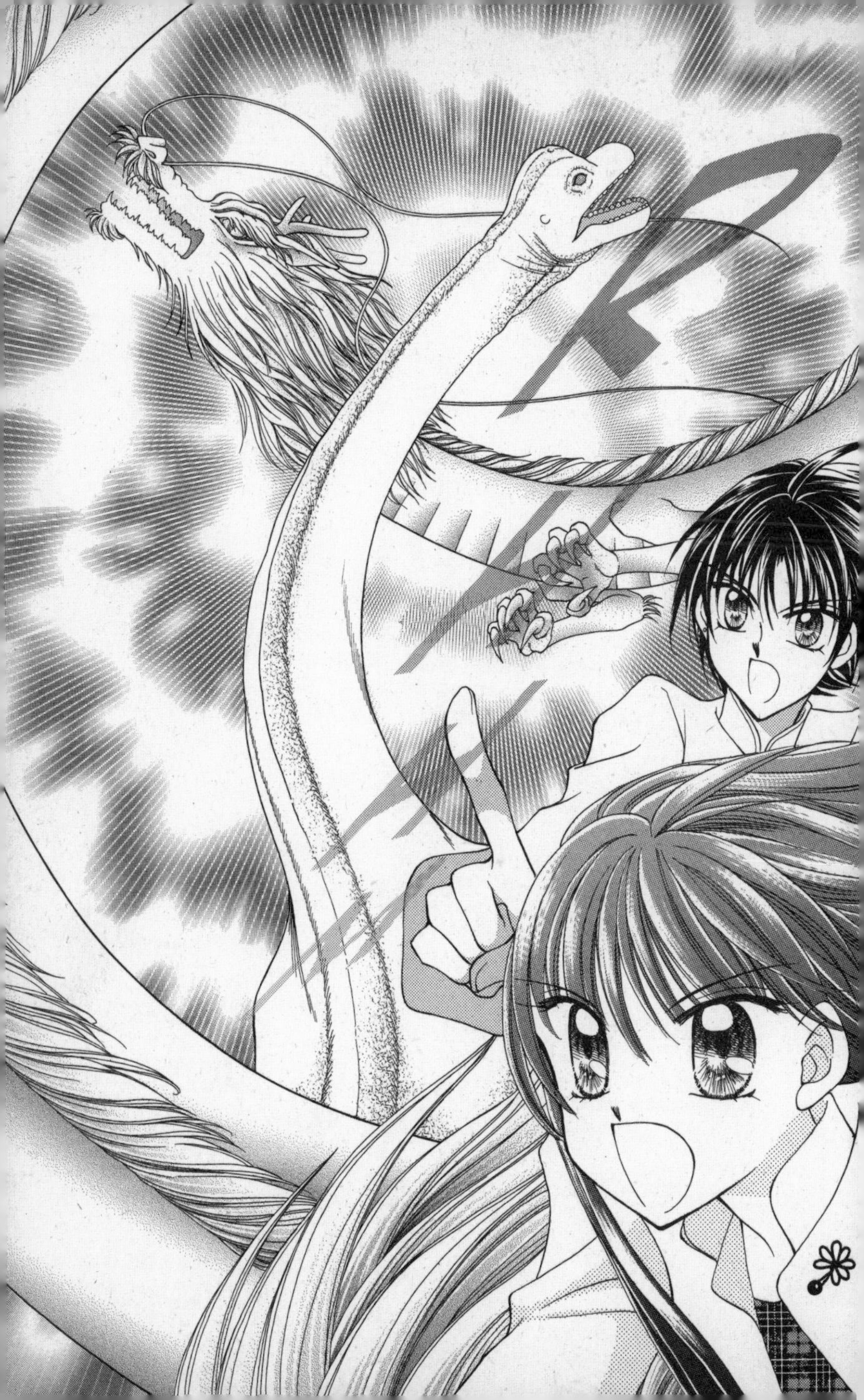

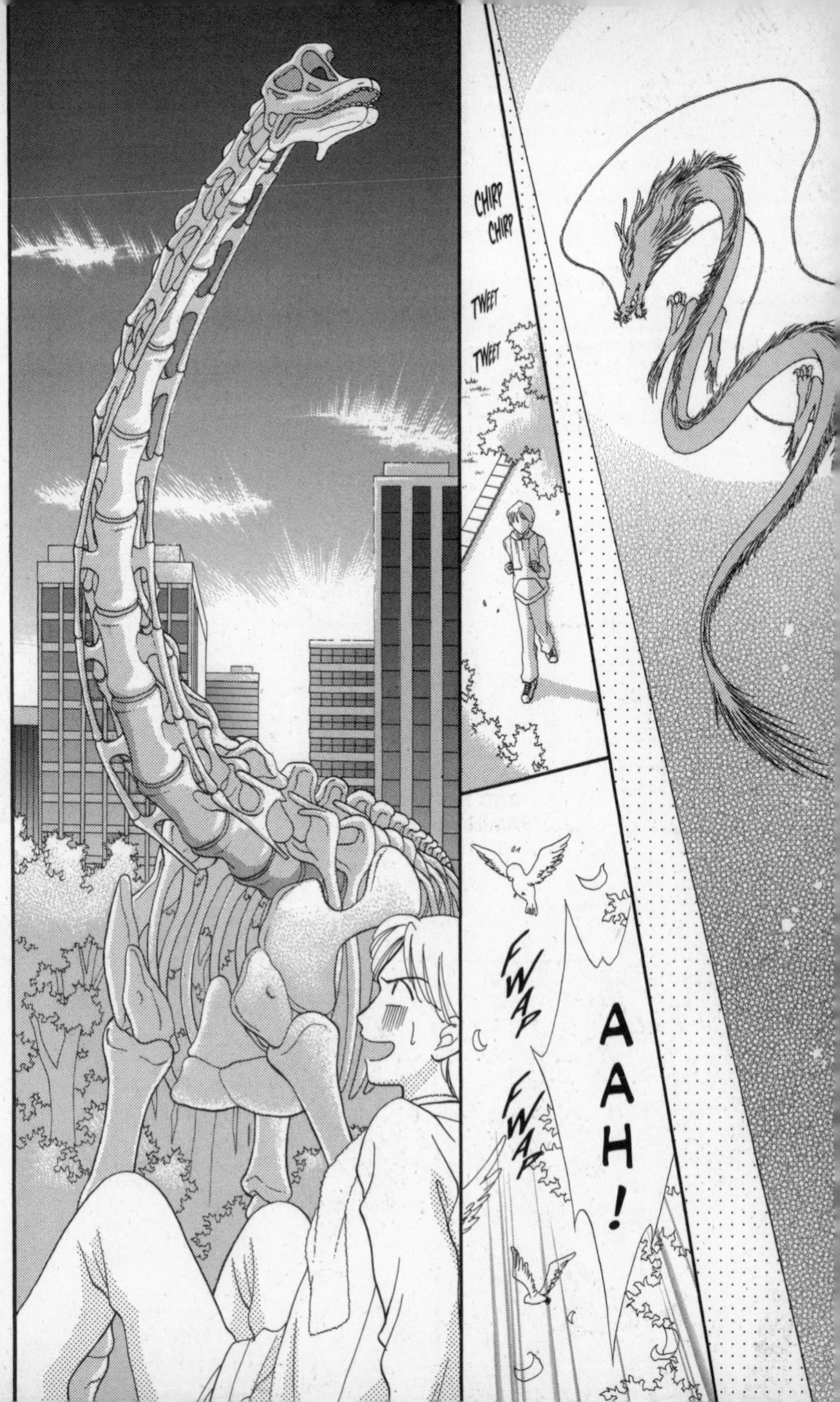
CHIRP CHIRP
TWEET TWEET
AAH!
FWAP FWAP

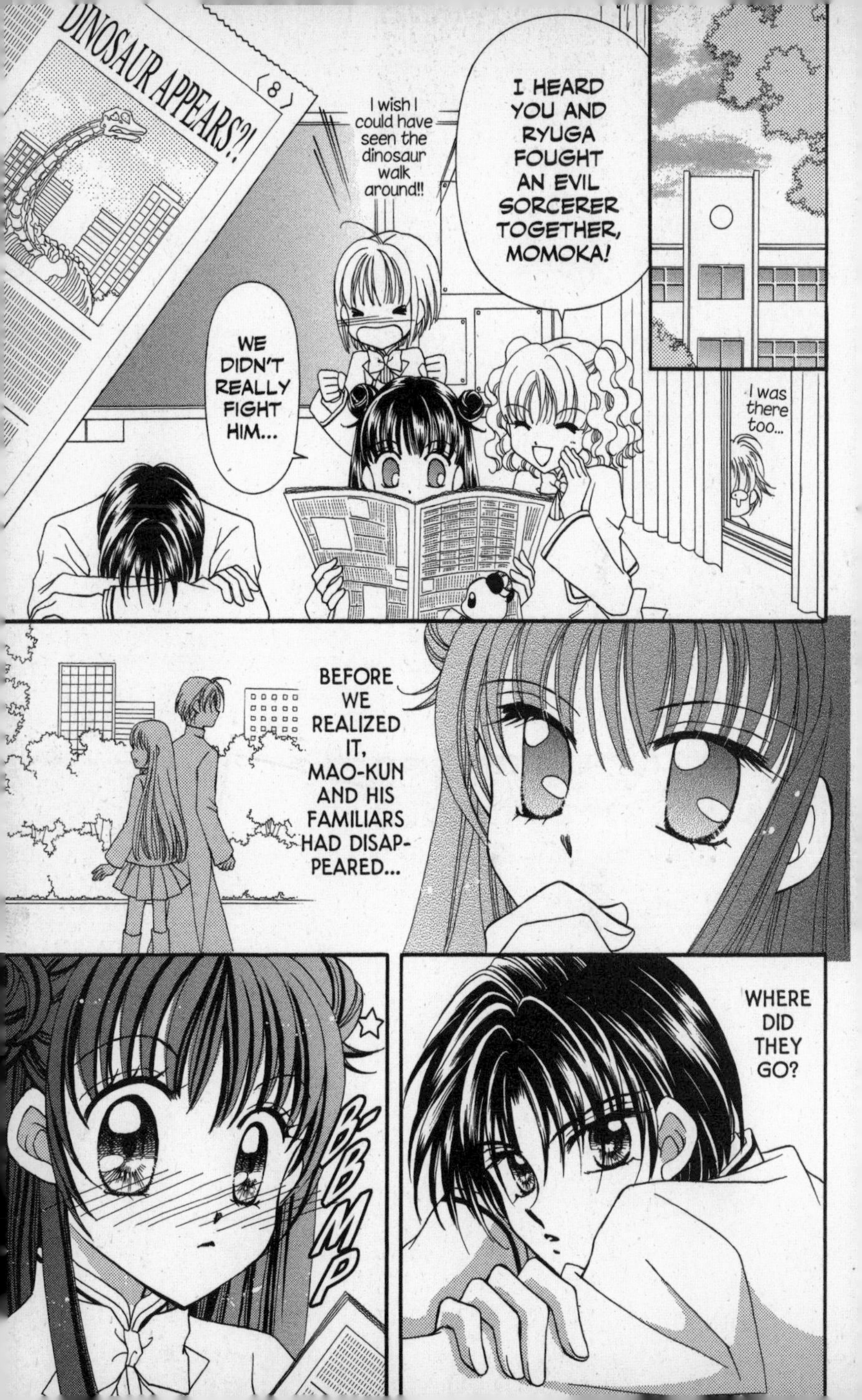
I HEARD YOU AND RYUGA FOUGHT AN EVIL SORCERER TOGETHER, MOMOKA!
I wish I could have seen the dinosaur walk around!!
DINOSAUR APPEARS?!
8
I was there too...
WE DIDN'T REALLY FIGHT HIM...
BEFORE WE REALIZED IT, MAO-KUN AND HIS FAMILIARS HAD DISAPPEARED...
WHERE DID THEY GO?
B-BMP

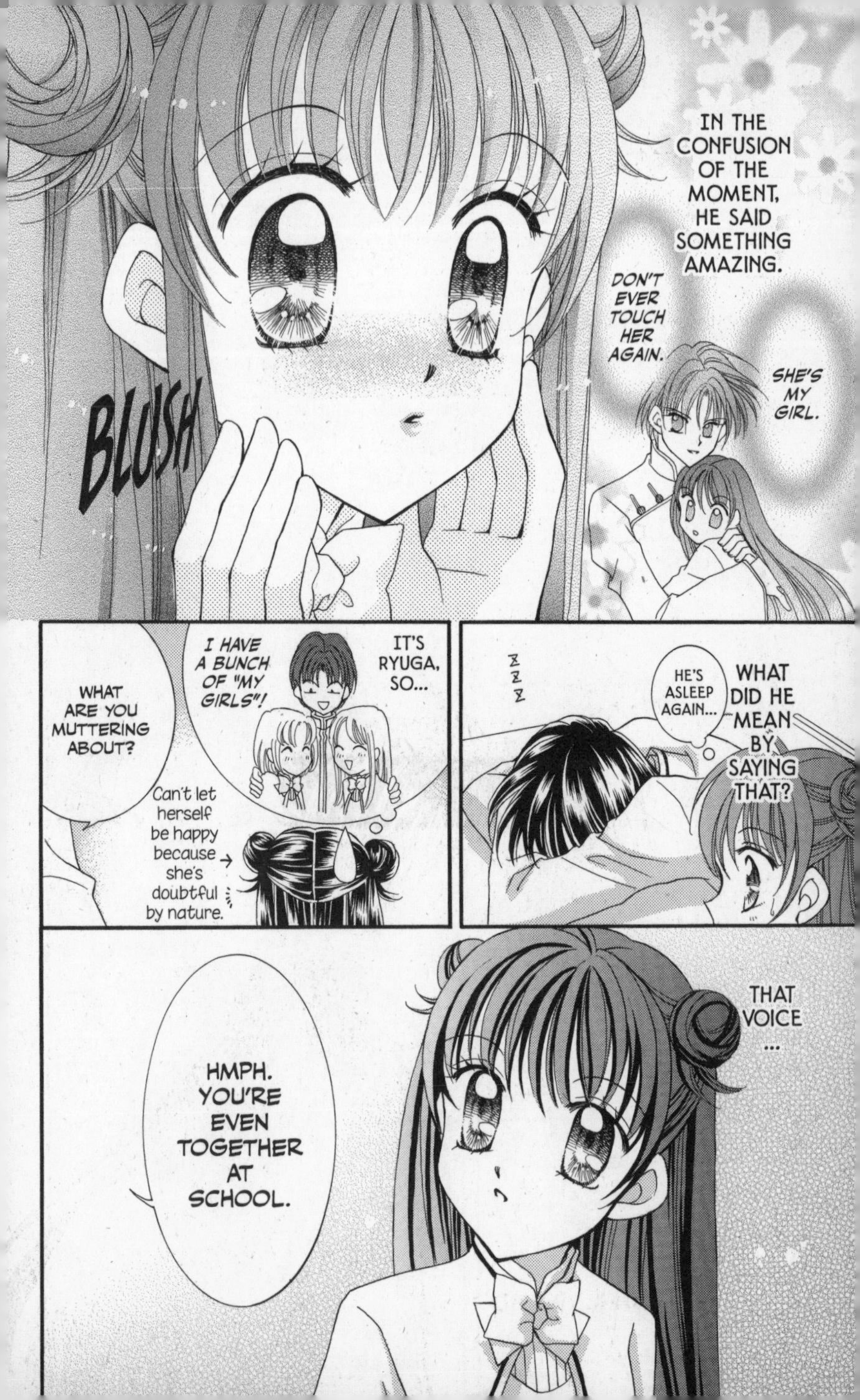

IN THE CONFUSION OF THE MOMENT, HE SAID SOMETHING AMAZING.
DON'T EVER TOUCH HER AGAIN.
SHE'S MY GIRL.
BLUSH
WHAT DID HE MEAN BY SAYING THAT?
HE'S ASLEEP AGAIN...
ZZZ
IT'S RYUGA, SO...
I HAVE A BUNCH OF "MY GIRLS"!
WHAT ARE YOU MUTTERING ABOUT?
Can't let herself be happy because she's doubtful by nature.
THAT VOICE ...
HMPH. YOU'RE EVEN TOGETHER AT SCHOOL.

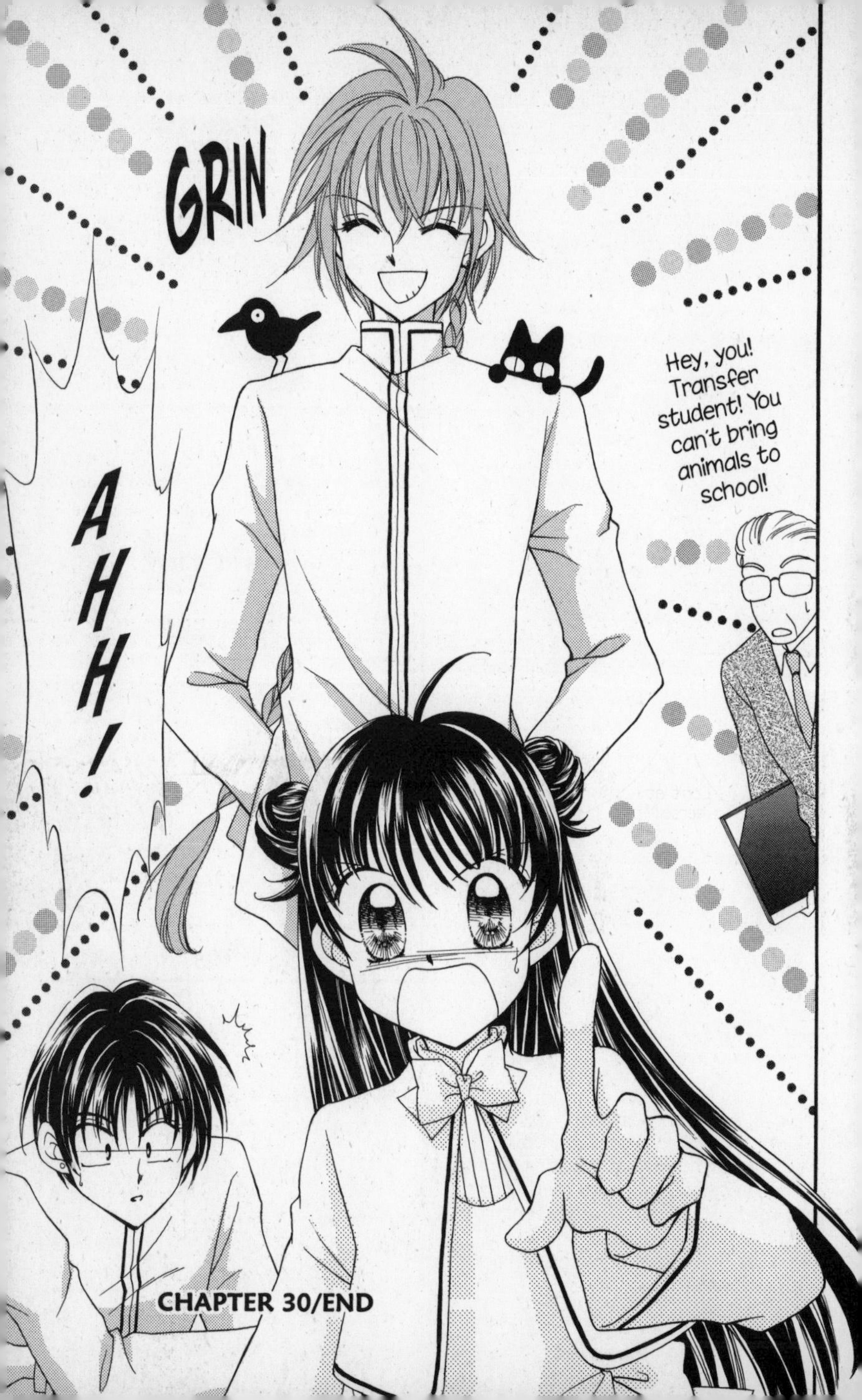
GRIN
Hey, you! Transfer student! You can't bring animals to school!
AHHH!
CHAPTER 30/END

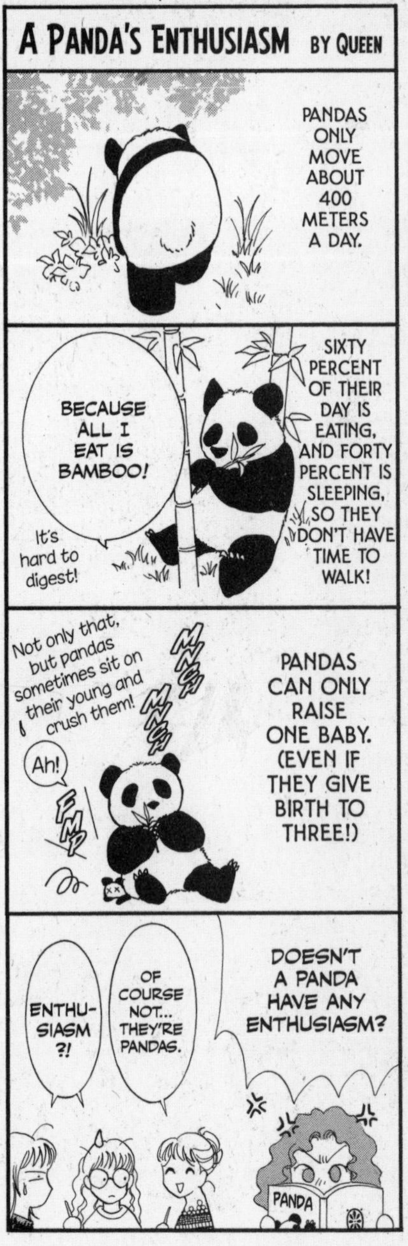
A PANDA'S ENTHUSIASM BY QUEEN
PANDAS ONLY MOVE ABOUT 400 METERS A DAY.
SIXTY PERCENT OF THEIR DAY IS EATING, AND FORTY PERCENT IS SLEEPING, SO THEY DON'T HAVE TIME TO WALK!
BECAUSE ALL I EAT IS BAMBOO!
It's hard to digest!
PANDAS CAN ONLY RAISE ONE BABY. (EVEN IF THEY GIVE BIRTH TO THREE!)
Not only that, but pandas sometimes sit on their young and crush them!
MNCH
MNCH
Ah!
FMP
DOESN'T A PANDA HAVE ANY ENTHUSIASM?
OF COURSE NOT... THEY'RE PANDAS.
ENTHU-SIASM?!
PANDA

By Queen ▸

When I began *St.♥Dragon Girl*, my knowledge of pandas increased. There were a lot of things I was really surprised about. I have an affinity for their laziness though... Pandas aren't going extinct anymore, so they can raise about two of their own babies now.

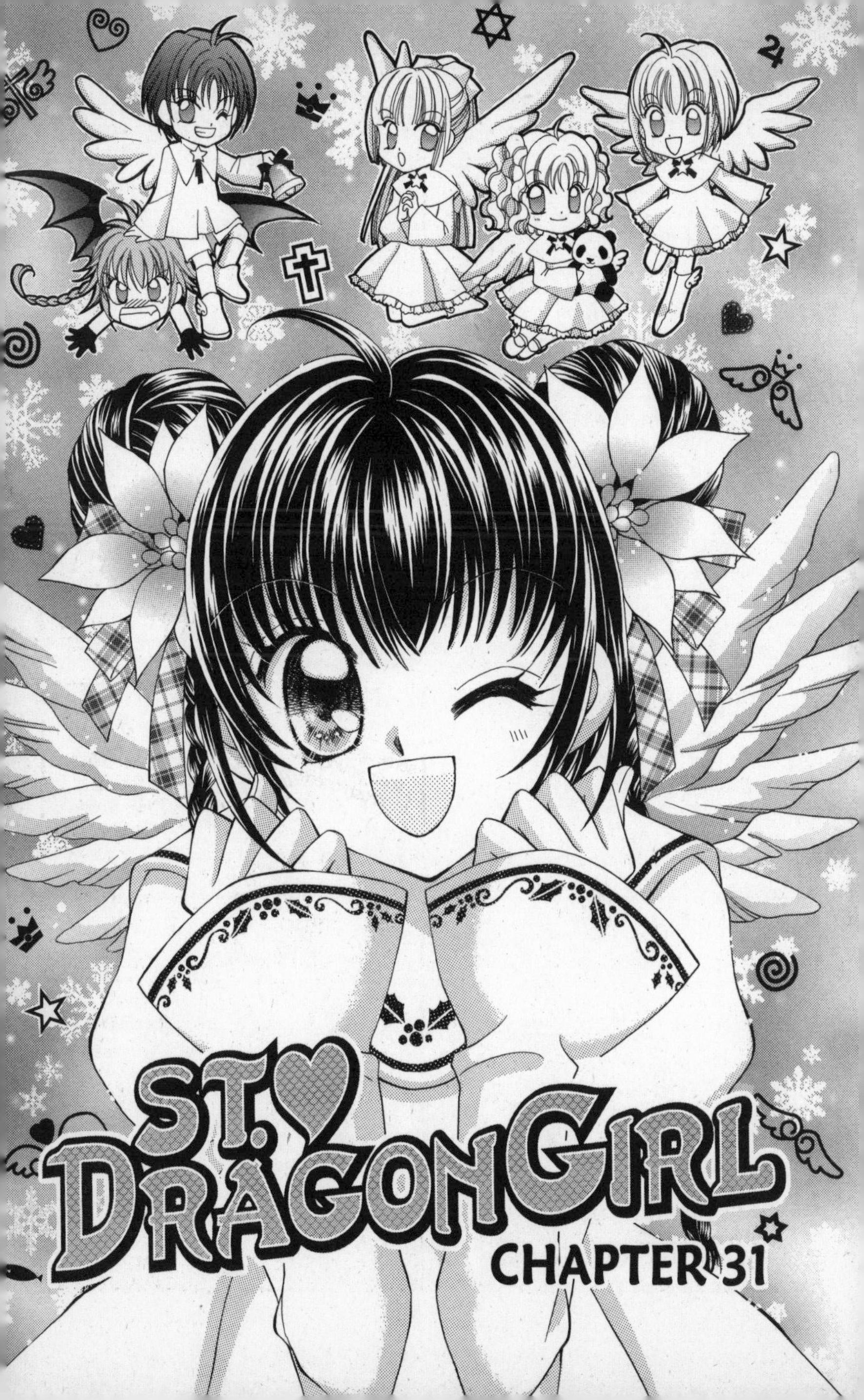
ST. DRAGON GIRL
CHAPTER 31

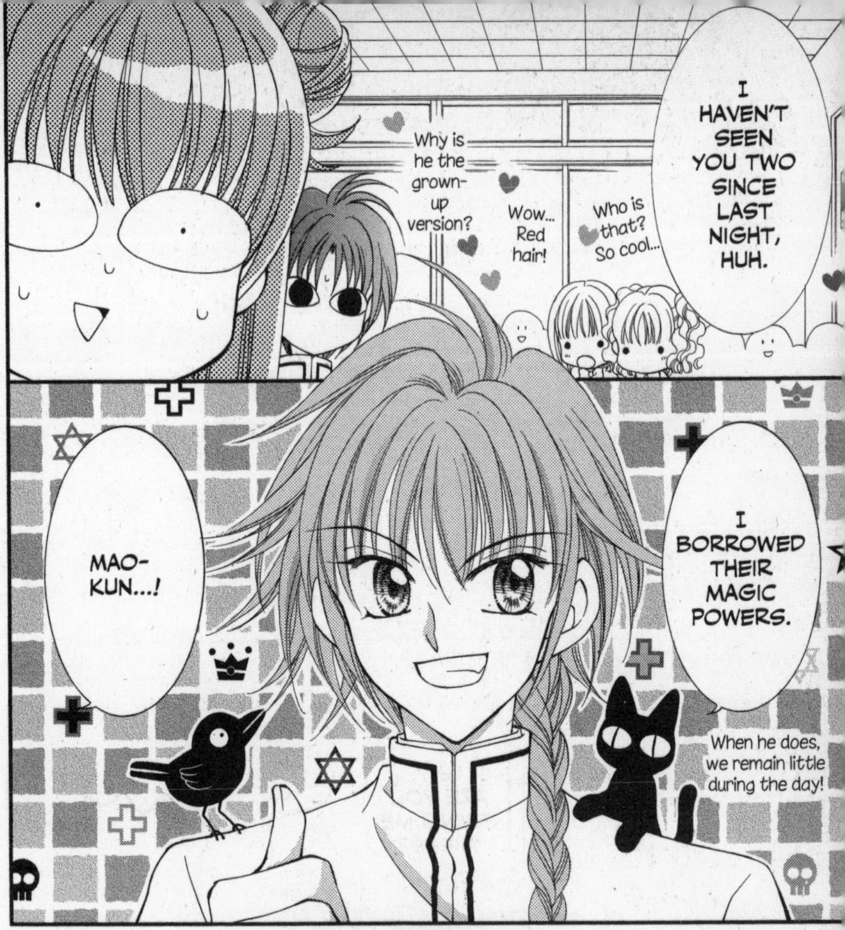
I HAVEN'T SEEN YOU TWO SINCE LAST NIGHT, HUH.
Who is that? So cool...
Wow... Red hair!
Why is he the grown-up version?
I BORROWED THEIR MAGIC POWERS.
When he does, we remain little during the day!
MAO-KUN...!

Kuu

He's a crow and one of Mao's familiars. He might be a Pisces. He's a little faint-hearted and easily surprised. He's very curious and loves shiny things.

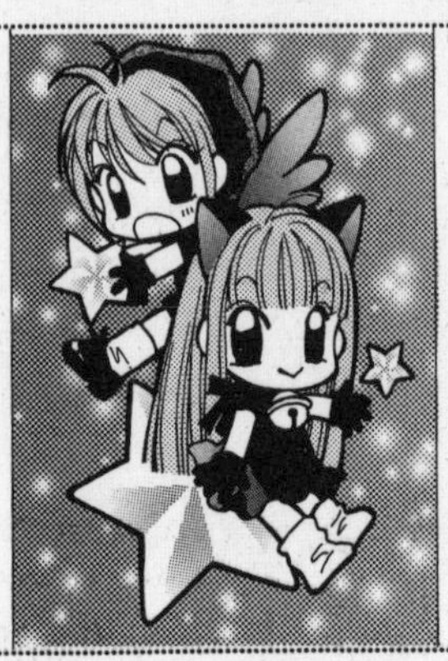

Miya

She's a cat and is one of Mao's familiars. She might be a Gemini. She's very whimsical, and she's very attached and devoted to Mao. Miya is full of curiousity. Sometimes she bullies Kuu, but they usually get along well. She loves fish cookies.

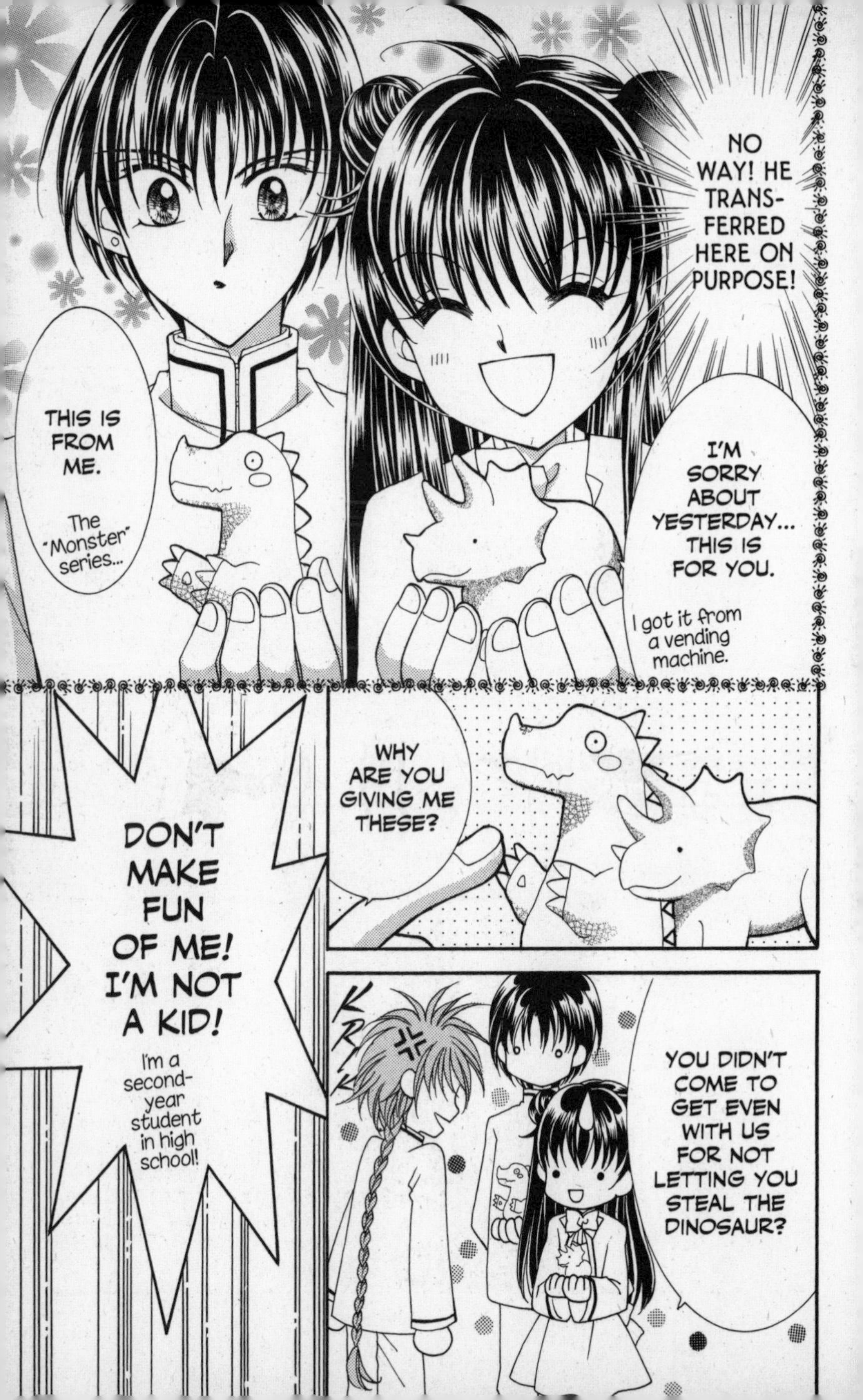
NO WAY! HE TRANSFERRED HERE ON PURPOSE!
I'M SORRY ABOUT YESTERDAY... THIS IS FOR YOU.
I got it from a vending machine.
THIS IS FROM ME.
The "Monster" series...
WHY ARE YOU GIVING ME THESE?
YOU DIDN'T COME TO GET EVEN WITH US FOR NOT LETTING YOU STEAL THE DINOSAUR?
DON'T MAKE FUN OF ME! I'M NOT A KID!
I'm a second-year student in high school!

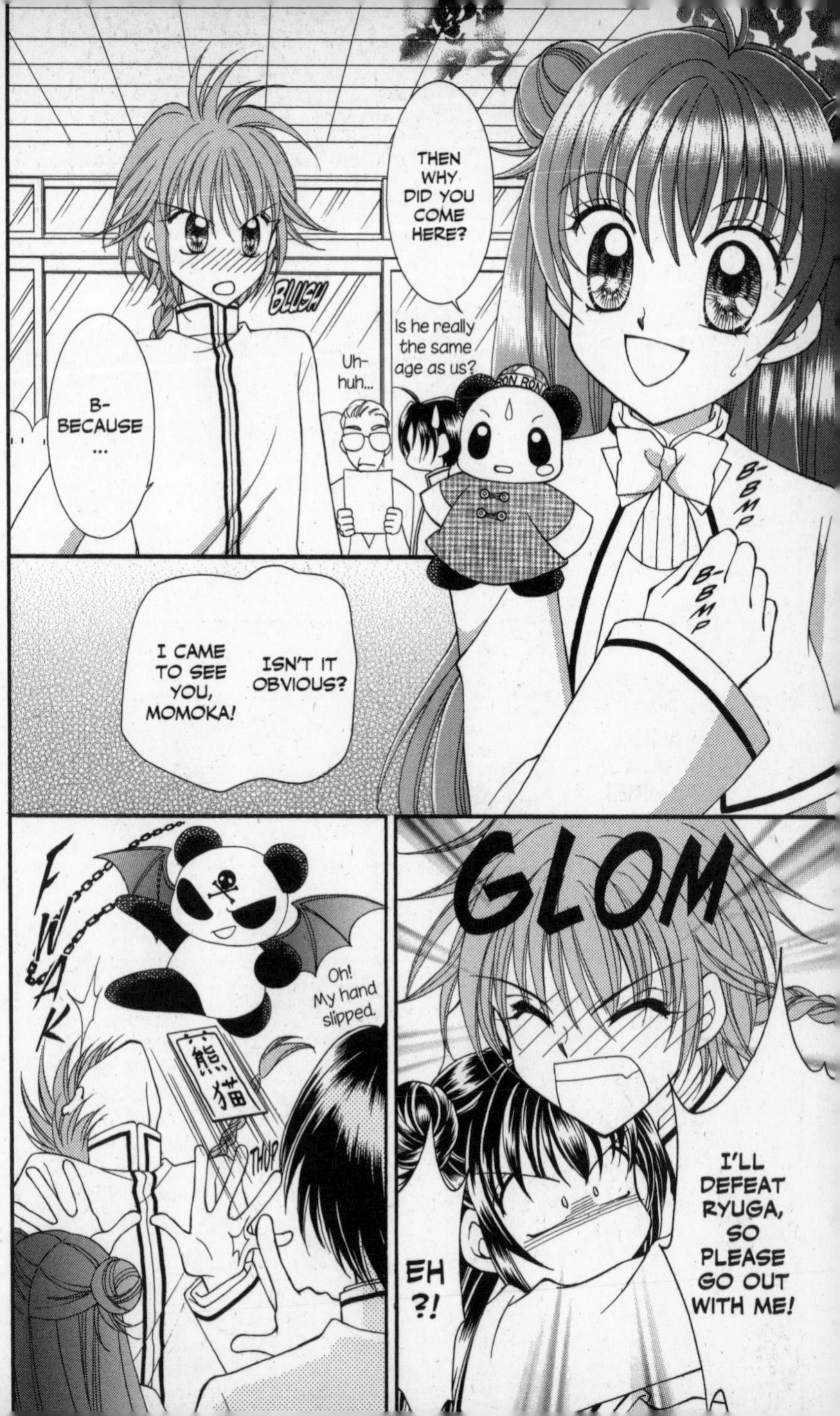
THEN WHY DID YOU COME HERE?
Is he really the same age as us?
RON RON
Uh-huh...
BLUSH
B-BECAUSE ...
B-BMP
B-BMP
I CAME TO SEE YOU, MOMOKA! ISN'T IT OBVIOUS?
GLOM
I'LL DEFEAT RYUGA, SO PLEASE GO OUT WITH ME!
EH?!
FWAK
Oh! My hand slipped.
熊猫
THUP

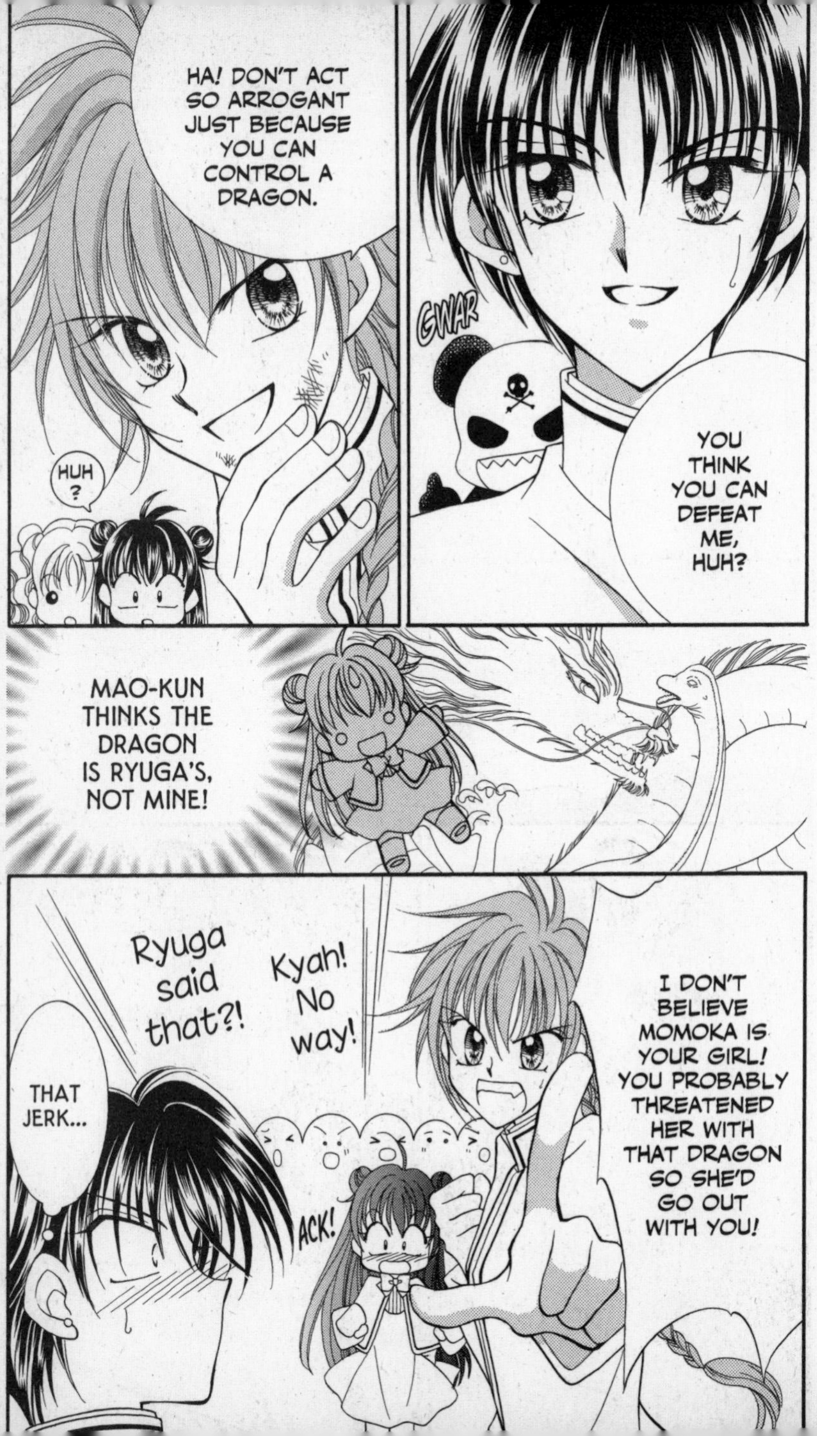
GWAR
YOU THINK YOU CAN DEFEAT ME, HUH?
HA! DON'T ACT SO ARROGANT JUST BECAUSE YOU CAN CONTROL A DRAGON.
HUH?
MAO-KUN THINKS THE DRAGON IS RYUGA'S, NOT MINE!
I DON'T BELIEVE MOMOKA IS YOUR GIRL! YOU PROBABLY THREATENED HER WITH THAT DRAGON SO SHE'D GO OUT WITH YOU!
Kyah! No way!
Ryuga said that?!
ACK!
THAT JERK...

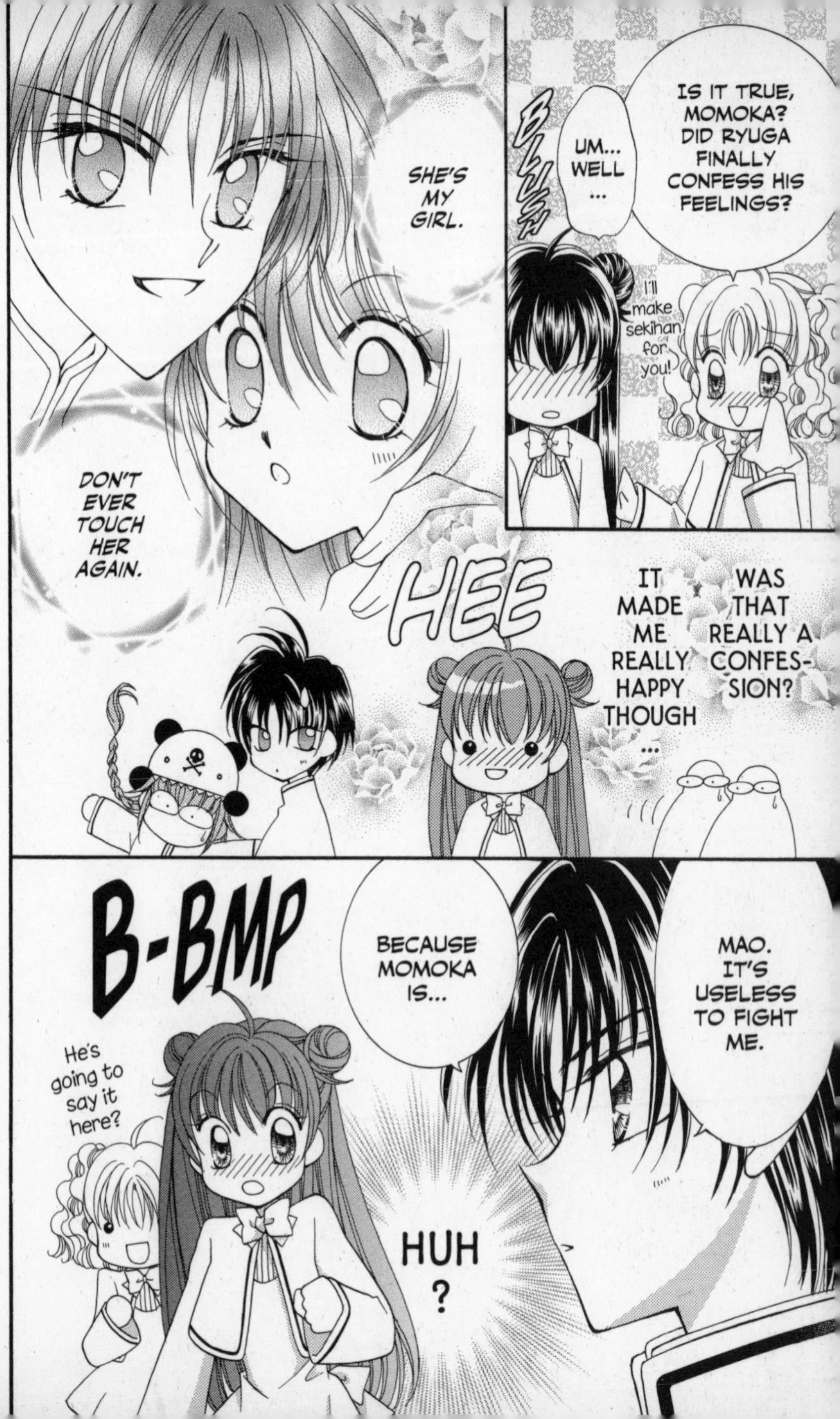
IS IT TRUE, MOMOKA? DID RYUGA FINALLY CONFESS HIS FEELINGS?
UM... WELL...
BLUSH
I'll make sekihan for you!
SHE'S MY GIRL.
DON'T EVER TOUCH HER AGAIN.
WAS THAT REALLY A CONFESSION?
IT MADE ME REALLY HAPPY THOUGH...
HEE
MAO. IT'S USELESS TO FIGHT ME.
BECAUSE MOMOKA IS...
B-BMP
HUH?
He's going to say it here?

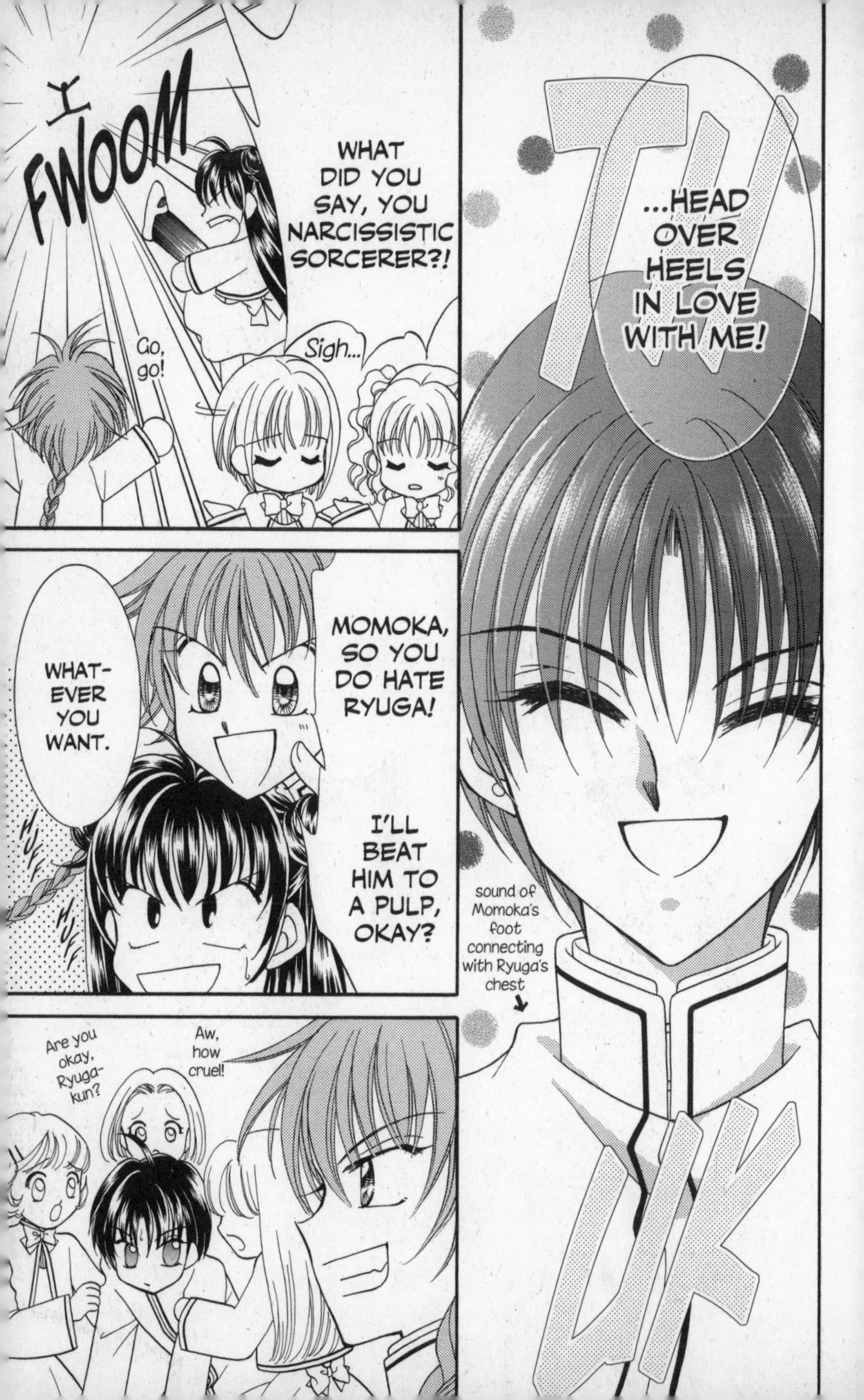
...HEAD OVER HEELS IN LOVE WITH ME!
sound of Momoka's foot connecting with Ryuga's chest
WHAT DID YOU SAY, YOU NARCISSISTIC SORCERER?!
Sigh...
Go, go!
FWOOM
MOMOKA, SO YOU DO HATE RYUGA!
WHAT-EVER YOU WANT.
I'LL BEAT HIM TO A PULP, OKAY?
HUFF
HUFF
Aw, how cruel!
Are you okay, Ryuga-kun?

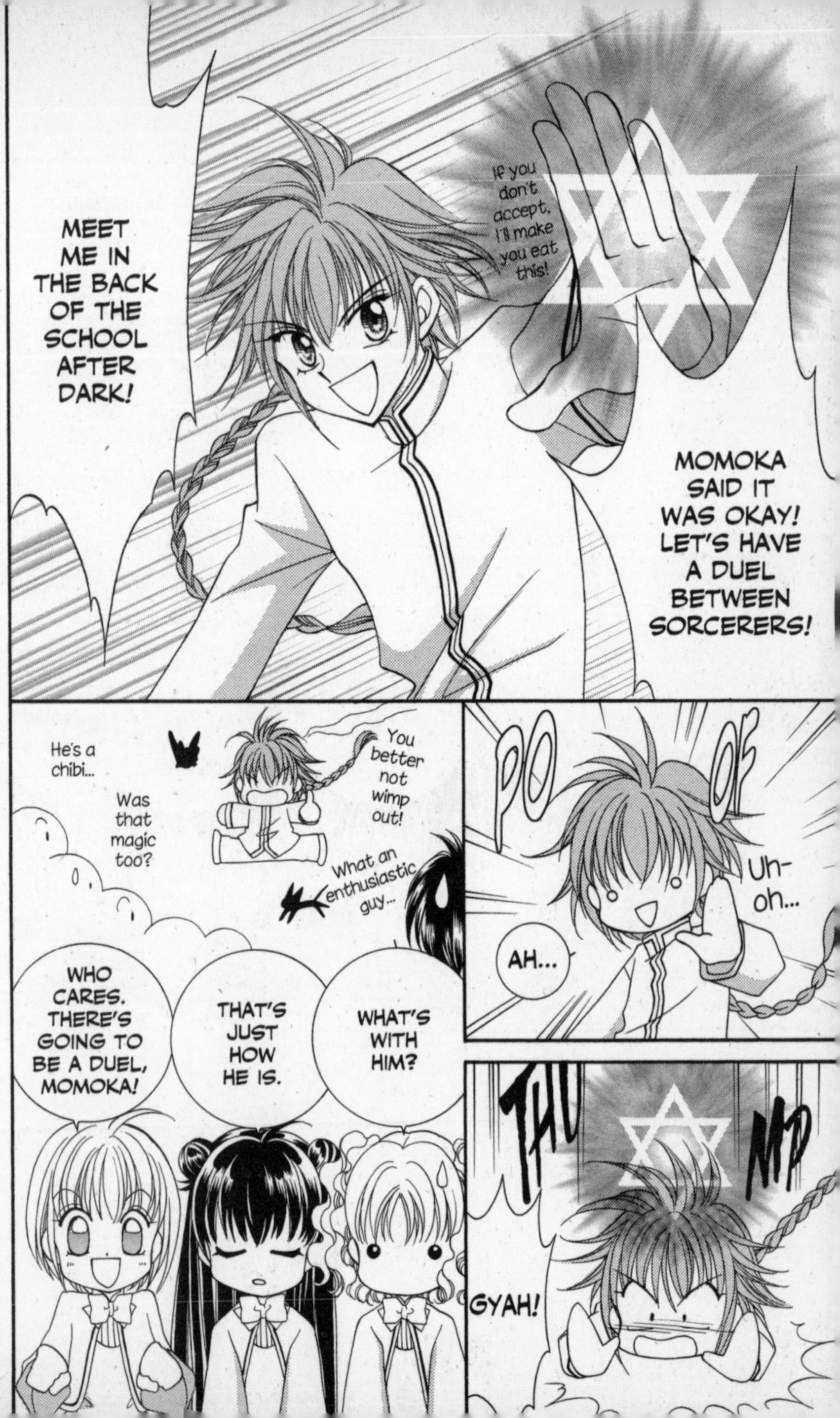
MOMOKA SAID IT WAS OKAY! LET'S HAVE A DUEL BETWEEN SORCERERS!
MEET ME IN THE BACK OF THE SCHOOL AFTER DARK!
If you don't accept, I'll make you eat this!
POOF
Uh-oh...
AH...
THUMP
GYAH!
You better not wimp out!
What an enthusiastic guy...
He's a chibi...
Was that magic too?
WHAT'S WITH HIM?
THAT'S JUST HOW HE IS.
WHO CARES. THERE'S GOING TO BE A DUEL, MOMOKA!

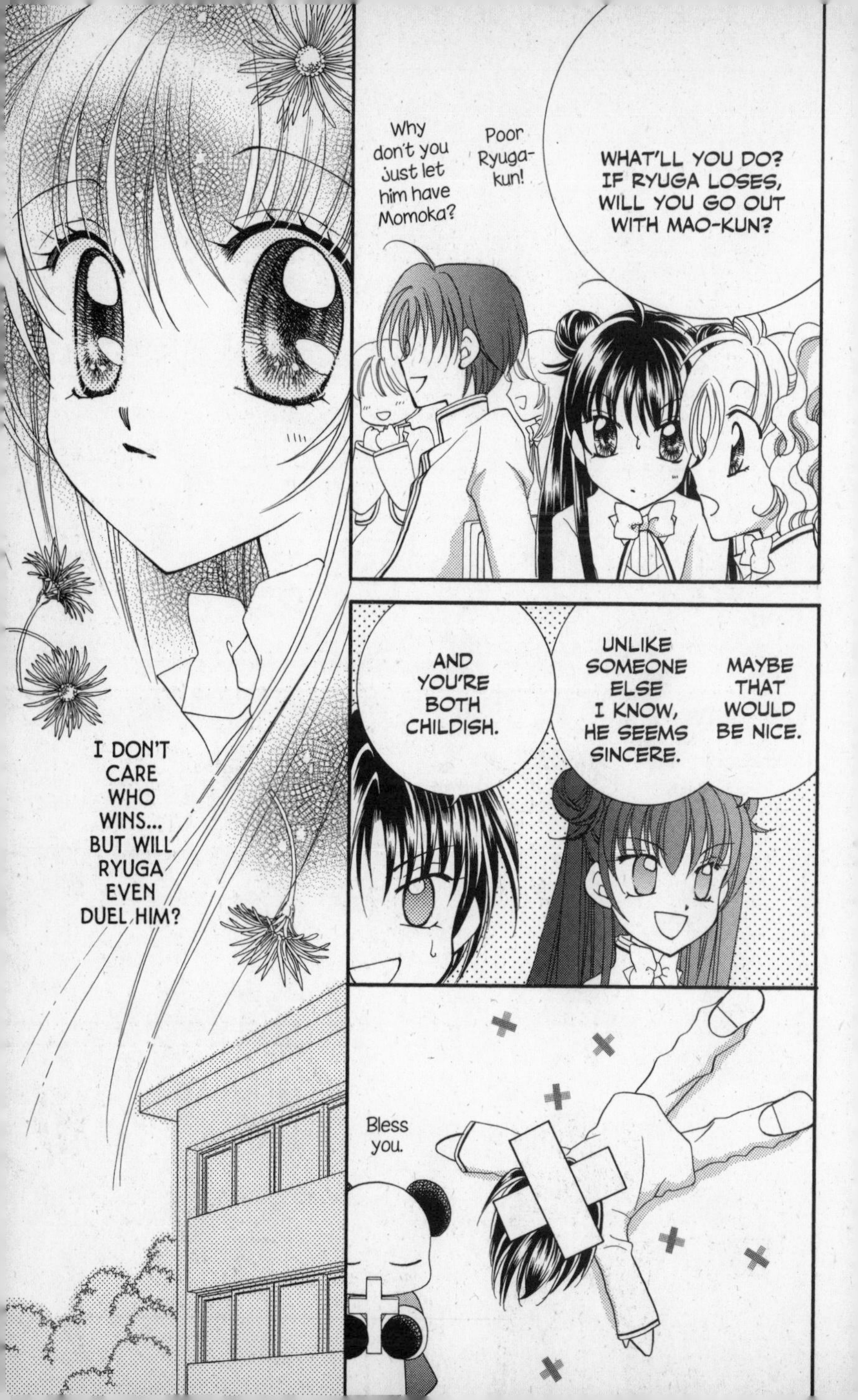
WHAT'LL YOU DO? IF RYUGA LOSES, WILL YOU GO OUT WITH MAO-KUN?
Poor Ryuga-kun!
Why don't you just let him have Momoka?
MAYBE THAT WOULD BE NICE.
UNLIKE SOMEONE ELSE I KNOW, HE SEEMS SINCERE.
AND YOU'RE BOTH CHILDISH.
Bless you.
I DON'T CARE WHO WINS... BUT WILL RYUGA EVEN DUEL HIM?

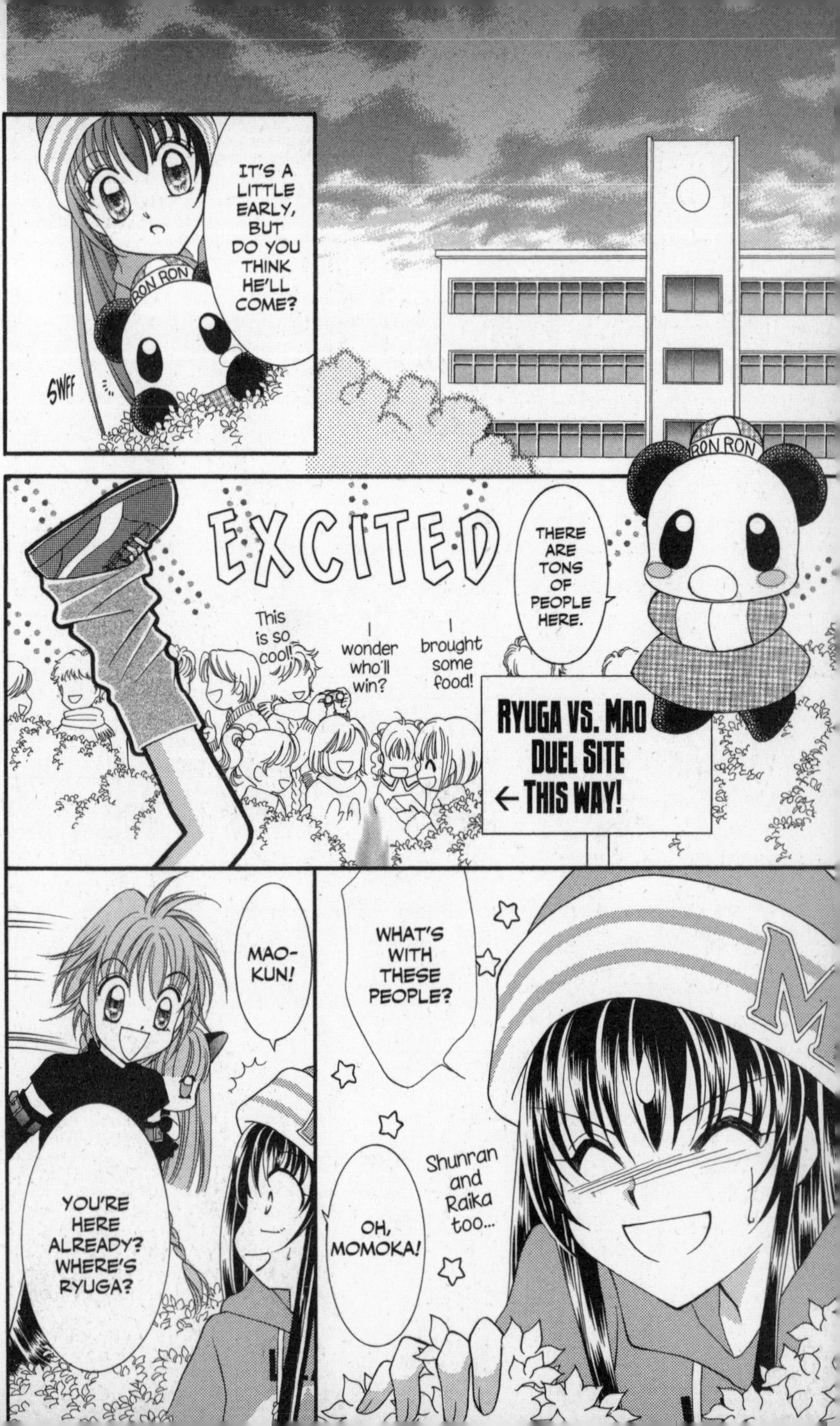

IT'S A LITTLE EARLY, BUT DO YOU THINK HE'LL COME?
RON RON
SWFF
THERE ARE TONS OF PEOPLE HERE.
RON RON
RYUGA VS. MAO DUEL SITE ← THIS WAY!
I brought some food!
I wonder who'll win?
This is so cool!
EXCITED
WHAT'S WITH THESE PEOPLE?
Shunran and Raika too...
OH, MOMOKA!
MAO-KUN!
YOU'RE HERE ALREADY? WHERE'S RYUGA?

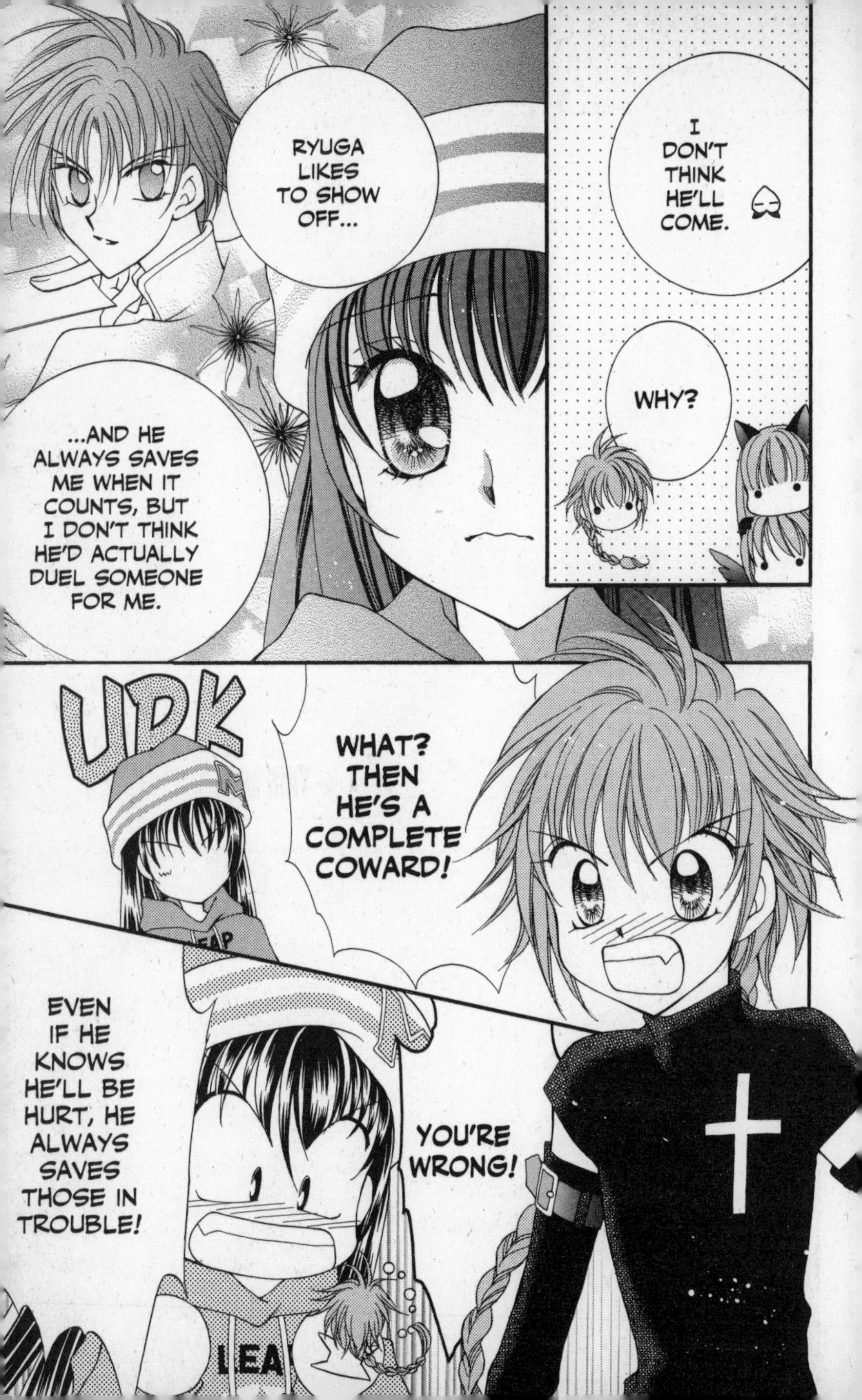
I DON'T THINK HE'LL COME.
WHY?
RYUGA LIKES TO SHOW OFF...
...AND HE ALWAYS SAVES ME WHEN IT COUNTS, BUT I DON'T THINK HE'D ACTUALLY DUEL SOMEONE FOR ME.
WHAT? THEN HE'S A COMPLETE COWARD!
UDK
YOU'RE WRONG!
EVEN IF HE KNOWS HE'LL BE HURT, HE ALWAYS SAVES THOSE IN TROUBLE!

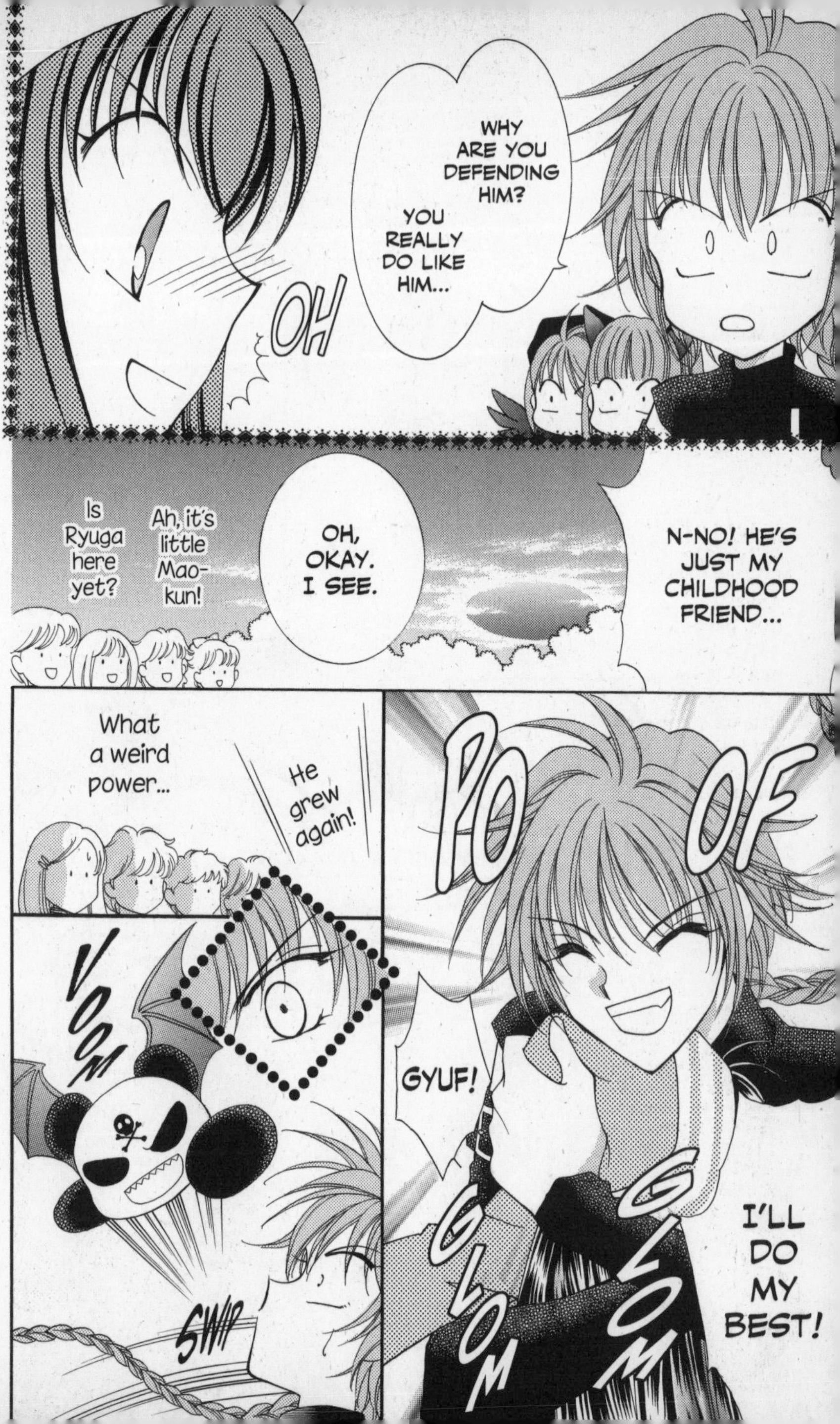
WHY ARE YOU DEFENDING HIM? YOU REALLY DO LIKE HIM...
OH
N-NO! HE'S JUST MY CHILDHOOD FRIEND...
OH, OKAY. I SEE.
Ah, it's little Mao-kun!
Is Ryuga here yet?
POOF
I'LL DO MY BEST!
GYUF!
GLOM GLOM
He grew again!
What a weird power...
VOOM
SWIP

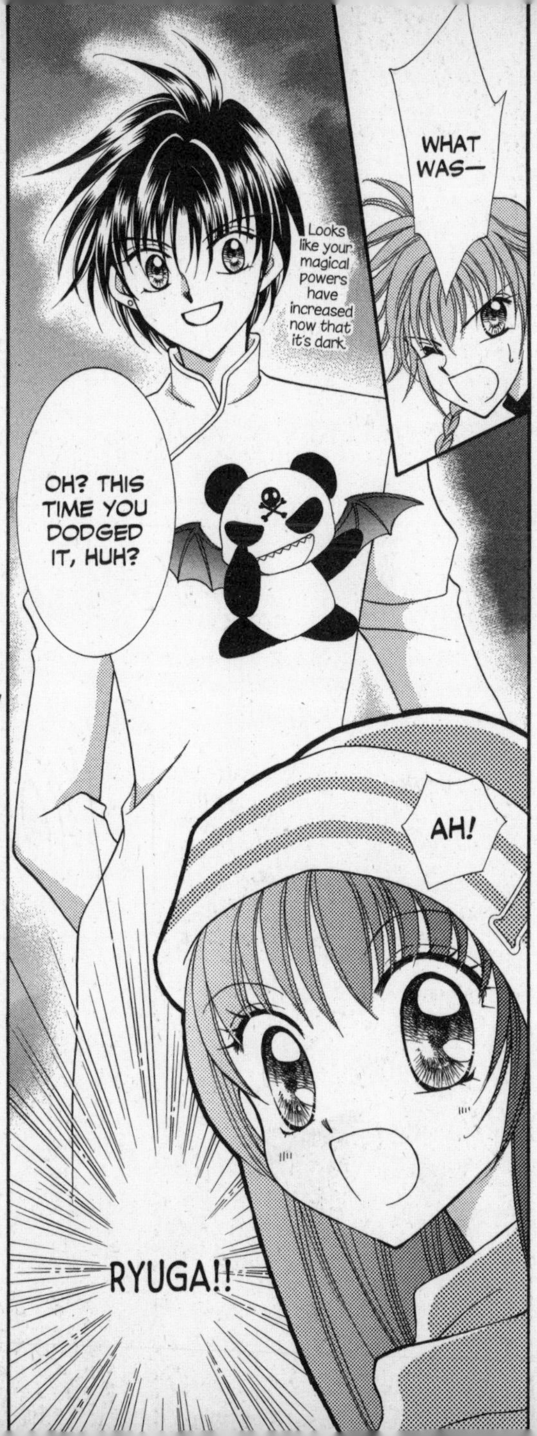
WHAT WAS—
Looks like your magical powers have increased now that it's dark.
OH? THIS TIME YOU DODGED IT, HUH?
AH!
RYUGA!!

10

The duel scenes with Ryuga and Mao were really lively with the crowd in the background. I'd always wanted to put a Western-style dragon in the story, so it was fun.

Note how stubborn Ryuga gets in this duel! (laugh) He's been worried about something ever since Mao's appearance. Those who are following along with the series in the monthly magazine probably already know what I'm talking about, but if you don't, you'll find out in volume 8.

I think the Western-style dragon has become Queen's pet.

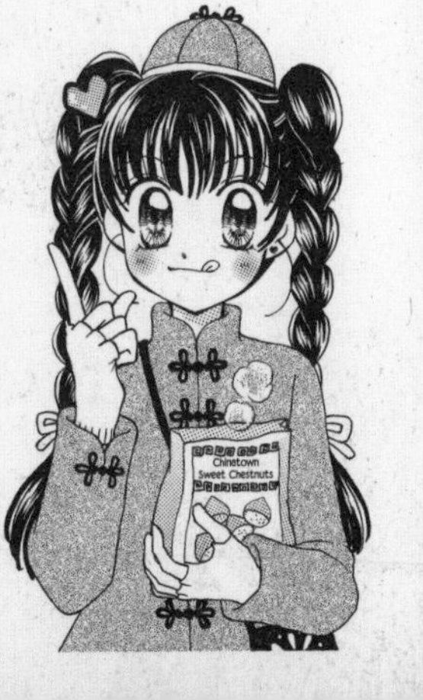
Chinatown Sweet Chestnuts

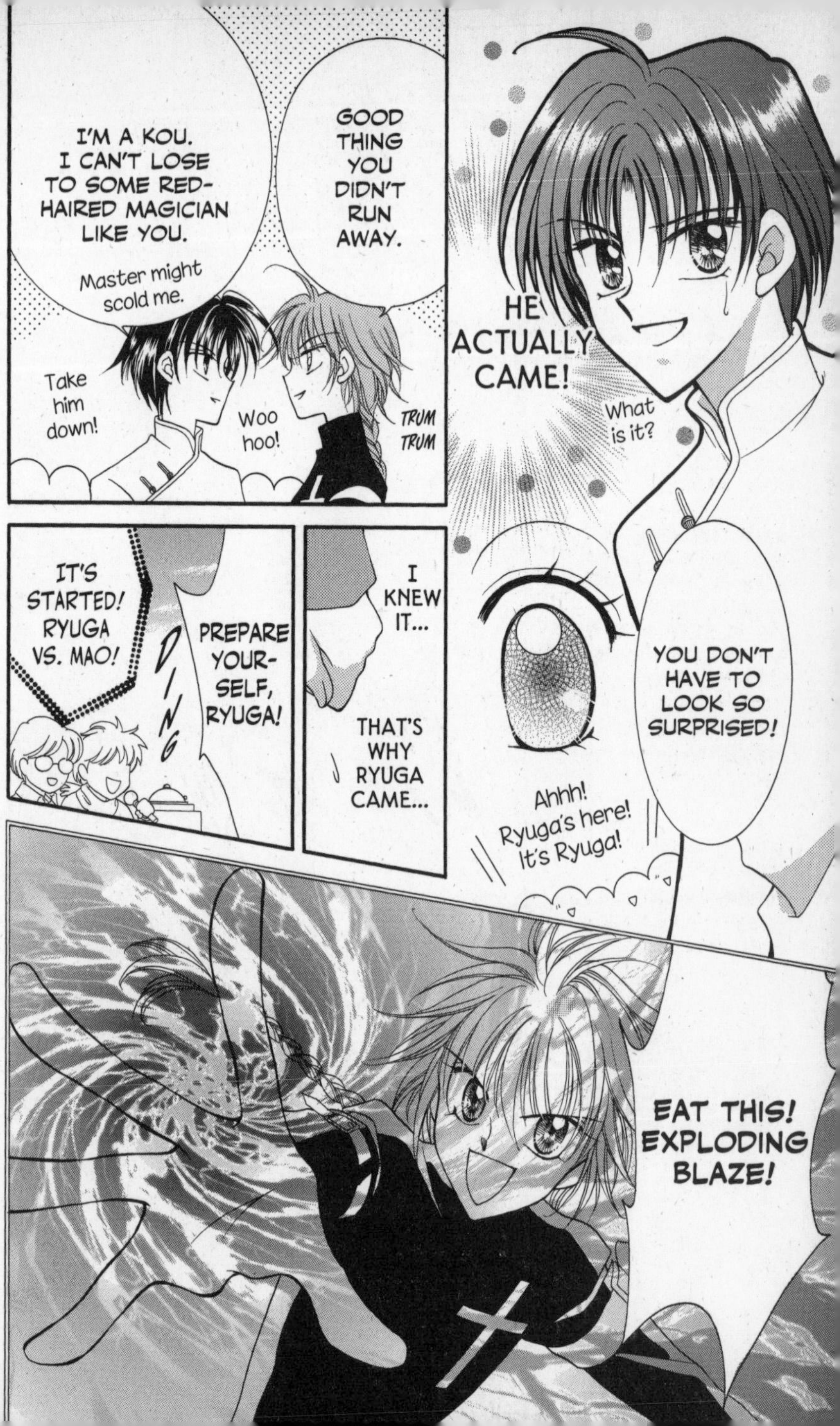
HE ACTUALLY CAME!
What is it?
YOU DON'T HAVE TO LOOK SO SURPRISED!
Ahhh! Ryuga's here! It's Ryuga!
GOOD THING YOU DIDN'T RUN AWAY.
I'M A KOU. I CAN'T LOSE TO SOME RED-HAIRED MAGICIAN LIKE YOU.
Master might scold me.
TRUM TRUM
Woo hoo!
Take him down!
I KNEW IT...
THAT'S WHY RYUGA CAME...
PREPARE YOURSELF, RYUGA!
DING
IT'S STARTED! RYUGA VS. MAO!
EAT THIS! EXPLODING BLAZE!

11

Lately fans have been asking in their letters which character is my favorite.

Since the series has been going on so long, a lot of people seem interested in this. It's really hard to decide. In my interview in *Ribon*, I said it was Momoka and Ron-Ron with the spirit of the Panda King inside him. For side characters, I really like Akira. (laugh)

The easiest to draw is Ryuga though. (Although I do love his personality too.) I like him as much as Momoka, I guess. Then I like Raika, Shunran, and Ageha. Ageha's blunt personality is really easy to write. I wish she was a friend of mine in real life. But... I guess I can't decide which one is my favorite!

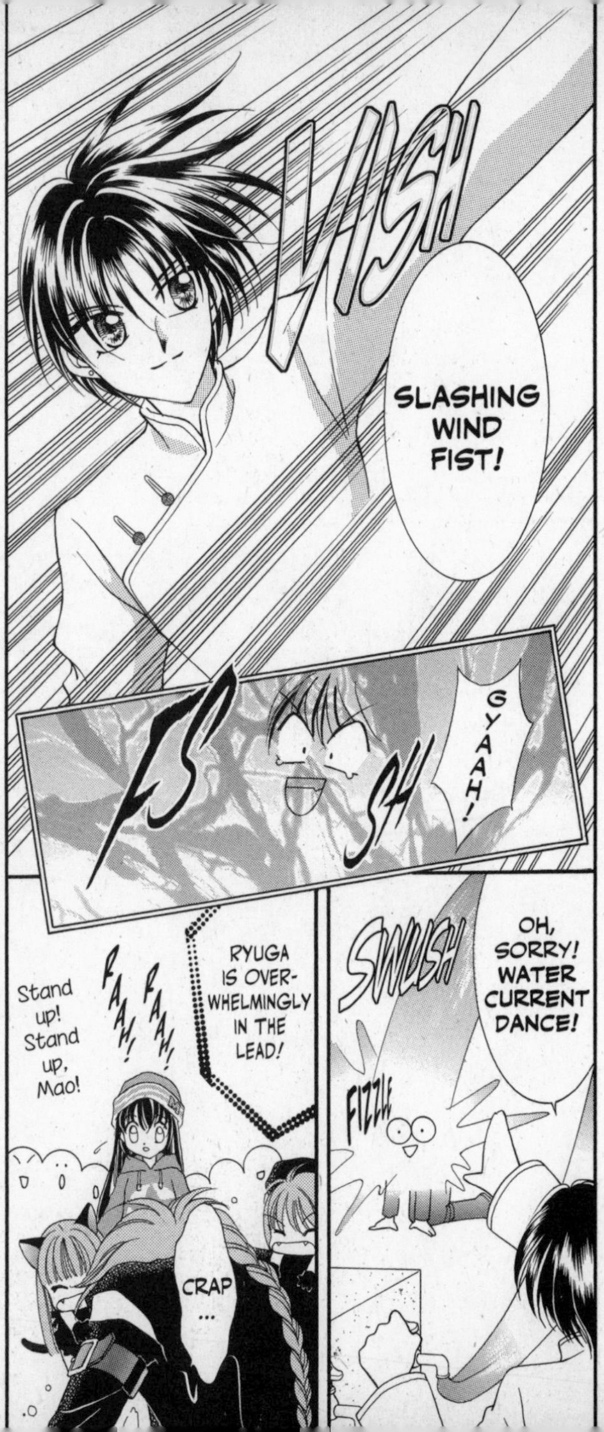
VISH
SLASHING WIND FIST!
FS
SH
GYAAH!
SWUSH
OH, SORRY! WATER CURRENT DANCE!
FIZZLE
RYUGA IS OVERWHELMINGLY IN THE LEAD!
RAAH!
RAAH!
Stand up! Stand up, Mao!
CRAP...

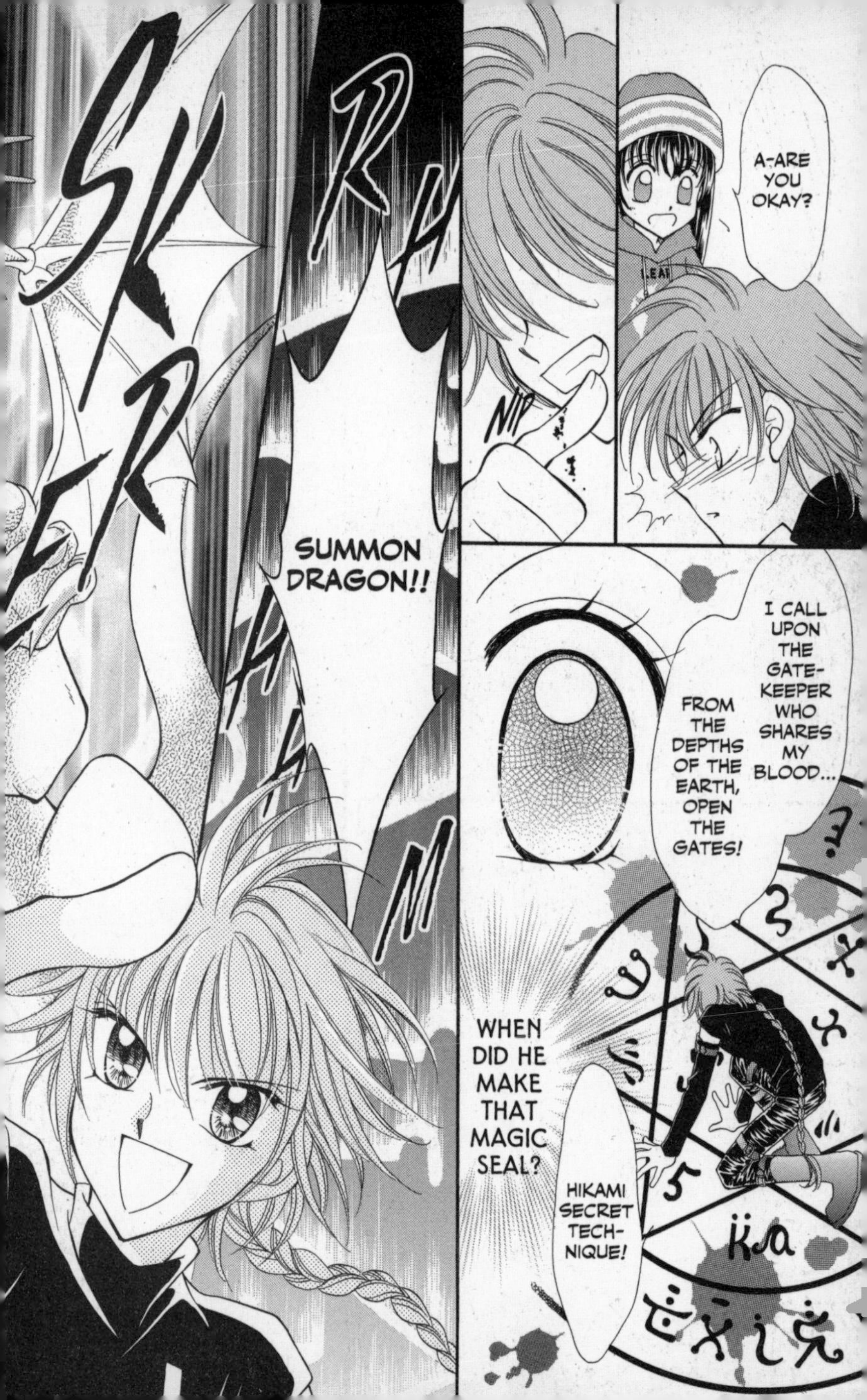
A-ARE YOU OKAY?
NIP
I CALL UPON THE GATE-KEEPER WHO SHARES MY BLOOD...
FROM THE DEPTHS OF THE EARTH, OPEN THE GATES!
HIKAMI SECRET TECH-NIQUE!
WHEN DID HE MAKE THAT MAGIC SEAL?
SUMMON DRAGON!!

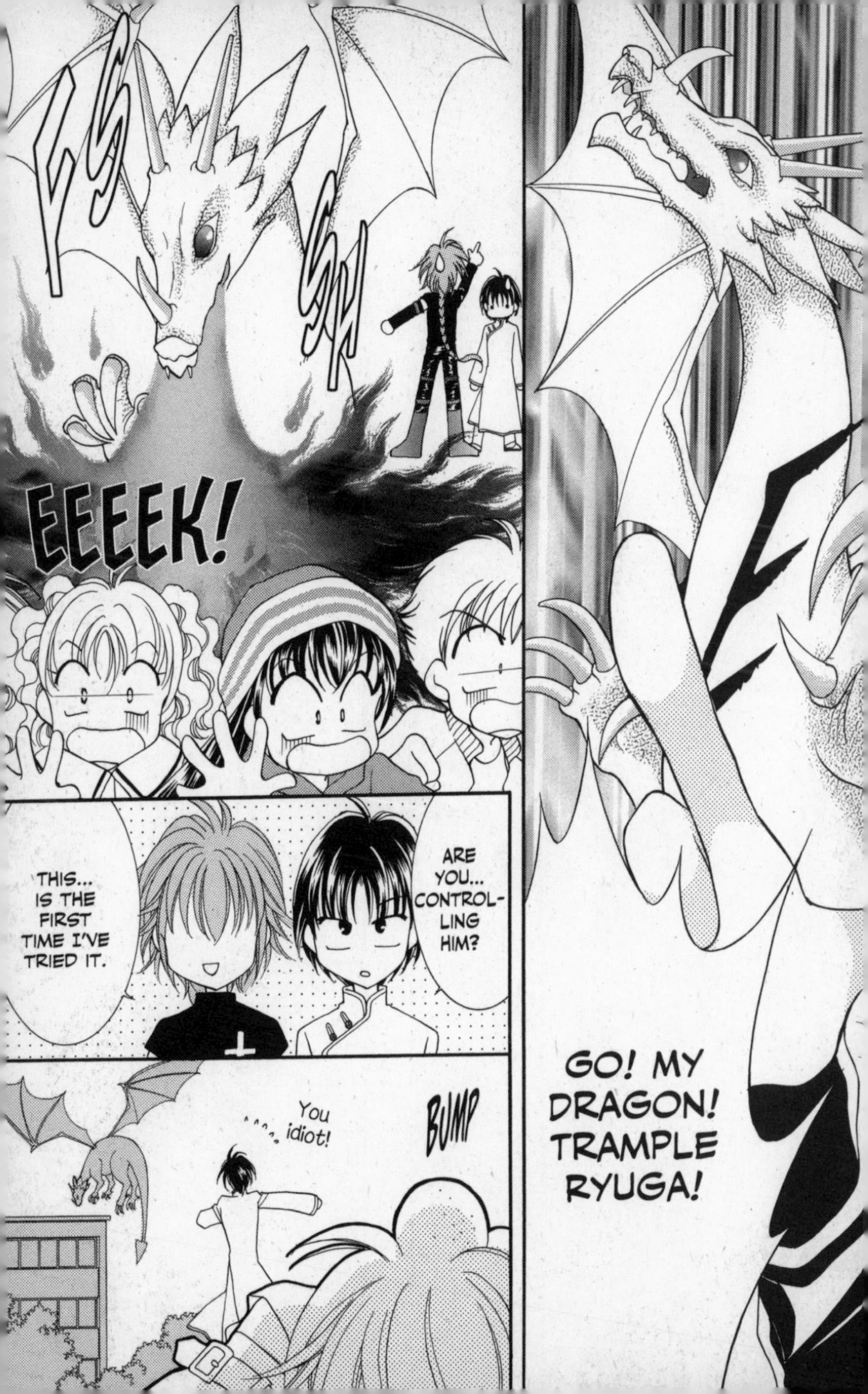
GO! MY DRAGON! TRAMPLE RYUGA!
EEEEK!
ARE YOU... CONTROL-LING HIM?
THIS... IS THE FIRST TIME I'VE TRIED IT.
BUMP
You idiot!

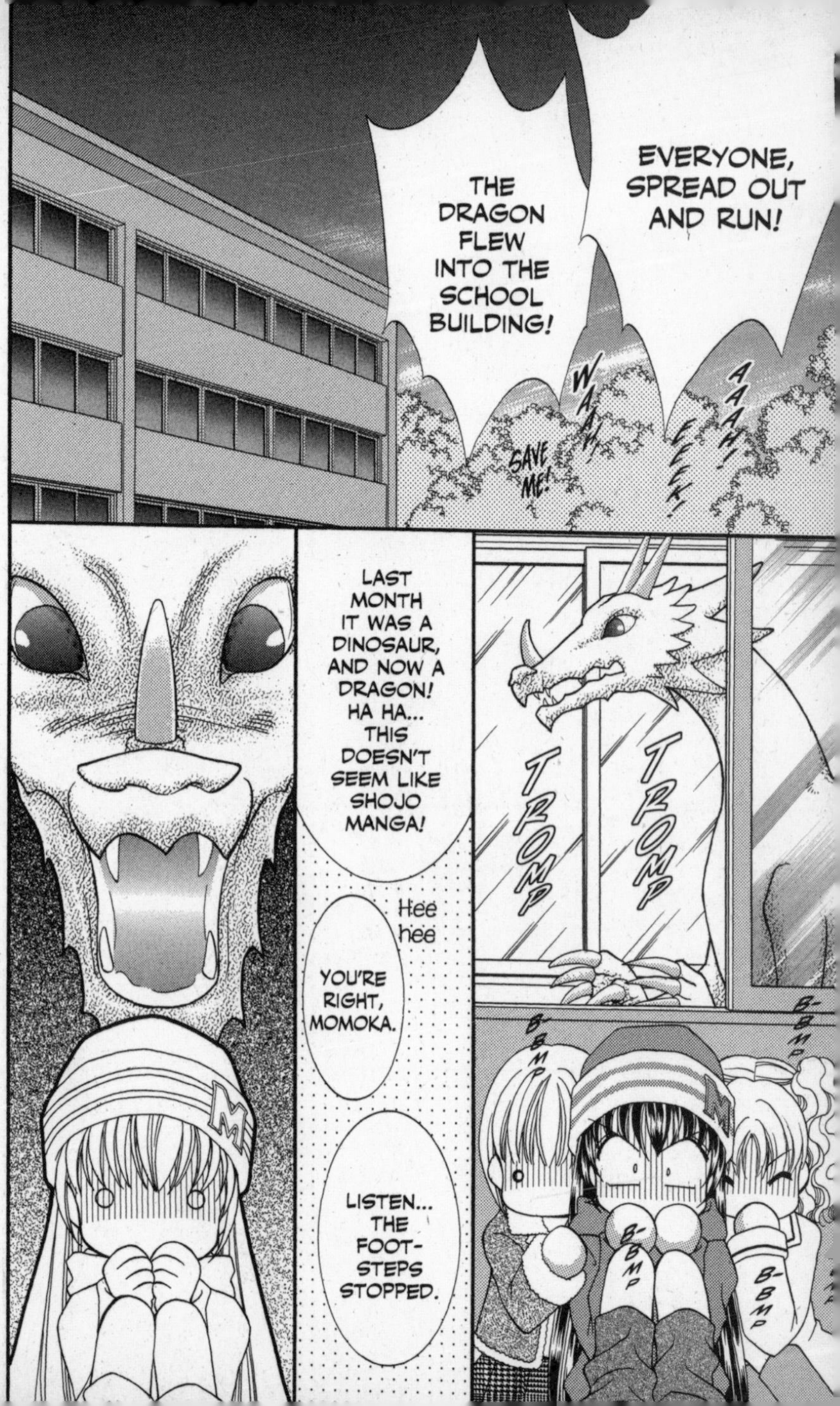
EVERYONE, SPREAD OUT AND RUN!
THE DRAGON FLEW INTO THE SCHOOL BUILDING!
AAAAH!
EEEK!
WAAAH
SAVE ME!
TROMP
TROMP
B-BMP
B-BMP
B-BMP
B-BMP
LAST MONTH IT WAS A DINOSAUR, AND NOW A DRAGON! HA HA... THIS DOESN'T SEEM LIKE SHOJO MANGA!
Hee hee
YOU'RE RIGHT, MOMOKA.
LISTEN... THE FOOT-STEPS STOPPED.

12

Another thing I read in fan letters often is "Momoka's personality is a lot like mine!" Basically the girls can't be straightforward in front of guys they like. They just get violent or something... A lot of other letters had "I love pandas too!" (laugh) I'm the same way.

I based Momoka's personality partly on mine and partly on a senpai of mine whom I admired. Before this, the boy characters were usually the most popular in my manga, but Momoka is probably the most popular character in *St.♥Dragon Girl*. It's really refreshing and it makes me happy! But Ryuga is pretty popular too. Ron-Ron was popular even before the Panda King possessed him! (laugh) Sometimes I wonder if he is the most popular of all! (laugh)

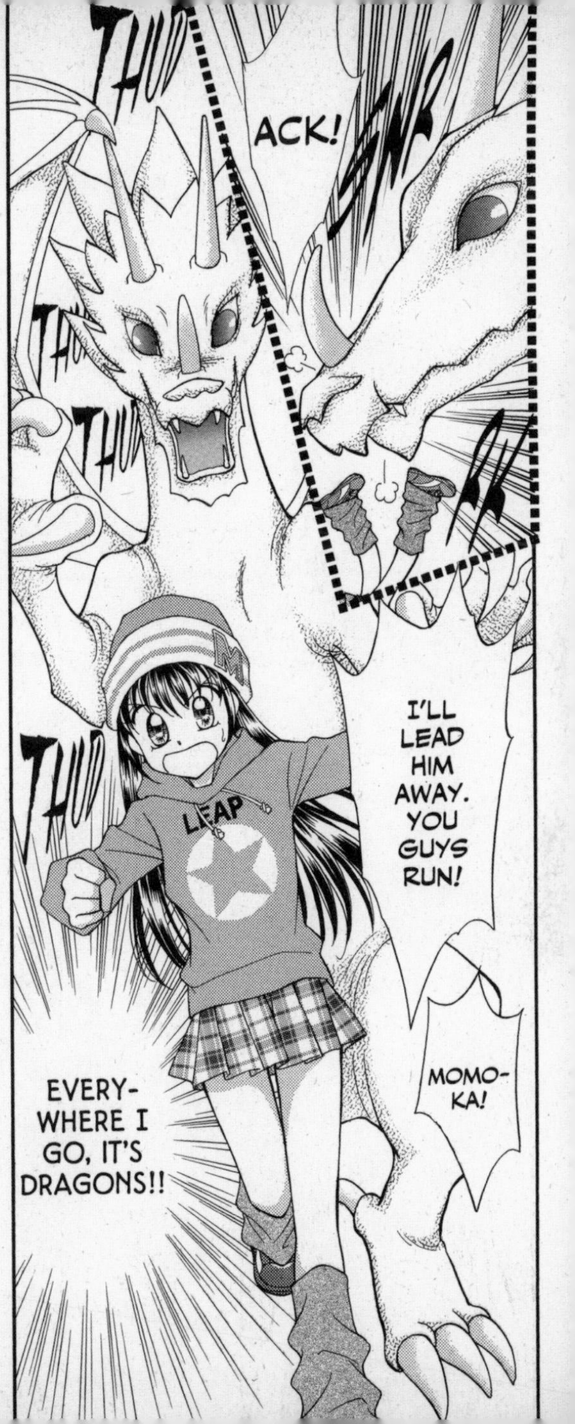
ACK!
THUD
THUD
THUD
I'LL LEAD HIM AWAY. YOU GUYS RUN!
THUD
MOMO-KA!
EVERY-WHERE I GO, IT'S DRAGONS!!

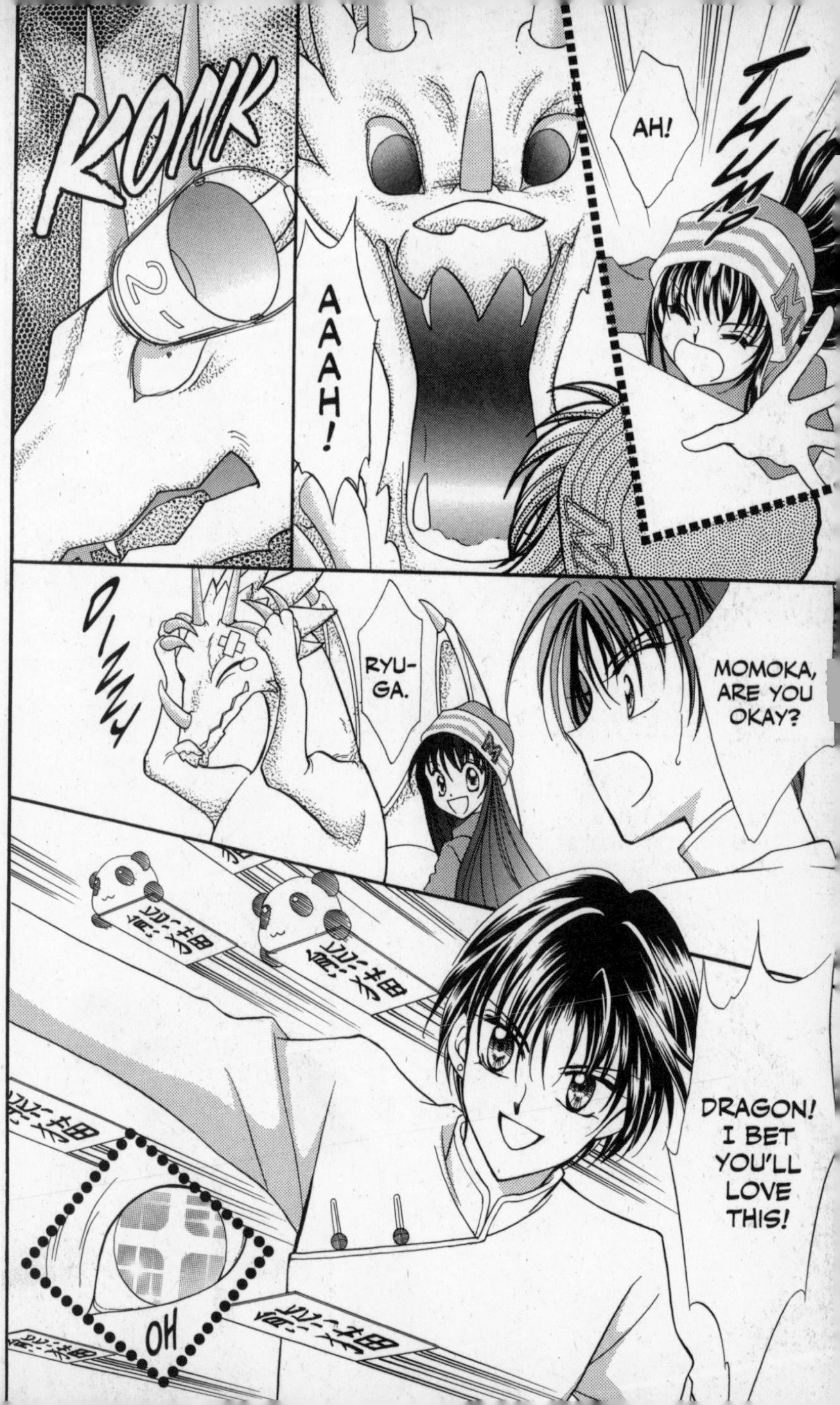
AH!
THUMP
AAAAH!
KONK
MOMOKA, ARE YOU OKAY?
RYU-GA.
DRAGON! I BET YOU'LL LOVE THIS!
OH

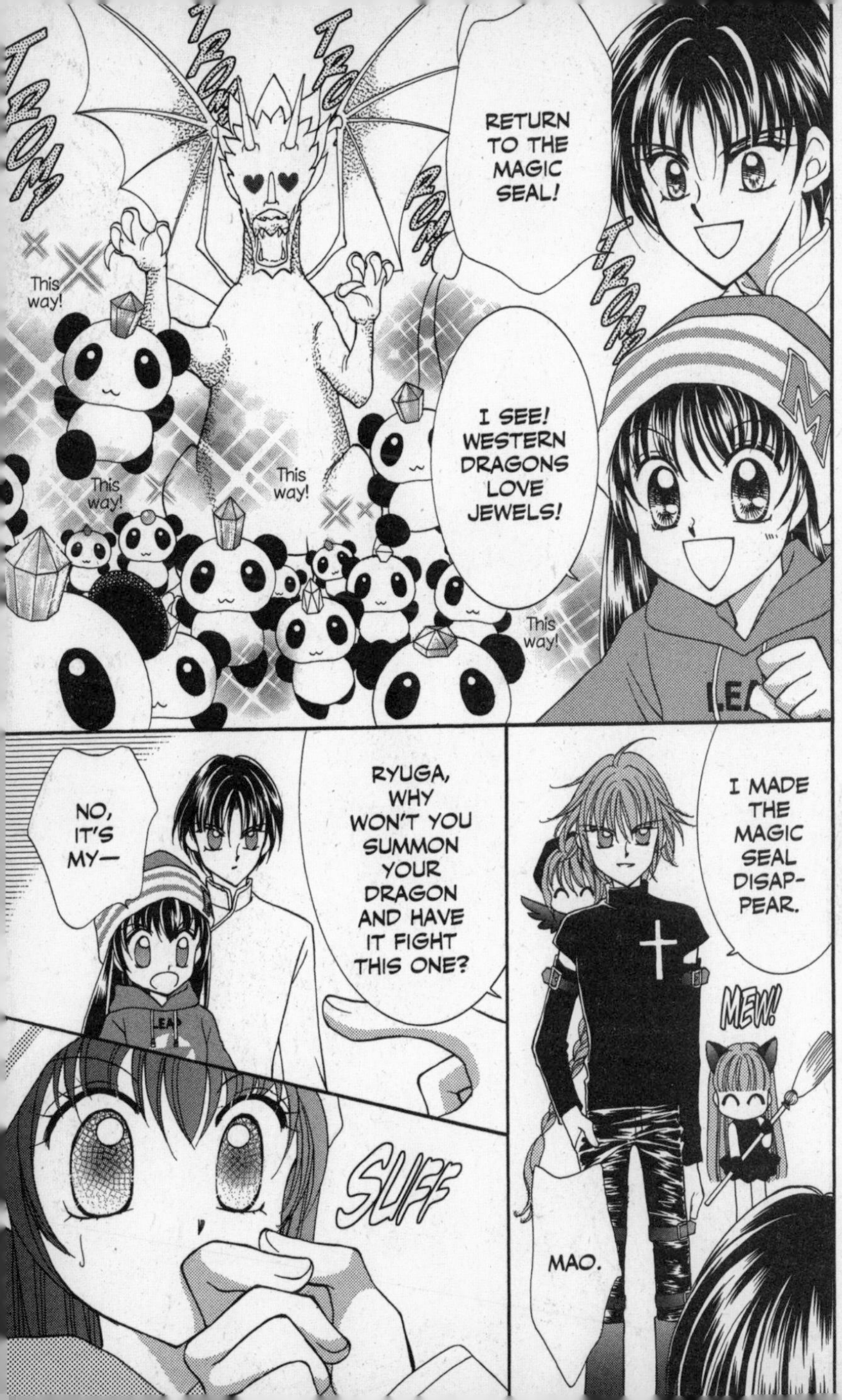
RETURN TO THE MAGIC SEAL!
TROM
I SEE! WESTERN DRAGONS LOVE JEWELS!
TROM
TROM
TROM
TROM
This way!
This way!
This way!
This way!
I MADE THE MAGIC SEAL DISAP-PEAR.
MEW!
MAO.
RYUGA, WHY WON'T YOU SUMMON YOUR DRAGON AND HAVE IT FIGHT THIS ONE?
NO, IT'S MY—
SUFF

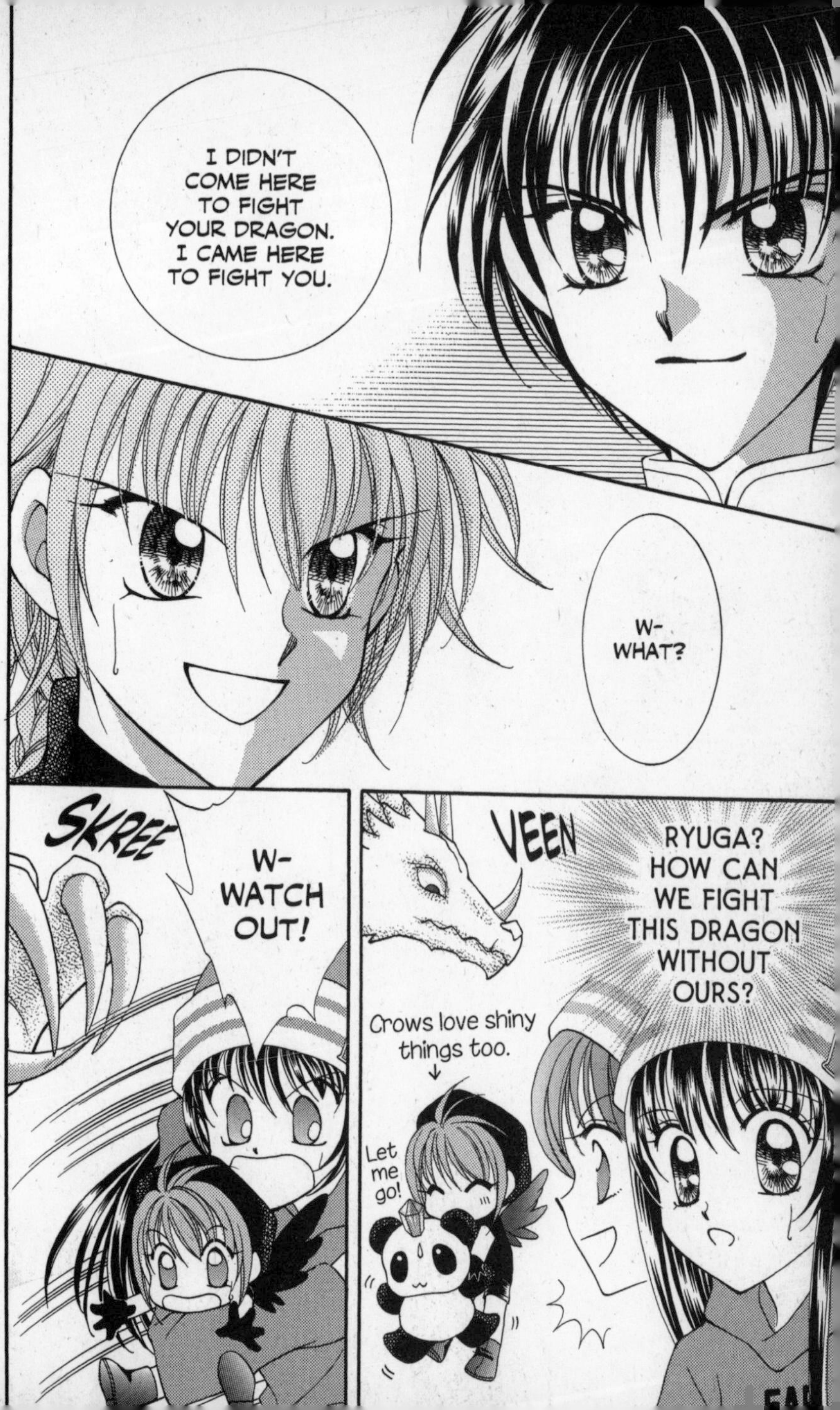
I DIDN'T COME HERE TO FIGHT YOUR DRAGON. I CAME HERE TO FIGHT YOU.
W- WHAT?
VEEN
RYUGA? HOW CAN WE FIGHT THIS DRAGON WITHOUT OURS?
Crows love shiny things too.
Let me go!
SKREE
W- WATCH OUT!

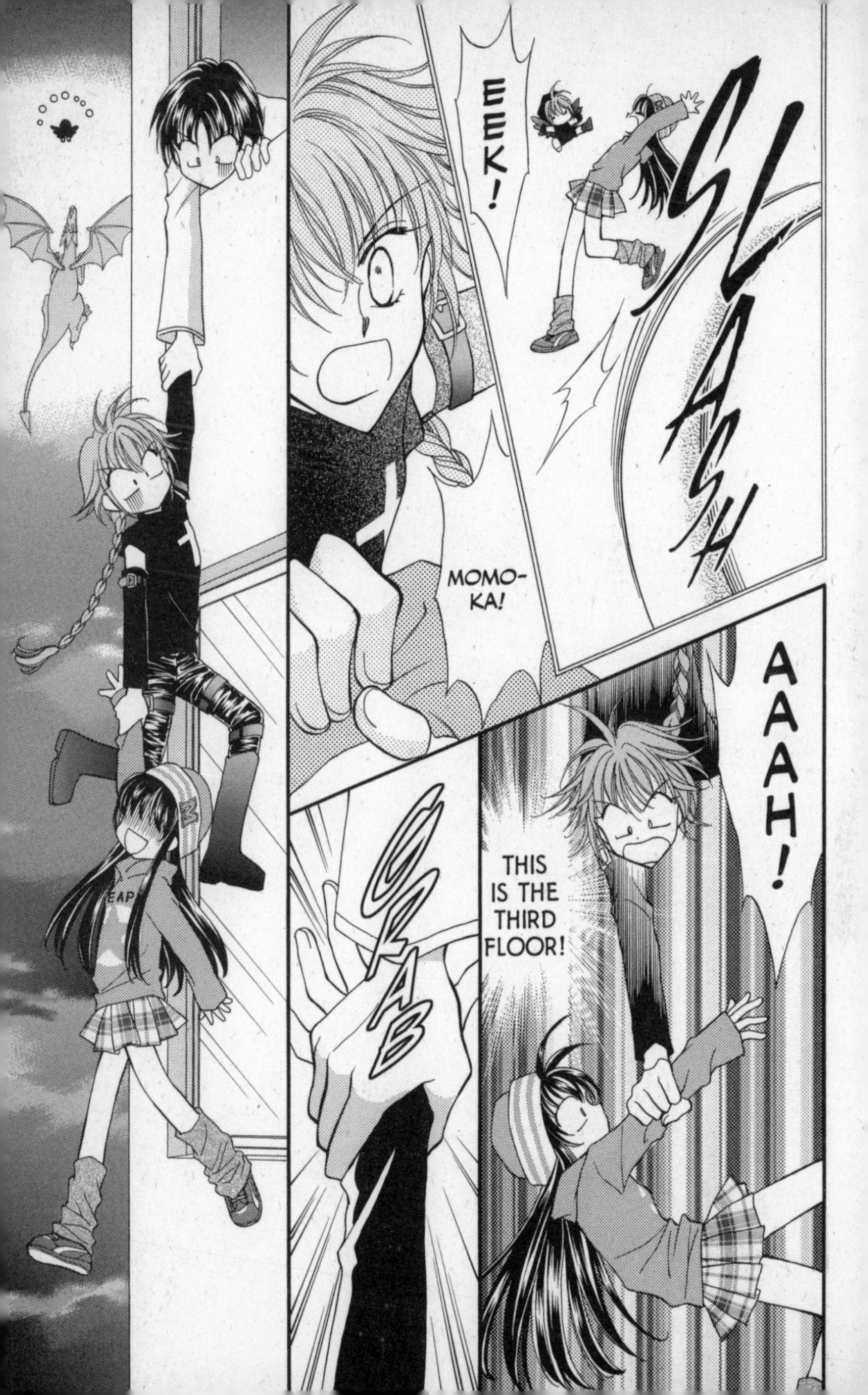
SLASH
EEK!
MOMO-KA!
AAAH!
THIS IS THE THIRD FLOOR!
GRAB

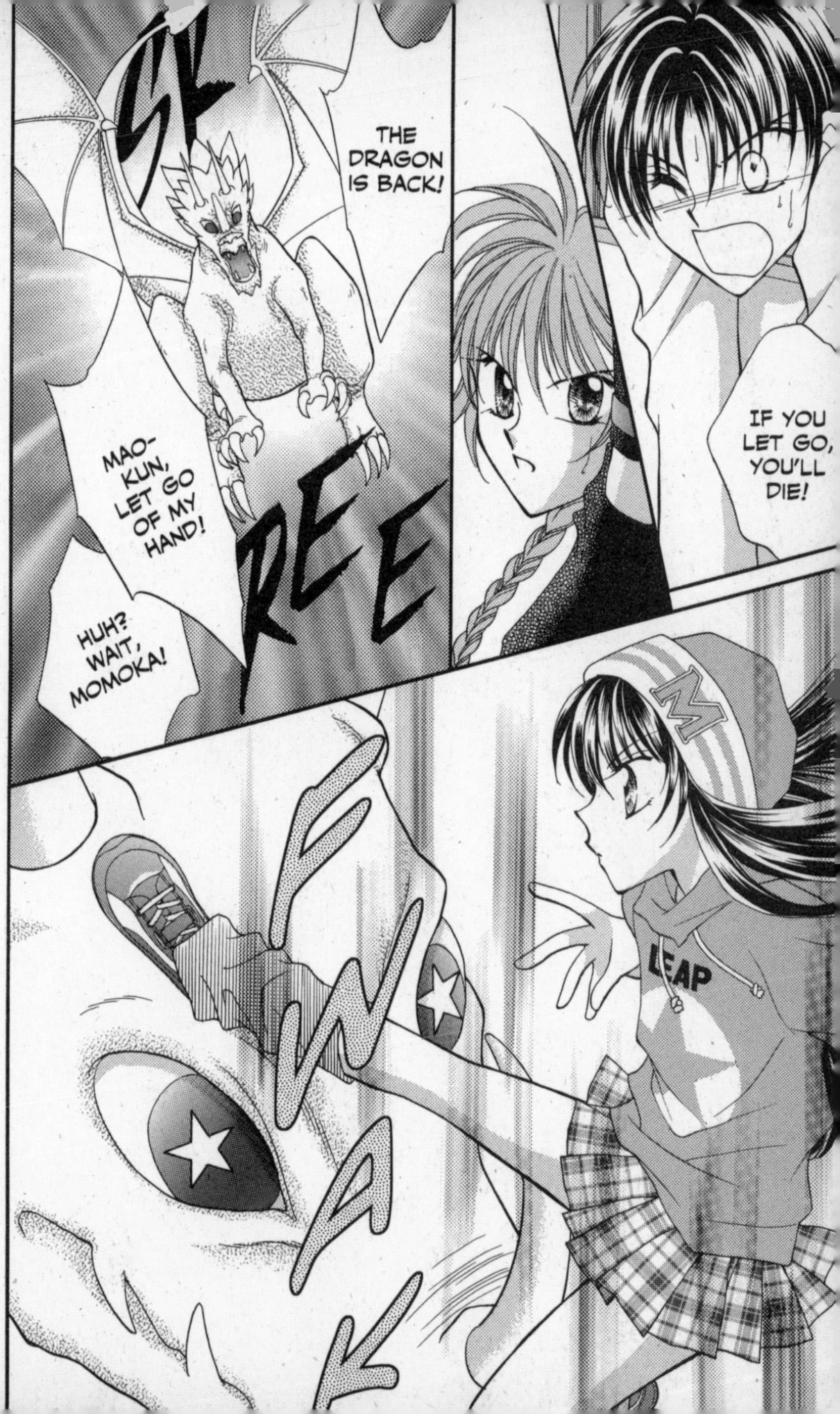
IF YOU LET GO, YOU'LL DIE!
THE DRAGON IS BACK!
SKREE
MAO-KUN, LET GO OF MY HAND!
HUH? WAIT, MOMOKA!
M
LEAP

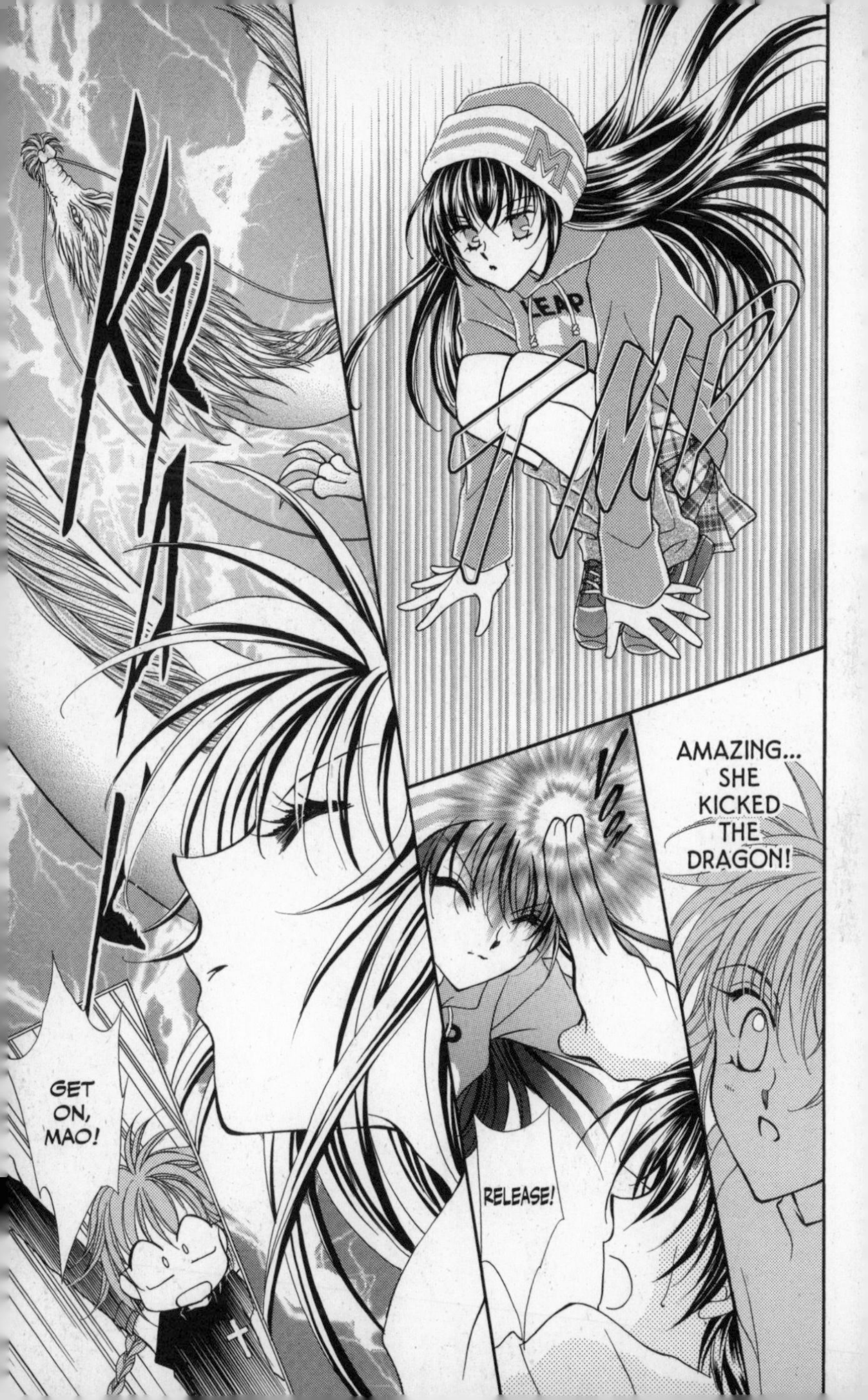
AMAZING... SHE KICKED THE DRAGON!
RELEASE!
GET ON, MAO!

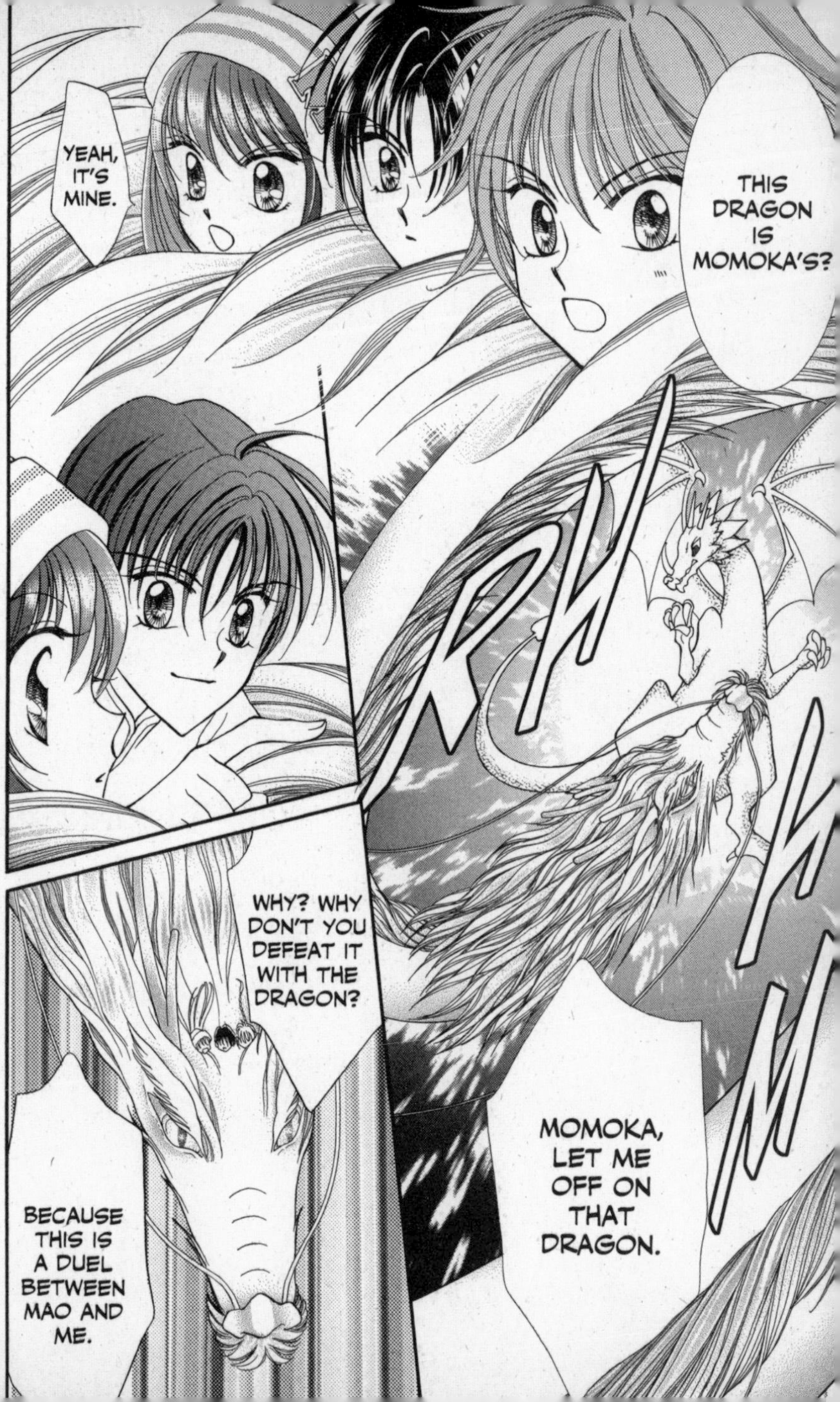
THIS DRAGON IS MOMOKA'S?
YEAH, IT'S MINE.
MOMOKA, LET ME OFF ON THAT DRAGON.
WHY? WHY DON'T YOU DEFEAT IT WITH THE DRAGON?
BECAUSE THIS IS A DUEL BETWEEN MAO AND ME.

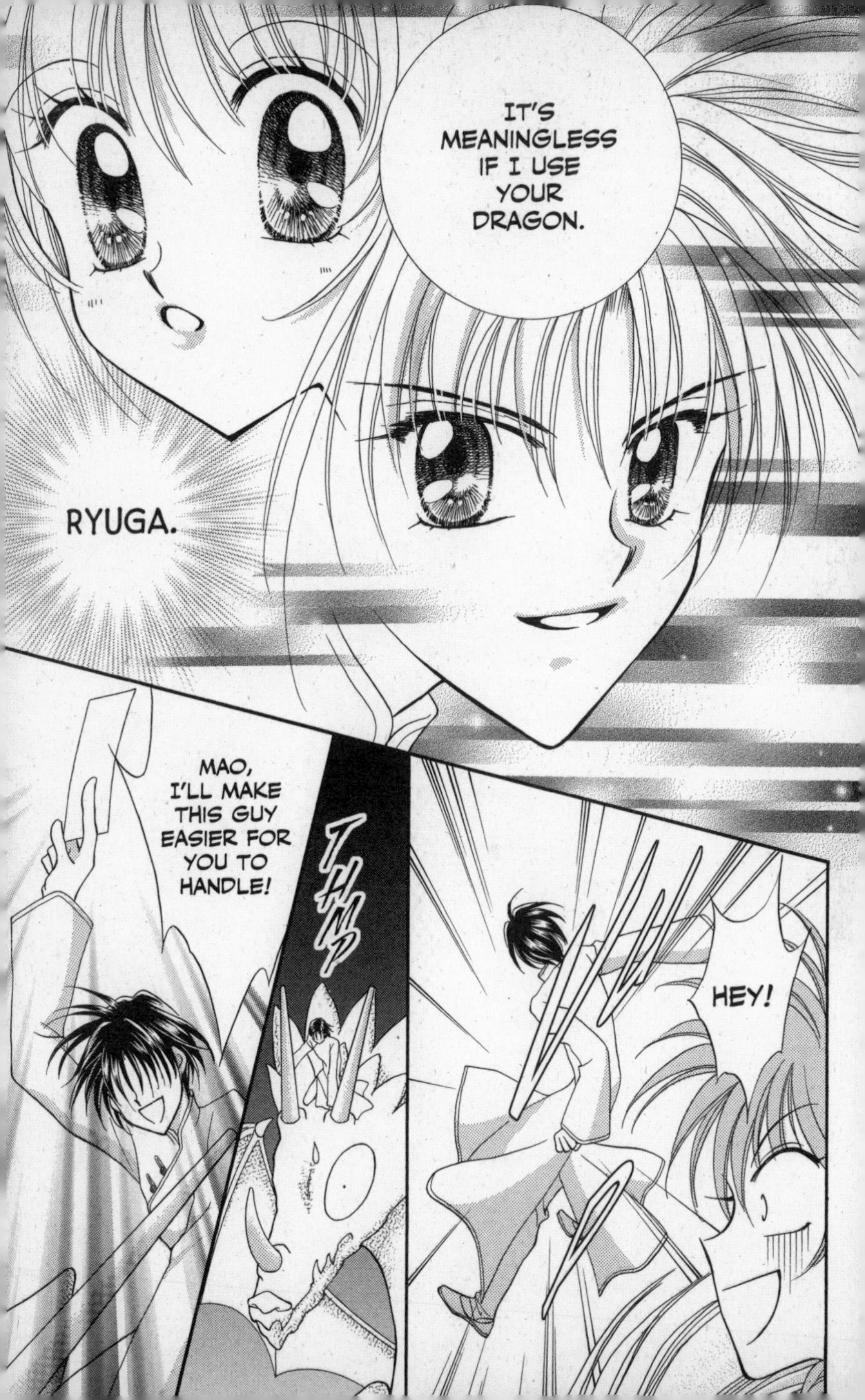
IT'S MEANINGLESS IF I USE YOUR DRAGON.
RYUGA.
HEY!
THMP
MAO, I'LL MAKE THIS GUY EASIER FOR YOU TO HANDLE!

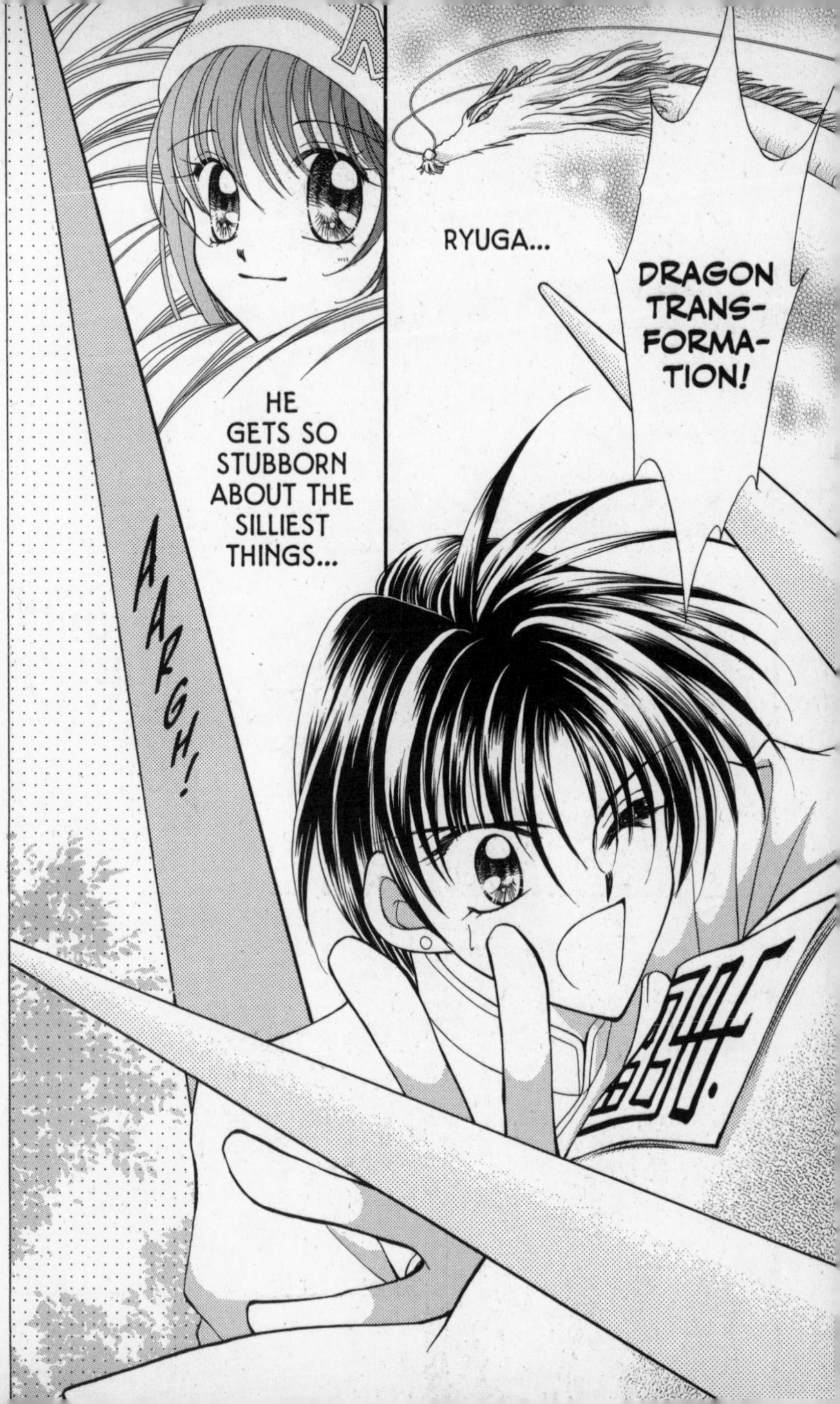
DRAGON TRANS-FORMA-TION!
RYUGA...
HE GETS SO STUBBORN ABOUT THE SILLIEST THINGS...
AARGH!

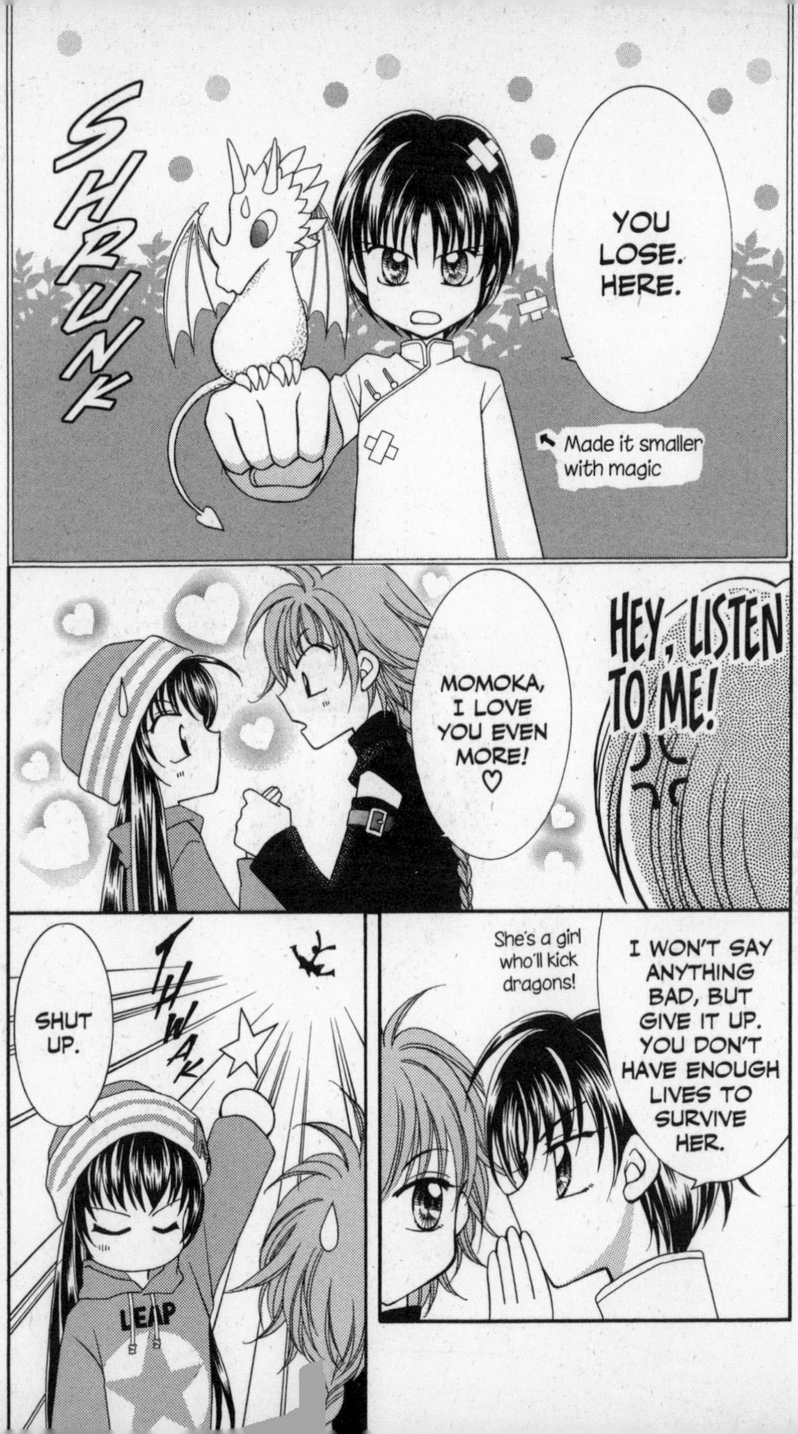
YOU LOSE. HERE.
Made it smaller with magic
SHRUNK
HEY, LISTEN TO ME!
MOMOKA, I LOVE YOU EVEN MORE! ♡
I WON'T SAY ANYTHING BAD, BUT GIVE IT UP. YOU DON'T HAVE ENOUGH LIVES TO SURVIVE HER.
She's a girl who'll kick dragons!
SHUT UP.
THWAK
LEAP

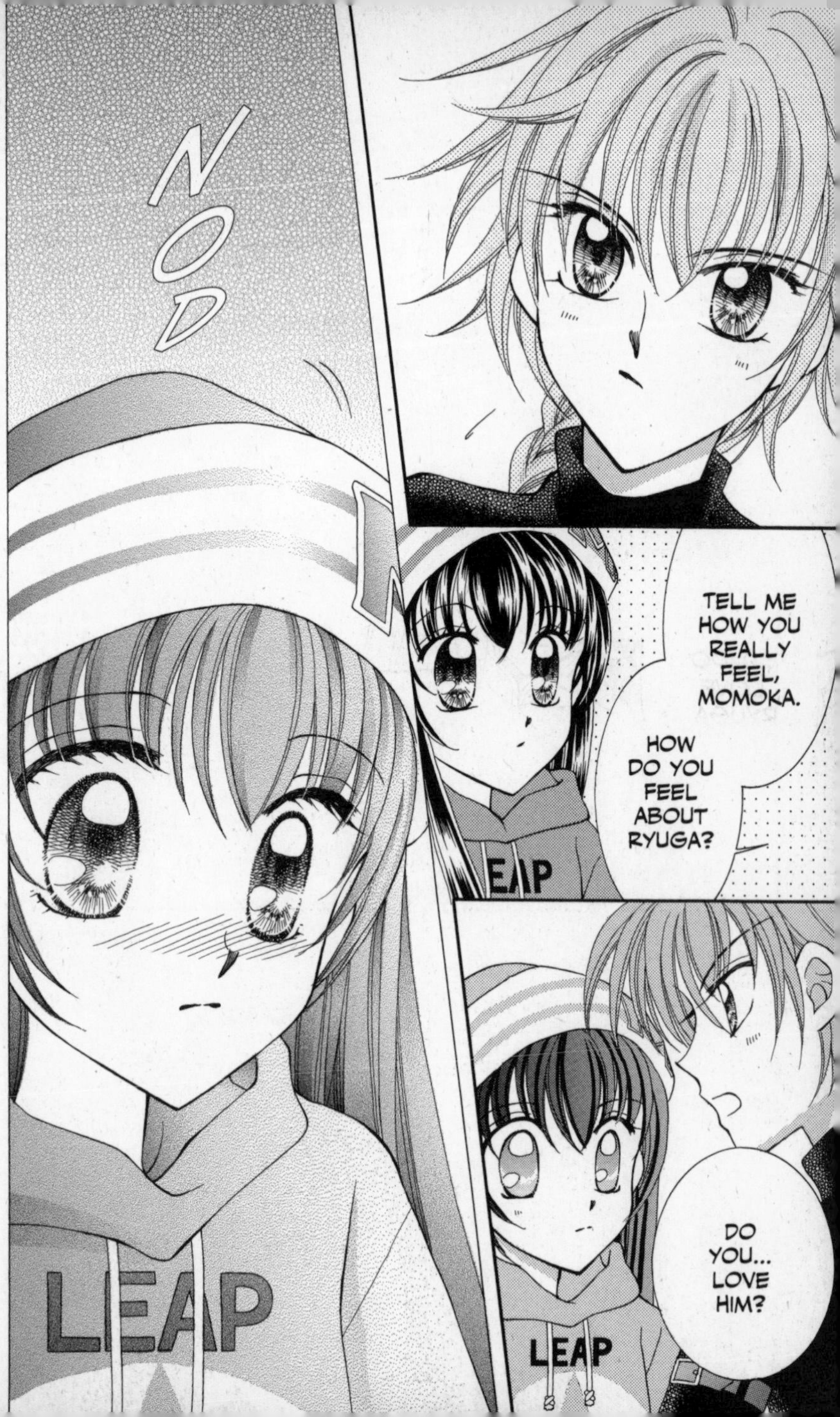
TELL ME HOW YOU REALLY FEEL, MOMOKA.
HOW DO YOU FEEL ABOUT RYUGA?
DO YOU... LOVE HIM?
NOD

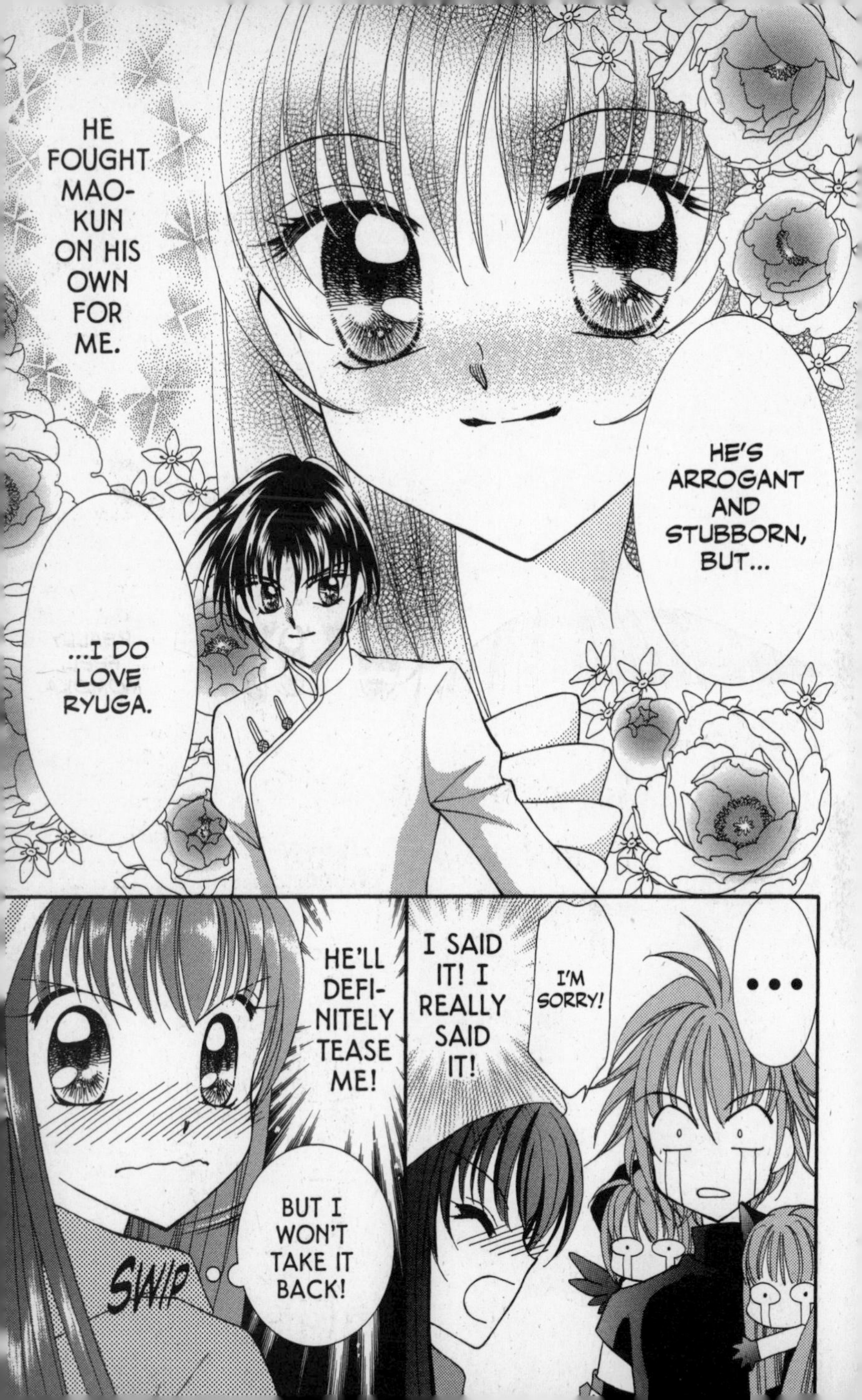
HE FOUGHT MAO-KUN ON HIS OWN FOR ME.
HE'S ARROGANT AND STUBBORN, BUT...
...I DO LOVE RYUGA.
...
I'M SORRY!
I SAID IT! I REALLY SAID IT!
HE'LL DEFINITELY TEASE ME!
BUT I WON'T TAKE IT BACK!
SWIP

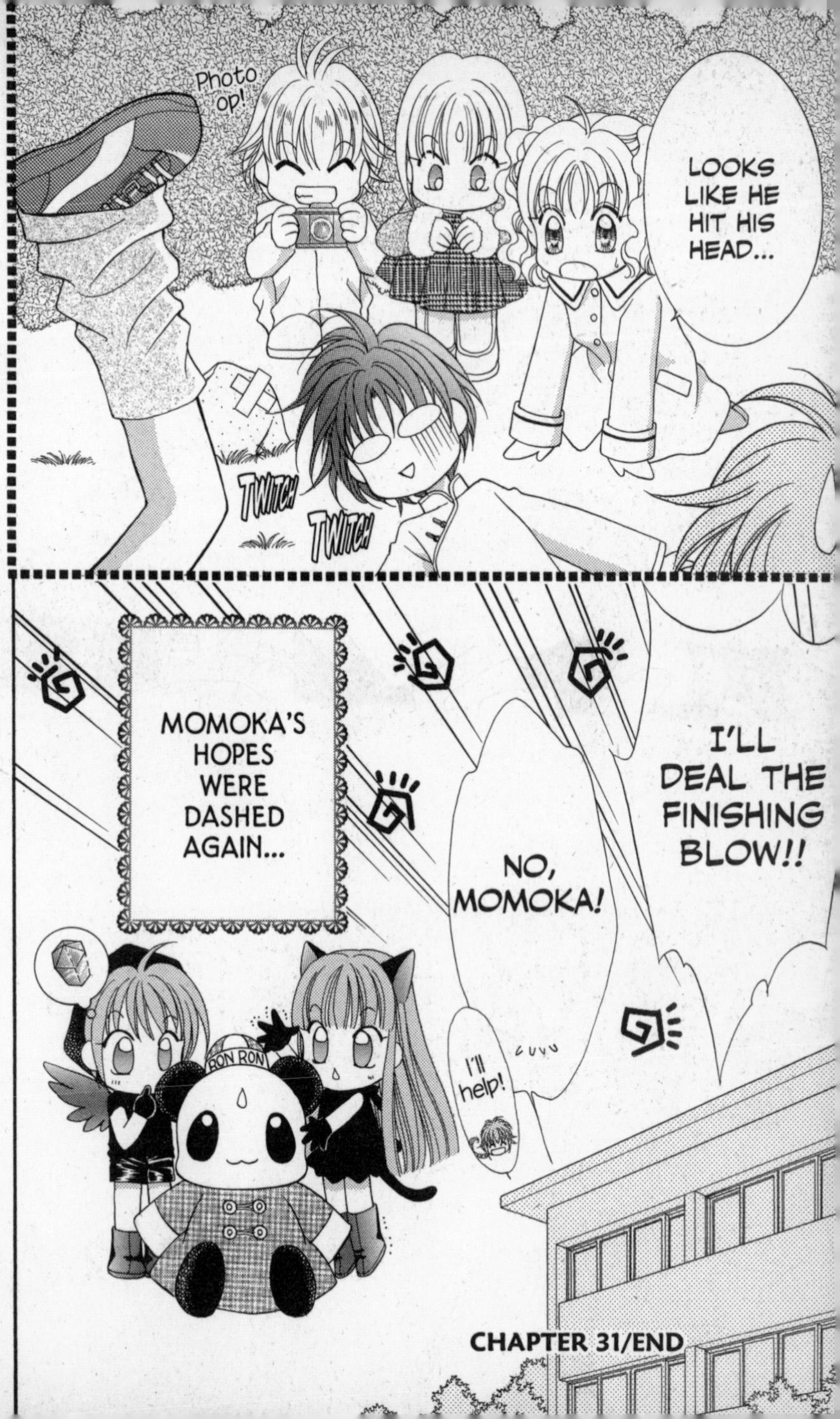
LOOKS LIKE HE HIT HIS HEAD...
Photo op!
TWITCH
TWITCH
I'LL DEAL THE FINISHING BLOW!!
NO, MOMOKA!
I'll help!
MOMOKA'S HOPES WERE DASHED AGAIN...
RON RON
CHAPTER 31/END

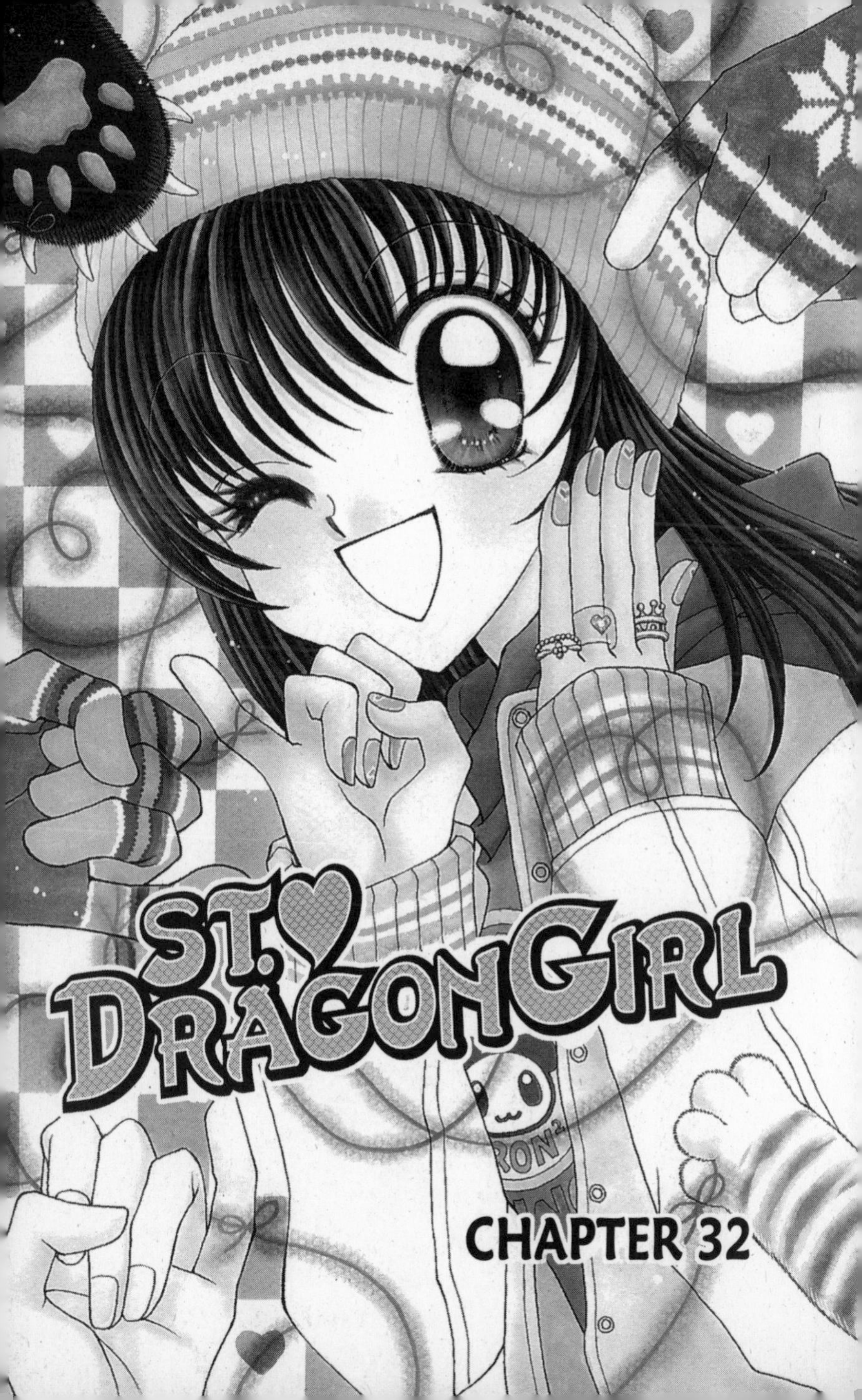
ST.♥ DRAGON GIRL
CHAPTER 32

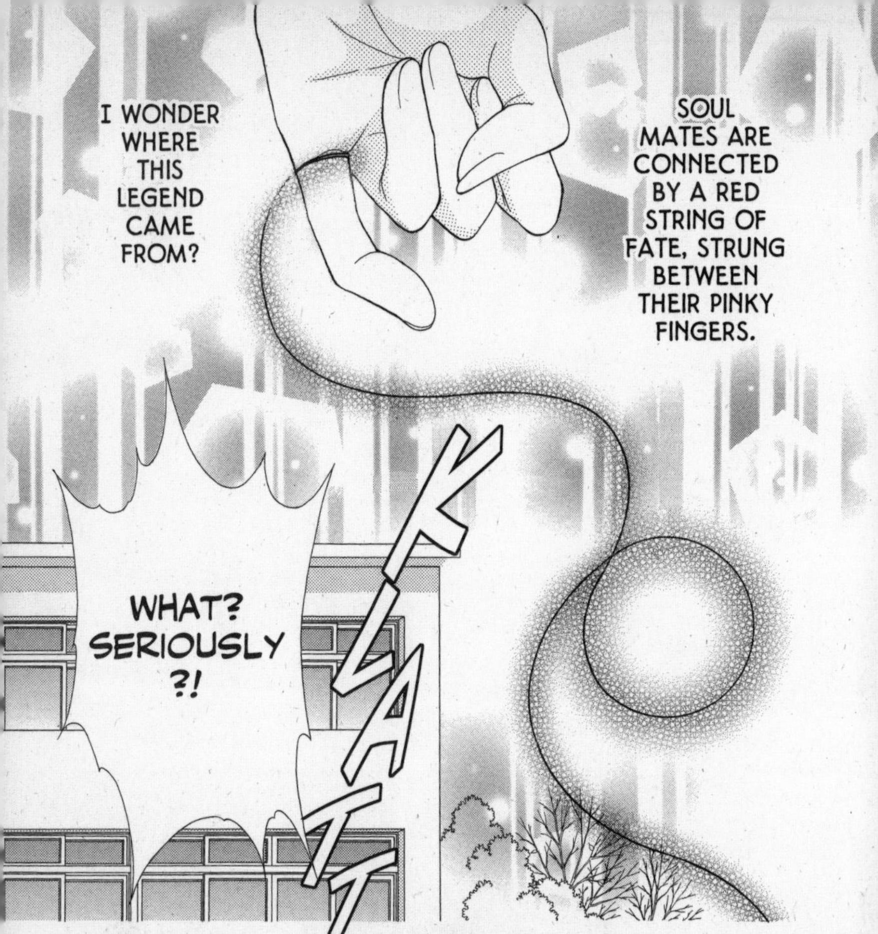
SOUL MATES ARE CONNECTED BY A RED STRING OF FATE, STRUNG BETWEEN THEIR PINKY FINGERS.
I WONDER WHERE THIS LEGEND CAME FROM?
WHAT? SERIOUSLY ?!

Mio Hikami

Birthday: April 10.
16 years old.
Aries. Blood Type: B.
Mao's little sister.
At night, her hair grows long. Her specialty is love magic. She doesn't have any familiars, but a small dragon (the one Mao summoned in the last chapter) is her pet.

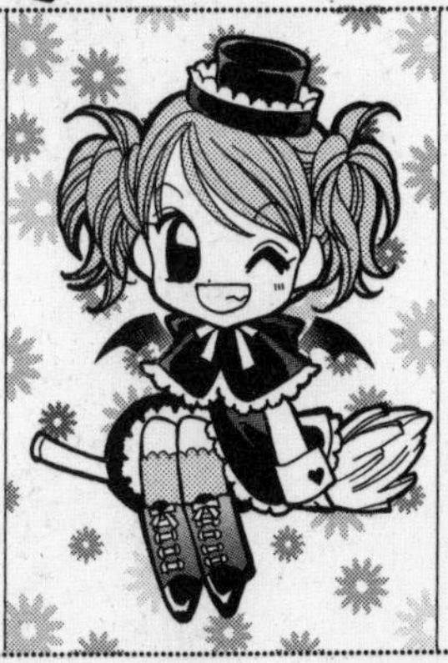

Unlike her brother, she's very levelheaded, and she's a powerful magic master. Maybe it's because of that, but she tries to get everything she wants by using magic! Her personality is strong, and she can be devilish sometimes. She likes being the pursuer in romantic relationships instead of waiting for guys to come to her.

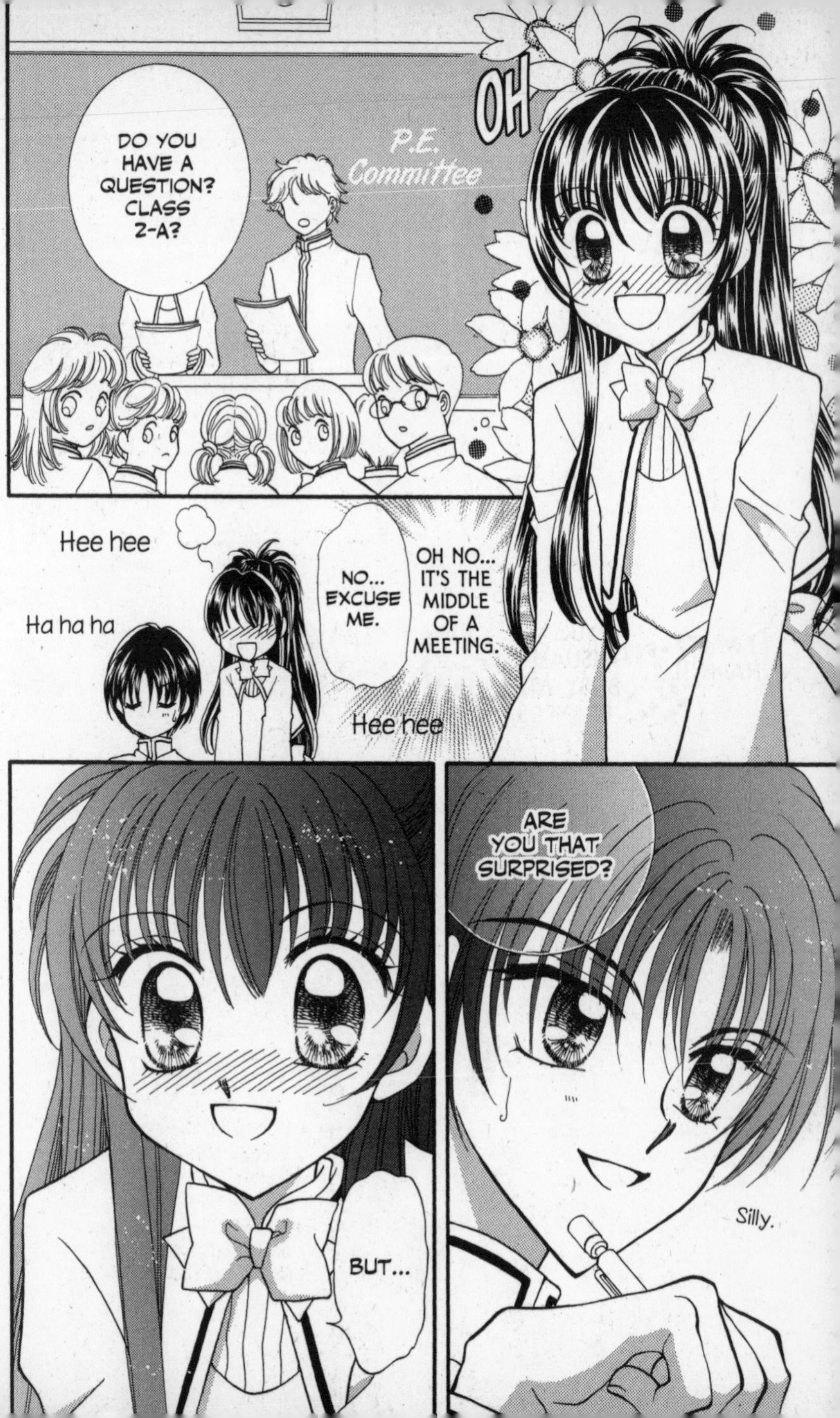
OH
DO YOU HAVE A QUESTION? CLASS 2-A?
P.E. Committee
OH NO... IT'S THE MIDDLE OF A MEETING.
NO... EXCUSE ME.
Hee hee
Ha ha ha
Hee hee
ARE YOU THAT SURPRISED?
Silly.
BUT...

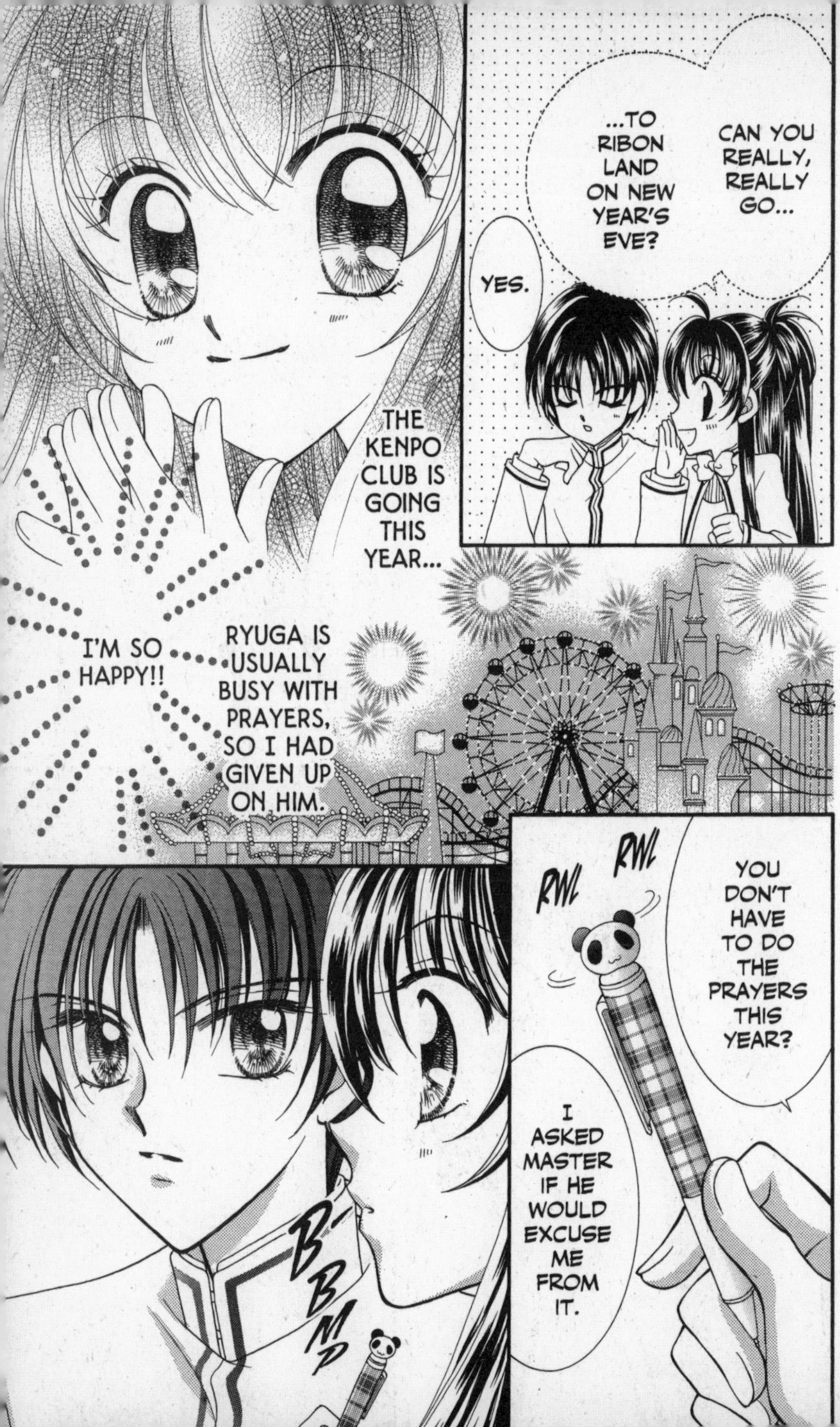
CAN YOU REALLY, REALLY GO...
...TO RIBON LAND ON NEW YEAR'S EVE?
YES.
THE KENPO CLUB IS GOING THIS YEAR...
RYUGA IS USUALLY BUSY WITH PRAYERS, SO I HAD GIVEN UP ON HIM.
I'M SO HAPPY!!
RWL
RWL
YOU DON'T HAVE TO DO THE PRAYERS THIS YEAR?
I ASKED MASTER IF HE WOULD EXCUSE ME FROM IT.
B-BMP

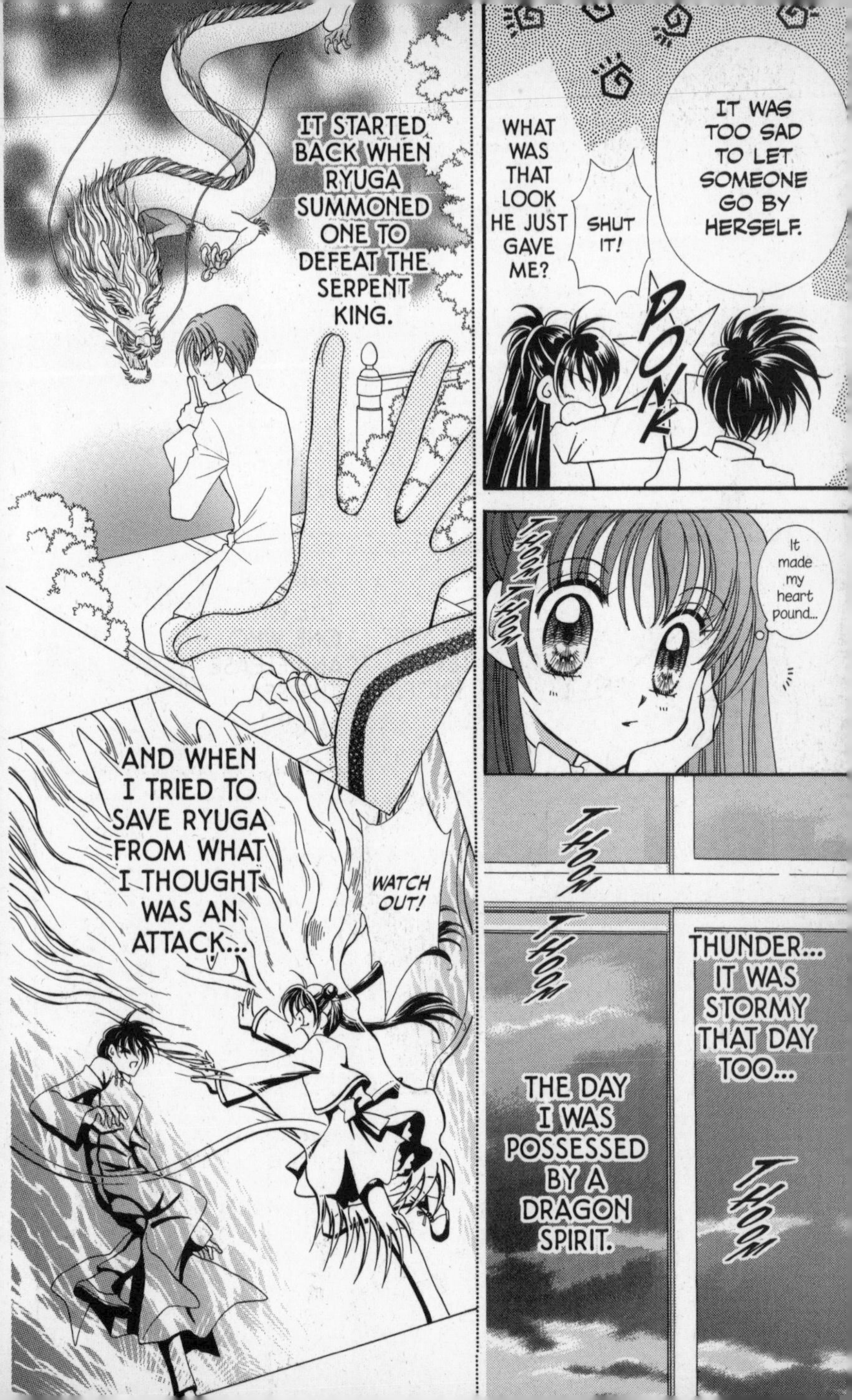
IT WAS TOO SAD TO LET SOMEONE GO BY HERSELF.
WHAT WAS THAT LOOK HE JUST GAVE ME?
SHUT IT!
PONK
THOOM THOOM
It made my heart pound...
THOOM
THUNDER... IT WAS STORMY THAT DAY TOO...
THOOM
THE DAY I WAS POSSESSED BY A DRAGON SPIRIT.
THOOM
IT STARTED BACK WHEN RYUGA SUMMONED ONE TO DEFEAT THE SERPENT KING.
AND WHEN I TRIED TO SAVE RYUGA FROM WHAT I THOUGHT WAS AN ATTACK...
WATCH OUT!

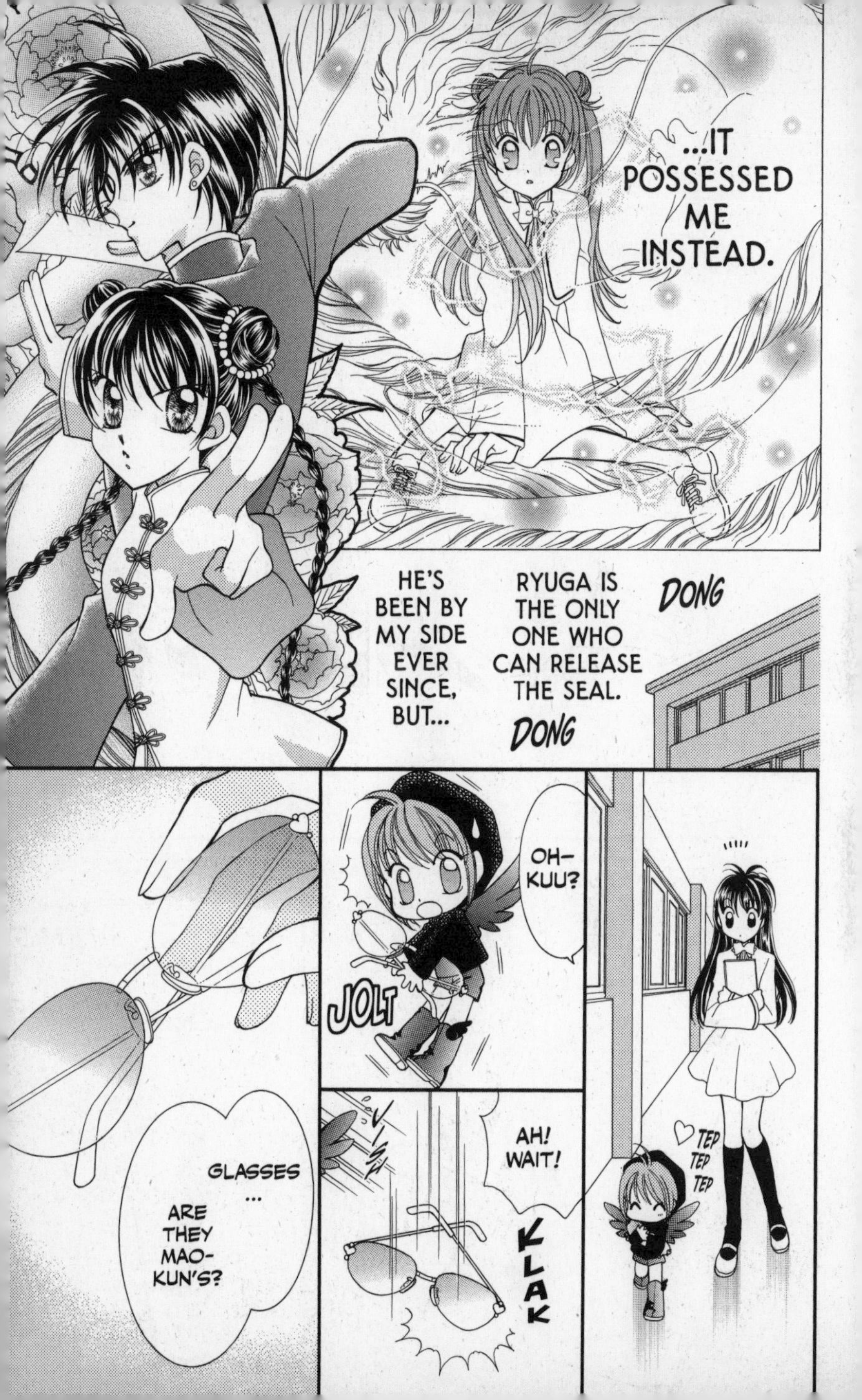
...IT POSSESSED ME INSTEAD.
DONG
RYUGA IS THE ONLY ONE WHO CAN RELEASE THE SEAL.
HE'S BEEN BY MY SIDE EVER SINCE, BUT...
DONG
TEP TEP TEP
OH-KUU?
JOLT
AH! WAIT!
KLAK
GLASSES ... ARE THEY MAO-KUN'S?

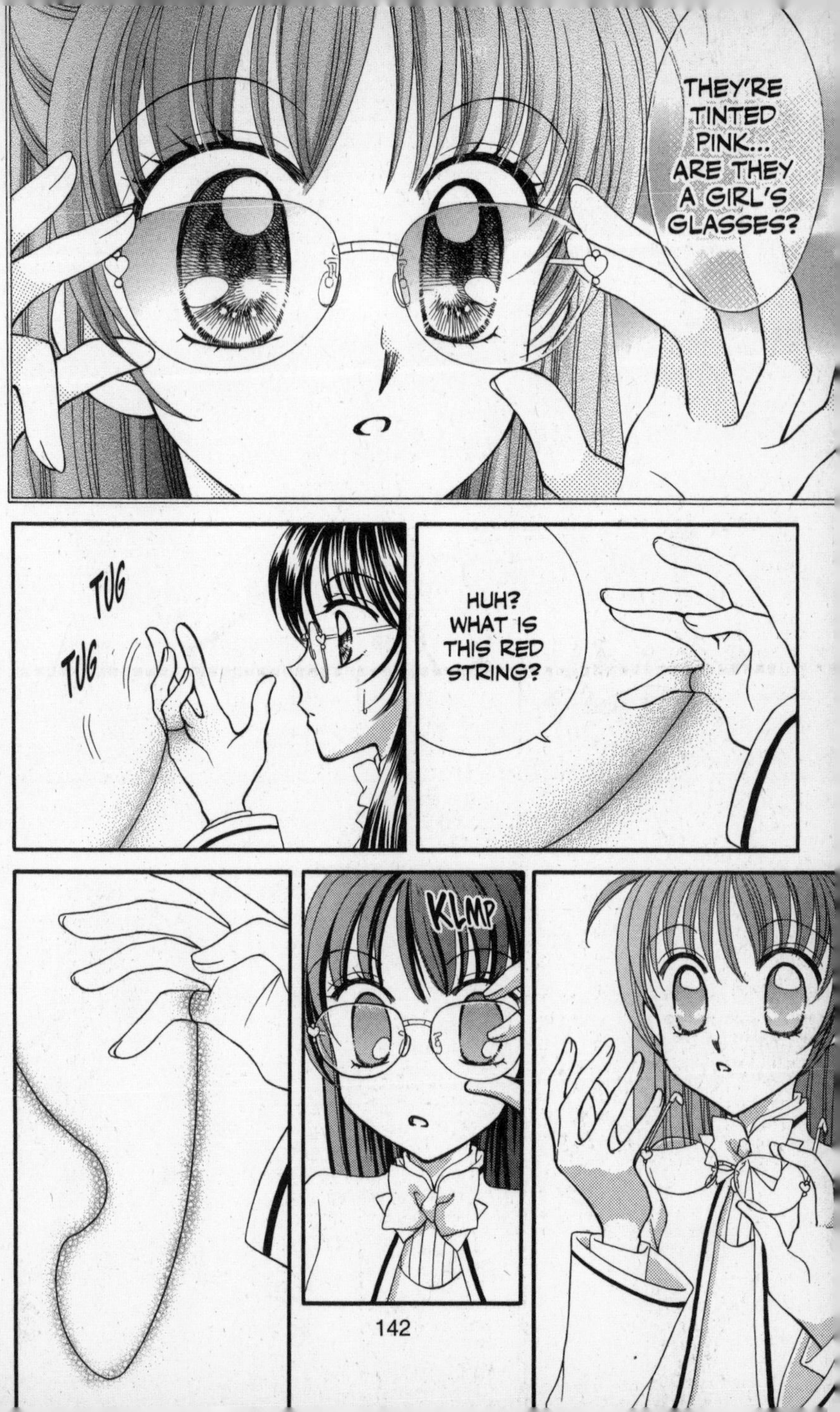
THEY'RE TINTED PINK... ARE THEY A GIRL'S GLASSES?
HUH? WHAT IS THIS RED STRING?
TUG
TUG
KLMP

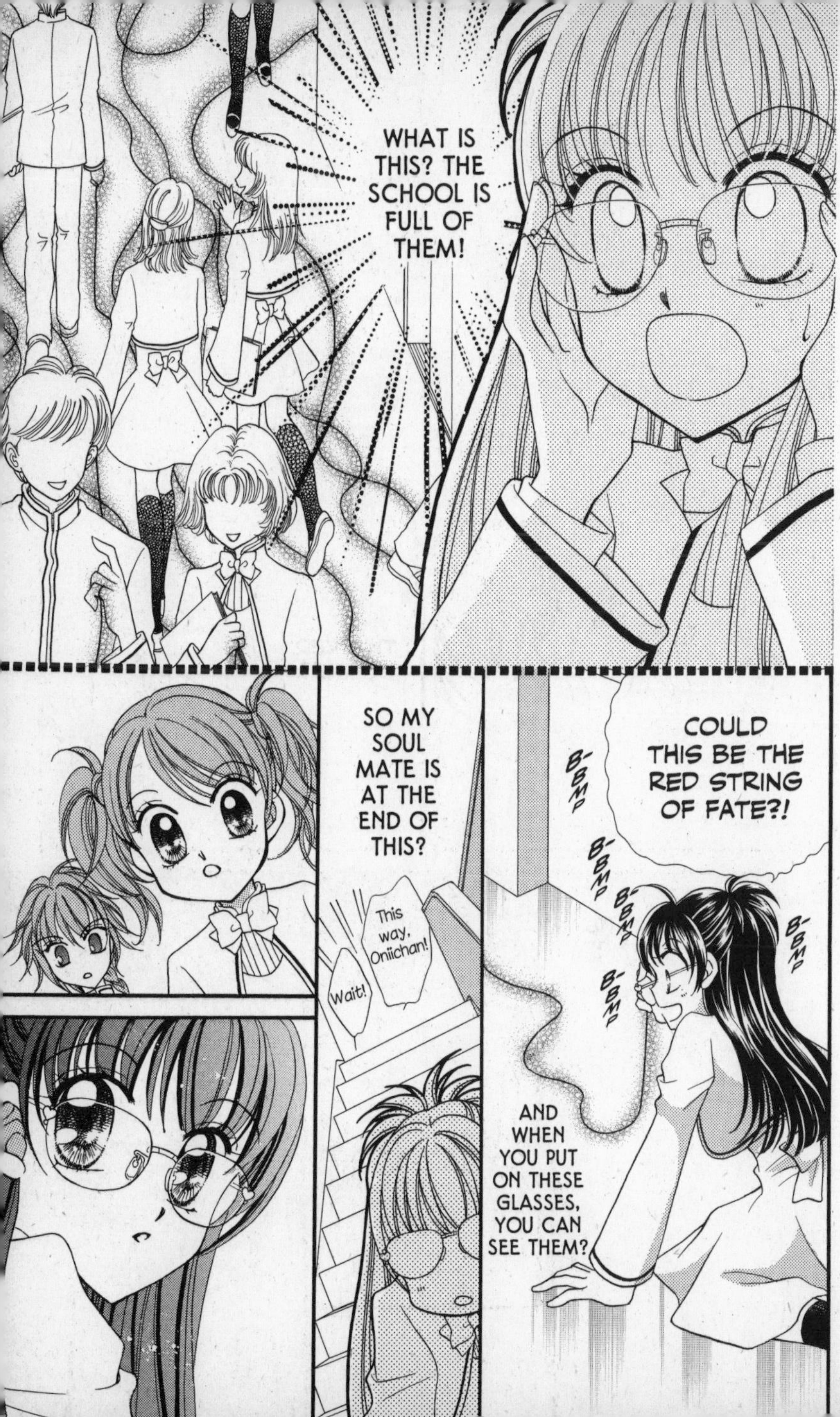
WHAT IS THIS? THE SCHOOL IS FULL OF THEM!
COULD THIS BE THE RED STRING OF FATE?!
B-BMP
B-BMP
B-BMP
B-BMP
B-BMP
AND WHEN YOU PUT ON THESE GLASSES, YOU CAN SEE THEM?
SO MY SOUL MATE IS AT THE END OF THIS?
This way, Oniichan!
Wait!

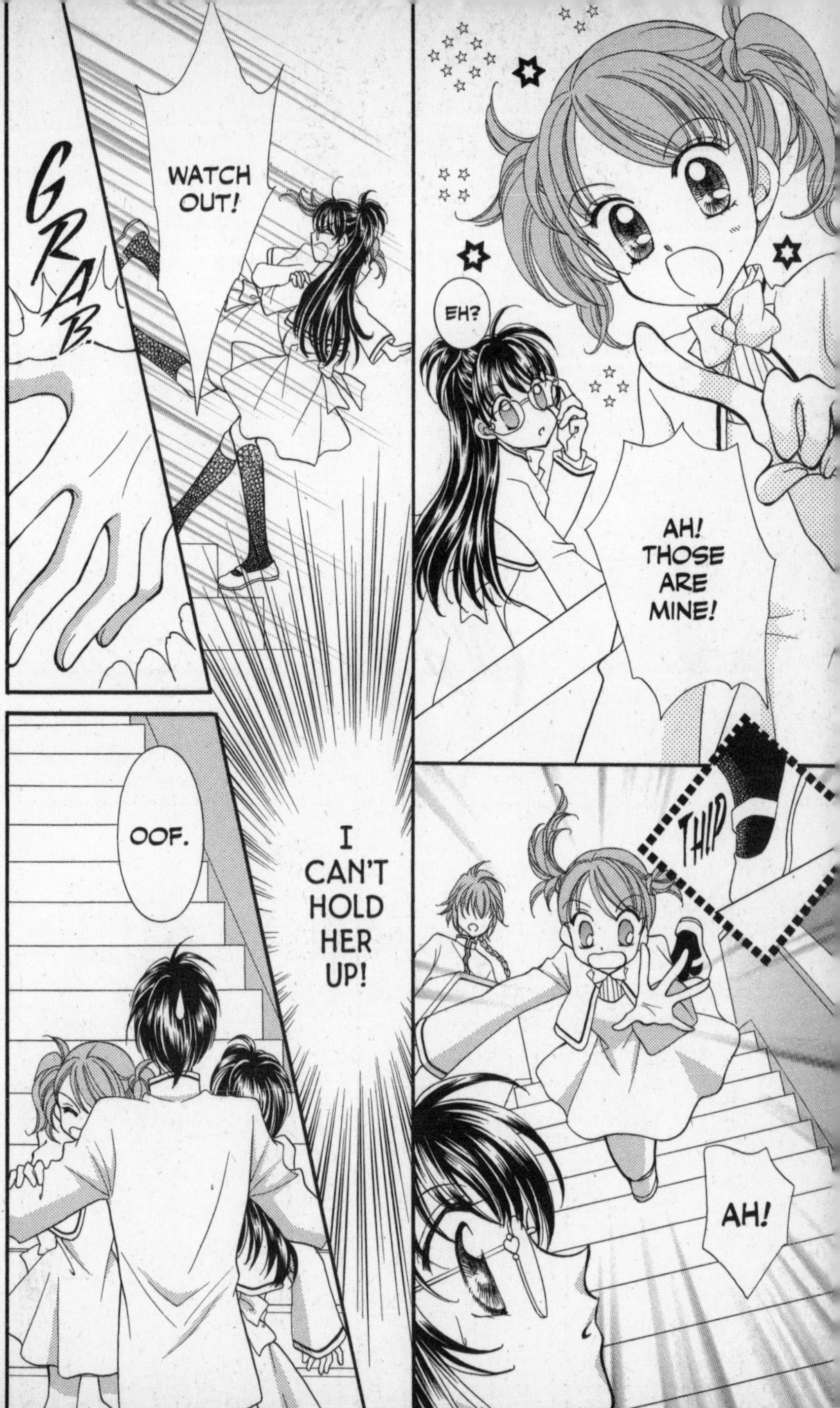
EH?
AH! THOSE ARE MINE!
THIP
AH!
WATCH OUT!
GRAB.
I CAN'T HOLD HER UP!
OOF.

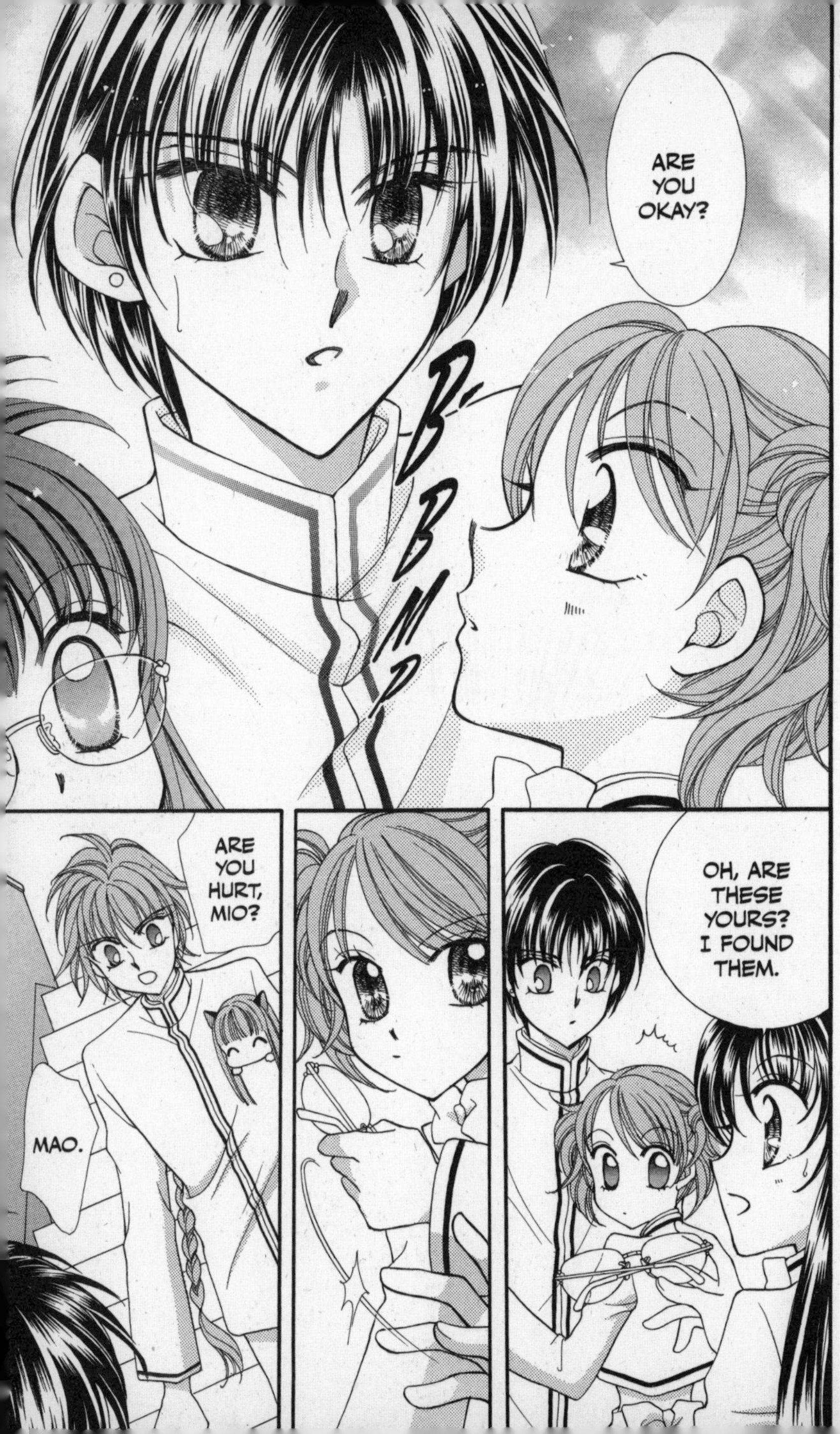
ARE YOU OKAY?
B-BMP
OH, ARE THESE YOURS? I FOUND THEM.
ARE YOU HURT, MIO?
MAO.

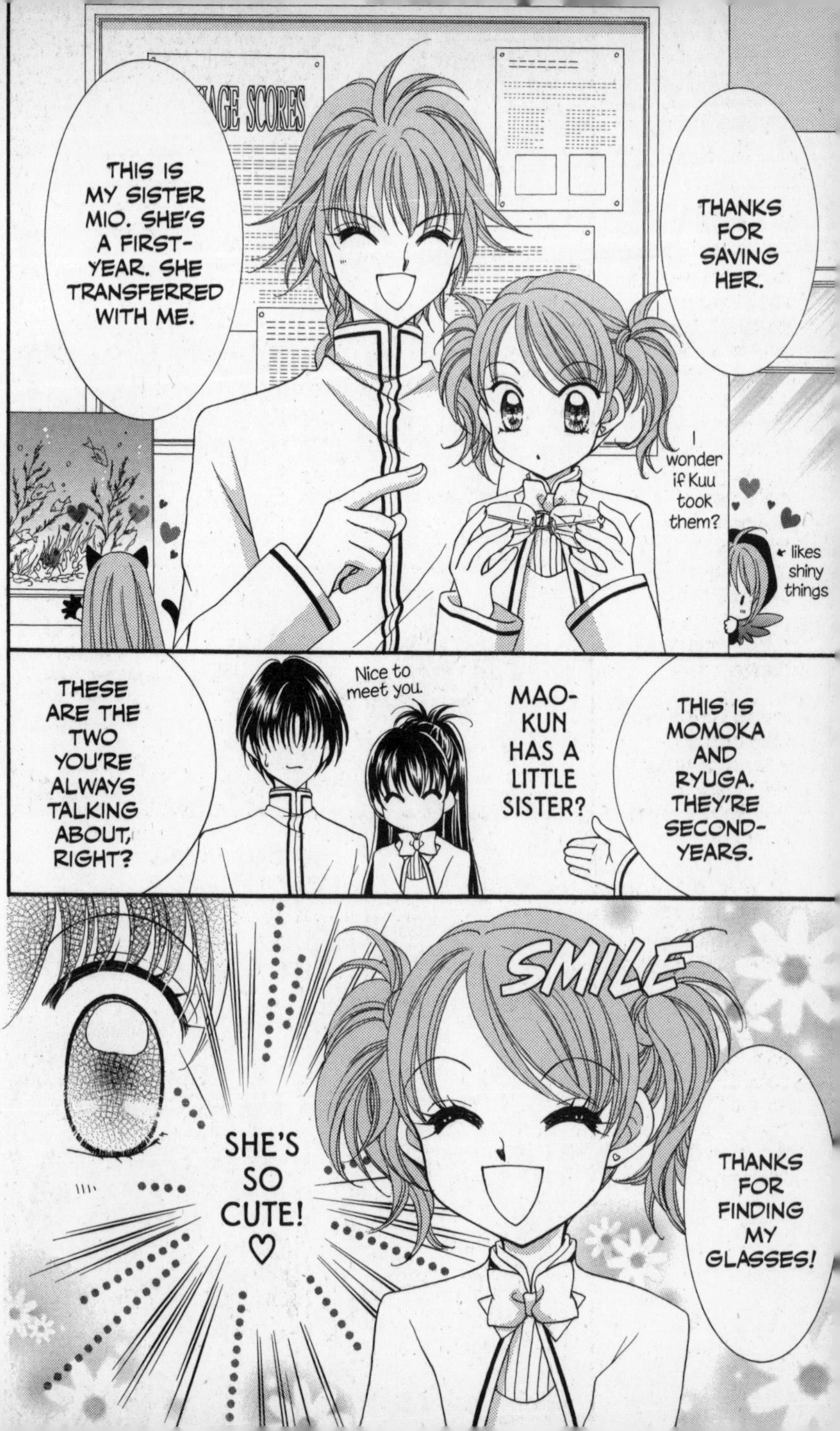
THIS IS MY SISTER MIO. SHE'S A FIRST-YEAR. SHE TRANSFERRED WITH ME.
THANKS FOR SAVING HER.
I wonder if Kuu took them?
likes shiny things
THIS IS MOMOKA AND RYUGA. THEY'RE SECOND-YEARS.
MAO-KUN HAS A LITTLE SISTER?
Nice to meet you.
THESE ARE THE TWO YOU'RE ALWAYS TALKING ABOUT, RIGHT?
THANKS FOR FINDING MY GLASSES!
SMILE
SHE'S SO CUTE! ♡

13

About characters I like... I really like Kouryu.♥ I haven't used him since this became a regular series though. But I get a lot of requests to draw him more. But he appears in this volume in a comic! Readers thought up those comics, but he's still arrogant as usual. It made me really happy.

I really like Kouryu's little brother, Houyru, but I don't think I have room for him in the story from now on.

Oh yeah, and there is also a comic involving Akira. Please read it.

There are a lot of popular characters I don't have room to put in anymore. Maybe I'll draw them in short bonus comics from now on?

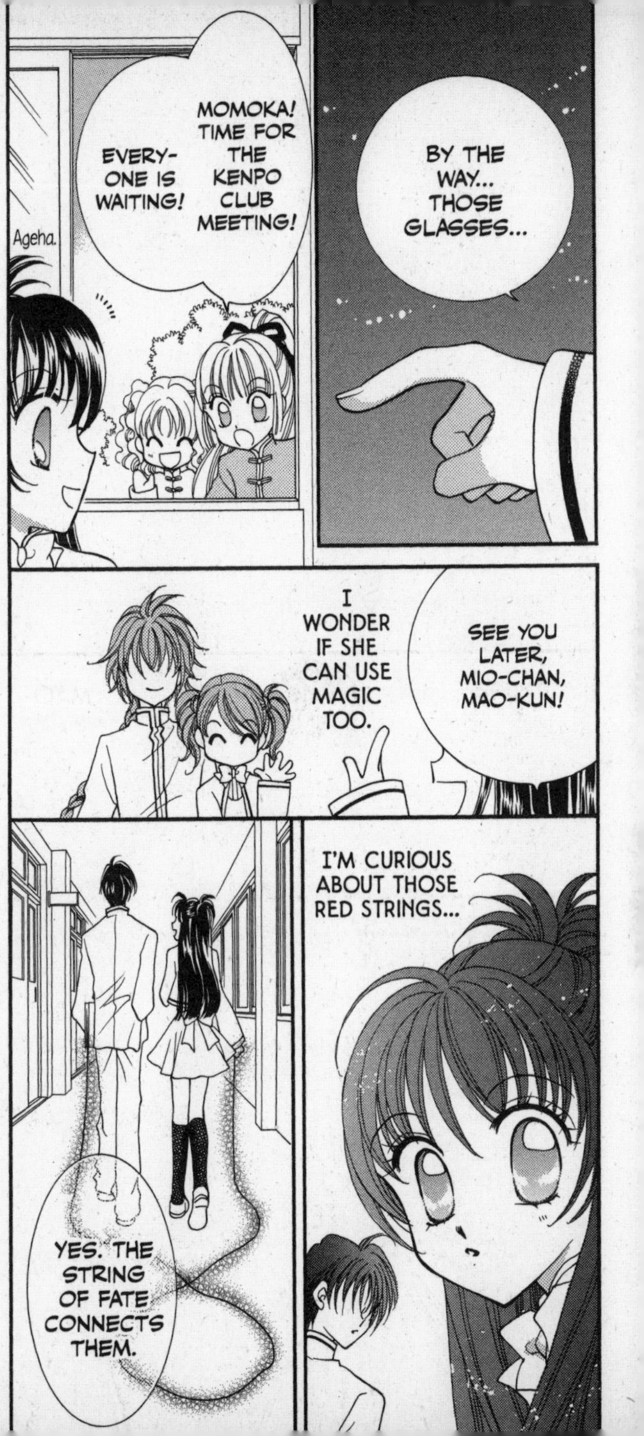
BY THE WAY... THOSE GLASSES...
MOMOKA! TIME FOR THE KENPO CLUB MEETING!
EVERY-ONE IS WAITING!
Ageha.
SEE YOU LATER, MIO-CHAN, MAO-KUN!
I WONDER IF SHE CAN USE MAGIC TOO.
I'M CURIOUS ABOUT THOSE RED STRINGS...
YES. THE STRING OF FATE CONNECTS THEM.

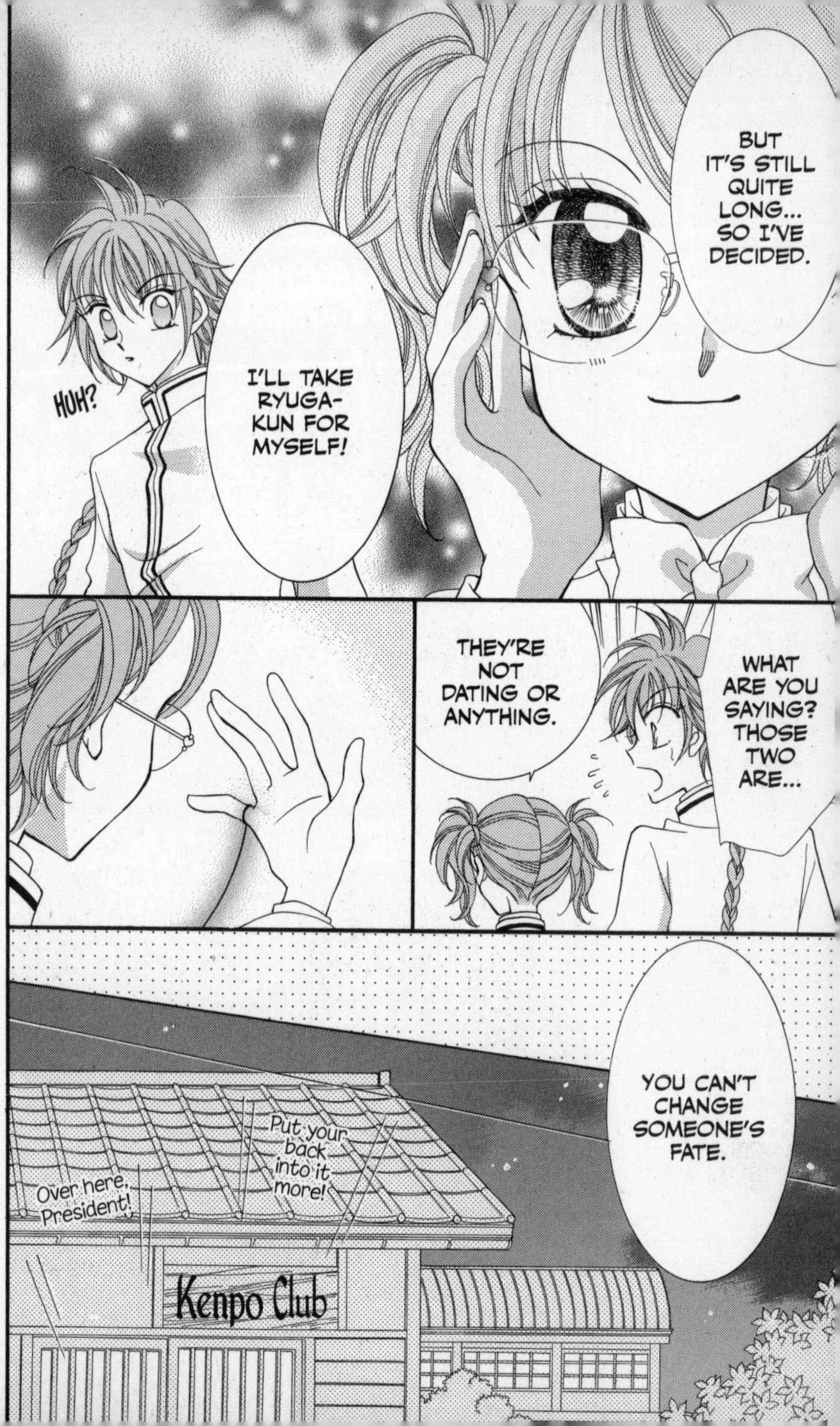
BUT IT'S STILL QUITE LONG... SO I'VE DECIDED.
I'LL TAKE RYUGA-KUN FOR MYSELF!
HUH?
WHAT ARE YOU SAYING? THOSE TWO ARE...
THEY'RE NOT DATING OR ANYTHING.
YOU CAN'T CHANGE SOMEONE'S FATE.
Put your back into it more!
Over here, President!
Kenpo Club

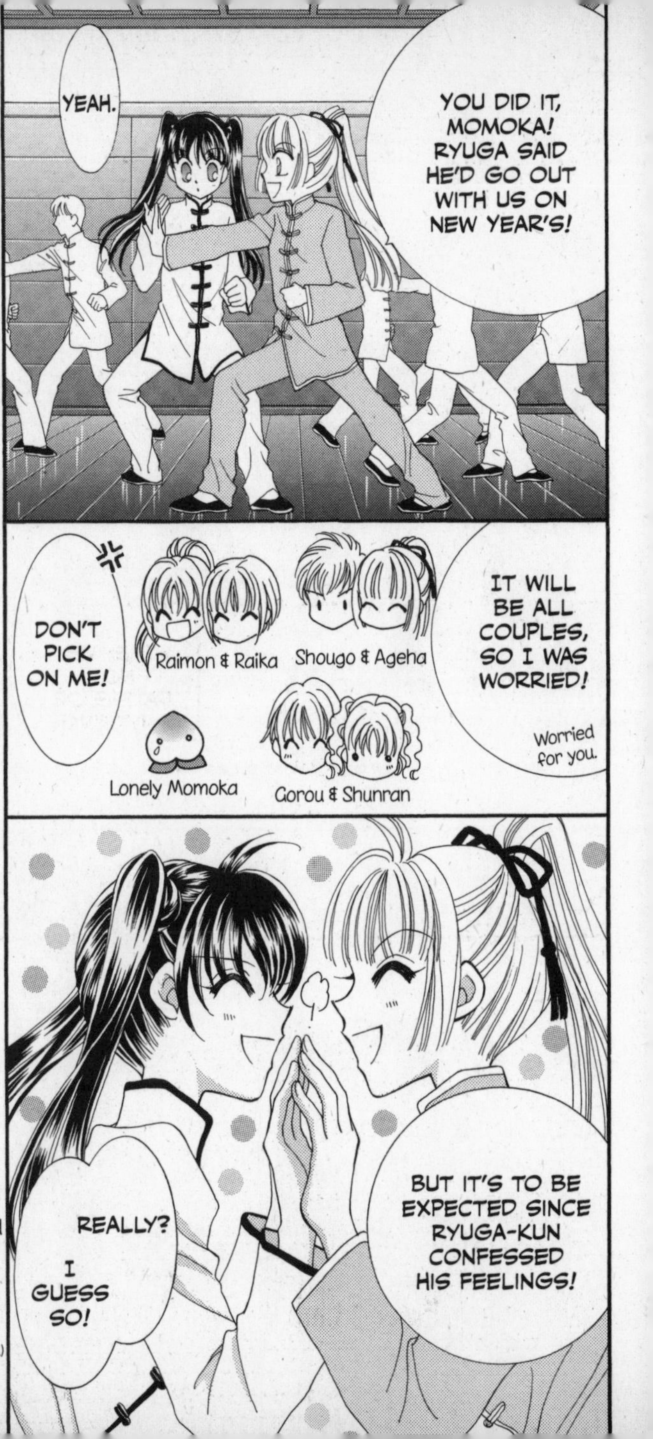
YOU DID IT, MOMOKA! RYUGA SAID HE'D GO OUT WITH US ON NEW YEAR'S!
YEAH.
IT WILL BE ALL COUPLES, SO I WAS WORRIED!
Worried for you.
Shougo & Ageha
Raimon & Raika
Gorou & Shunran
Lonely Momoka
DON'T PICK ON ME!
BUT IT'S TO BE EXPECTED SINCE RYUGA-KUN CONFESSED HIS FEELINGS!
REALLY?
I GUESS SO!

14

This is when Mio first appears, but now that I've brought up the "red string of fate" legend, doesn't it seem more like a shojo manga?

I researched this legend a lot, and it seems its origins are in China and Japan.

In China, the story goes that an old person put a piece of red rope in a bag, and any girl and boy who got their ankles tied up with that rope would marry in the future. So it's called "the red rope of fate," not "the red string of fate."

In Japan, there was a girl who got pregnant, but she wasn't married. When she investigated, she found out a guy kept sneaking in every night. She tried to find out his identity, and noticed a red thread had unraveled from his kimono. She decided to follow it the next day...

(Continues...)

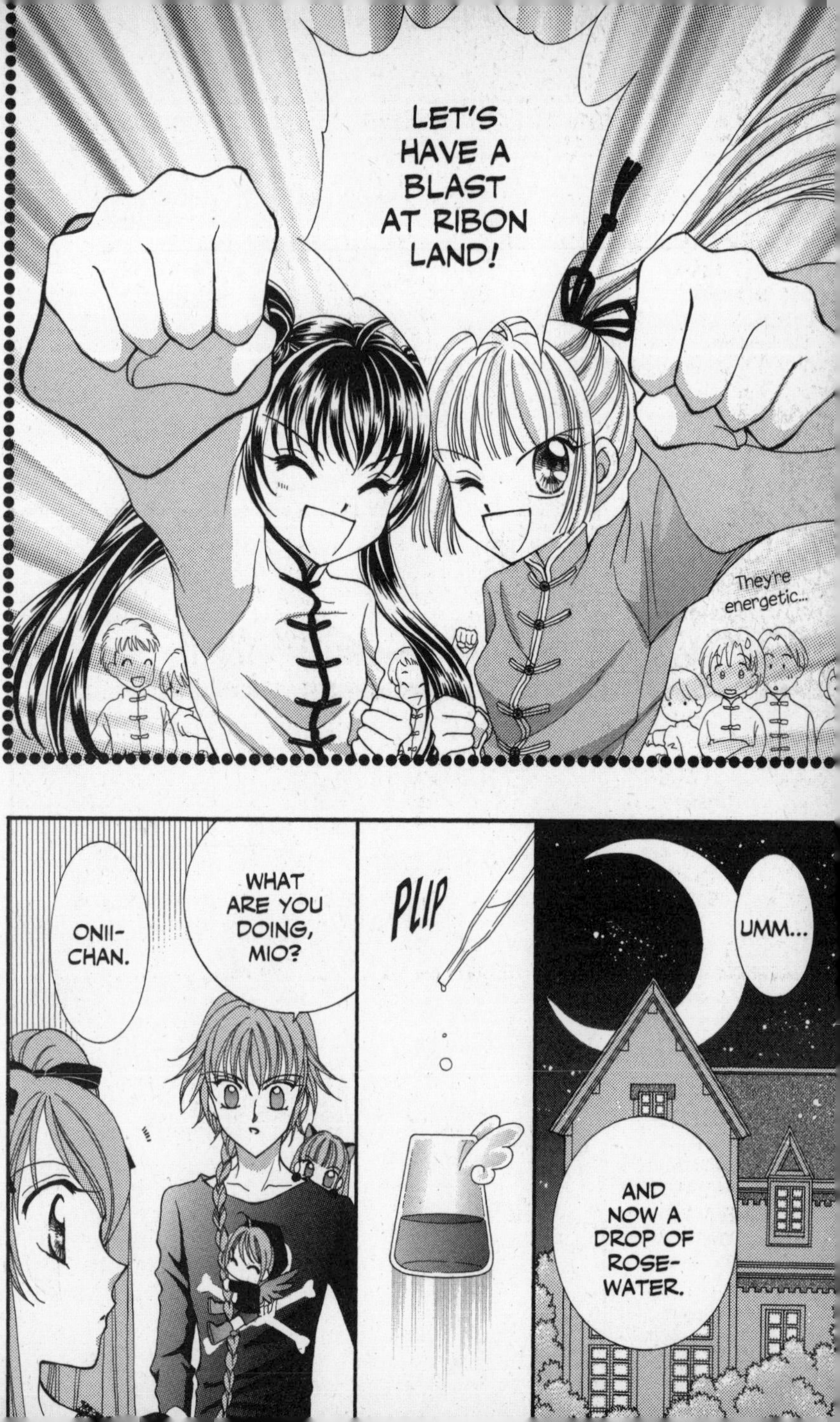
LET'S HAVE A BLAST AT RIBON LAND!
They're energetic...
UMM...
AND NOW A DROP OF ROSE-WATER.
PLIP
WHAT ARE YOU DOING, MIO?
ONII-CHAN.

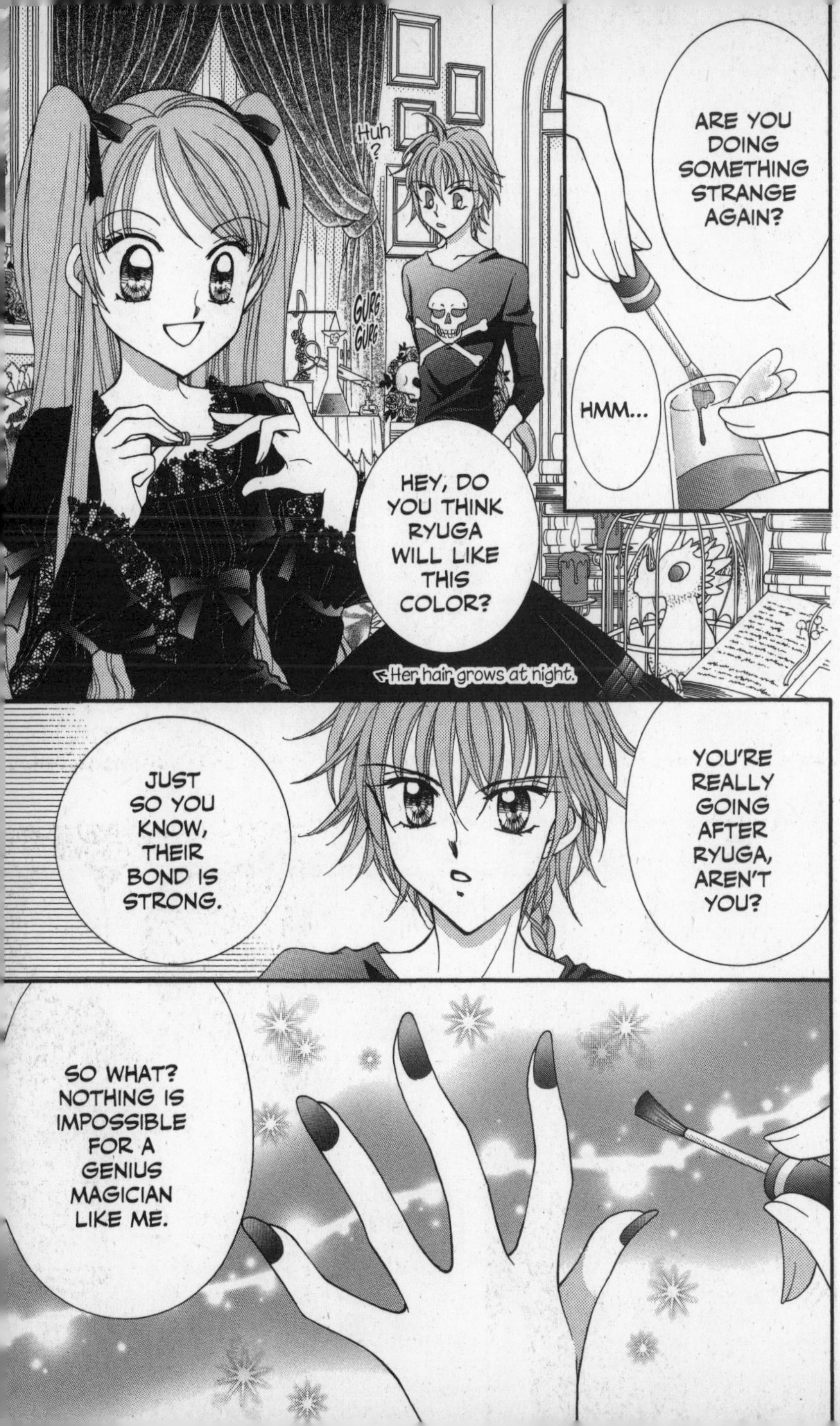
ARE YOU DOING SOMETHING STRANGE AGAIN?
HMM...
Huh?
GURG GURG
HEY, DO YOU THINK RYUGA WILL LIKE THIS COLOR?
Her hair grows at night.
YOU'RE REALLY GOING AFTER RYUGA, AREN'T YOU?
JUST SO YOU KNOW, THEIR BOND IS STRONG.
SO WHAT? NOTHING IS IMPOSSIBLE FOR A GENIUS MAGICIAN LIKE ME.

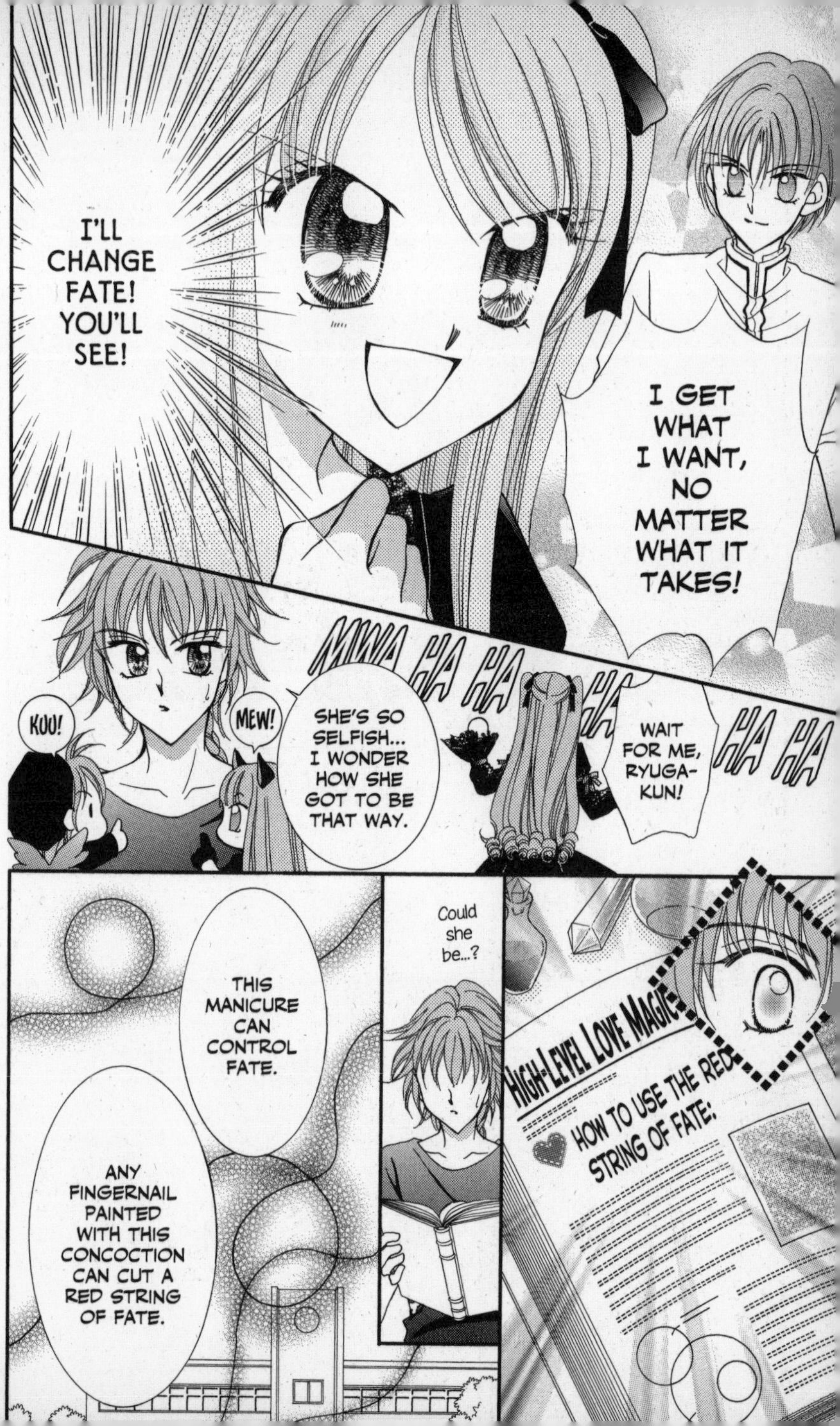
I GET WHAT I WANT, NO MATTER WHAT IT TAKES!
I'LL CHANGE FATE! YOU'LL SEE!
MWA HA HA HA HA HA
WAIT FOR ME, RYUGA-KUN!
SHE'S SO SELFISH... I WONDER HOW SHE GOT TO BE THAT WAY.
MEW!
KUU!
HIGH-LEVEL LOVE MAGIC
HOW TO USE THE RED STRING OF FATE:
Could she be...?
THIS MANICURE CAN CONTROL FATE.
ANY FINGERNAIL PAINTED WITH THIS CONCOCTION CAN CUT A RED STRING OF FATE.

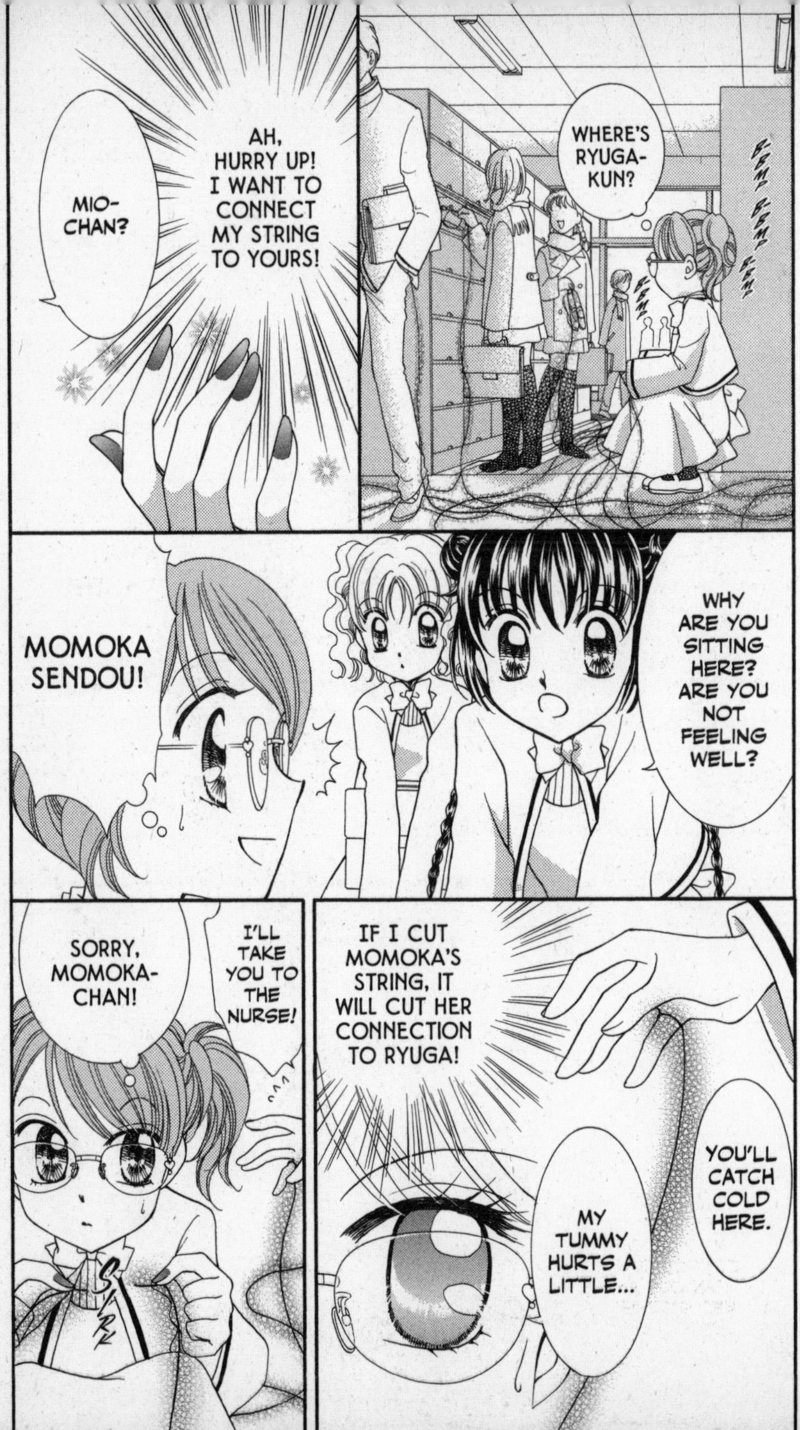
WHERE'S RYUGA-KUN?
AH, HURRY UP! I WANT TO CONNECT MY STRING TO YOURS!
MIO-CHAN?
WHY ARE YOU SITTING HERE? ARE YOU NOT FEELING WELL?
MOMOKA SENDOU!
IF I CUT MOMOKA'S STRING, IT WILL CUT HER CONNECTION TO RYUGA!
YOU'LL CATCH COLD HERE.
MY TUMMY HURTS A LITTLE...
I'LL TAKE YOU TO THE NURSE!
SORRY, MOMOKA-CHAN!

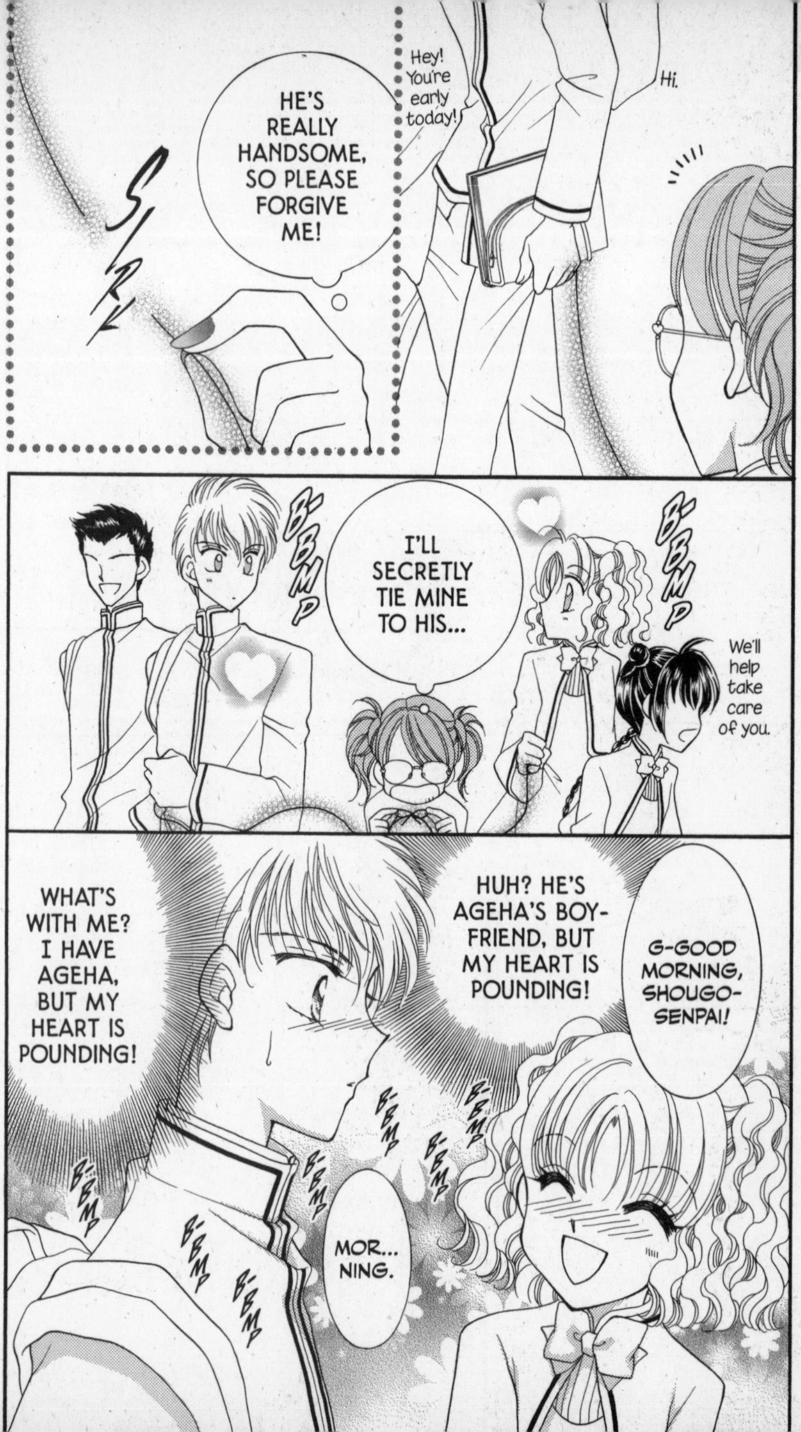
Hey! You're early today!
Hi.
HE'S REALLY HANDSOME, SO PLEASE FORGIVE ME!
SIRK
B-BMP
We'll help take care of you.
I'LL SECRETLY TIE MINE TO HIS...
B-BMP
G-GOOD MORNING, SHOUGO-SENPAI!
HUH? HE'S AGEHA'S BOY-FRIEND, BUT MY HEART IS POUNDING!
WHAT'S WITH ME? I HAVE AGEHA, BUT MY HEART IS POUNDING!
B-BMP
B-BMP
B-BMP
MOR... NING.
B-BMP
B-BMP
B-BMP
B-BMP

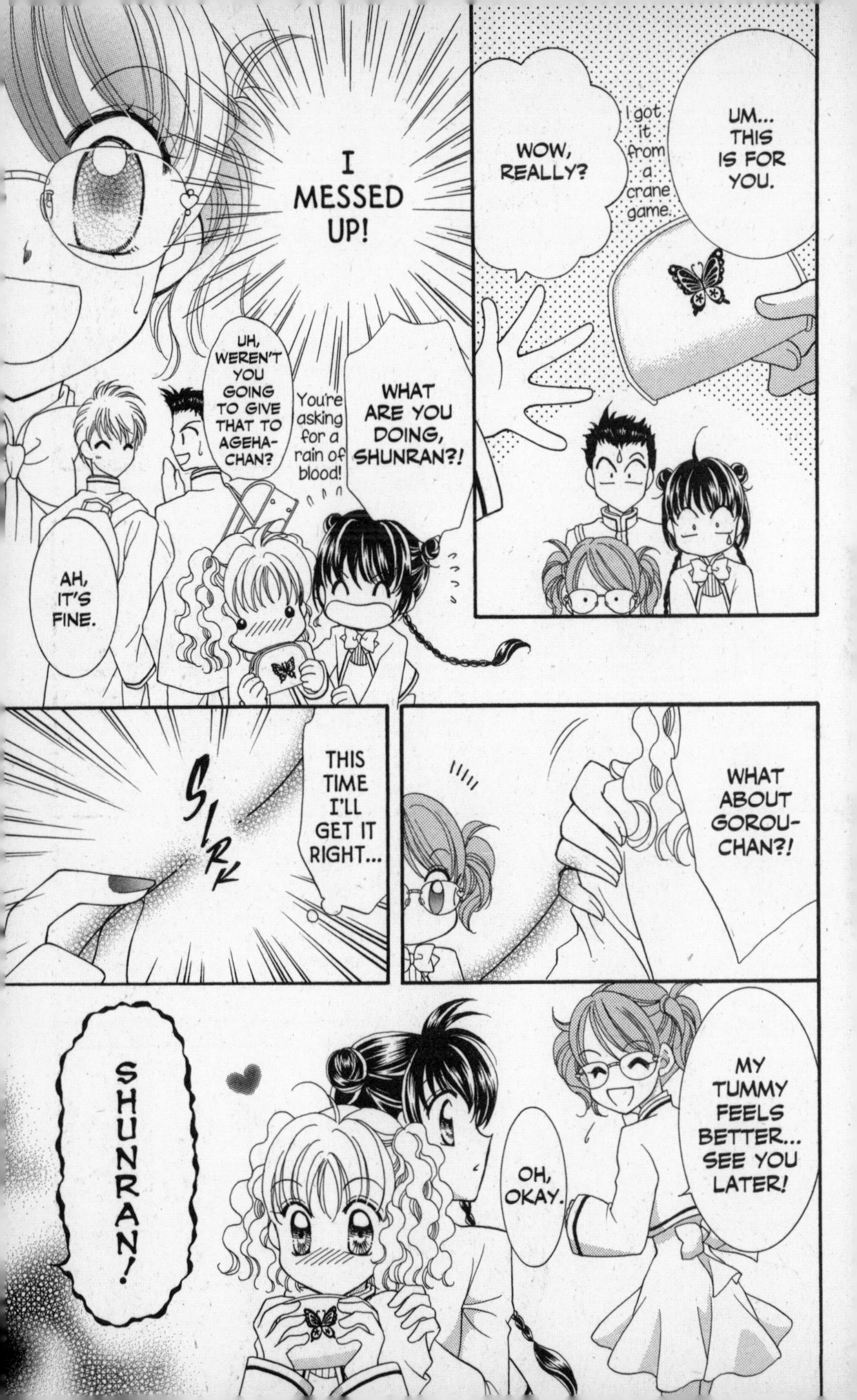
UM... THIS IS FOR YOU.
I got it from a crane game.
WOW, REALLY?
I MESSED UP!
WHAT ARE YOU DOING, SHUNRAN?!
You're asking for a rain of blood!
UH, WEREN'T YOU GOING TO GIVE THAT TO AGEHA-CHAN?
AH, IT'S FINE.
WHAT ABOUT GOROU-CHAN?!
THIS TIME I'LL GET IT RIGHT...
SIRK
MY TUMMY FEELS BETTER... SEE YOU LATER!
OH, OKAY.
SHUNRAN!

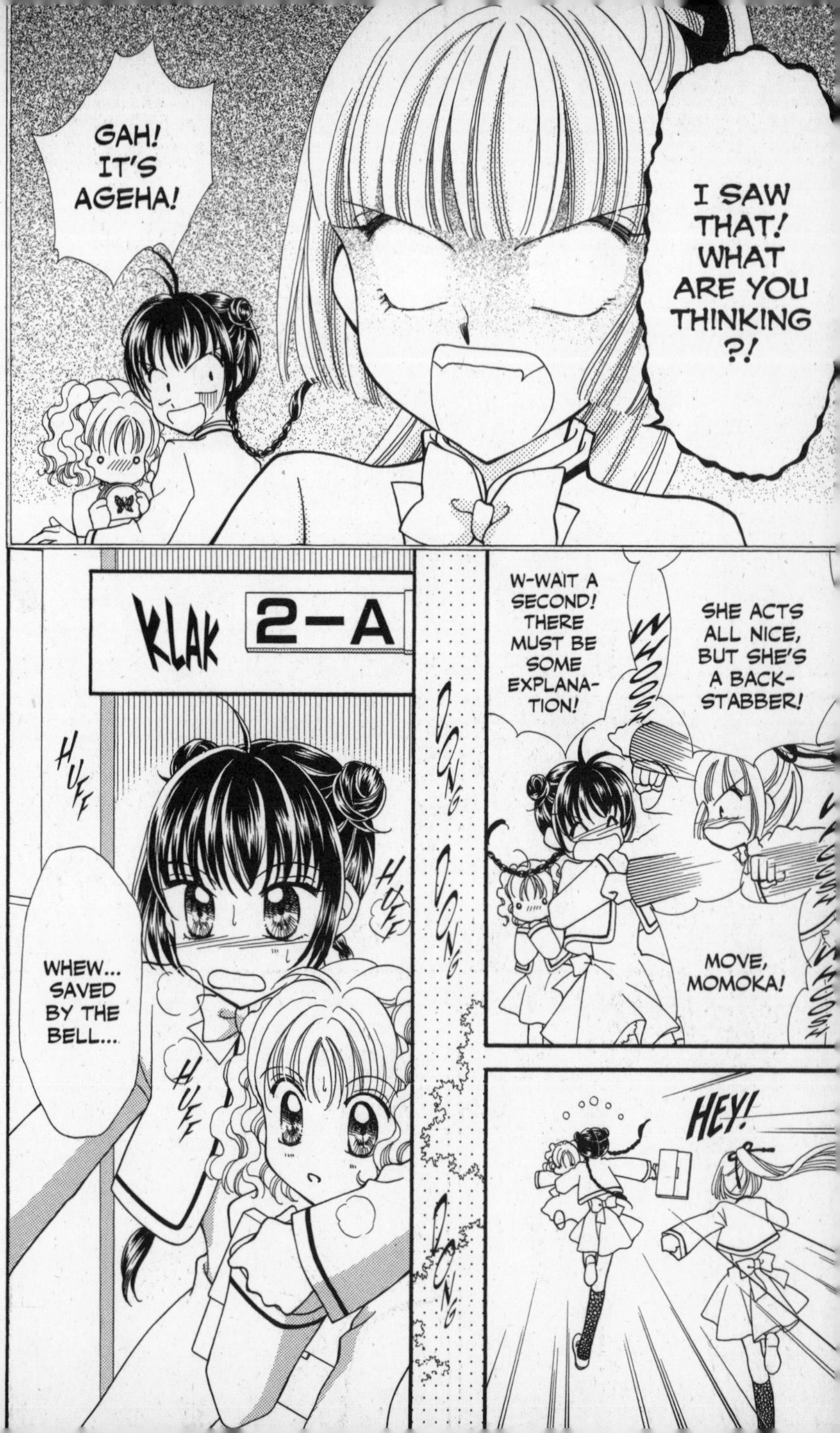
I SAW THAT! WHAT ARE YOU THINKING ?!
GAH! IT'S AGEHA!
SHE ACTS ALL NICE, BUT SHE'S A BACK-STABBER!
W-WAIT A SECOND! THERE MUST BE SOME EXPLANA-TION!
MOVE, MOMOKA!
HEY!
DONG DONG DONG
2-A
KLAK
HUFF
HUFF
HUFF
WHEW... SAVED BY THE BELL...

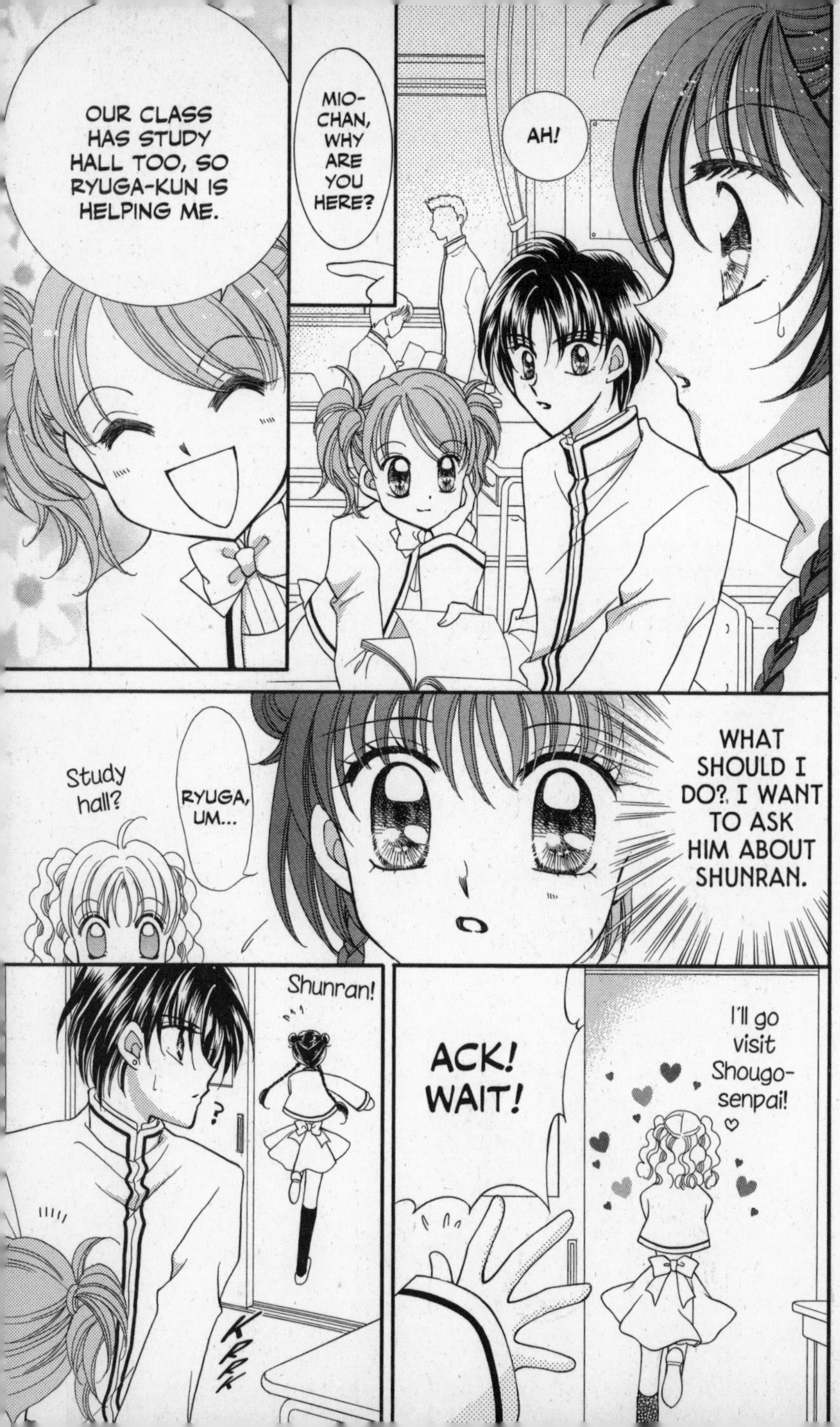
AH!
MIO-CHAN, WHY ARE YOU HERE?
OUR CLASS HAS STUDY HALL TOO, SO RYUGA-KUN IS HELPING ME.
WHAT SHOULD I DO?. I WANT TO ASK HIM ABOUT SHUNRAN.
RYUGA, UM...
Study hall?
I'll go visit Shougo-senpai!
ACK! WAIT!
Shunran!
?
KRRK

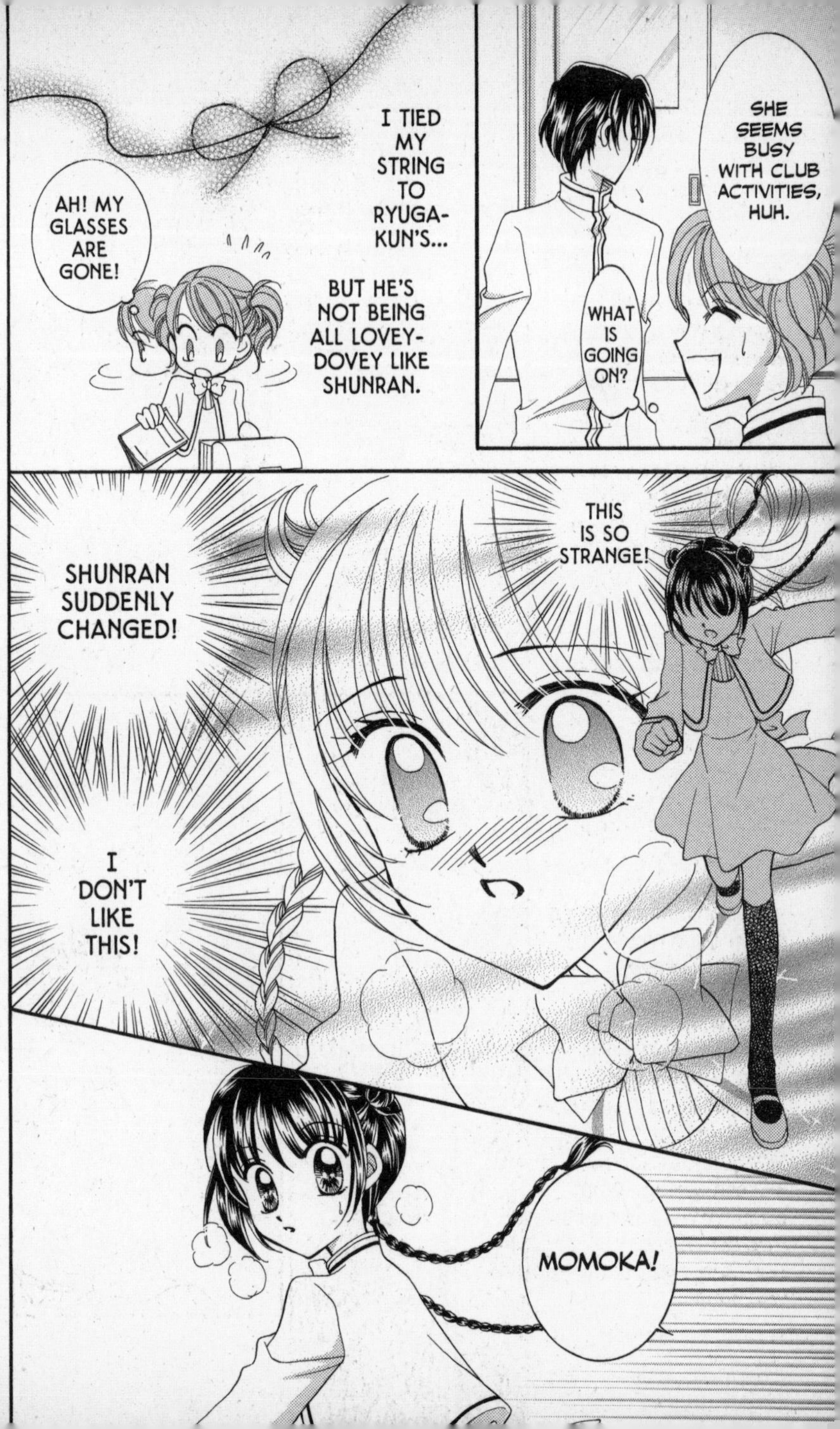
SHE SEEMS BUSY WITH CLUB ACTIVITIES, HUH.
WHAT IS GOING ON?
I TIED MY STRING TO RYUGA-KUN'S...
BUT HE'S NOT BEING ALL LOVEY-DOVEY LIKE SHUNRAN.
AH! MY GLASSES ARE GONE!
THIS IS SO STRANGE!
SHUNRAN SUDDENLY CHANGED!
I DON'T LIKE THIS!
MOMOKA!

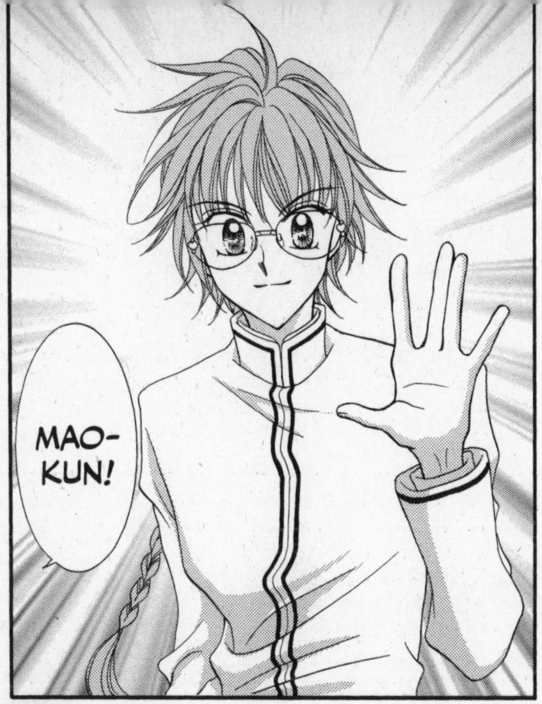
MAO-KUN!

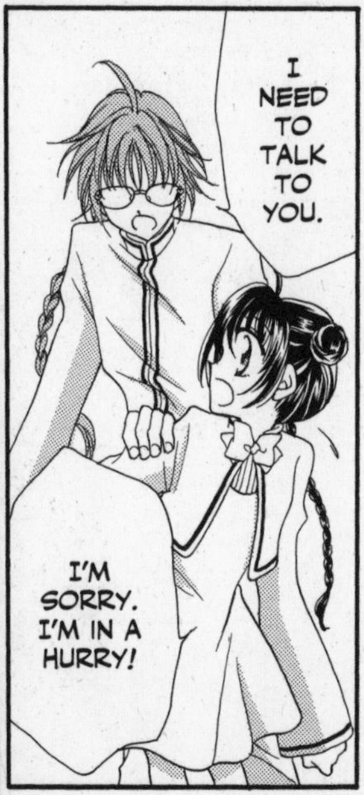
I NEED TO TALK TO YOU.
I'M SORRY. I'M IN A HURRY!

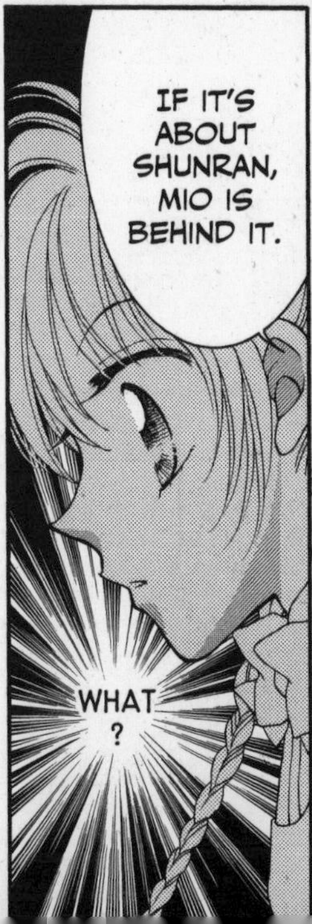
IF IT'S ABOUT SHUNRAN, MIO IS BEHIND IT.
WHAT?

15

So she follows the thread all the way up Miwayama, and she finds out he's actually a god! There are other variations of the story, but that's basically the one that "the red string of fate" legend comes from. But I really thought it was from Western folklore.

In the Chinese legend, it says no matter how old they are, no matter how different they are, no matter how wide the class difference, they'll be together one day. Am I the only one who thinks that's more scary than romantic? If you could see your own red string, what would you do? I'd probably follow mine! What would I do if it was someone famous? ♥ But that won't happen. Sorry. I got a lot of letters asking, "What about Mio's soul mate?" He's coming up! Heh. Just wait until volume 8!

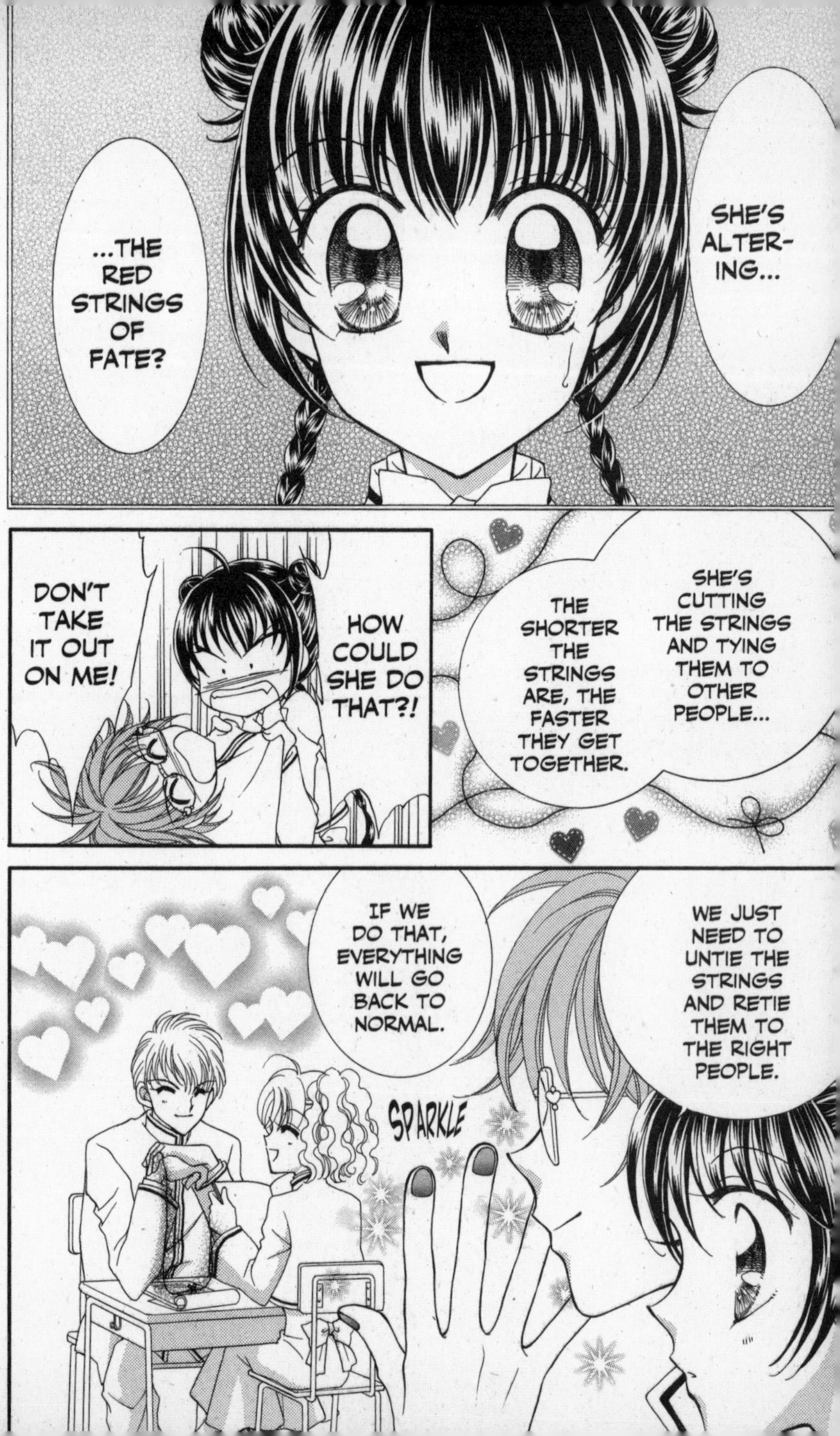
SHE'S ALTERING...
...THE RED STRINGS OF FATE?
SHE'S CUTTING THE STRINGS AND TYING THEM TO OTHER PEOPLE...
THE SHORTER THE STRINGS ARE, THE FASTER THEY GET TOGETHER.
HOW COULD SHE DO THAT?!
DON'T TAKE IT OUT ON ME!
WE JUST NEED TO UNTIE THE STRINGS AND RETIE THEM TO THE RIGHT PEOPLE.
IF WE DO THAT, EVERYTHING WILL GO BACK TO NORMAL.
SPARKLE

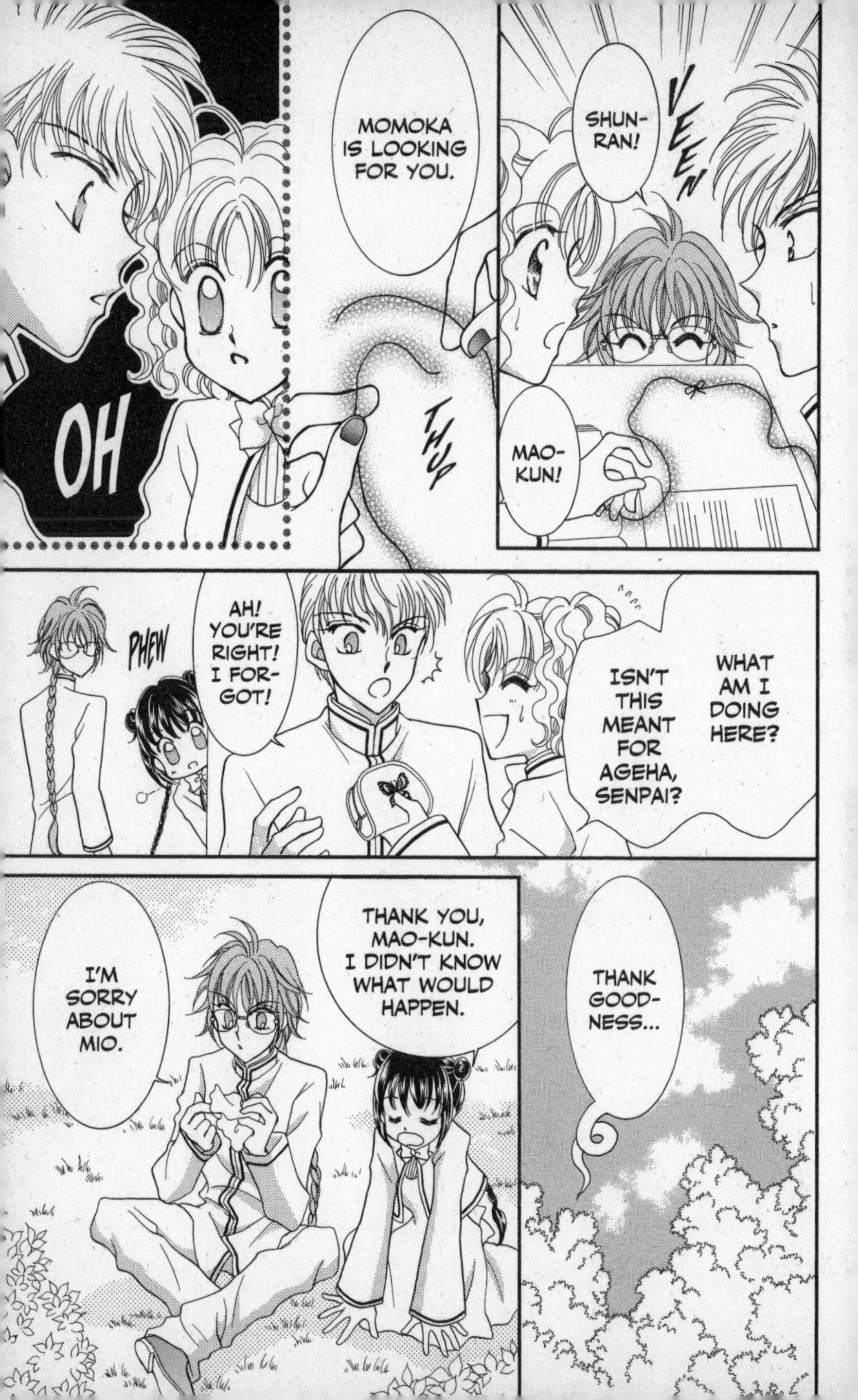
SHUN-RAN!
VEEN
MAO-KUN!
MOMOKA IS LOOKING FOR YOU.
THUP
OH
WHAT AM I DOING HERE?
ISN'T THIS MEANT FOR AGEHA, SENPAI?
AH! YOU'RE RIGHT! I FOR-GOT!
PHEW
THANK GOOD-NESS...
THANK YOU, MAO-KUN. I DIDN'T KNOW WHAT WOULD HAPPEN.
I'M SORRY ABOUT MIO.

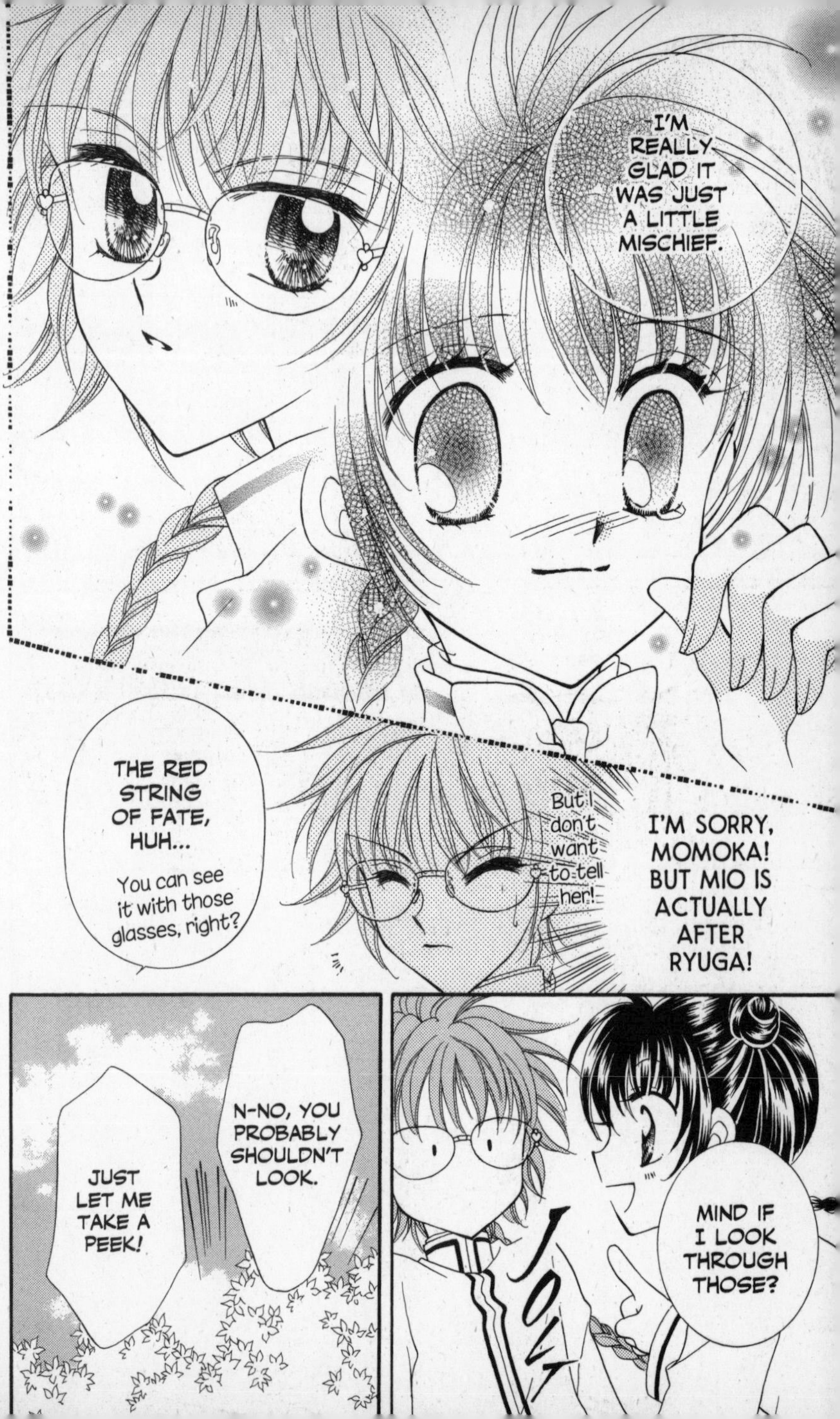
I'M REALLY GLAD IT WAS JUST A LITTLE MISCHIEF.
I'M SORRY, MOMOKA! BUT MIO IS ACTUALLY AFTER RYUGA!
But I don't want to tell her!
THE RED STRING OF FATE, HUH...
You can see it with those glasses, right?
MIND IF I LOOK THROUGH THOSE?
JOLT
N-NO, YOU PROBABLY SHOULDN'T LOOK.
JUST LET ME TAKE A PEEK!

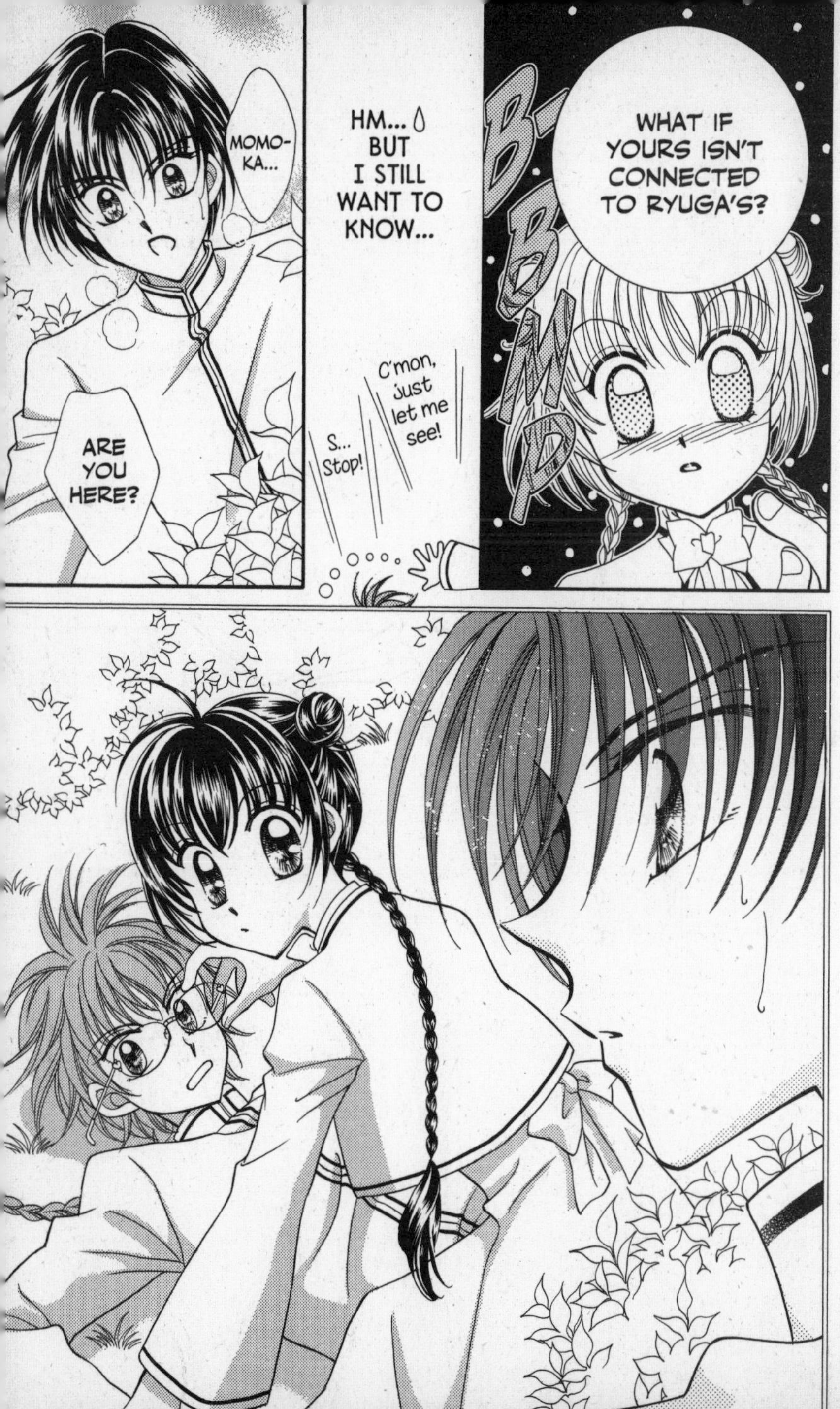
WHAT IF YOURS ISN'T CONNECTED TO RYUGA'S?
HM... BUT I STILL WANT TO KNOW...
C'mon, just let me see!
S... Stop!
MOMO-KA...
ARE YOU HERE?

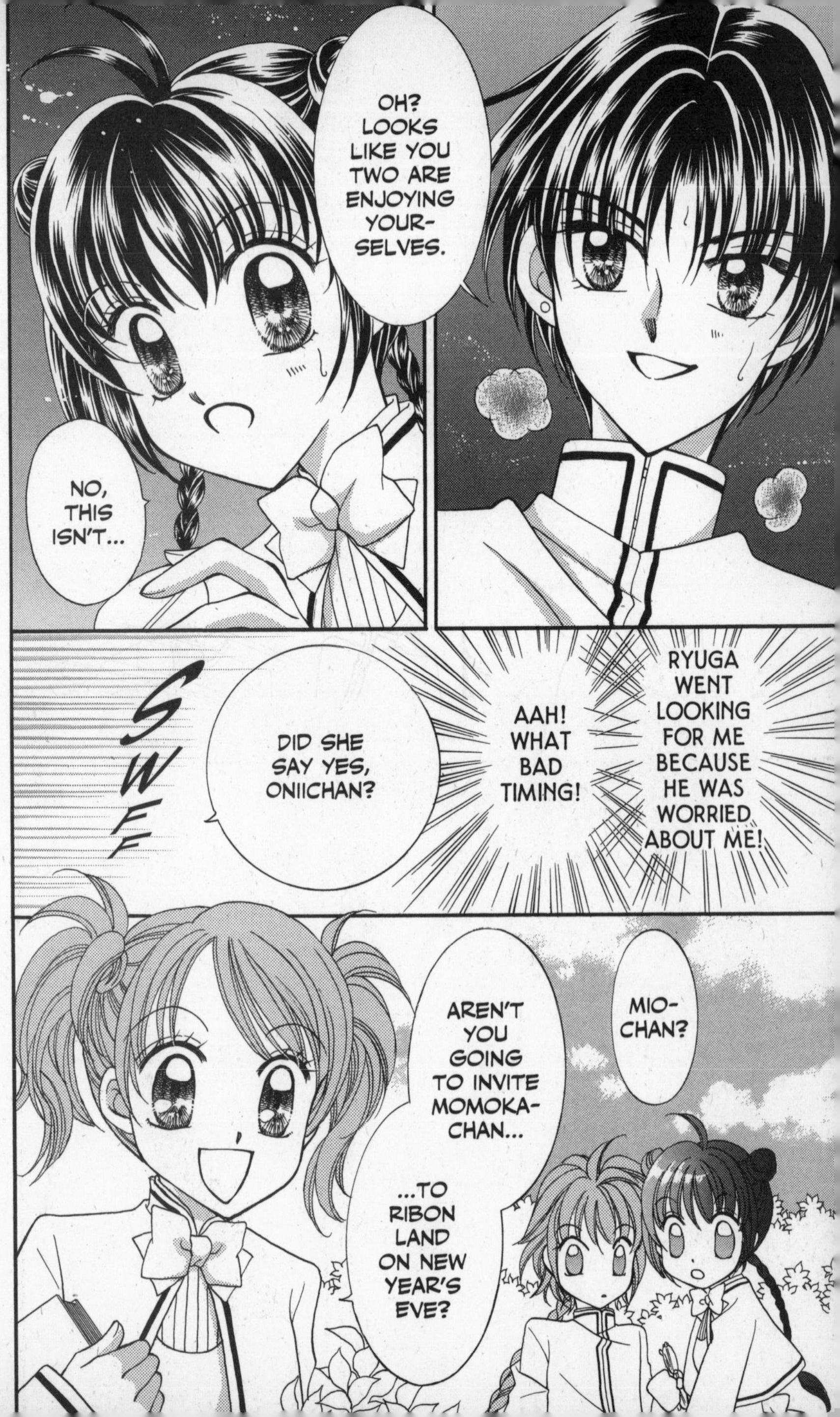
OH? LOOKS LIKE YOU TWO ARE ENJOYING YOUR-SELVES.
NO, THIS ISN'T...
RYUGA WENT LOOKING FOR ME BECAUSE HE WAS WORRIED ABOUT ME!
AAH! WHAT BAD TIMING!
DID SHE SAY YES, ONIICHAN?
SWFF
MIO-CHAN?
AREN'T YOU GOING TO INVITE MOMOKA-CHAN...
...TO RIBON LAND ON NEW YEAR'S EVE?

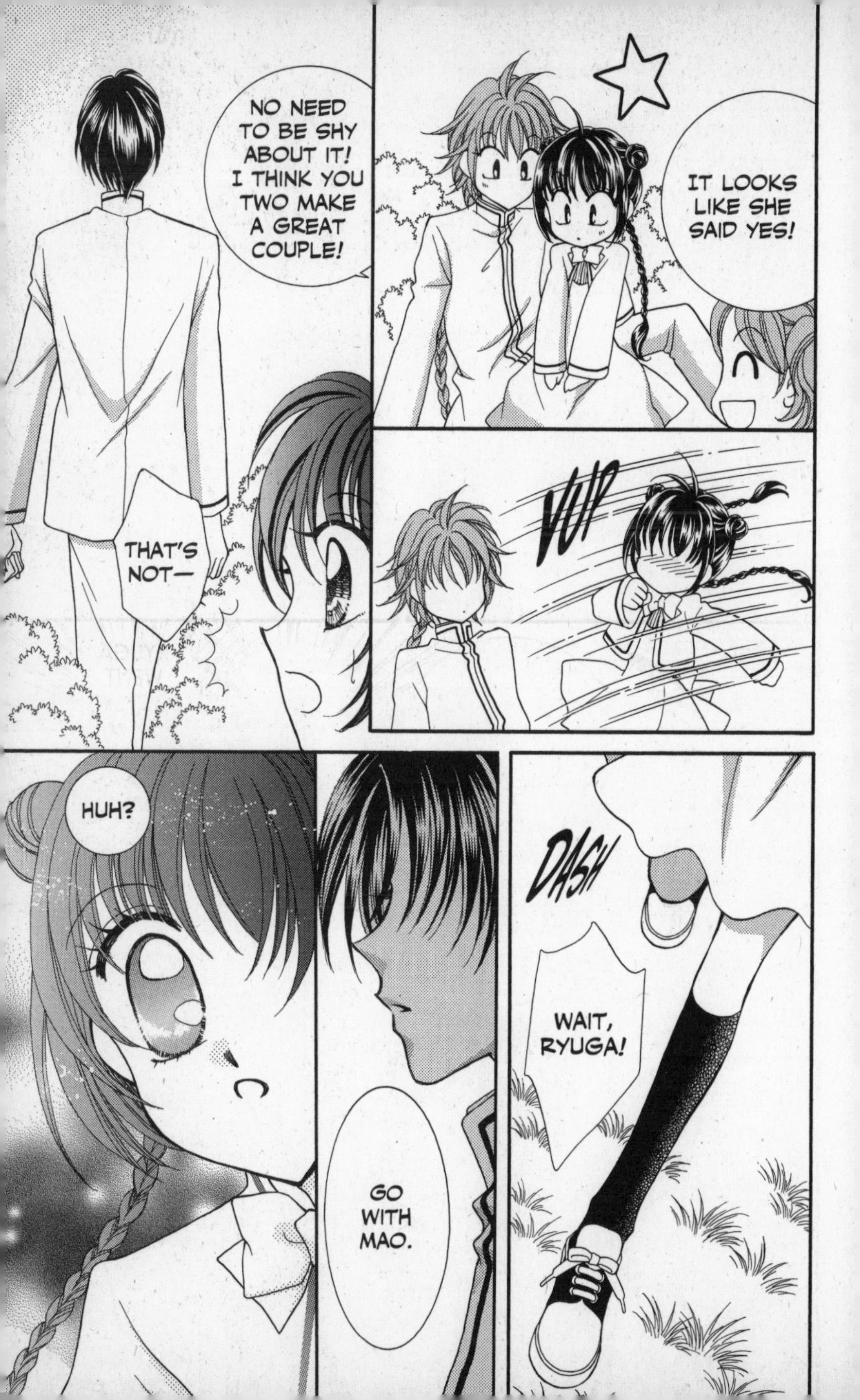
IT LOOKS LIKE SHE SAID YES!
VUIP
NO NEED TO BE SHY ABOUT IT! I THINK YOU TWO MAKE A GREAT COUPLE!
THAT'S NOT—
DASH
WAIT, RYUGA!
GO WITH MAO.
HUH?

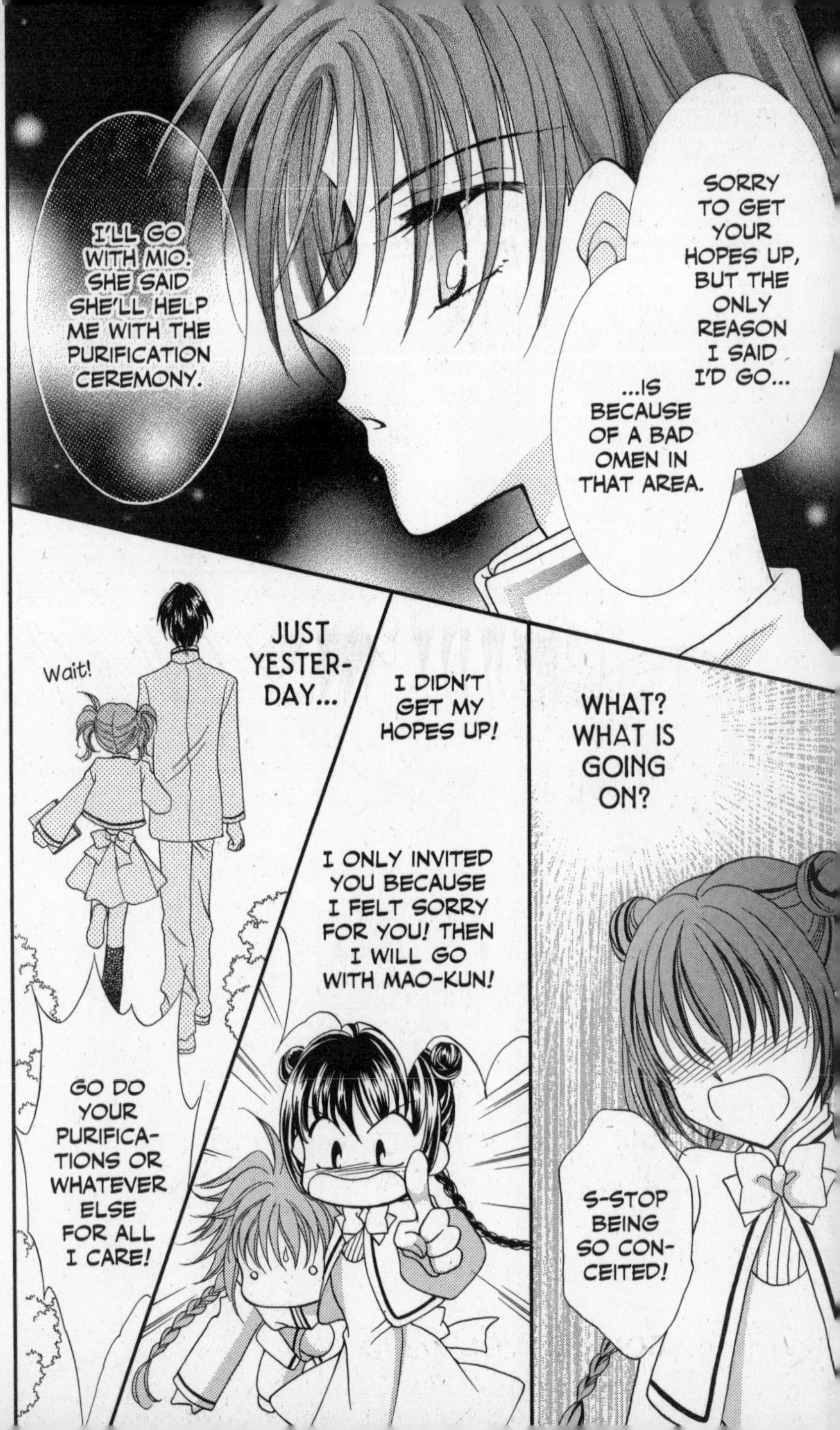
SORRY TO GET YOUR HOPES UP, BUT THE ONLY REASON I SAID I'D GO...
...IS BECAUSE OF A BAD OMEN IN THAT AREA.
I'LL GO WITH MIO. SHE SAID SHE'LL HELP ME WITH THE PURIFICATION CEREMONY.
WHAT? WHAT IS GOING ON?
S-STOP BEING SO CONCEITED!
I DIDN'T GET MY HOPES UP!
I ONLY INVITED YOU BECAUSE I FELT SORRY FOR YOU! THEN I WILL GO WITH MAO-KUN!
JUST YESTER-DAY...
Wait!
GO DO YOUR PURIFICA-TIONS OR WHATEVER ELSE FOR ALL I CARE!

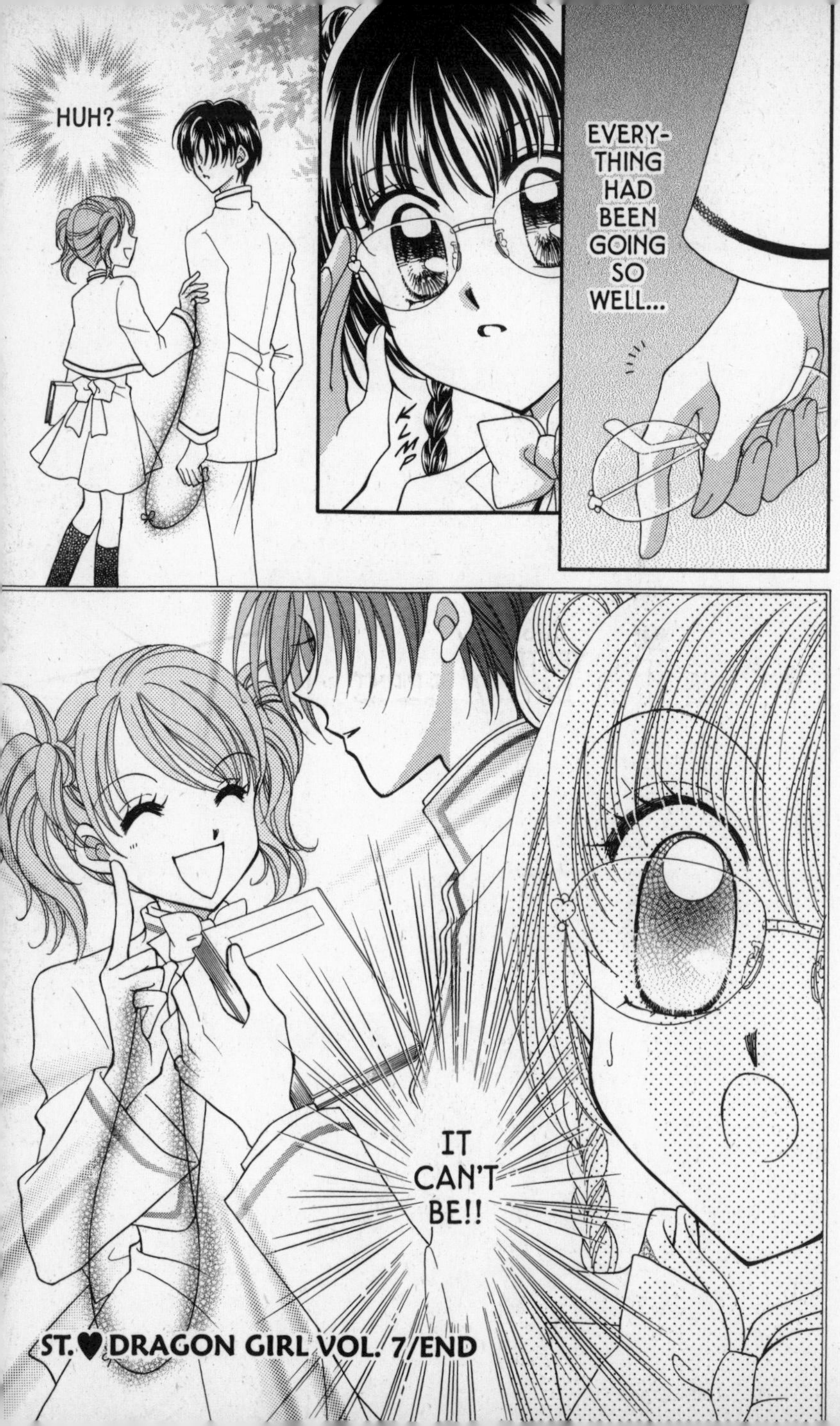
EVERY-THING HAD BEEN GOING SO WELL...
KLMP
HUH?
IT CAN'T BE!!
ST.♥DRAGON GIRL VOL. 7/END

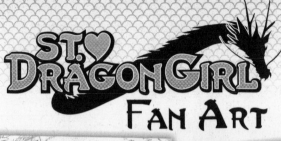

St. Dragon Girl
Fan Art

Holly Leialoha

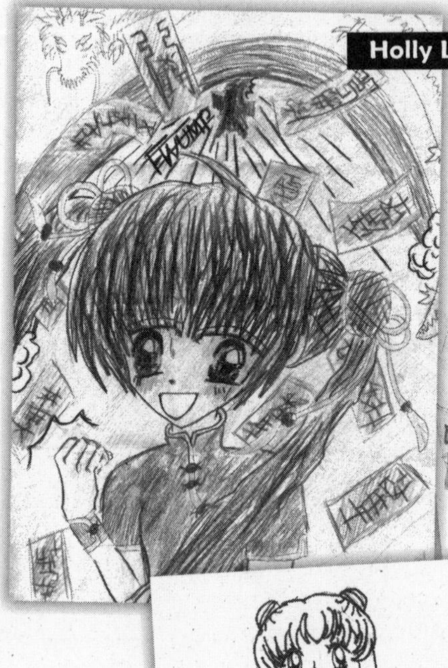

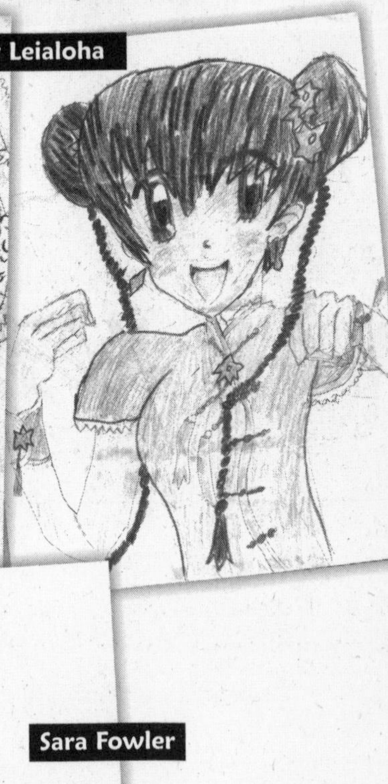

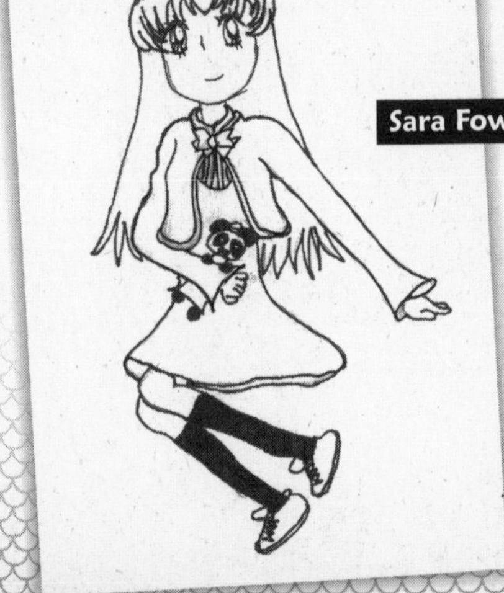

Sara Fowler

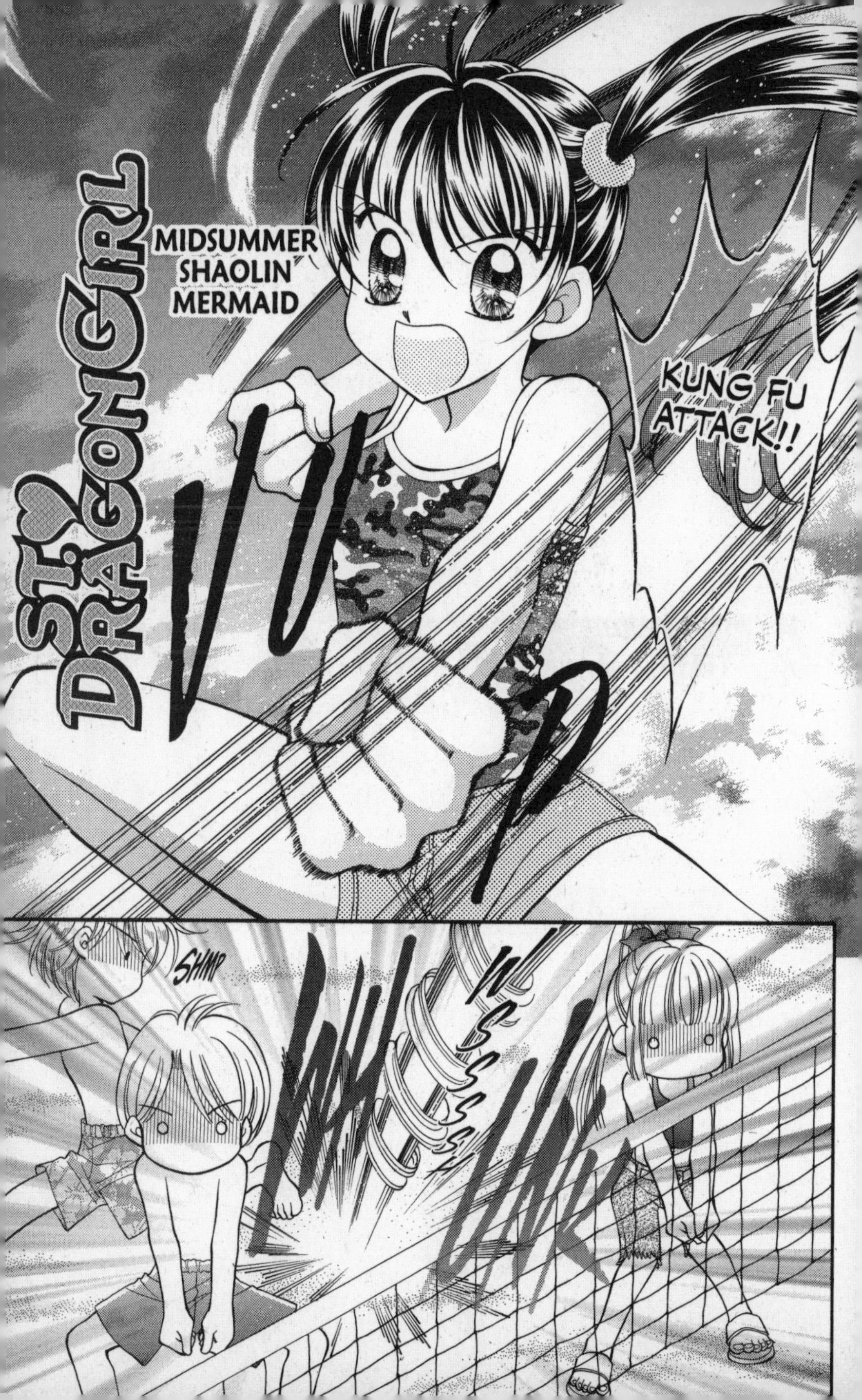
KUNG FU ATTACK!!
ST. DRAGON GIRL
MIDSUMMER SHAOLIN MERMAID
WSSSSSH
SHMP

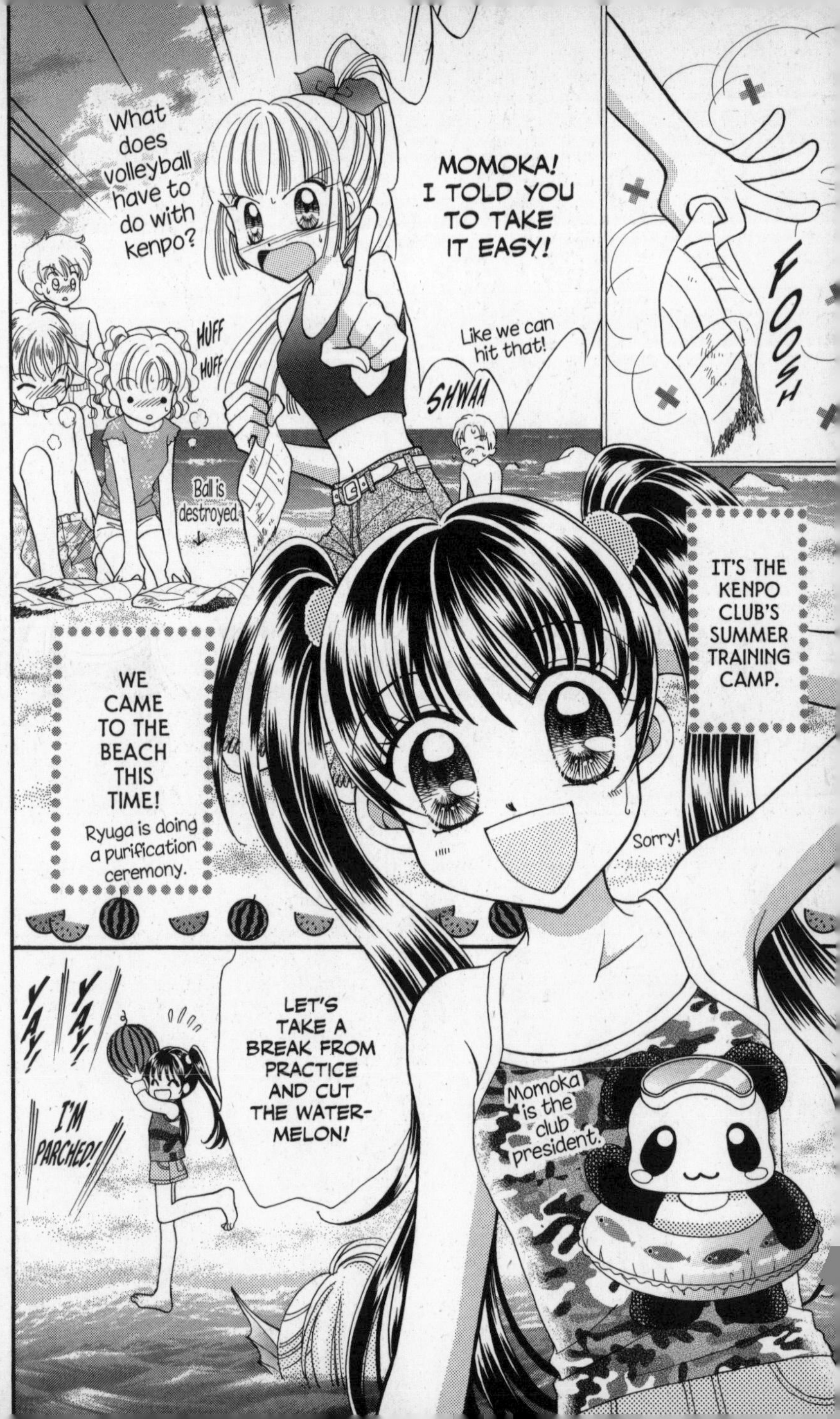
FOOOSH
MOMOKA! I TOLD YOU TO TAKE IT EASY!
What does volleyball have to do with kenpo?
Like we can hit that!
SHWAA
HUFF HUFF
Ball is destroyed.
IT'S THE KENPO CLUB'S SUMMER TRAINING CAMP.
Sorry!
WE CAME TO THE BEACH THIS TIME!
Ryuga is doing a purification ceremony.
Momoka is the club president.
LET'S TAKE A BREAK FROM PRACTICE AND CUT THE WATER-MELON!
YAY! YAY!
I'M PARCHED!

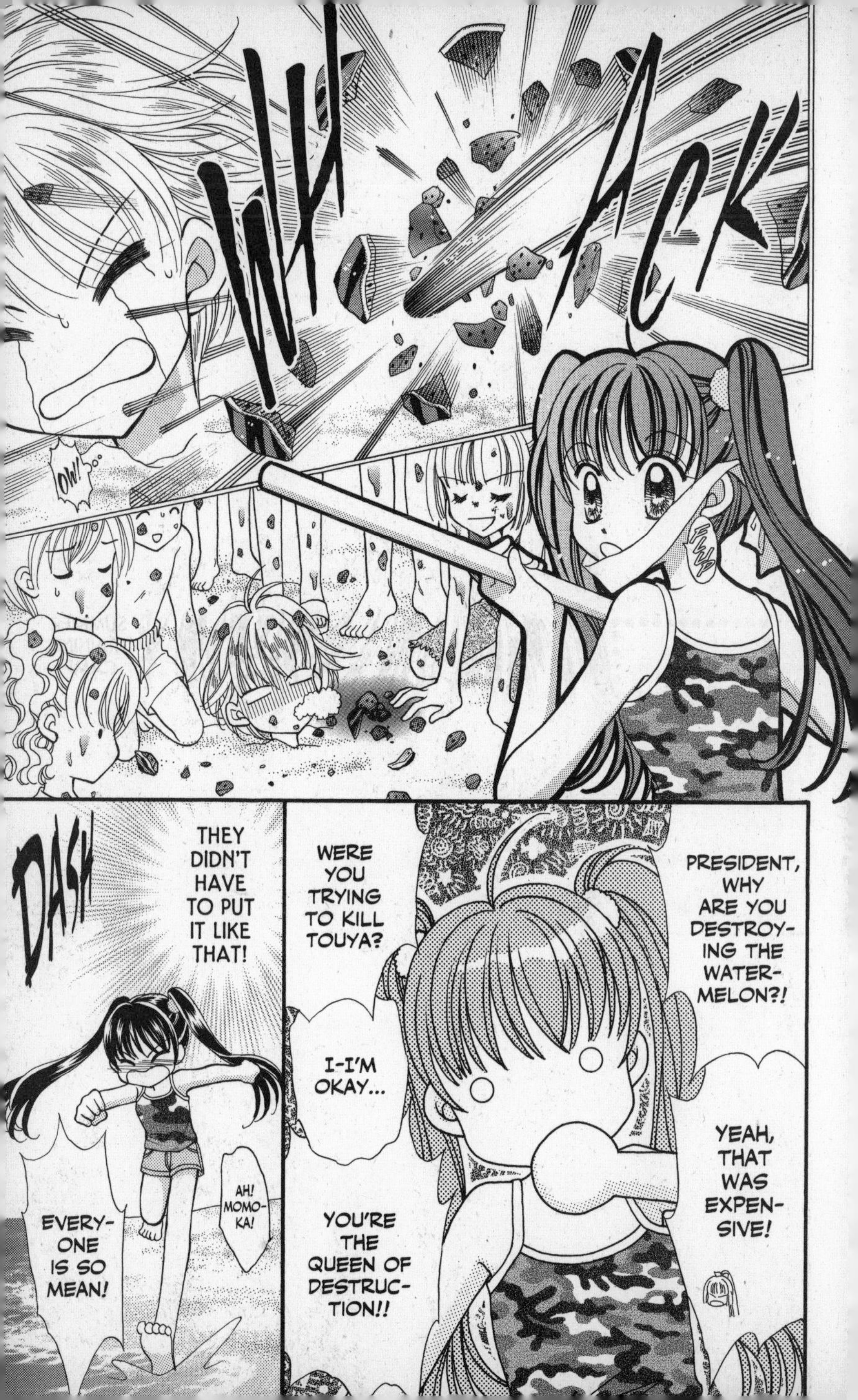
WHACK
OW!
PRESIDENT, WHY ARE YOU DESTROYING THE WATERMELON?!
WERE YOU TRYING TO KILL TOUYA?
YEAH, THAT WAS EXPENSIVE!
I-I'M OKAY...
YOU'RE THE QUEEN OF DESTRUCTION!!
THEY DIDN'T HAVE TO PUT IT LIKE THAT!
DASH
AH! MOMOKA!
EVERYONE IS SO MEAN!

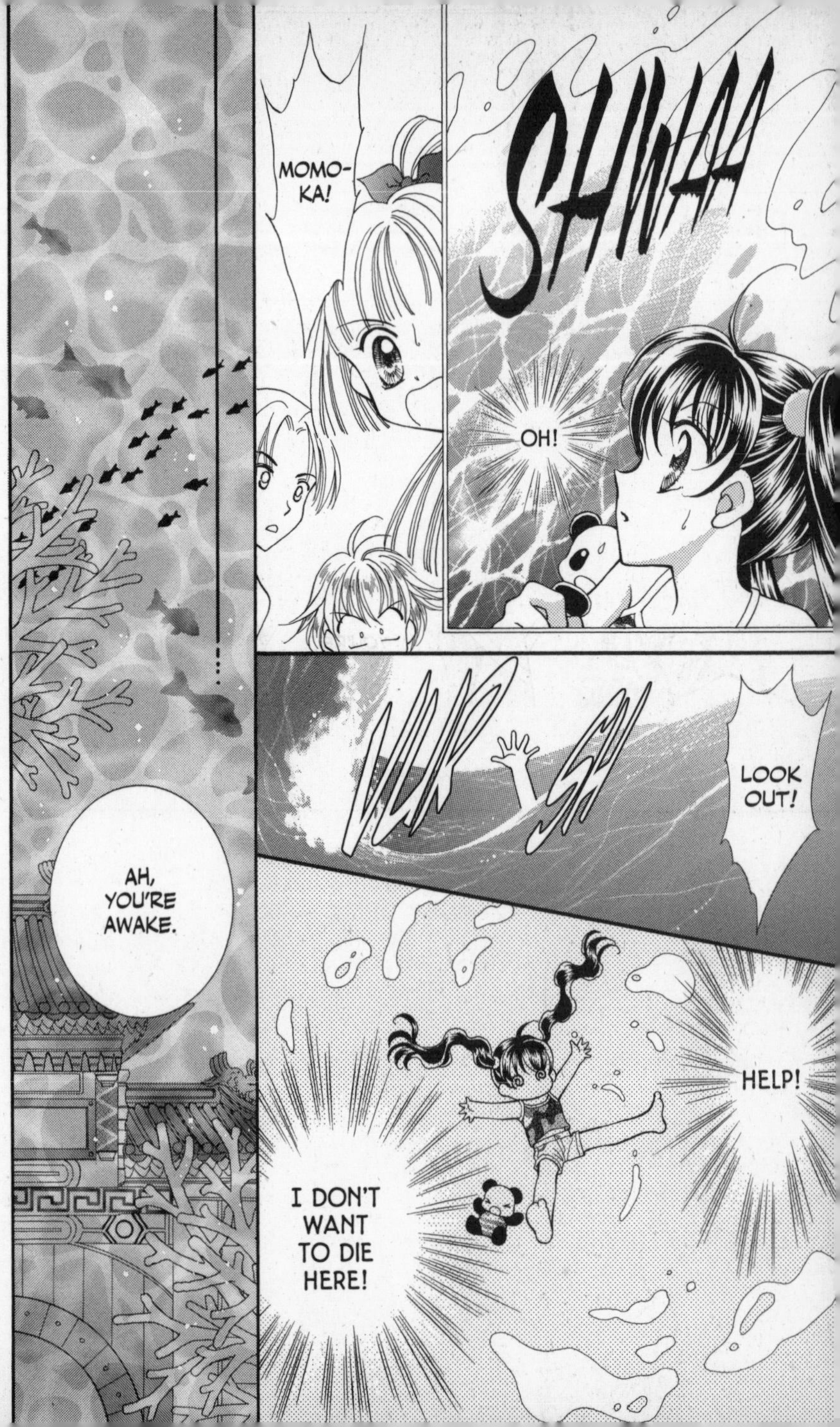
SHWAA
OH!
MOMO-KA!
LOOK OUT!
HELP!
I DON'T WANT TO DIE HERE!
.....
AH, YOU'RE AWAKE.

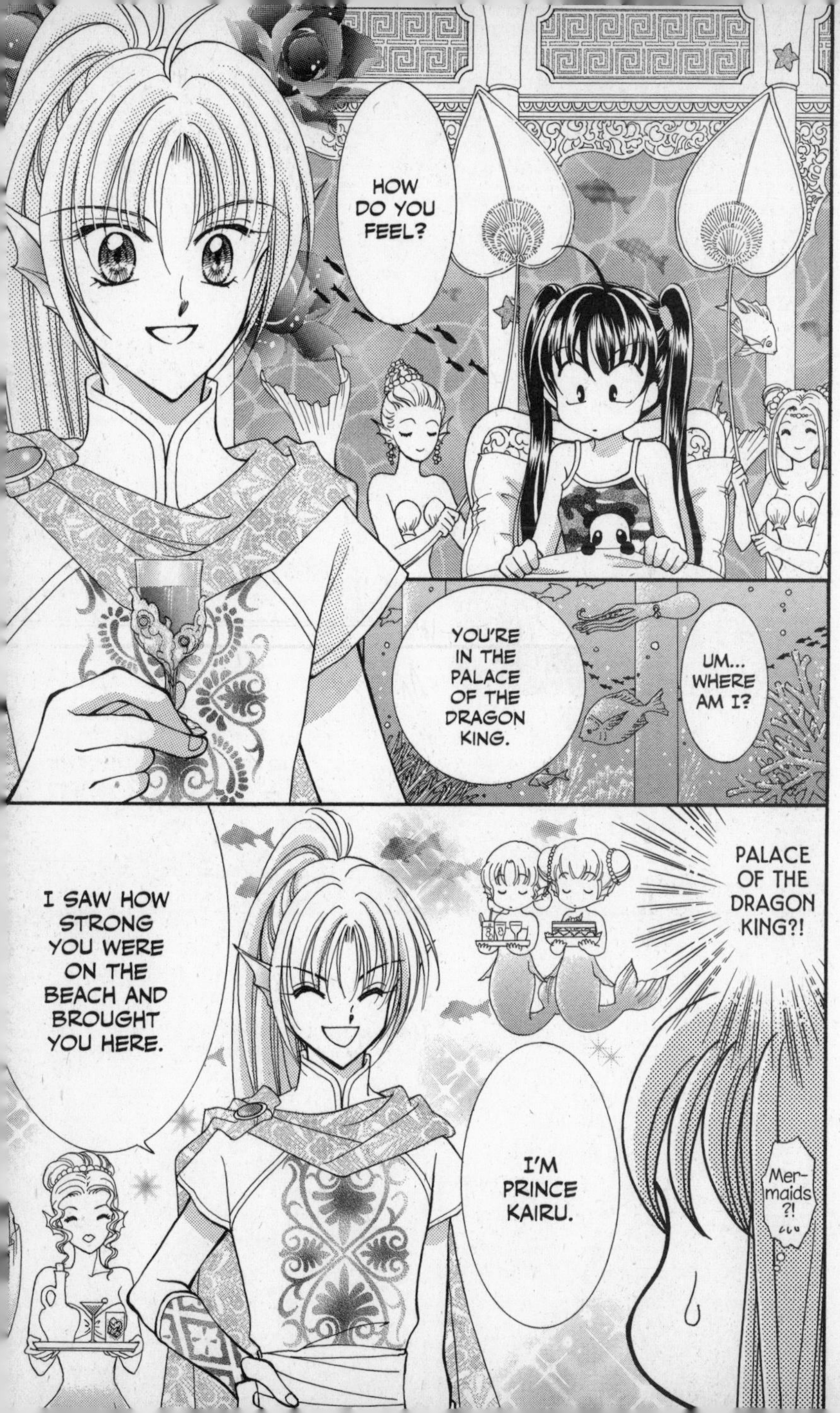
HOW DO YOU FEEL?
UM... WHERE AM I?
YOU'RE IN THE PALACE OF THE DRAGON KING.
PALACE OF THE DRAGON KING?!
Mer-maids?!
I'M PRINCE KAIRU.
I SAW HOW STRONG YOU WERE ON THE BEACH AND BROUGHT YOU HERE.

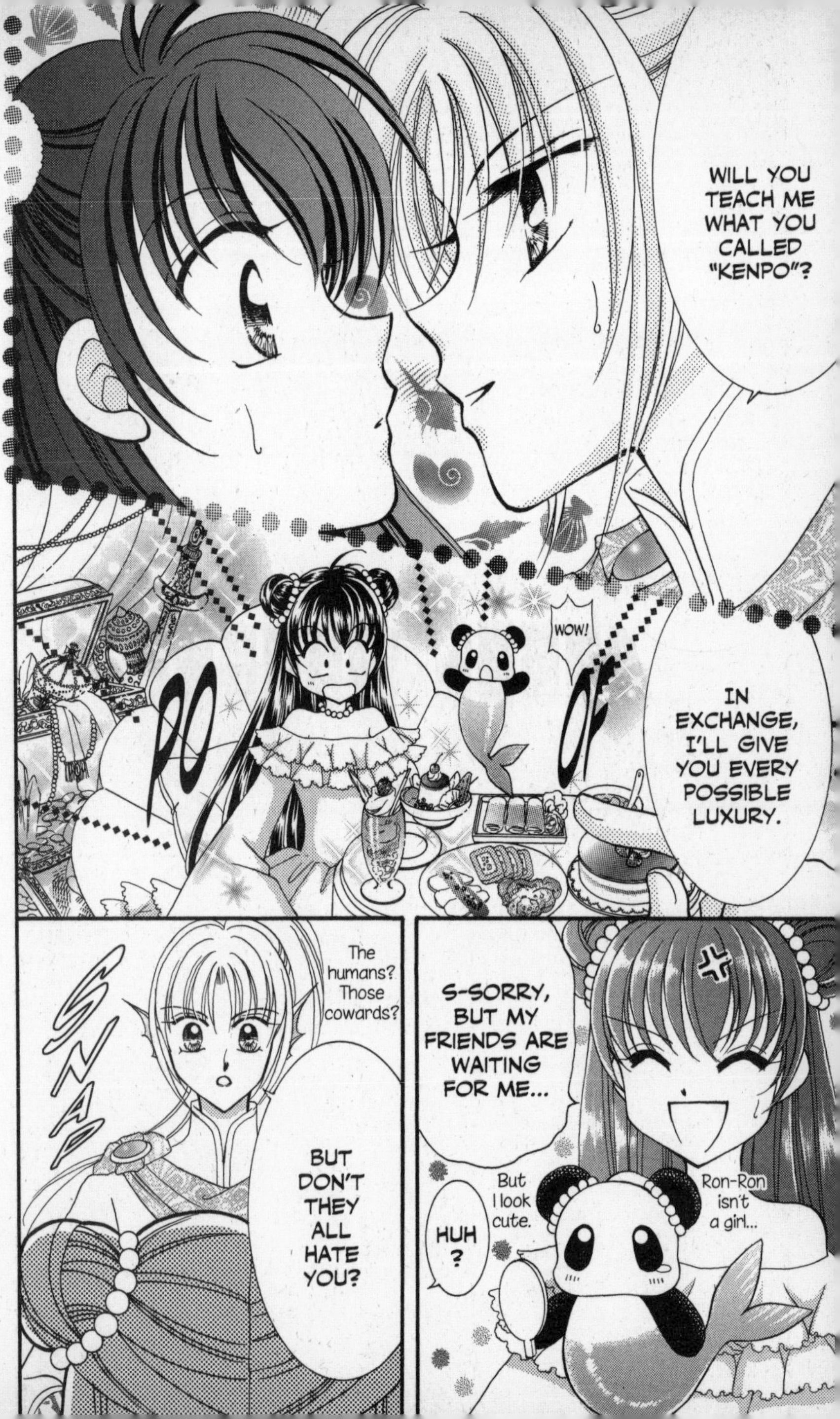
WILL YOU TEACH ME WHAT YOU CALLED "KENPO"?
IN EXCHANGE, I'LL GIVE YOU EVERY POSSIBLE LUXURY.
WOW!
OF
PO
S-SORRY, BUT MY FRIENDS ARE WAITING FOR ME...
Ron-Ron isn't a girl...
But I look cute.
HUH?
The humans? Those cowards?
BUT DON'T THEY ALL HATE YOU?
SNAP

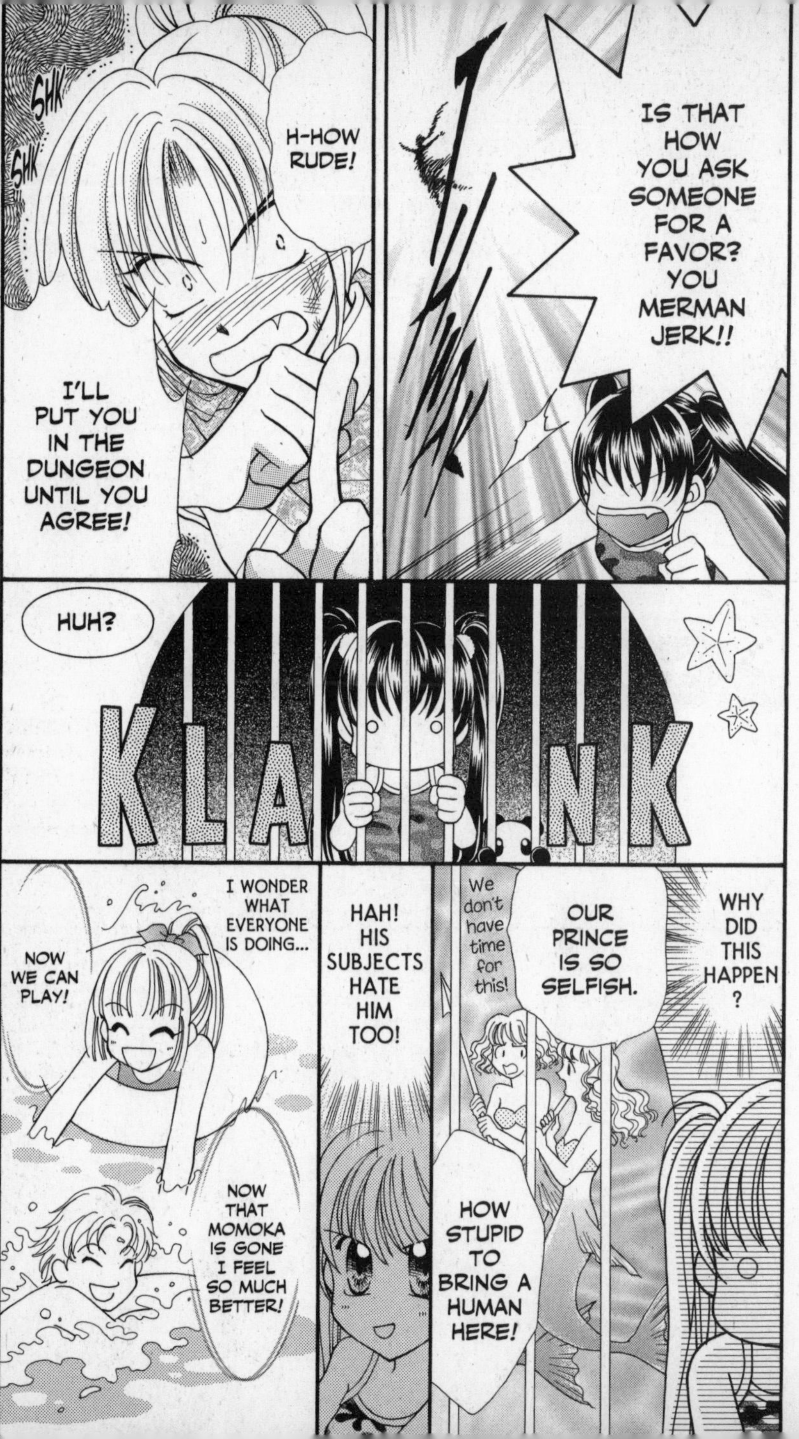

IS THAT HOW YOU ASK SOMEONE FOR A FAVOR? YOU MERMAN JERK!!
SHK
SHK
H-HOW RUDE!
I'LL PUT YOU IN THE DUNGEON UNTIL YOU AGREE!
KLANK
HUH?
WHY DID THIS HAPPEN ?
OUR PRINCE IS SO SELFISH.
We don't have time for this!
HOW STUPID TO BRING A HUMAN HERE!
HAH! HIS SUBJECTS HATE HIM TOO!
I WONDER WHAT EVERYONE IS DOING...
NOW WE CAN PLAY!
NOW THAT MOMOKA IS GONE I FEEL SO MUCH BETTER!

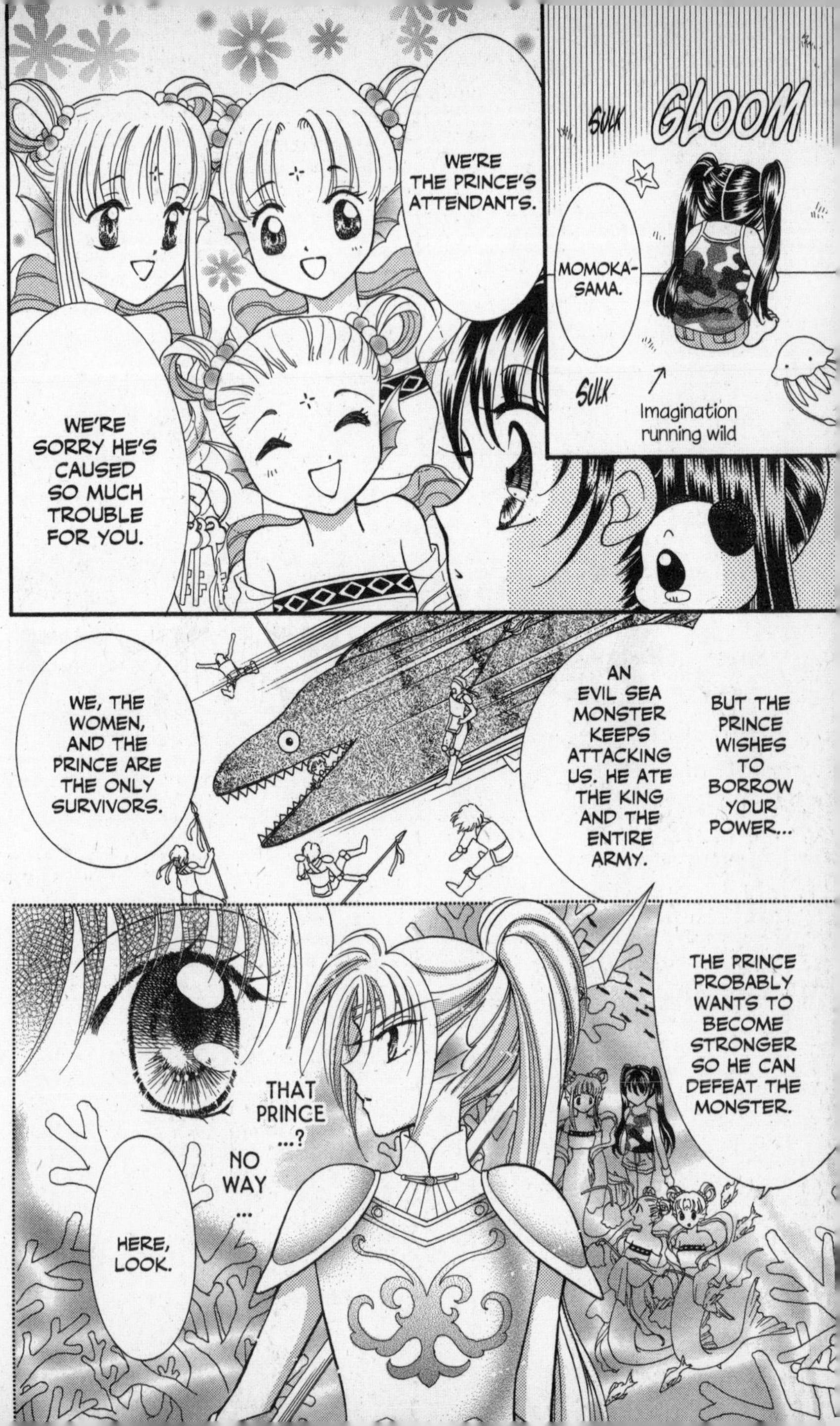
GLOOM
SULK
MOMOKA-SAMA.
SULK
Imagination running wild
WE'RE THE PRINCE'S ATTENDANTS.
WE'RE SORRY HE'S CAUSED SO MUCH TROUBLE FOR YOU.
AN EVIL SEA MONSTER KEEPS ATTACKING US. HE ATE THE KING AND THE ENTIRE ARMY.
BUT THE PRINCE WISHES TO BORROW YOUR POWER...
WE, THE WOMEN, AND THE PRINCE ARE THE ONLY SURVIVORS.
THE PRINCE PROBABLY WANTS TO BECOME STRONGER SO HE CAN DEFEAT THE MONSTER.
THAT PRINCE ...?
NO WAY ...
HERE, LOOK.

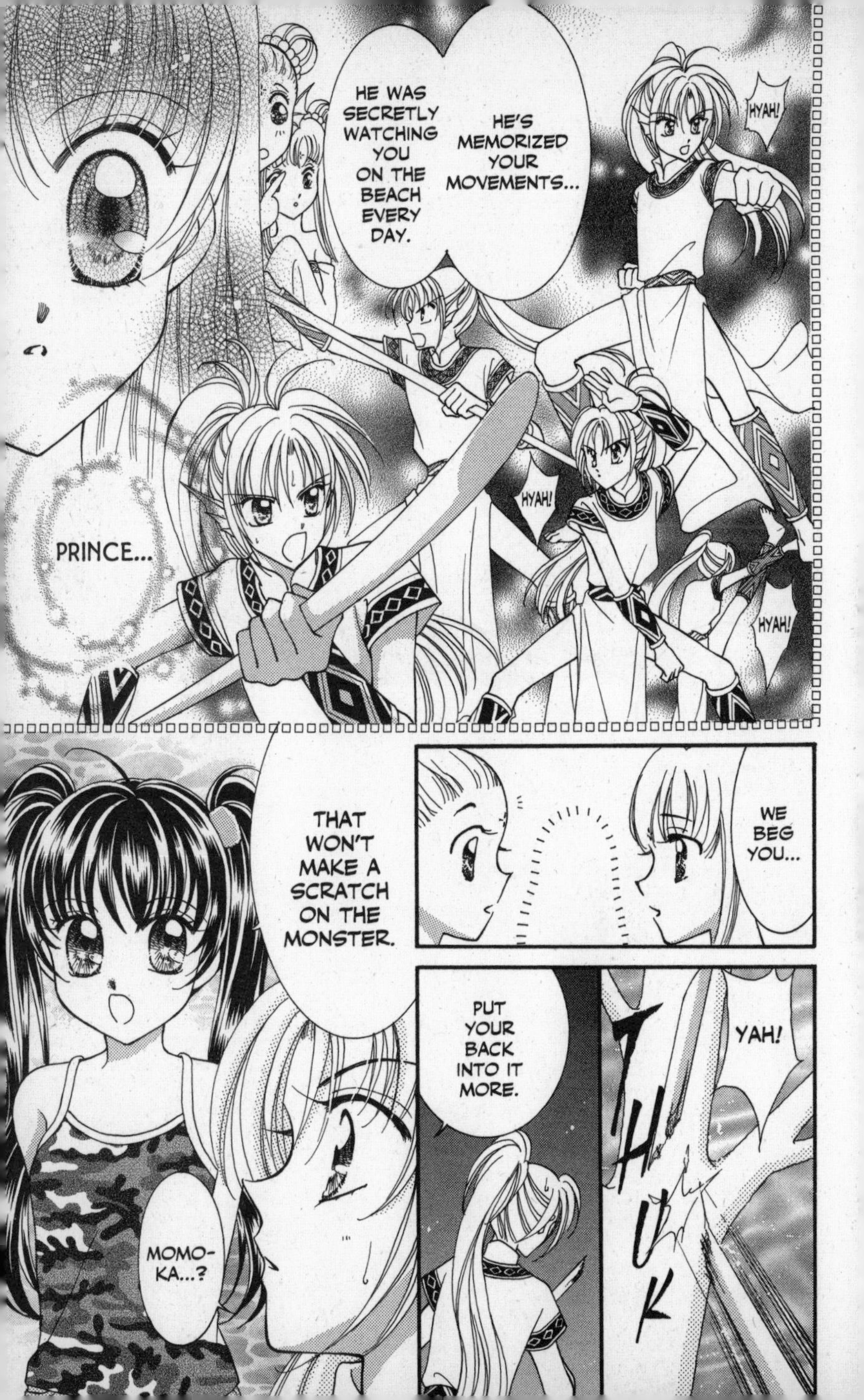
HYAH!
HE'S MEMORIZED YOUR MOVEMENTS...
HE WAS SECRETLY WATCHING YOU ON THE BEACH EVERY DAY.
HYAH!
HYAH!
PRINCE...
WE BEG YOU...
YAH!
THUK
PUT YOUR BACK INTO IT MORE.
THAT WON'T MAKE A SCRATCH ON THE MONSTER.
MOMO-KA...?

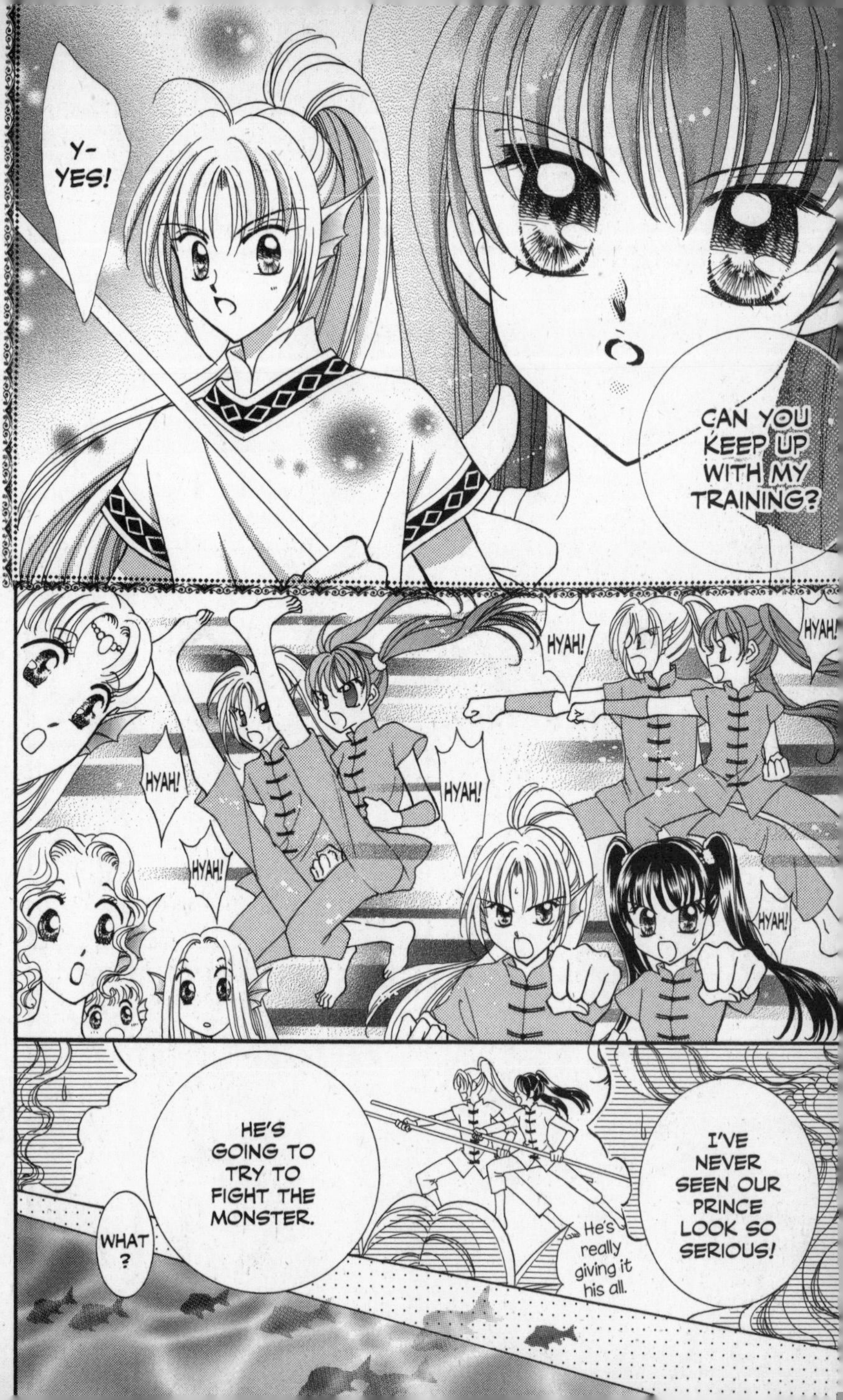
CAN YOU KEEP UP WITH MY TRAINING?
Y-YES!
HYAH!
HYAH!
HYAH!
HYAH!
HYAH!
HYAH!
I'VE NEVER SEEN OUR PRINCE LOOK SO SERIOUS!
He's really giving it his all.
HE'S GOING TO TRY TO FIGHT THE MONSTER.
WHAT?

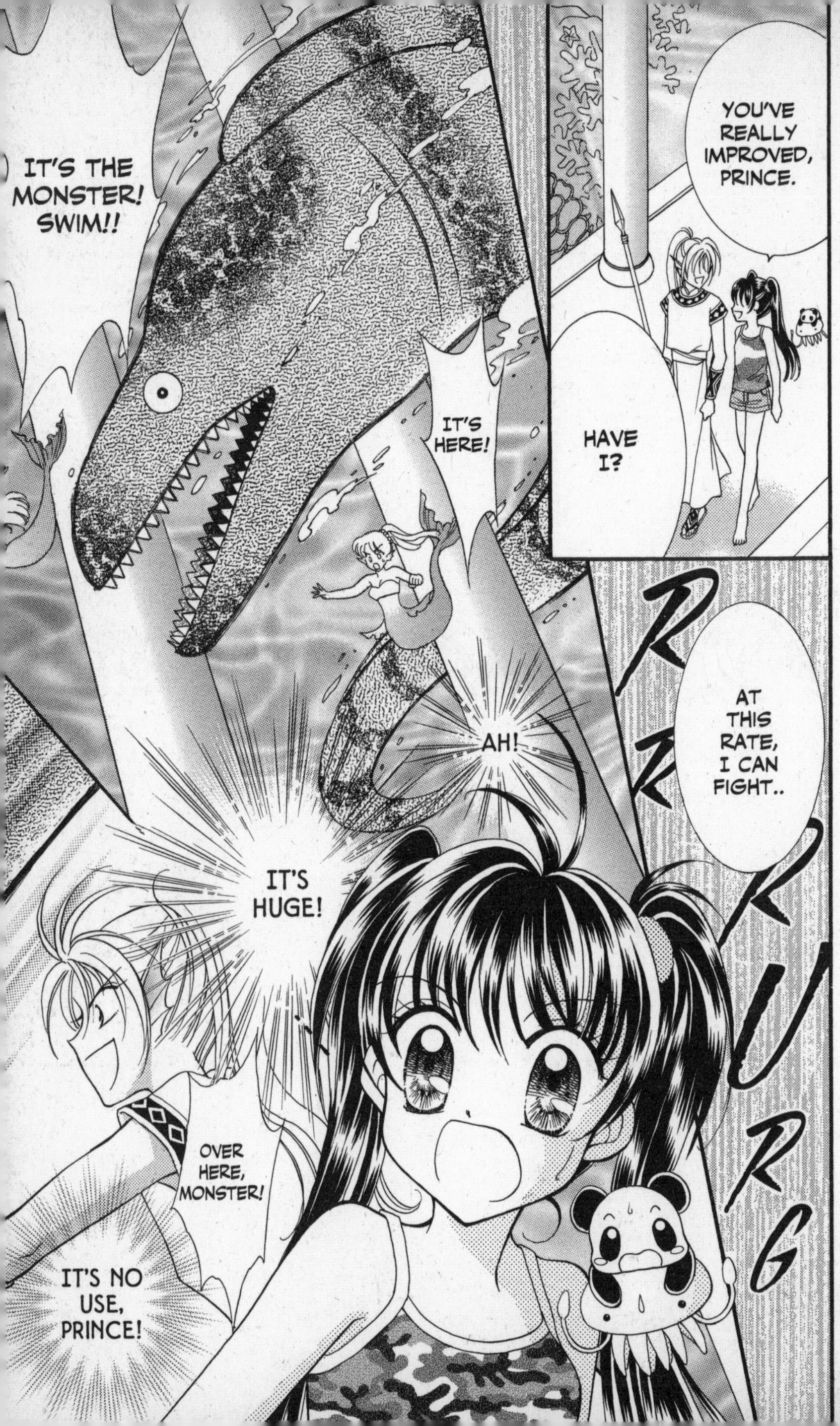
YOU'VE REALLY IMPROVED, PRINCE.
HAVE I?
AT THIS RATE, I CAN FIGHT..
RRRURG
IT'S HERE!
IT'S THE MONSTER! SWIM!!
AH!
IT'S HUGE!
OVER HERE, MONSTER!
IT'S NO USE, PRINCE!

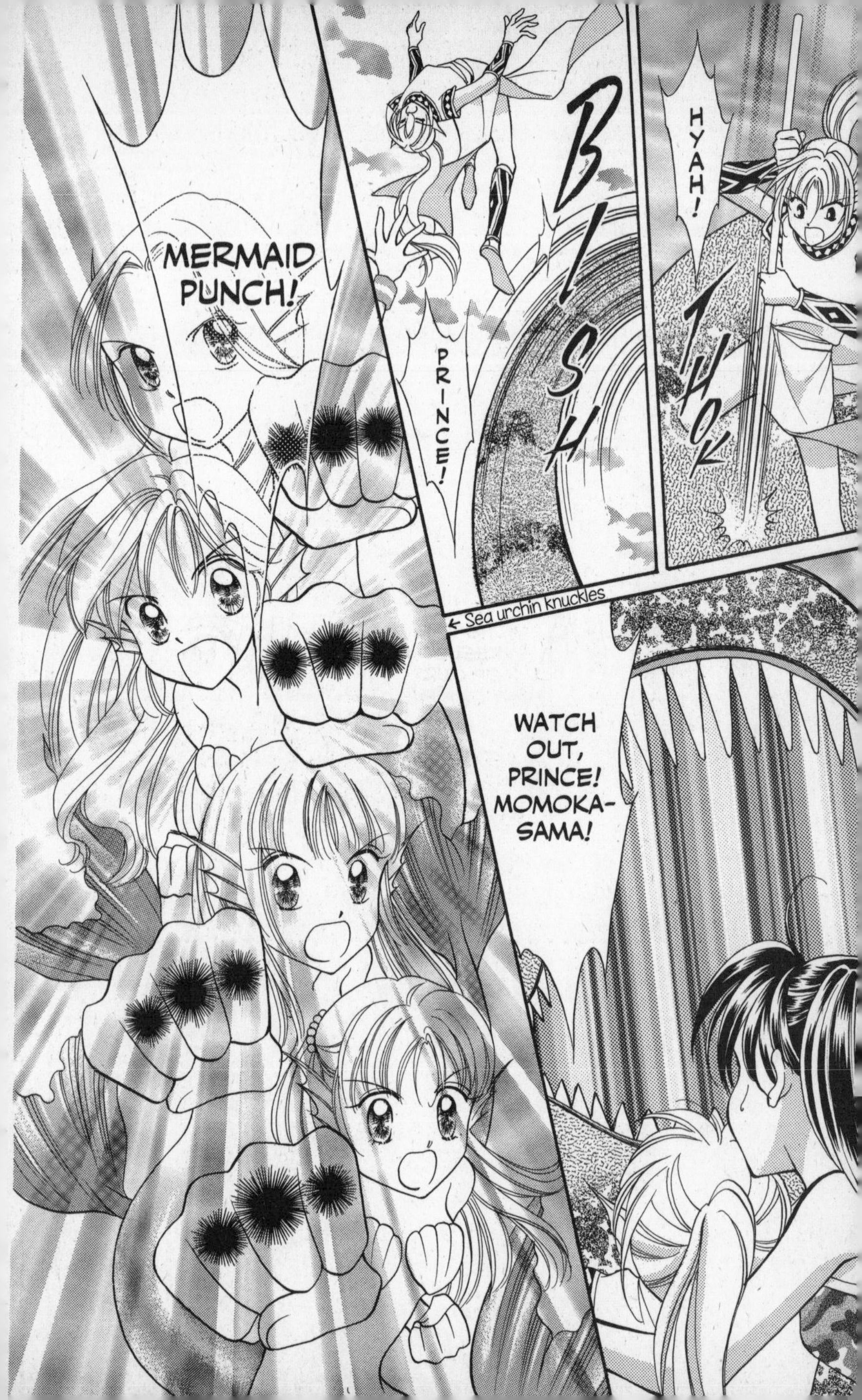
HYAH!
THOK
BISH
PRINCE!
WATCH OUT, PRINCE! MOMOKA-SAMA!
MERMAID PUNCH!
← Sea urchin knuckles

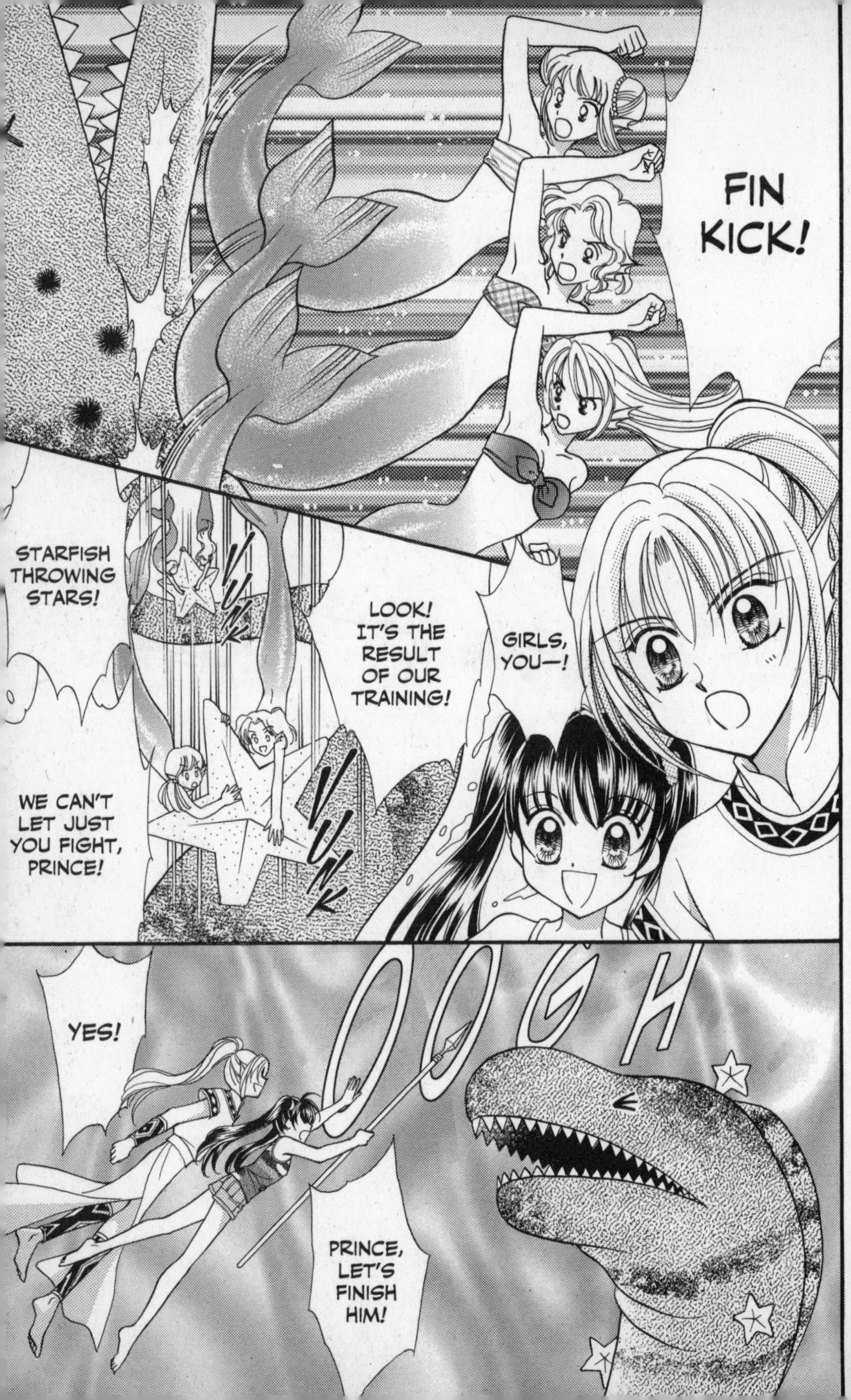
FIN KICK!
GIRLS, YOU—!
LOOK! IT'S THE RESULT OF OUR TRAINING!
VUNK
STARFISH THROWING STARS!
VUNK
WE CAN'T LET JUST YOU FIGHT, PRINCE!
OOGH
PRINCE, LET'S FINISH HIM!
YES!

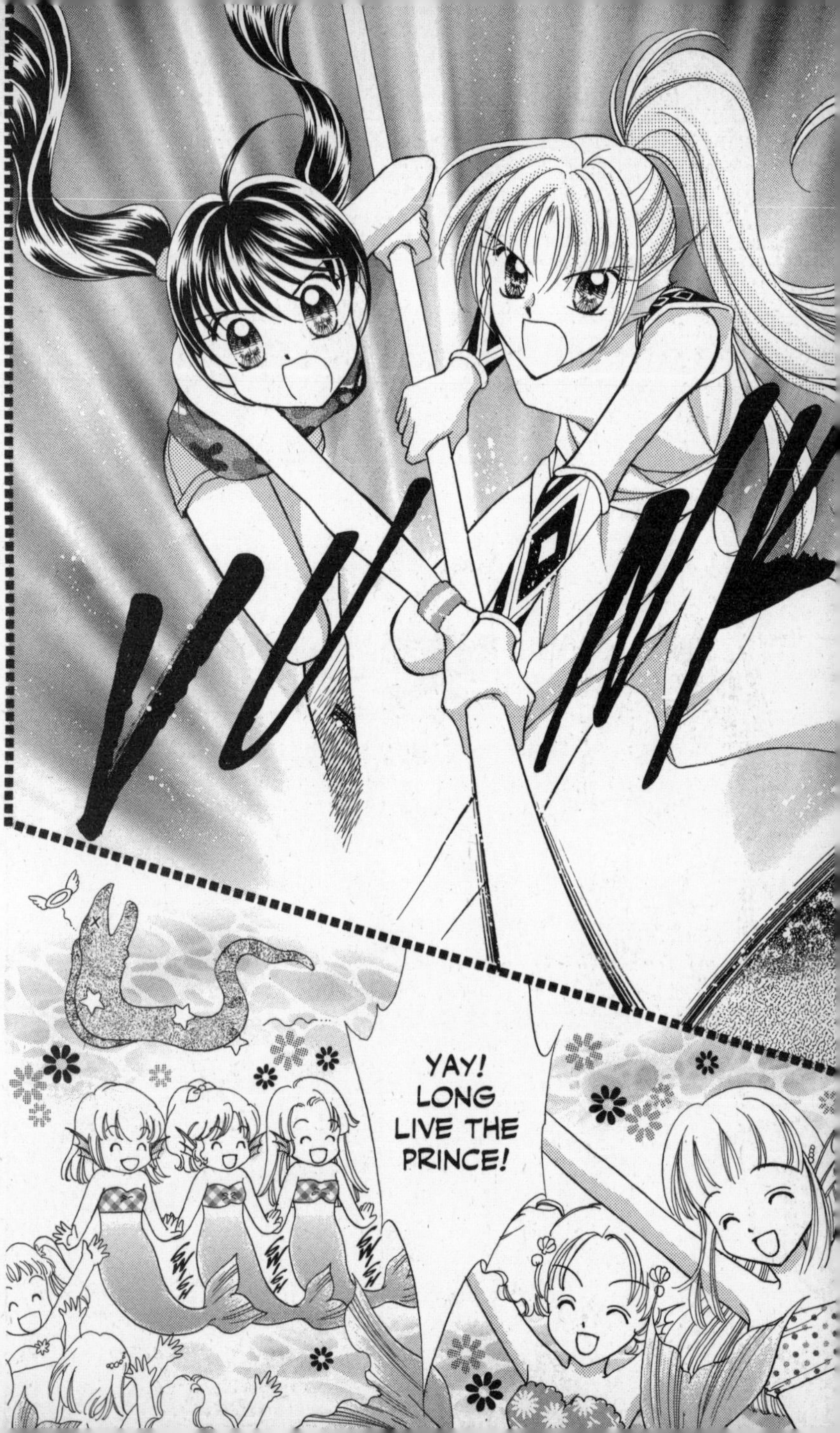
YAY! LONG LIVE THE PRINCE!

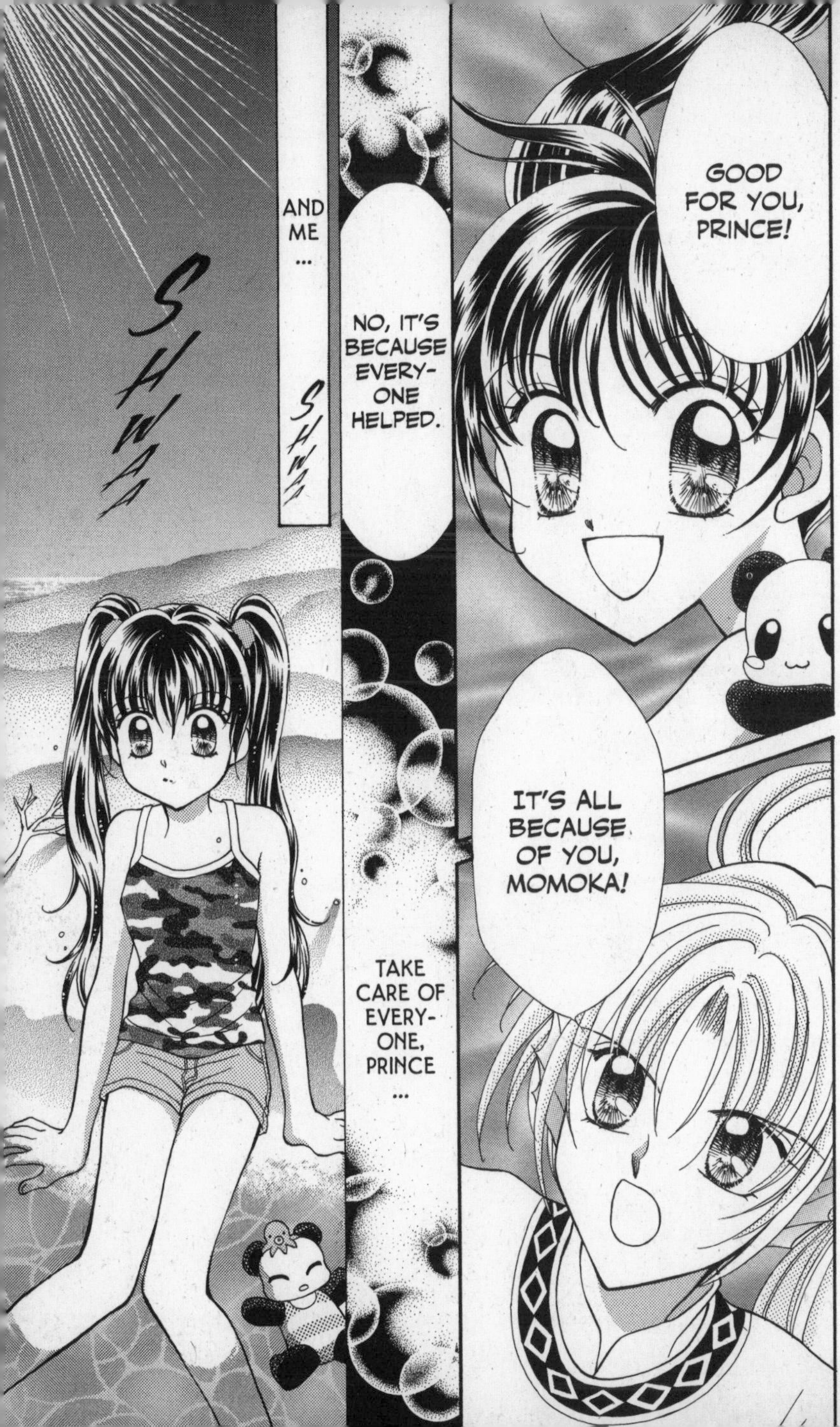
GOOD FOR YOU, PRINCE!
IT'S ALL BECAUSE OF YOU, MOMOKA!
NO, IT'S BECAUSE EVERY-ONE HELPED.
TAKE CARE OF EVERY-ONE, PRINCE ...
AND ME ...
SHWAA
SHWAA

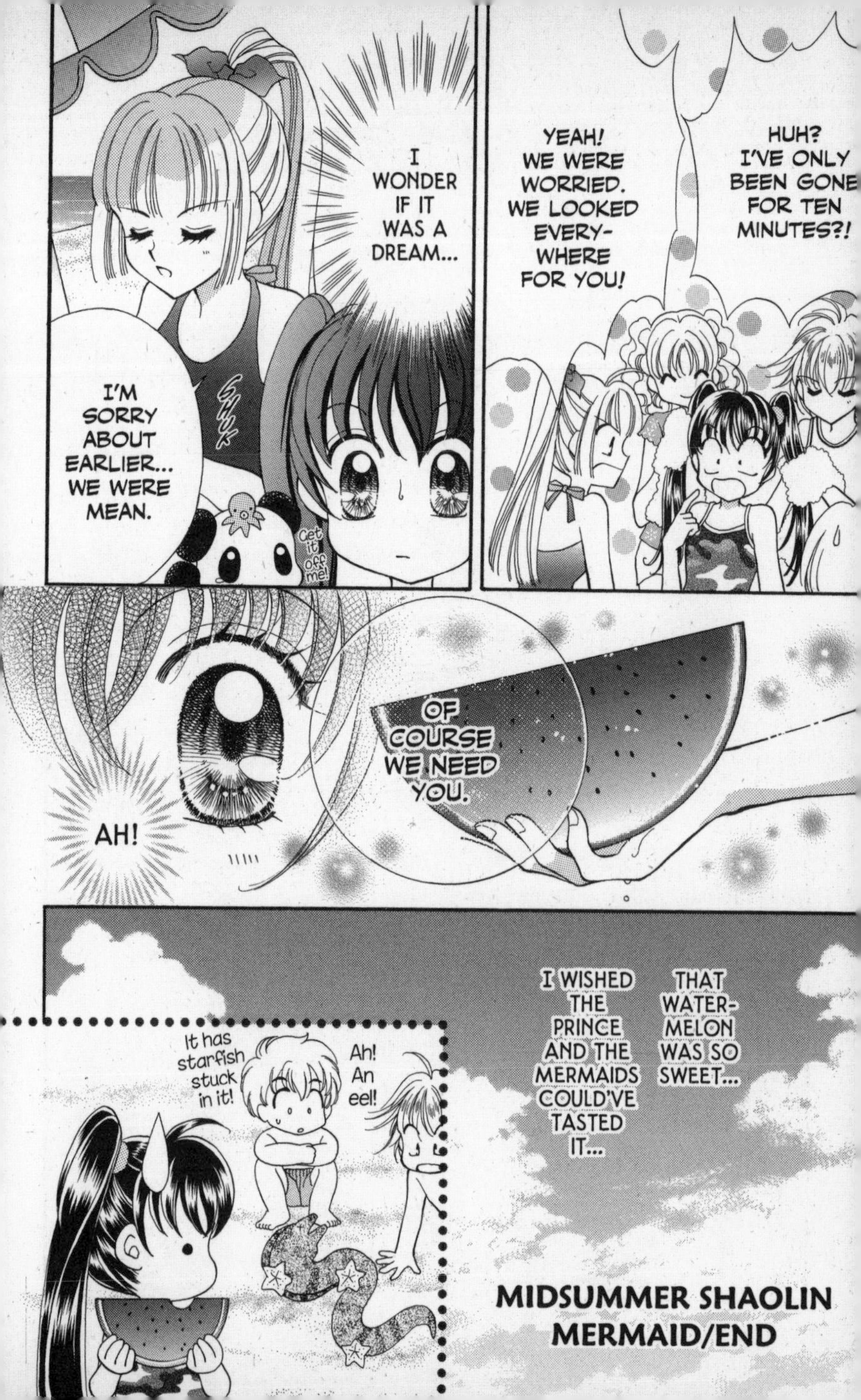
HUH? I'VE ONLY BEEN GONE FOR TEN MINUTES?!
YEAH! WE WERE WORRIED. WE LOOKED EVERY-WHERE FOR YOU!
I WONDER IF IT WAS A DREAM...
I'M SORRY ABOUT EARLIER... WE WERE MEAN.
Get it off me!
OF COURSE WE NEED YOU.
AH!
THAT WATER-MELON WAS SO SWEET...
I WISHED THE PRINCE AND THE MERMAIDS COULD'VE TASTED IT...
Ah! An eel!
It has starfish stuck in it!
MIDSUMMER SHAOLIN MERMAID/END

Bonus Pages

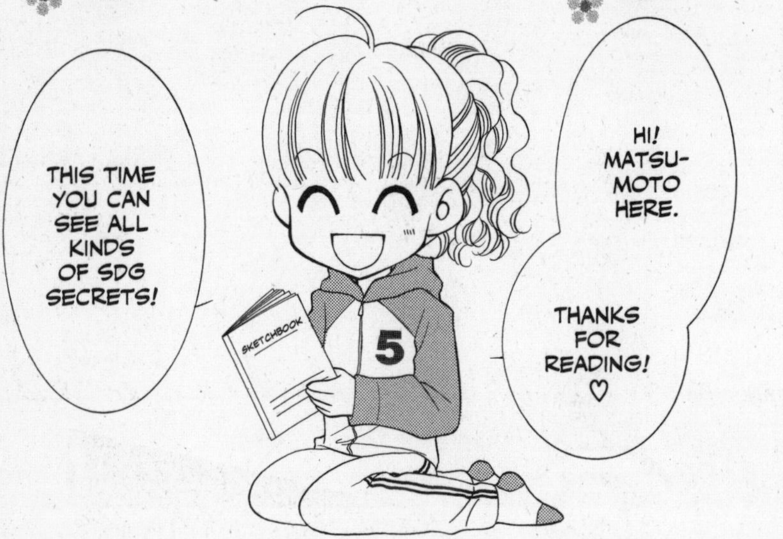
HI! MATSU-MOTO HERE.
THANKS FOR READING! ♡
THIS TIME YOU CAN SEE ALL KINDS OF SDG SECRETS!
SKETCHBOOK
5

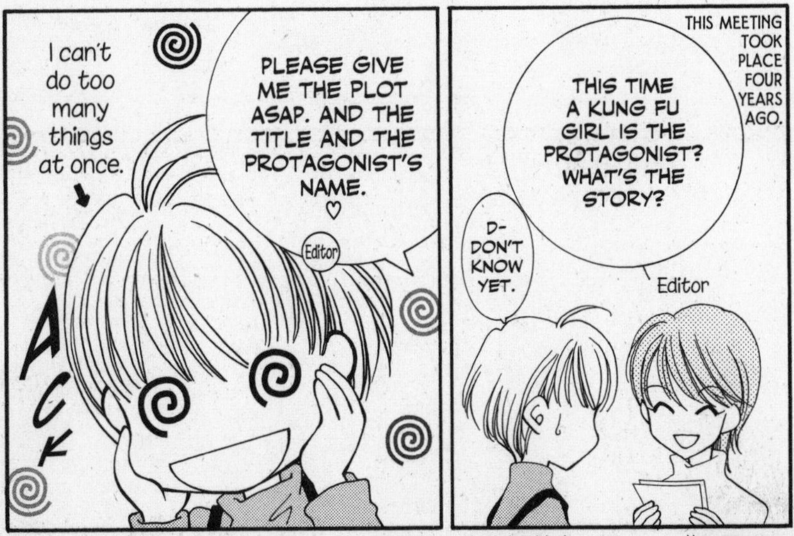
THIS MEETING TOOK PLACE FOUR YEARS AGO.
THIS TIME A KUNG FU GIRL IS THE PROTAGONIST? WHAT'S THE STORY?
Editor
D-DON'T KNOW YET.
PLEASE GIVE ME THE PLOT ASAP. AND THE TITLE AND THE PROTAGONIST'S NAME. ♡
Editor
I can't do too many things at once.
ACK

How are you, Ishikawa-san?

I had short hair at the time.

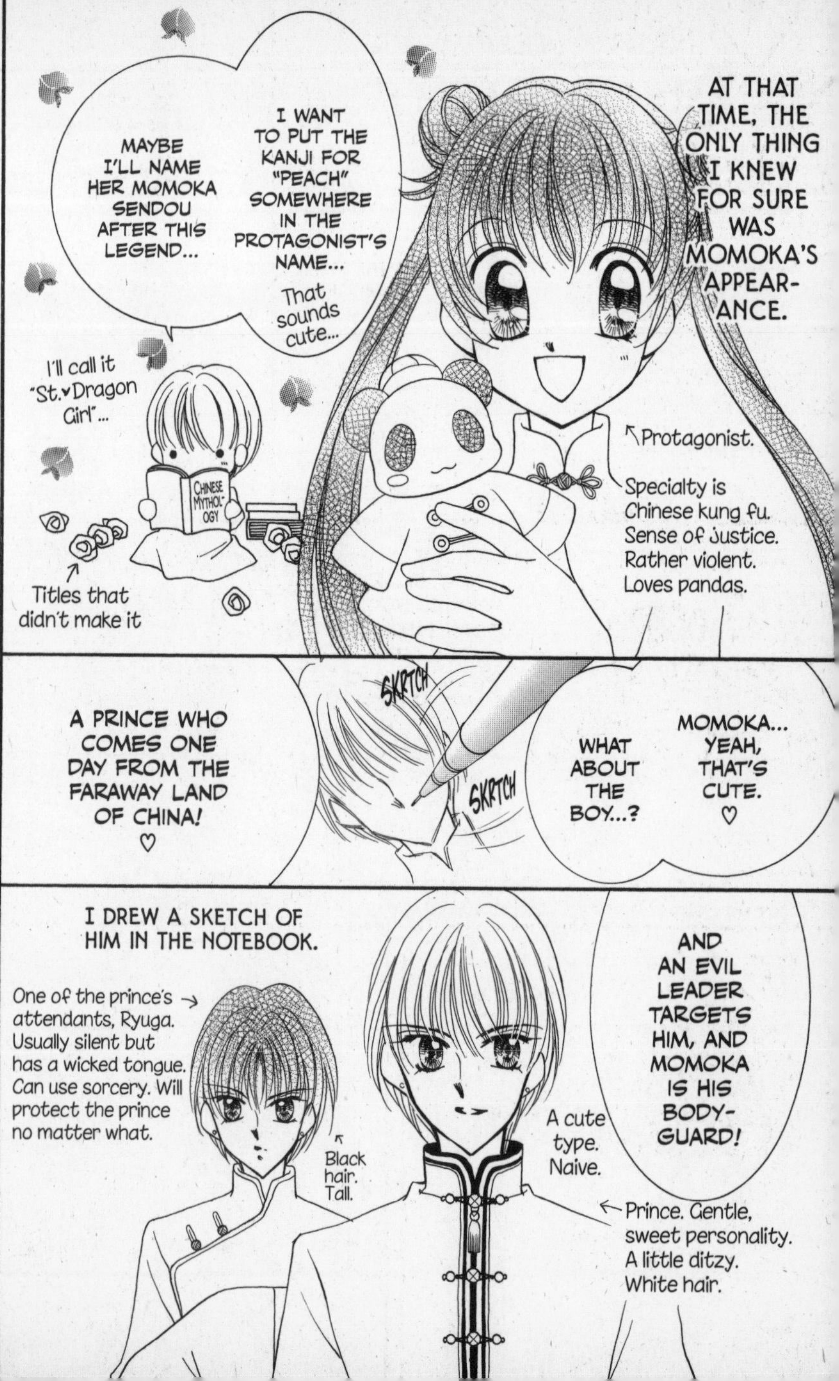
AT THAT TIME, THE ONLY THING I KNEW FOR SURE WAS MOMOKA'S APPEARANCE.
I WANT TO PUT THE KANJI FOR "PEACH" SOMEWHERE IN THE PROTAGONIST'S NAME...
MAYBE I'LL NAME HER MOMOKA SENDOU AFTER THIS LEGEND...
That sounds cute...
↖Protagonist.
Specialty is Chinese kung fu. Sense of justice. Rather violent. Loves pandas.
I'll call it "St.♥Dragon Girl"...
CHINESE MYTHOLOGY
Titles that didn't make it
MOMOKA... YEAH, THAT'S CUTE. ♡
WHAT ABOUT THE BOY...?
SKRTCH
SKRTCH
A PRINCE WHO COMES ONE DAY FROM THE FARAWAY LAND OF CHINA! ♡
AND AN EVIL LEADER TARGETS HIM, AND MOMOKA IS HIS BODYGUARD!
I DREW A SKETCH OF HIM IN THE NOTEBOOK.
A cute type. Naive.
← Prince. Gentle, sweet personality. A little ditzy. White hair.
↖ Black hair. Tall.
One of the prince's → attendants, Ryuga. Usually silent but has a wicked tongue. Can use sorcery. Will protect the prince no matter what.

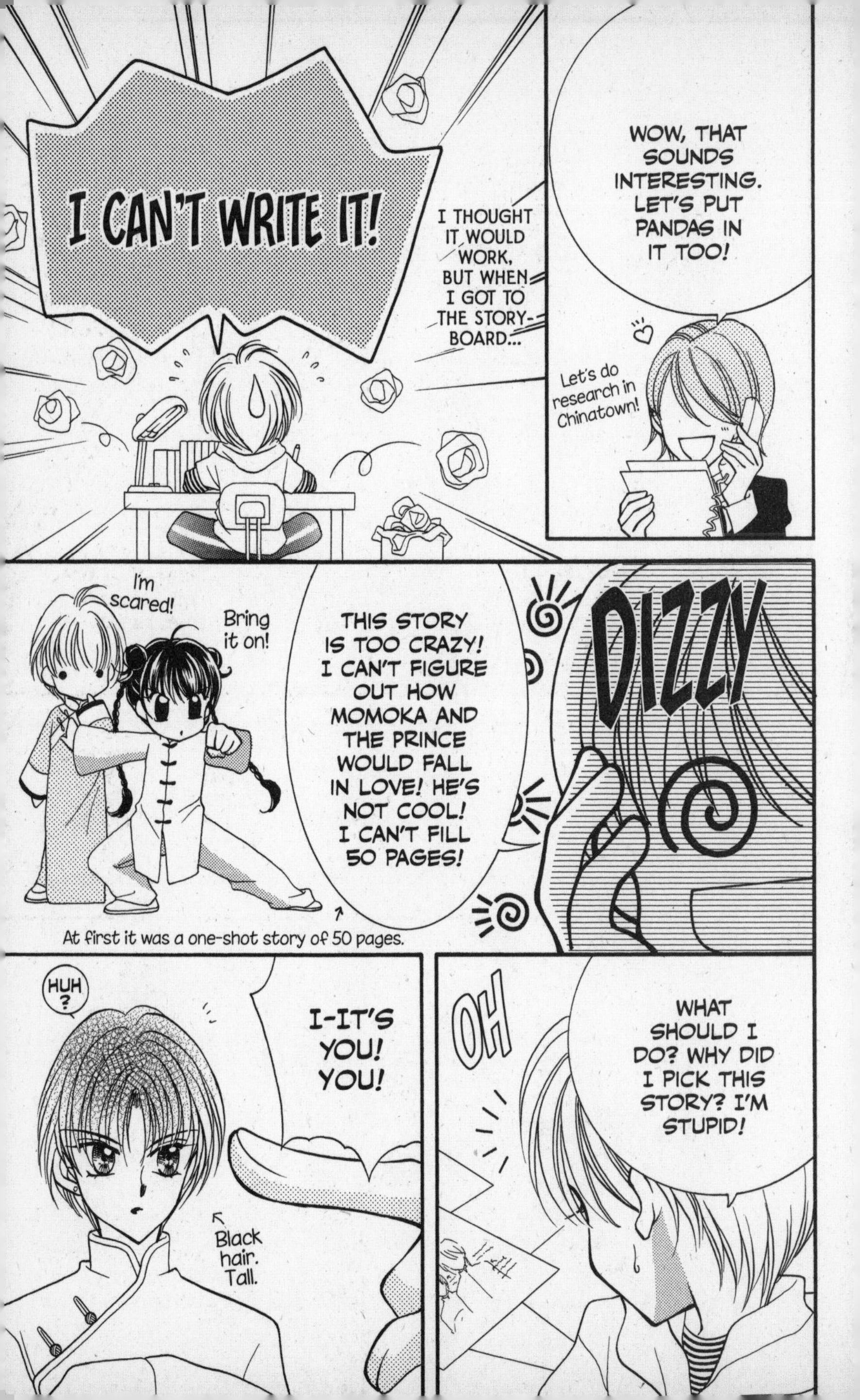
WOW, THAT SOUNDS INTERESTING. LET'S PUT PANDAS IN IT TOO!
Let's do research in Chinatown!
I THOUGHT IT WOULD WORK, BUT WHEN I GOT TO THE STORY-BOARD...
I CAN'T WRITE IT!
DIZZY
THIS STORY IS TOO CRAZY! I CAN'T FIGURE OUT HOW MOMOKA AND THE PRINCE WOULD FALL IN LOVE! HE'S NOT COOL! I CAN'T FILL 50 PAGES!
Bring it on!
I'm scared!
At first it was a one-shot story of 50 pages.
OH
WHAT SHOULD I DO? WHY DID I PICK THIS STORY? I'M STUPID!
I-IT'S YOU! YOU!
HUH?
Black hair. Tall.

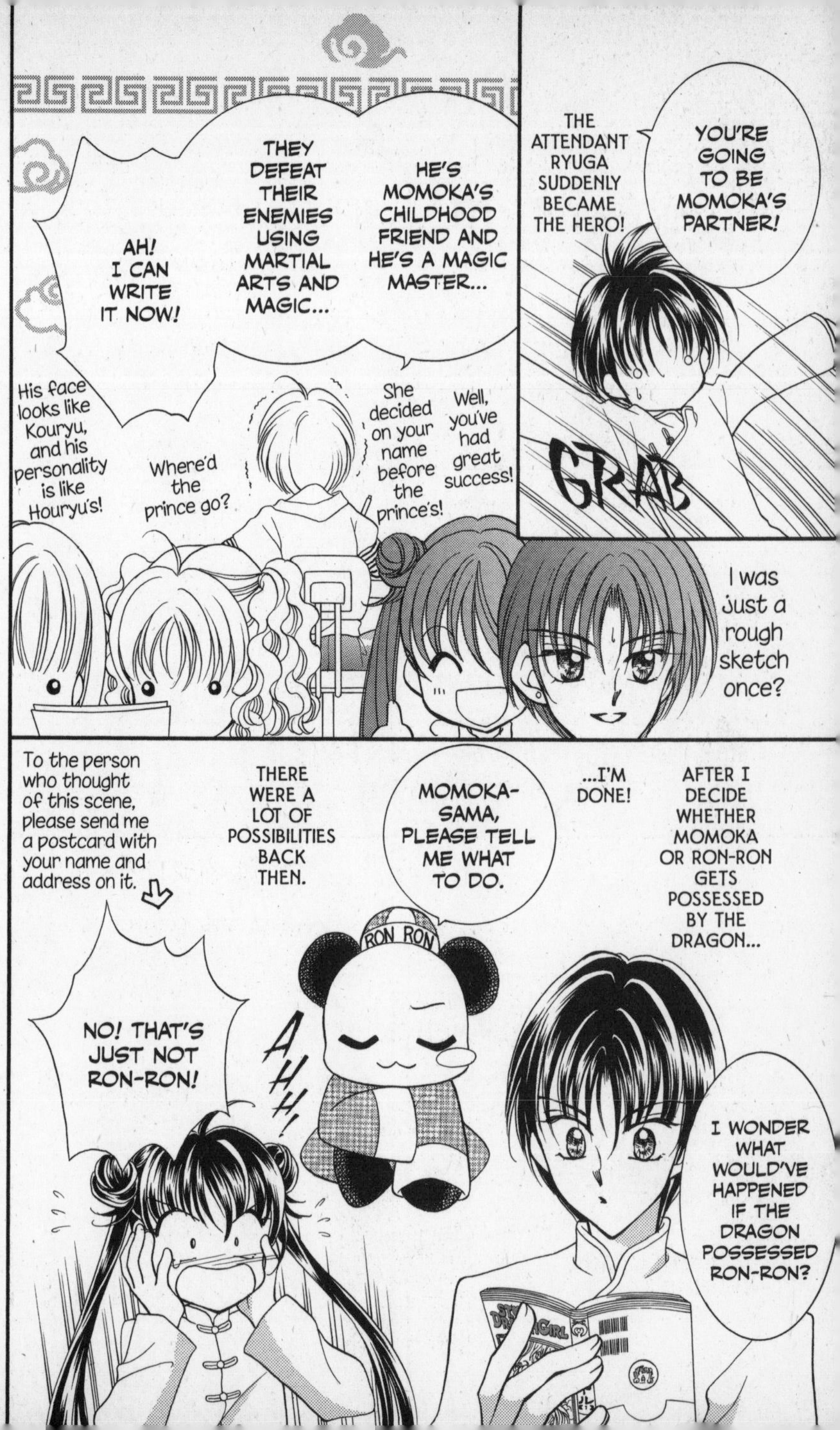
YOU'RE GOING TO BE MOMOKA'S PARTNER!
THE ATTENDANT RYUGA SUDDENLY BECAME THE HERO!
GRAB
HE'S MOMOKA'S CHILDHOOD FRIEND AND HE'S A MAGIC MASTER...
THEY DEFEAT THEIR ENEMIES USING MARTIAL ARTS AND MAGIC...
AH! I CAN WRITE IT NOW!
I was just a rough sketch once?
Well, you've had great success!
She decided on your name before the prince's!
Where'd the prince go?
His face looks like Kouryu, and his personality is like Houryu's!
AFTER I DECIDE WHETHER MOMOKA OR RON-RON GETS POSSESSED BY THE DRAGON...
...I'M DONE!
MOMOKA-SAMA, PLEASE TELL ME WHAT TO DO.
THERE WERE A LOT OF POSSIBILITIES BACK THEN.
To the person who thought of this scene, please send me a postcard with your name and address on it.
RON RON
I WONDER WHAT WOULD'VE HAPPENED IF THE DRAGON POSSESSED RON-RON?
AHH!
NO! THAT'S JUST NOT RON-RON!

BUT BEFORE I KNEW IT, SDG WAS ON ITS SEVENTH VOLUME!
I'M SO THANKFUL TO HAVE MADE IT THIS FAR.
PLEASE KEEP SUPPORTING THESE TWO! ♡
RON RON

Special Thanks:

Assistants: Kodaka
Sasaki
Hiromasa
Itsumi
Kasuya
Wakamatsu

Advisors: Sanjou
Osabe
&
My parents

PLEASE SEND US YOUR COMMENTS!
Natsumi-kun is waiting for your letters!
RON RON

Nancy Thistlethwaite, Editor
VIZ Media, LLC
P.O. Box 77010
San Francisco, CA 94107

HONORIFICS
In Japan, people are usually addressed by their name followed by a suffix. The suffix shows familiarity or respect, depending on the relationship.

Male (familiar): first or last name + kun
Female (familiar): first or last name + chan
Adult (polite): last name + san
Upperclassman (polite): last name + senpai
Teacher or professional: last name + sensei
Close friends or lovers: first name only, no suffix

TERMS

Oneesan means "older sister" but can also be used to address a female who is older than the speaker.

Morning Musume is an all-girl Japanese pop group.

Oniisan means "older brother" but can also be used to address a male who is older than the speaker.

Chibi here refers to small, stylized versions of manga characters.

Sekihan is a red-rice dish made with azuki beans that is often served on special occasions.

I've started practicing tai chi seriously. Even though the movements are very slow, the next morning my muscles always ache. Apparently it takes years to learn everything. The life of a mangaka is pretty hectic, so I'm enjoying the relaxed pace of tai chi, and I hope to continue it.

—Natsumi Matsumoto

Natsumi Matsumoto debuted with the manga *Guuzen Janai Yo!* (No Coincidence!) in *Ribon Original* magazine. *St.* ♥ *Dragon Girl* was such a hit that it spawned a sequel, *St.* ♥ *Dragon Girl Miracle*. Her other series from *Ribon* include *Alice kara Magic* and *Yumeiro Patisserie*. The popular *Yumeiro Patisserie* was made into an animated TV series in Japan. In her free time, Natsumi studies Chinese and practices tai chi. She also likes visiting aquariums and collecting the toy prizes that come with snack food in Japan.

St. ♥ Dragon Girl

Vol. 7
Shojo Beat Edition

STORY AND ART BY | **Natsumi Matsumoto**

Translation | **Andria Cheng**
Touch-up Art & Lettering | **Gia Cam Luc**
Design | **Fawn Lau**
Editor | **Nancy Thistlethwaite**

VP, Production | **Alvin Lu**
VP, Sales & Product Marketing | **Gonzalo Ferreyra**
VP, Creative | **Linda Espinosa**
Publisher | **Hyoe Narita**

SAINT DRAGON GIRL © 1999 by Natsumi Matsumoto. All rights reserved. First published in Japan in 1999 by SHUEISHA Inc., Tokyo. English translation rights arranged by SHUEISHA Inc.

The stories, characters and incidents mentioned in this publication are entirely fictional.

Printed in Canada

Published by VIZ Media, LLC
P.O. Box 77010
San Francisco, CA 94107

10 9 8 7 6 5 4 3 2 1
First printing, June 2010

www.viz.com

PARENTAL ADVISORY
ST. ♥ DRAGON GIRL is rated T for Teen and is recommended for ages 13 and up. This volume contains mild violence.
ratings.viz.com

www.shojobeat.com

HUDSON BRANCH